The Future of Food

The Future of Food

Biotechnology Markets and Policies in an International Setting

Edited by Philip G. Pardey

Published by the International Food Policy Research Institute
Washington, D.C.

Distributed by The Johns Hopkins University Press

Library of Congress Cataloging-in-Publication Data available.

International Food Policy Research Institute
2033 K Street, N.W., Washington, D.C. 20006-1002, U.S.A.
Telephone: +1-202-862-5600; Fax: +1-202-467-4439
www.ifpri.org

To John Louis Dillon, 1931–2001,

*who cared about people generally
and the poor in particular,
and never shied away from controversy,
sometimes helping to create it.*

Contents

Tables

Figures

Foreword

What is the future of food? Looking forward, a thinking person could adopt either a pessimistic or an optimistic outlook. On the bleak side many hundreds of millions of poor people are still malnourished, and there will be an additional 1.5 million mouths to feed by 2020. Little new land remains to bring into agriculture, and the water and other natural resources needed for agriculture are being degraded and siphoned off for use in other sectors. Being upbeat, one can marvel at the productivity gains seen over the past several decades and be reassured the same will hold true for the decades to come. The sense that a new technological era in agriculture is upon us bolsters the optimists but the latest crop of biotechnologies, and the context in which they are being developed and used, are attracting much controversy and criticism.

In the minds of many, agriculture is a natural endeavor and should remain so: yet in many ways it is the antithesis of "natural." Farmers managed and manipulated the genetic makeup of crops for the first 10,000 years of agriculture, giving rise to slow, but by contemporary standards only modest, gains in crop function and yield. The science of genetics took off in the early twentieth century and so did crop performance, with unprecedented increases in yields over much of the world in the second half of the last century. Yet these efforts came with their fair share of controversy. Some saw the hybrid corn technologies that spread rapidly beginning in the 1930s in the United States as a thoroughly unwelcome change. The technology was deemed "unnatural" and deprived farmers of the chance to save seed for next year's crop. It also heralded the privatization of large parts of the seed sectors in many developed counties. The new semi-dwarf (short statured) rice and wheat varieties that became available to farmers in the 1960s were tarred with the same brush. Unfamiliarity bred contempt, and similar sounding arguments swirl around the transgenic crops and other biotechnologies science is just beginning to provide.

There is no question of the need for substantial yield gains over the decades to come, nor that genetic manipulation in tandem with other technologies is necessary to achieve these boosts in productivity. What is in question is the part biotechnology will play in achieving food security for all and especially for the world's poor who are yet to gain access to the food many of us simply take for granted.

The ramifications of the market and policy choices taken now regarding agricultural biotechnologies will reverberate for decades to come. The consequences will be global, and the choices controversial. The chapters in this book confront this controversy with new analyses and insights from economists and technologists. The topics covered include an assessment of differences in perceptions among rich and poor countries; a quantitative investigation of the effects of rich-country restrictions on international trade in GMO crops on the welfare of poorer parts of the world; an analysis of alternative technology trajectories; an exploration of the effects of intellectual property rights on the bioscience done by public agencies the world over; and several economic appraisals of the economic impacts of the technologies—past, present, and future.

Once in a while, those making policies confront choices with profound long-term consequences; today's policy choices about biotechnology are such. They will affect the future of food for many years to come. I recommend that those who are concerned about these policies read this book. It will inform and affect your views; it did mine.

Per Pinstrup-Andersen
Director General, IFPRI

Acknowledgments

On January 22, 2001, a workshop on "Agricultural Biotechnology: Markets and Policies in an International Setting" was held in Adelaide, Australia. The event was convened jointly by the Australian Agricultural and Resource Economic Society (AARES) and the International Food Policy Research Institute (IFPRI) of Washington, D.C., in conjunction with the annual AARES meetings. This book includes revised versions of the papers presented at that workshop.

Agriculture, Fisheries and Forestry—Australia, the Grains Research and Development Corporation, and the U.S. Farm Foundation generously provided financial support for the workshop and the production of this book. In addition to this specific support, significant general support was provided to IFPRI's research on agricultural biotechnology and genetic resource policy by the Swedish International Development Agency (Sida), the Canadian International Development Agency (CIDA), the European Commission (EC), and the U.S. Agency for International Development (USAID); results of that research are represented in some of the chapters that follow.

The workshop could not have been organized from half way around the world without the dedication of the chair of the AARES local organizing committee, Doug Young, assisted by members of that committee, especially Kym Jervois, Andrew Manson, and Randy Stringer, all of whom went above and beyond their duty in providing logistical and practical help. Julian Alston, 2001 president of the AARES, sowed the seed of the idea for the workshop and also helped to make it happen.

The editor gratefully acknowledges the help of several IFPRI staff in preparing this manuscript, in particular Patricia Zambrano for her excellent research assistance, Heidi Fritschel, Uday Mohan, and Joanna Berkman for their very effective editorial assistance, and Evelyn Banda for the layout and cover design. Above all, thanks go to Mary-Jane Banks, who oversaw the logistics for the workshop and helped organize and edit the material for this manuscript, ably seeing it through several rounds of revision. Final thanks are offered to the chapter authors for their contributions and consideration in meeting the tight deadlines required to produce this book.

Part 1

Introduction

Chapter 1

Biotechnology Markets and Policies— Overview

Philip G. Pardey

Context

Sorting the wheat from the chaff is something farmers have done for eons. Sorting the truth from the tales—and ultimately the payoffs from the pitfalls—of the new agricultural biotechnologies is a much tougher task. The latest, most exhilarating, and most controversial chapter in agricultural science is the biotechnology revolution. Science has now moved beyond understanding the structure of DNA to analyzing the complete sequence of genes in humans, plants, animals, and other organisms. The mapping of this genetic landscape, known as genomics, includes the recently completed gene sequences for *Arabidopsis thaliana,* a weed in the mustard family of Brassicaceae, and for rice. Both plants provide genomic blueprints for a host of basic plant functions, dramatically accelerating crop improvement efforts.

By coupling the biosciences with new computing and informatics technologies, researchers are developing databanks of DNA·sequences for individual plants and animals and are linking them to various functions and traits. To the new science of functional genomics, genes are recipes for proteins, and proteins are the workhorses of living cells. The even newer science of proteomics catalogues proteins within living things and probes deeper to understand the molecular structure of these proteins and the complex biology linking specific genes to specific proteins. Like the more conventional breeding efforts preceding them, the modern biosciences open up more options for improving plants' resistance to certain pests and diseases; their tolerance to drought, waterlogging, frosts, and saline or acid soils; and the overall quality of grain. These plant traits can reduce crop losses and the costs of production, raise crop yields and the returns to growers (and others in the food marketing chain), and expand choices available to consumers. The biosciences are also expanding options for improving the agricultural performance of animals and providing avenues for agriculture to grow new pharmacological and nutraceutical products.

All these discoveries have spurred a rapid restructuring of the institutions and industries engaged in the science that affects agriculture, at least in the United States and other rich countries. Incentives for research are changing, as are public and private research roles, ultimately shifting the balance between locally provided and internationally traded goods—part and parcel of the globalization of agricultural research.

The disquiet over these new biotechnologies both reflects and affects these many changes. Some critics are concerned over environmental and human health consequences. In Europe, consumer resistance to transgenic plants and animals has engendered trade bans and restrictive labeling. The majority of consumers in other markets, including Argentina, China, and the United States, seem less concerned and more accepting. Other critics of biotechnology focus on its relationship to the consolidation and concentration of the agriculture industry, most noticeably the many mergers and acquisitions in the seed and agricultural chemical companies during the 1990s. The concern is that oligopoly will stifle competition, shift profits away from farmers, and drive research toward private profitability, but not necessarily society's food security interests. An additional criticism is that the proliferation of patents and other forms of intellectual property protection demanded by large biotechnology companies will slow progress in the agricultural sciences and make new innovations inaccessible to farmers and scientists in developing countries. Joined to this is the worry that many of the less-developed countries (LDCs) lack the capacity to regulate and monitor the use of modern biotechnologies in ways that will satisfy consumers in rich export markets, further impeding their development. Each of these criticisms merits attention in the context of science and food security.

Perhaps because the preponderance of agricultural biotechnologies have been developed and most extensively commercialized in the United States and other rich countries, the debate has had a distinctly rich-country bias. The concerns of and opportunities for producers and consumers in poor countries have been less prominent, yet the issues involved are global. Countries are inextricably linked through international markets—either through trade in agricultural technologies or the food products these technologies bring about—and through a host of institutional arrangements and international policy and legal agreements.

The chapters in this book highlight these international aspects, reporting recent work done mainly (but not exclusively) by economists. Economists think in terms of tradeoffs: in this case balancing the risks and rewards posed by using these new technologies. Part of the policy problem is that many of these biotechnologies and the collective experience with them are nascent, providing only a partial picture of the possibilities and their consequences. This makes it difficult to identify the nature and magnitude of the costs, benefits, and tradeoffs involved—doubly difficult because the essence of science is its unpredictability.

Notwithstanding these uncertainties, marshaling the available evidence and subjecting it to economic scrutiny with an eye to problems of common interest or those with international ramifications should prove useful for policymaking—at least that was the premise in putting together this volume. Key questions and concerns beg inherently economic answers: How much should be invested in the new biosciences? Who should perform the research and pay for it? Who are the likely users—as well as the likely winners and losers?

Chapter Overview

In the second chapter of this introduction, Michael Taylor provides an Australian perspective, recognizing Australian agriculture's reliance on global markets, both for exporting its primary and processed food products and for importing biotechnologies or the technological tools required to further the country's own research.

In Chapter 3, Per Pinstrup-Andersen and Marc Cohen compare and contrast rich versus poor country perspectives on agricultural biotechnology. They delve into how and why these perspectives differ, highlighting the consequences of the differences. Many poor people live on the edge of subsistence, spending much of their meager incomes on food. For genetically modified (GM) foods their risk-benefit calculus is entirely different than it is for rich people. The market power of agricultural interests also differs between rich and poor countries and advocacy groups are active too. Pinstrup-Andersen and Cohen build a strong case for making choices about GM food and agriculture based on sound scientific testing and evidence-based approaches, and above all stress leaving the choices to those who are ultimately affected by them.

The confluence of rich and poor country concerns is most pronounced in the area of trade. Some see the push for stricter labeling regimes and import controls (and the product segregation strategies they entail) as a prudent precaution to perceived health concerns; others see it as a back door to protecting domestic agricultural interests from products produced elsewhere. Whatever the reasons, markets are moving toward more regulations concerning the sale and international movement of GM foods. In Chapter 4, Kym Anderson and colleagues provide a range of results using various global models to explore the economywide consequences of stricter controls on the trade in GM varieties. There is an inherent tension between the gains flowing from the productivity consequences of GM crops and the increased costs that come from restricting the production or sale of these crops; these changes have ripple effects throughout economies worldwide. Anderson et al. investigate the worldwide production, consumption, trade, and price effects of restricting the local production of genetically modified organisms (GMOs), for example GM maize and soybeans in western Europe, or sale of GM crops, including a ban on imports—the most extreme application of the precautionary principle within the scope of the Biosafety Protocol. The authors find the potential global economic gains from growing GM coarse grain and oilseed crops to be sizable and the economic costs to Europe from banning the imports of GM crops significant (to be weighed against the perceived benefits from implementing the precautionary principle in this fashion). A less costly alternative would be to allow consumers access to both GM and non-GM foods, using market mechanisms instead of import bans to express their preferences. An important finding is that developing countries can respond to the GM preferences of rich countries, and redirect their trade flows accordingly. Whether developing (and other) countries ultimately gain or lose, and by how much, depends on (a) the degree of substitutability between GM and non-GM varieties and the price differentials between the two types of crops (aspects that were explicitly modeled), and (b) the costs of labeling and segregation, and implications for research and development (R&D) and seed markets globally (aspects that were not dealt with explicitly in the models).

We have barely begun to tap the potential of these new technologies. In Chapter 5, Richard Jefferson goes beyond the current crop of transgenic technologies, providing intriguing insights into some strategic technological options facing the biosciences, both in the near and longer term. Developing a clearer and structured sense of these options, their implications, and the links to other areas of the agricultural sciences puts the current, single transgene technologies (like *Bacillus thuringiensis [Bt]* cotton and corn or Roundup Ready® soybeans) into proper perspective, making for more informed policy choices.

The elaborate web of patent protection in western countries, and its extension to international trade law, has provoked anxiety that the "genetic commons" may be enclosed by biotechnology companies seeking to protect their profits, locking developing countries out and blocking their access to new developments by public and nonprofit researchers. The chapters in Part 3 deal with the policy and practical consequences of changing intellectual property regimes on agricultural R&D. In Chapter 6, my colleagues Carol Nottenburg and Brian Wright and I confront the "lockout" apprehension by assessing the geographical extent of the intellectual property and the pattern of trade flows for crops grown in poor countries and consumed in rich ones. We conclude that as things stand now the concerns that patents and other forms of intellectual property are stifling research done for or in developing countries are largely misplaced, diverting attention from more crucial issues like lack of funding and scientific and regulatory wherewithal to access and tap the promise that modern biotechnologies offer. As the extent of patent protection expands, access to proprietary science is bound to become a bigger problem. We broach some of the options by which public agencies may take advantage of proprietary technologies, emphasizing the international and developing-country aspects.

In Chapter 7, Peter Phillips and Dan Dierker go beyond issues of access to intellectual property, expanding on the theme of the problems posed for public research from an increasingly private approach to agricultural innovation. They suggest parts of the public research agenda are beginning to mimic the private portfolio, shifting to shorter-term research done increasingly on a commercial or fee-for-service basis and seeking patent protection on the results. Moreover, this is happening at the expense of the more basic research that underpins tomorrow's applied R&D. According to Phillips and Dierker, putting publicly performed R&D increasingly in the pockets of private interests undermines the independence of public research, hinders the provision of technology assessments by disinterested parties, and confounds efforts of regulatory agencies to credibly oversee the introduction and use of these technologies. They conclude their chapter with a number of suggestions to revitalize the public good parts of publicly performed R&D.

More than two thirds of U.S. cotton and soybean acres were planted to transgenic varieties within six years of initial introduction. Farmers in other countries like Argentina and China have also been quick to take up these technologies, given the chance. The adoption rates, themselves, are strong evidence that these crops are profitable for farmers. In Chapter 8, Michele Marra systematically scrutinizes all the empirical evidence available in the public domain of the impacts of the first generation of transgenic crops in the United States and elsewhere. The types of potential benefits are described and discussed as well as the systematic biases introduced into some of the estimates because input quantities are not set at the relevant technology-specific optimum. Overall, the evidence indicates these technologies are profitable for farmers although the impacts vary by year and location. Transgenic cotton (containing DNA from soil bacteria that produce proteins to control the types of caterpillars that attack cotton plants) shows reduced pesticide use in most years in most U.S. states; pest-resistant corn shows small but significant yield increases in most years across the U.S. Corn Belt (and for some places in some years the increase is substantial); and, despite evidence of small yield losses in Roundup Ready® soybean varieties in many U.S. states, other cost savings seem to more than offset the lost revenue from the yield discrepancy. Evidence of the effects of transgenic crops in other countries is provided as well.

There are different ways to introduce the same trait into a crop. In Chapter 9, Richard Gray describes an economic model for assessing the effects of two types of herbicide-tolerant wheat that may both be ready for commercial release in 2002. One is a non-GM variant produced by mutagenesis (a chemical or radioactive process to induce mutation used by breeders for decades); the other is a GM variant developed by the Monsanto Corporation that is tolerant of the glyphosate herbicide marketed as Roundup®. Gray investigates the likely economic consequences of these two technologies, taking explicit account of possible economic externality and costly segregation effects. The externality effects include the additional costs GM producers may impose on non-GM producers (from increased weed control costs or price discounts for non-GM crops grown in unsegregated markets), and possible (but, based on current evidence, seemingly improbable) increases in health care costs for consumers of GM products. The issue of segregation costs arises because there are many sources for mixing different wheat varieties, and it is costly to maintain and test for the purity of the product. Indeed, Gray speculates that it is unlikely segregation systems will develop at a low enough cost to maintain parallel GM and non-GM product streams, possibly causing countries to bifurcate into GM and non-GM producers.

The modern biosciences affect not only the costs of growing and marketing new varieties, but also the costs of research to breed new crop varieties. In Chapter 10, Michael Morris and colleagues assess the economics of biotechnology-assisted plant breeding programs, particularly those in developing countries. They focus on marker-assisted selection methods, whereby short pieces of DNA within or close to gene sequences with traits of interest are identified and used to track the movement of these traits from one plant to another during a breeding cycle. The private sector makes extensive use of these techniques in their crop breeding work; less is done in the public domain, partly because of the costs involved. Decisions to invest in these new technologies involve economic choices, typically trading off increased costs (compared with conventional breeding techniques) against the benefits from speeding up the breeding cycle or spinning off new findings. The economic choices involved rely on empirical results; thus Morris et al. use an analysis of marker-assisted selection methods in maize breeding at the International Maize and Wheat Improvement Center (CIMMYT) to illustrate the issues involved. They also provide an assessment of the future, both in terms of marker technologies and their potential impacts on breeding programs worldwide, giving guidance to developing countries faced with using their scarce research resources wisely in light of these new crop-improvement possibilities.

Part 5 groups together chapters that provide different regional and national policy perspectives. The first two chapters, Chapter 11 by Eduardo Trigo and colleagues and Chapter 12 by John Skerritt, summarize two separate but parallel efforts led by the respective regional banks (specifically the Inter-American Development Bank and the Asian Development Bank) to take stock of agricultural biotechnology throughout Latin America and Asia and to recommend regional policy and investment initiatives. In Chapter 13, Nicole Ballenger uses a chronological listing of op-ed pieces published by *The Washington Post* between January 1999 and November 2000 as a way of tracking public interest in and U.S. perspectives on agricultural biotechnology during this period. Ballenger also documents how research economists at the U.S. Department of Agriculture have responded to and sought to inform the policy and public discourse on these issues. Although the central concern is "agricultural biotechnology" the topics at issue are ever-changing (at least in terms of the emphasis placed on any one issue at any particular point in time) and wide-ranging.

Part 6 presents some concluding commentary from Jock Anderson, Walter Armbruster, and Bob Richardson, complementing that of Brian Fisher, Bob Lindner, and Ron Duncan presented in earlier parts of the book. The three commentators in Part 6 have very different institutional vantage points: an international financial institution, a nonprofit agency representing U.S. agricultural interests, and an Australian academic institution. Their comments reflect these differences but also raise concerns held more widely. Policymaking is usually a messy, often short-term, exercise. Many sense that in this case the stakes are particularly high, with potentially profound long-term consequences for the future of agriculture and food security worldwide. It also seems those making these policies are confronted with more than the usual dose of uncertainty and partisanship. I hope this book removes some of these uncertainties and injects useful economic ways of thinking into the biotech policy process.

Chapter 2

Agricultural Biotechnology—
An Australian Perspective
on a Global Science

Michael J. Taylor

Biotechnology is without doubt a revolution as far as agriculture and the food processing industries are concerned. This is as true in Australia as it is elsewhere in the world. Whenever the status quo is challenged, differences of opinion can result. With the introduction of biotechnology to agriculture and food processing, the Australian experience is no exception. High levels of emotion and misinformation feature in the public debate about the technology in Australia including, unfortunately, reporting by the nation's electronic and print media. This makes it difficult to have a reasoned public discussion about the potential importance of biotechnology for agriculture—not to mention our overall economic bottom line.

Food security in the developing world, and biotechnology's role, have not featured strongly in the public debate in Australia. I suspect this is true elsewhere in the developed world. Australians, like others, need to understand that biotechnology offers millions of people the promise of something that we all take for granted. By rejecting food products developed through biotechnology, we place at risk the continued development of the technology and its availability to others who are not in our fortunate position.

Importantly for Australia, the benefits of biotechnology are not confined to agriculture and food processing. The capacity of biotechnology to contribute to the sustainable use of the natural resource base upon which Australian agriculture depends has not been fully recognized in the broader community. Real potential exists to use the technology to increase the management tools available to deal with serious environmental problems such as soil and water salinity. Biotechnology may well be a significant aid to how we manage these problems in the future, but the precursor must be improved public understanding and acceptance of the technology.

For a globally oriented country like Australia, which exports more than two thirds of its agricultural production, being able to meet market demands and be competitive are important challenges. It is also important to understand the type of qualifications that might be placed on our products. This is something we are grappling with, along with other western countries.

Australian investment in biotechnology is small compared with the countries of North America and Europe. The performance of the local biotechnology sector is nevertheless impressive. Australia has around 190 biotechnology companies operating across the economy. Currently about 35 biotechnology companies are listed on the Australian Stock Exchange, representing an increase of more that 40 percent from 1999. Over the past two years, the value of most listed Australian biotechnology companies has grown strongly with a number showing a significant increase in their share price. In 1998–99, biotechnology companies in Australia earned about AU\$965 million, almost half of that derived from export sales. U.S. biotechnology patents granted to Australians have increased 250 percent in recent years. This is more than double the rate of increase of such patents for the rest of the world.

Traditional biotechnology such as plant and animal breeding have long been the mainstay of Australian agriculture. They will position the nation well to capitalize on modern biotechnology. Australia has already approved two genetically modified (GM) cotton varieties for commercial production, one an insect-resistant *Bacillus thuringiensis (Bt)* type and the other a cotton tolerant to a major herbicide. In both cases, the vehicle that brought these new biotechnologies into commercial production was improved local cotton germplasm. Future commercial releases of genetically modified crops in Australia are likely to be among those currently being field tested. More than 100 field trials of GM crops, mostly cotton and canola, have taken place in Australia.

Australia's commitment to biotechnology research and development (R&D) is significant. The public sector spends in excess of AU\$250 million per year on biotechnology research. CSIRO (the Commonwealth Scientific and Industrial Research Organisation), Australia's premier, publicly funded research agency, is investing AU\$145 million in biotechnology research over three years from the year 2000. Australia's rural R&D corporations, a unique industry-government partnership, invest about 8 percent of their combined budgets, or AU\$19 million per year, in research into agriculture and food applications of biotechnology. Other major areas of Commonwealth funding for biotechnology research include the higher education, health, and medical sectors, and the Cooperative Research Centres (CRCs) involving collaborative partnership between government, industry, and universities.

Commonwealth government policy for biotechnology is multifaceted. First and foremost, Australia is committed to maintaining the highest possible public health and environmental safety standards. The establishment of a national gene technology regulatory system is a case in point. Commonwealth, state, and territory governments worked together for some time to establish the Office of the Gene Technology Regulator to protect the health and safety of people and to protect the environment by identifying and managing risks posed by gene technology. This new system replaced a voluntary system of oversight that served Australia well for a decade and a half. Legislation to establish the new regulator was passed by the Commonwealth Parliament late in 2000 and the office became fully operational in June 2001.

The Commonwealth Government believes that information is a key to addressing community and consumer concerns about biotechnology. In 2000, the Australian and New Zealand governments agreed through their health ministers to a new labeling regime for GM food. Australia's food standard will require that foods containing GM protein or DNA in the final product be labeled. While the standard is comprehensive and informative, it is practical in that products such as minor ingredients and highly refined oils are exempt and there is a 1 percent tolerance for unintended mixture. By any definition Australia's new GM food labeling regime is tight. This will raise important issues for Australia, both domestically and in a trade sense.

In terms of nonregulatory policy, the Commonwealth government has adopted a whole-of-government rather than a sector-by-sector approach. A national biotechnology strategy has been developed as a framework for Australia's approach to biotechnology. The strategy is intended to realize a greater return on the already substantial public investment in biotechnology. Under the strategy, the Commonwealth government will deliver an additional AU$30 million. Of this, AU$20 million will provide support to help bridge the commercialization gap, the most critical barrier to biotechnology development in Australia. More recently, the Commonwealth government has announced further support for biotechnology through the establishment of a new center, or centers, of excellence in biotechnology research and the expansion of a biotechnology innovation fund. These measures are part of the Commonwealth government's overall approach to innovation.

Unlike the United States, Australia has yet to adopt GM crops on a large scale with the exception of cotton. Canola is likely to be the next major GM crop to be produced commercially in Australia. For local farmers, deciding to adopt GM canola will not be easy, given the domestic and international market uncertainty about the oil and products derived from the seed, including meat products from livestock that have been fed GM meal. Australian farmers will need to decide if it is in their best interest to continue to produce traditional crops and to forego advantages offered by biotechnology, or perhaps seek to spread their risk and do both. Such a decision will require information on markets for GM and non-GM products. Identity preservation, segregation, and certification must be key elements of any decision by Australian agriculture and food industries to supply GM and non-GM products.

The whole area of biotechnology, particularly as it involves the modern techniques, is challenging the way government policy paradigms are structured in Australia and elsewhere. The chapters in this volume look at these issues on a global scale and consider a number of different perspectives.

Part 2

Looking Forward on a Global Scale

Chapter 3

Rich and Poor Country Perspectives on Biotechnology

Per Pinstrup-Andersen and Marc J. Cohen

Introduction

The current debate about the potential utility of modern biotechnology for food and agriculture and the associated risks and opportunities often ignores the differences between conditions in rich and poor countries. Positions for or against the use of genetic engineering in food and agriculture in industrialized countries are frequently extrapolated directly to the developing world. But food and agriculture problems differ widely between poor and rich countries, and one would expect the most appropriate solutions to also differ. It is important that each country, and population groups within countries, be in a position to make their own decisions regarding modern biotechnology. Attempts by wealthy countries, population groups, and advocacy groups to decide for poor farmers and consumers are paternalistic and unethical. This chapter first discusses the different perspectives and the reasoning behind them. It then discusses in more detail the risks and benefits associated with the use of modern biotechnology in developing-country food and agriculture. It concludes with a look at issues requiring future action.

Why Should Perspectives Differ?

Rich and poor country perspectives on the use of modern biotechnology for food and agriculture differ for many reasons. Similarly, within any given country views

Table 3.1   Illustrative impact of a 33 percent reduction of food commodity prices on poor
            and rich consumers

	Poor consumers	Rich consumers
	(percent)	
Assumed budget share on food	80.00	10.00
Assumed commodity cost share	70.00	10.00
Impact on consumer purchasing power[a]	19.00	0.33

Source: Authors' calculations.

a. The budget and commodity shares used to estimate the impact of a 33 percent reduction in price are hypothetical, but deemed representative of typical poor and rich consumers. To illustrate the calculation, a poor person is assumed to spend 80 cents of every dollar of income on food, and 70 percent of that 80-cent expenditure entails the cost of commodities; thus, the commodity costs per dollar of expenditure are 56 cents. Reducing the price of those commodities by 33 percent is equivalent to a 19 percent (0.33 x 56) increase in the income of the poor. The same method, with different budget and commodity shares, was used to estimate the income effect of a food price reduction on the rich.

likely differ between poor people and the nonpoor. The factors deemed most important in determining these different perspectives are discussed below.

The Budget Share for Food

Application of modern biotechnology in food and agriculture may increase productivity and reduce unit costs in production and marketing. This may lead to higher incomes for innovative producers, reduced prices for consumers, or most likely a combination of the two. Consumers spending a large share of their budget on food are thus likely to be more interested in such productivity increases than consumers who spend a relatively small share of their budget on food.

Low-income people in developing countries often spend 50–80 percent of their total disposable income on food whereas Americans, Australians, and Europeans spend 10–15 percent on average. Furthermore, the cost of the food commodity occupies a much larger share of the consumer price among the poor. Costs of processing and marketing tend to dominate in foods consumed by the rich. Unit cost savings in the production of food commodities are therefore likely to result in a larger price reduction for poor consumers (see Table 3.1). For these reasons, one would expect poor people and poor countries to emphasize reduced unit costs and prices for food.

The Importance of Agriculture

Insofar as farmers can capture the benefits of increased productivity, reduced unit costs, and lower production risks, they would likely favor the use of modern biotechnology in production. More than 70 percent of the world's poor reside in rural areas, and it is not uncommon for 50–80 percent of a low-income country's population to depend directly or indirectly on agriculture. In contrast, 2–5 percent of the populations of most industrialized nations depend on agriculture for their livelihoods. Therefore, it is reasonable to expect that the application of modern biotechnology in food and agriculture would be far more favorably received by low-income countries than by high-income ones.

Another closely related aspect is the relative importance of the agricultural sector in generating broad-based economic growth in society as a whole. Agricultural growth is essential in promoting rapid overall growth in low-income countries, while it may be of limited importance in industrialized nations.

Market Power and Political Power

Insofar as farmers expect to gain from the introduction of modern biotechnology in food and agriculture, they will try to influence political decisionmaking in favor of such technology. Farmers in industrialized nations have used political power effectively to gain access to large farm subsidies supported by fiscal resources and artificially high consumer prices. At the same time, however, the market power of industrialized-world farmers has gradually deteriorated, as consumers gain a greater say. Thus, while European farmers continue to receive large subsidies by exercising their political power, they have been unable to exercise similar power in questions related to genetically modified (GM) food. On the other hand, farmers in low-income developing countries possess very limited political power and generally have been taxed rather than subsidized by their governments. Domestically, however, they continue to exercise a great deal of market power, as poor consumers seek low-cost foods instead of the more expensive products demanded by consumers in European domestic markets. Like European farmers, farmers in the United States have also managed to maintain large farm subsidies, but unlike their European colleagues, they have not met strong opposition by consumers or government to GM food in the marketplace—at least not yet.

Strong opposition to GM food in the European Union (E.U.) has resulted in severe restrictions on modern agricultural biotechnology, including limited approval for commercial use of new GM agricultural products. The opposition is driven in part by perceived lack of consumer benefits, uncertainty about possible negative health and environmental effects, widespread perception that a few large corporations will be the primary beneficiaries, and ethical concerns.

While European governments have tended to follow the desires expressed by advocacy groups, and most consumers are opposed to genetically engineered food, the U.S. government supports the farm sector and the private sector engaged in developing and distributing modern biotechnology for food and agriculture. One could argue that European consumers have gained a great deal of political power over agriculture in their capacity as consumers, while still agreeing to provide large subsidies to agriculture in their capacity as taxpayers. The possibility that the application of modern biotechnology in European agriculture could reduce the need for farm subsidies does not seem to enter into the European debate. To the extent that this potential contradiction has been considered by consumers and government, consumers seems to prefer to pay farmers not to produce GM food either through additional subsidies or through higher food prices. Such a contradiction is not prevalent in the United States.

The Power of Advocacy Groups

Another factor that has led to differing perspectives between rich and poor countries is the relative political power of civil society groups, including advocacy groups opposed to genetic engineering in food and agriculture. Such groups have successfully influenced the debate and consumer and government attitudes towards GM food in Europe. Advocacy groups opposed to genetic engineering in food and agriculture are also gaining power in developing countries such as the Philippines. The groups in developing countries often maintain close contact with European and international counterparts such as Greenpeace, Friends of the Earth, and the Soils Association.

Those responsible for food and agriculture in developing countries do not always welcome efforts by multinational advocacy groups based in high-income countries to groom opposition to modern biotechnology in their countries. In a recent op-ed in *The Washington Post*, Nigerian Minister of Agriculture Hassan Adamu states:

> We do not want to be denied this technology [agricultural biotechnology] because of a misguided notion that we do not understand the dangers or the future consequences. We understand. . . .We will proceed carefully and thoughtfully, but we want to have the opportunity to save the lives of millions of people and change the course of history in many nations. That is our right, and we should not be denied by those with a mistaken idea that they know best how everyone should live or that they have the right to impose their values on us. The harsh reality is that, without the help of agricultural biotechnology, many will not live (Adamu 2000, A23).

One might expect a similar statement from a European minister of health if Africans tried to spur opposition in Europe to the use of modern biotechnology to develop a cure for cancer.

Professor Thomson of the University of Cape Town, South Africa, puts it this way:

> Rich countries may engage in lengthy disputes about real or imagined risks. We suggest that is largely a luxury debate. From the perspectives of many developing and newly industrialized countries, agricultural biotechnology's benefits are very real and urgently needed today and indispensable tomorrow. The developing world cannot afford to let Europe's homemade problems negatively impact the future growth in our countries (Thomson 2000, 1).

The African Biotechnology Stakeholders Forum also expresses concern about "mounting attempts to curb the evolution and development of biotechnology in Africa" and states "that those in the industrialized countries continue to assume they know what is best for Kenya and the rest of Africa" (ABSF 1999, 3).

The president of the Federation of Farmers Associations in Andhra Pradesh, India, also expresses great concern about the failure of "certain well-known activist organizations in developed countries" to consider how modern agricultural technology could improve the well-being of the poor in Asia. He suggests that we should "leave the choice of selecting modern agricultural technologies to the wisdom of Indian farmers" (Reddy 2000).

However, while some advocacy groups fail to distinguish between rich and poor countries in their position on modern biotechnology for agriculture, many are beginning to recognize the opportunities this technology offers for improving food security and reducing poverty in developing countries. For example, in a recent position paper, Oxfam GB recommends donor support for "(1) public research into applications of GM technology of benefit to smaller farmers and low-income consumers in developing countries, and (2) regulatory and monitoring systems in developing countries" (Oxfam 1999, 3).

Paarlberg summarizes what appears to be the position of many in developing countries:

> It would be unfortunate if the same environmental activists in rich countries, who previously waged an inspired and courageous battle to prevent the dumping of toxic wastes in developing countries, should now use their reputation to deny those same countries access to modern agribiotechnology. This is a powerful tool of science, not a toxic waste. It is the toxic quality of the current industrial world debate regarding GM seeds that the developing countries should perhaps choose not to import (Paarlberg 2000b, 26).

Willingness to Take Risks

The willingness to take certain risks is expected to differ between the poor and the rich, primarily because the consequences of taking or not taking these risks differ between the two groups. This relates to the levels of food safety demanded by the poor and those demanded by the rich. One would expect that increasing levels of food safety would tend to increase food prices. Thus, consumers may be faced with a trade-off between the quantity and quality of food they can acquire. Poor people would tend to place a higher premium on quantity until basic nutritional requirements are met, even if it implies lower levels of food safety. On the other hand, American, Australian, and European households, spending 10–15 percent of their budget on food, are prepared to pay a premium for even small increases in food safety and reduced uncertainty.

The relationship between a society's income level and its desired level of food safety is illustrated not only across countries but also over time in any given country. The food-safety level demanded by high-income countries today is quite different from that demanded by those same countries 50–100 years ago, when incomes were lower and food-budget shares higher. The implication for the introduction of modern biotechnology in food and agriculture is that higher-income people and higher-income countries would be less willing to take risks associated with genetically engineered food, even if those risks are very small or nonexistent. Globalization may impose the levels of food safety preferred by the rich on the poor at the expense of the latter's food security.

The rich are likely to accept biotechnology that improves food safety—even if it raises food prices—although this does not seem to be the case for GM seed that reduces the use of chemical pesticides such as *Bt* food crops. The possibility of reducing or eliminating pesticide residues in food through genetic engineering has not played a significant role in the European debate, even though European farmers rely heavily on synthetic pesticides. As shown in Figure 3.1, 75–80 percent of nationally representative samples in Canada, China, India, and the United States favored using modern biotechnology to develop pest resistance in crops and reduce the use of chemical pesticides. The percentage was considerably lower in Japan, and significantly lower in Europe.

Different Health Problems

While poor people in poor countries worry about their ability to acquire sufficient food to feed their families, rich households in rich countries are concerned about health problems such as obesity, cancer, diabetes, and heart disease. This explains at least in part why Europeans strongly support the use of modern science to develop pharmaceuticals to prevent or cure diseases of concern to them, while they oppose

Figure 3.1   Selected countries of 25 surveyed on the use of biotechnology to grow pest-resistant crops that require fewer farm chemicals

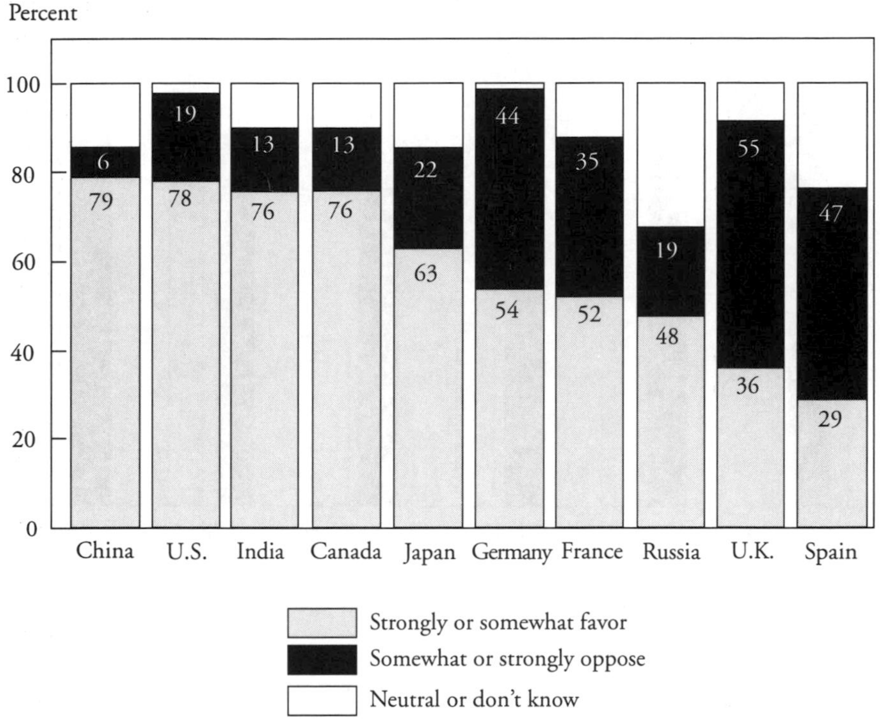

Percent

Strongly or somewhat favor
Somewhat or strongly oppose
Neutral or don't know

Source: Environics International, Ltd. (1998).

use of such science to improve food and agriculture. Few people seeking a cure for cancer are likely to reject a cure developed through genetic engineering, and GM insulin is widely accepted to control diabetes. West African farmers unable to grow or purchase enough food to feed their children are much more concerned about improvements in food and agriculture than about developing a cure for cancer.

One would then certainly expect the rich and poor to differ on the priorities of modern science. This is borne out by an assessment of public opinion in selected countries (Figure 3.2). While a large majority of people in China and India favor the use of modern biotechnology both for treating human diseases and for developing pest-resistant crops, European populations are much more in favor of using modern biotechnology to treat human diseases than for food and agriculture.

In addition to concern about obtaining enough food for the family, the low-income mother in a developing country also worries about other health

Figure 3.2   Public opinion on the use of modern biotechnology in selected countries

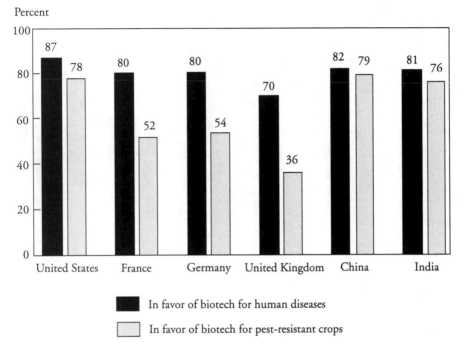

Source: Environics International, Ltd. (1998).

problems. These tend to be related to infectious diseases, many of which are associated with unclean water, poor hygiene, and extremely low food-safety standards. She is thus likely to favor the use of modern science to solve problems related to infectious diseases rather than those related to chronic diseases.

The Importance of Environmental Concerns

Finally, differing environmental concerns between rich and poor countries are likely to lead to different perspectives on the use of modern biotechnology. Modern biotechnology, which would increase productivity in staple food production but with a potentially negative environmental impact, is more likely to be accepted by the poor than by the rich, simply because of the pressing food problems facing the poor. High-income countries are less likely to approve of the application of modern biotechnology in agriculture if there is even a small or unknown environmental risk, because concerns about impact on biodiversity are much more prevalent there than concerns about hunger and malnutrition. The opposite is likely to be true in poor countries.

Figure 3.3   Percentage of adults who "agree" that benefits of using biotechnology in food crops are greater than the risks

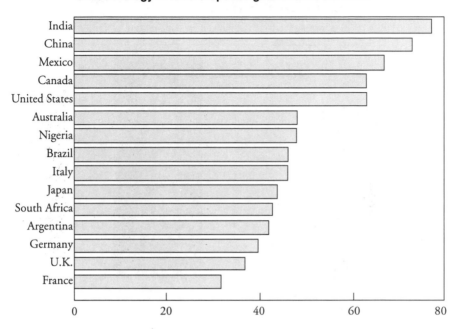

Source: Environics International, Ltd. (1998).

Do the Perspectives Differ as Expected?

The answer to the above question is generally "yes" but with some significant exceptions. For the most part, governments of low-income countries and individuals responsible for facilitating food security for people in those countries favor the use of modern biotechnology in food and agriculture. Public opinion surveys indicate that a larger share of the populations of some developing countries favor using biotechnology in food and agriculture than is the case for western European countries and Japan. However, in some high-income countries that rely heavily on agricultural exports for foreign exchange, such as Australia, Canada, and the United States, there is stronger support for the technology (Figure 3.3). Moreover, there is increasing opposition from various advocacy groups in a number of poorer countries, notably India and the Philippines.

While most developing-country governments seem to favor the use of modern biotechnology, including genetic engineering for food and agriculture, enthusiasm for the new technology differs significantly among countries. The Chinese government is eagerly promoting research based on molecular biology to develop GM food and other agricultural commodities, and it perhaps needs to strengthen its

**Figure 3.4   European support for the application of biotechnology in the
production of foods and development of crops with increased
resistance to pests, 1996 and 1999**

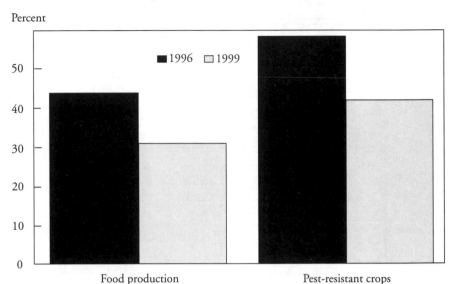

Percent

Food production   Pest-resistant crops

Source: European Commission (2000).

regulatory system. India has yet to approve its first GM seed for commercial planting, yet it has accepted food aid that is likely to be genetically modified. Large,
middle-income developing countries such as Brazil, Egypt, India, and South Africa
are promoting molecular biology-based agricultural research, but approval for commercial production is still very limited.

Views on using modern biotechnology for food and agriculture also differ
among high-income countries. While most E.U. citizens oppose the production and
consumption of GM food, such opposition is less prevalent in Australia, Canada,
and the United States, perhaps because of the importance of export agriculture to
their economies. A recent study by Gaskell et al. (1999) showed that about 40 percent of the E.U. population and 60 percent of the U.S. population support the use
of biotechnology in food production. European support for applying modern
biotechnology in food and agriculture deteriorated from 1996 to 1999 (Figure 3.4).
The viewpoint expressed in Japan seems close to that of the Europeans, maybe
because of Japan's substantial reliance on food and feed imports. A perceived health
risk partly explains the opposition in Europe (Figure 3.5). However, the perceptions
of risks and benefits are based on very limited knowledge of basic biology, as Figures
3.6 and 3.7 illustrate.

Figure 3.5   Percentage of sample population that perceives a serious health risk associated with consumption of GM foods, 1995

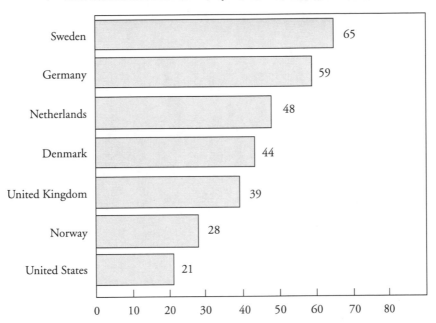

Source: Hoban (2000).

Why Does It Matter That Perspectives Differ?

Different perspectives leading to different policies and standards may conflict with current globalization trends. For globalization to continue in food and agriculture, certain policies and standards need to be synchronized. The biggest threat is that low-income countries will have to adopt policies and standards appropriate only for high-income country situations.

Opposition to the use of genetic engineering in food and agriculture by the rich countries may harm poor people in developing countries for at least three reasons. First, governments and high-income people in developing countries may follow the leads of the industrialized countries in accepting or rejecting the use of modern science for food and agriculture. A coalition is possible between those with decision-making power in developing countries, who are generally nonpoor, and governments and other decisionmakers in high-income countries. Such a coalition would behave much like a high-income country and might establish policies and standards that would harm the majority of the populations of developing countries, which are poor. This situation of course is not limited to the application of modern biotechnology. It can be argued that rich people in developing countries may have more in

Figure 3.6   Ordinary tomatoes do not contain genes, while genetically modified ones do: True or False?

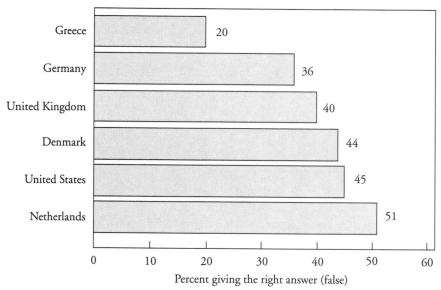

Source: Hoban (2000).

common with the populations of high-income countries than with poor people in their own countries.

Second, most developing countries will be unable to undertake agricultural research to develop the technology needed by their farmers and consumers without research collaboration and financial support from industrialized countries. If industrialized countries decide to limit their molecular biology-based research to solving the health problems of greatest concern to them, developing countries will not get the support they need to apply molecular biology-based research to food and agriculture. A few large developing countries including Brazil, China, India, and South Africa do have the capability to develop the necessary research capacity in food and agriculture; their efforts could provide some of the support needed by other developing countries.

Third, different standards among countries with respect to GM food are likely to hamper trade liberalization and agricultural exports from developing countries. This could be harmful to low-income people in developing nations because most of them depend on agricultural growth, which in turn, is likely to depend in part on expanded export earnings. Some developing countries that are considering the commercialization of GM crops have been warned by the E.U. that they may lose access to the European market not only for the commodities that have been genetically modified but possibly also for those that have not been modified.

Figure 3.7   By eating a genetically modified fruit, a person's genes can be changed: True or False?

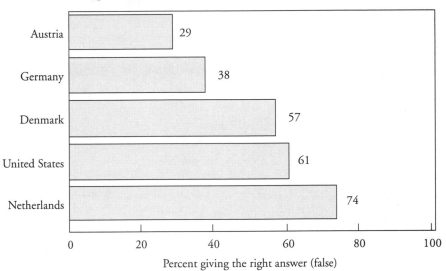

Percent giving the right answer (false)

Source: Hoban (2000).

Presumably, the reason for possibly not discriminating between GM commodities and others is that most countries would have great difficulty keeping the commodities separate. This was recently illustrated in the United States, where GM maize approved for animal feed but not for human consumption ended up in processed food sold for direct human consumption. The GM maize (Starlink®) was simply mixed with other maize either on the farm or in grain elevators. Even if developing countries agreed to label all GM food, the existence of GM food in a developing country could preclude that country from exporting labeled non-GM food to the E.U. This possibility has put pressure on governments of such countries as China and Thailand not to approve the use of GM seed for commercial production.

Developing countries that might wish to use genetic modification to improve agricultural productivity and the nutritional quality of their foods might be faced with a choice: either use genetic modification for the domestic market and lose export opportunities, or forego the potential benefits to domestic consumers while maintaining export opportunities.

The Importance of Productivity Increases in Developing-Country Agriculture

In low-income developing countries, agriculture is the driving force for broad-based economic growth and poverty alleviation. A healthy agricultural economy also offers farmers incentives to soundly manage natural resources. To facilitate agricultural and rural growth, accelerated public investment is needed in a number of areas:

- environmentally friendly, yield-increasing crop varieties, including pest-resistant and drought- and salt-tolerant varieties, and improved livestock;

- access to productive resources (such as land) and appropriate inputs and credit;

- extension services and technical assistance;

- improved rural infrastructure and effective markets;

- attention to the needs of women farmers, who grow much of the locally produced food in many developing countries; and

- primary education and health care, clean water, safe sanitation, and good nutrition for all.

These investments need to be supported by an enabling policy environment including good governance as well as trade, macroeconomic, and sectoral policies that do not discriminate against agriculture. Development efforts must engage small farmers and other low-income people as active participants, not passive recipients; unless the affected people have a sense of ownership, development schemes are not likely to succeed.

Public investment in agricultural research that can improve the productivity of small farmers in developing countries is especially important. The research should develop and draw upon the most appropriate technologies, including making better use of the insights to be gained from traditional indigenous knowledge. The private sector is unlikely to devote substantial resources to such work because it cannot expect sufficient returns to cover costs. Even minor increases in agricultural research aimed at the problems of small farmers in developing countries can significantly boost food supplies, while relatively small cuts can have serious negative effects. Benefits to society from such research generally exceed 20 percent per year, compared with long-run real interest rates of 3–5 percent for government borrowing. Yet these returns will not be obtained without public investment, and average annual growth rates of public agricultural research expenditures in the developing world have slowed since the 1970s (Alston et al. 2000; Alston, Pardey, and Smith 1999; Rosegrant, Agcaoili-Sombilla, and Perez 1995). Low-income developing countries invest less than 0.5 percent of the value of farm production in agricultural research, compared with 2 percent in higher-income countries (Pardey and Alston 1996).

Continued low productivity in agriculture contributes not only to gaps between food production and demand in poor countries, but also prevents the broad-based income growth and lower unit costs in food production needed to improve food security. Efforts to raise longer term productivity on small-scale farms, emphasizing staple food crops and high-value cash crops, must be accelerated.

Research and technology alone will not drive agricultural growth however. The full and beneficial effects of agricultural research and technological change will materialize only if government policies foster and support poverty alleviation and sustainable management of natural resources. Also, it is critical that small farmers are put in decisionmaking roles and that they are informed about their options for improving productivity, reducing risks, and increasing the well-being of the farm family.

The Role of Agricultural Biotechnology in Achieving Food Security

Although tissue culture and other biotechnological work is under way in several developing countries, very little transgenic seed material has been grown in the developing world. Only a few countries—Argentina, Brazil, China, Egypt, India, and South Africa—account for almost all the current developing-country research in agricultural biotechnology; therefore ex post assessment of its risks and benefits, and its relevance for the problems outlined above, is virtually impossible. Identifying similarities and differences between conventional breeding and modern biotechnology can help ex ante assessment of the latter's likely risks and benefits.

Comparing Conventional Breeding with Modern Biotechnology

Within-species versus transgenic breeding. Molecular biology-based research includes both within-species and between-species research. The former may include tissue culture and marker-assisted conventional breeding, while gene transfer between species is usually referred to as "genetic engineering" or "transgenic" work. Although the terms "modern biotechnology" and "genetic engineering" are often used interchangeably, the opposition, concerns, and uncertainties usually refer to the latter.

There are four major differences between conventional plant breeding and genetic engineering. First, the human-induced transfer of one or more genes between species and from microorganisms and animals to plants is relatively new. While all plant breeding arguably involves "genetic modification," conventional breeding crosses different varieties within a single species. Because of their recent origin, there is considerable debate about whether gene transfers across species boundaries entail significant risks to human health and the environment.

A shift to private-sector research. The public sector, with support from philanthropic institutions, has traditionally taken the lead in conventional crop research, especially in developing countries. As a direct consequence, improved seed was usually freely available for multiplication and distribution. In other instances, the improved material was subject to breeders' rights, which may permit a royalty charge. But even in these instances, intellectual property rights (IPR) often did not extend beyond the initial varietal release. Having acquired the seed, farmers could reuse it without further payment, although reuse of hybrid seed would drastically reduce the yield advantage. Such practices are in keeping with the principle of "farmers' rights" included in the International Undertaking on Plant Genetic Resources. Negotiations are currently under way to incorporate the Undertaking into the Convention on Biological Diversity.[1]

In contrast, private-sector firms undertake the bulk of modern agricultural biotechnology research. Consolidation has proceeded rapidly in the agricultural biotechnology industry, with more than 25 major acquisitions and alliances worth US$15 billion between 1996 and 1998 (Serageldin 1999). Transnational life science companies protect IPR through patents that extend beyond the first release of a variety that contains patented technologies. Thus, farmers cannot legally plant or sell for planting the crop produced with the patented seed without the permission of the patent holder. Patent holders are currently seeking to enforce IPR through legal agreements and technologies that will deactivate specific genes.

Use of legal instruments is widespread for industrialized country agriculture, but it does not presently appear viable for poor developing countries. Monitoring and enforcing contracts that prohibit large numbers of small farmers from using the crops they produce as seed would be expensive and difficult.

Genetic use-restriction technology (the "terminator" gene) is the first patented component of the technological approach to intellectual property (IP) protection. Seeds containing this gene produce plants with sterile seed. This technology is inappropriate for small farmers in developing countries, however, because existing infrastructure and production processes cannot keep fertile and infertile seeds apart. Small farmers could face dire consequences if they inadvertently planted infertile seeds. The Consultative Group on International Agricultural Research (CGIAR), which supports 16 Future Harvest international agricultural research centers, has officially rejected use of "any genetic system designed to prevent seed germination" (CGIAR 1998, 52) as a means of protecting IPR. In its October 1998 statement the CGIAR cited concerns about the spread of the trait through pollen, the possibility of the sale or exchange of nonviable seed for planting, the importance for poor farmers of saving seed, potential negative impacts on genetic diversity, and the importance of selection and breeding by farmers for sustainable agriculture.

Rise of proprietary research processes and technologies. A third and related distinction between conventional crop breeding and modern biotechnology relates to the patenting of processes as well as products. Most conventional breeding technology lies in the public domain and is frequently employed by public institutions. The processes used in modern agricultural biotechnology are increasingly subject to IP protection, along with the resulting products.

As the global agricultural research environment becomes increasingly proprietary, will public agencies be able to maintain free access to the fruits of their research for poor farmers in developing countries? Basic but proprietary knowledge and processes may be needed in research, for example, on the so-called "orphaned crops," such as cassava and millet. These are critical staples in the diets of many poor people, but they do not offer promising economic returns to private-sector research and development efforts. So the public sector will need to develop disease-resistant cassava or drought-tolerant millet, whether through genetic modification or conventional breeding.

So far, international agricultural research centers have acquired access to proprietary technologies through commercial licenses, formal agreements providing limited-use rights for specific research, and informal arrangements. Sometimes, technology owners have permitted research but not distribution of the resulting products.

Patent applications are country-specific, and most existing patents related to agricultural research are held in the industrialized countries (Nottenburg, Pardey, and Wright this volume). Thus, if a patent is not obtained in a particular developing country, that country's national agricultural research system (NARS) is free to use the research processes and traits in further research, adaptation, and commercialization. An international agricultural research center located in the country would have the same freedom to operate locally. Farmers in the country are free to use commercialized improved seed even though it may be patented in other countries. The country, however, may not be able to export commodities produced by such seeds to countries where patents are in effect. Private-sector corporations are likely to take out patents only in countries where they expect a sufficiently large commercial demand for the patented product. Similarly, since patenting is costly, holders of patents on specific aspects of a research process may limit their patent applications to a few countries where they can obtain significant economic gains by providing access to the patented processes.

Thus, while all members of the World Trade Organization (WTO) must develop acceptable IPR regimes, many of the poorest and smallest developing countries may not be greatly affected by the rapid increase in patenting of agricultural research processes and outputs simply because the patent holders will not take out patents in those countries. Furthermore, countries need not permit patenting of living organisms, other than microorganisms, to comply with WTO requirements. Less restrictive property rights regimes suffice. An implicit market segmentation is thus developing where research processes and traits patented elsewhere may be freely available in countries and for agricultural commodities of little interest to the private sector.

Where required, agreements should be reached between developing-country NARSs and the major private-sector patent holders. These would explicitly segment markets and make available the output of modern biotechnology for further research and adaptation to benefit poor farmers and consumers in developing countries. Appropriate technology would become public goods in the poor and unprofitable markets while remaining private goods in profitable markets. Future Harvest centers could help facilitate such agreements while continuing to collaborate with NARSs.

Some firms have agreed to transfer proprietary technologies without charging royalties to developing countries where there are few potential commercial prospects. Monsanto, for example, has agreed to place its map of the rice genome in the public domain. The company has also agreed to transfer virus resistance technology to public research institutes in Mexico and Kenya working on potatoes and sweet potatoes, respectively. But so far such arrangements are few and generally involve the philanthropic arms of the private firms (Serageldin 1999; Qaim 1999).

Adaptation versus direct transfer. A final difference involves the adaptation of developed-country agricultural research to developing-country conditions. Conventional breeding efforts that focused on solving specific problems in developing countries (such as low rice yields) adapted developed-country technology to local conditions. Most current applications of modern biotechnology focus on developed-country agriculture.

In 2000, 76 percent of the land planted to GM crops was in developed countries, with the United States alone accounting for 68 percent of global GM crop area. Australia, with 150,000 hectares of commercial GM crops, accounted for 0.3 percent of 2000's total area. Among developing countries, the bulk of the hectares planted to GM crops were in Argentina and China, although Mexico, South Africa, and Uruguay also had commercial plantings. The GM crop area in the developing world increased by more than 50 percent over 1999 levels. Developing countries other than China with commercial GM plantings have a substantial number of large-scale, capital-intensive farms and produce primarily for industrialized-country markets. Herbicide-tolerant cotton, maize, and soybeans and insect-resistant cotton and maize account for 94 percent of global GM plantings. Both the area planted to GM crops and the value of the harvests grew dramatically between 1995 and 2000, from under a million hectares to more than 44 million. The global market for transgenic seed grew from US$1 million to US$3 billion between 1995 and 1999 (James 2000a and 2000b).

To date, little private-sector agricultural biotechnology research has focused on developing-country food crops other than maize. Moreover, little adaptation of the research to developing-country crops and conditions has occurred through the not-for-profit, public-goods-oriented channels prominent in conventional breeding efforts in the developing countries. Except for limited work on rice, maize, and cassava, mostly done by Future Harvest centers, little biotechnology research focuses on the productivity and nutrition of poor people. The Rockefeller Foundation's agriculture program is one of the few examples. In 1998, it provided about US$7.4 million for biotechnology research relevant to developing countries, mainly through international agricultural research centers and developing-country NARSs, with a major emphasis on rice. This sum pales in comparison with the multibillion-dollar research and development budgets of the life sciences companies (Rockefeller Foundation 1999; Monsanto Company 1999).

As with conventional breeding, the challenge is to move from the scientific foundation established by research efforts oriented toward developed countries to research focused on the needs of poor farmers and consumers in developing countries. Direct transfer of much of the current crop of agricultural biotechnologies to the developing world is inappropriate. For example, poor farmers in developing countries may not be able to afford herbicides. More appropriate research for the developing world might focus on biotechnology and conventional breeding to develop alternative forms of weed resistance. The West African Rice Development Association (WARDA), a Future Harvest center based in Côte d'Ivoire, used a combination of conventional breeding and tissue culture to cross African and Asian rice varieties. This resulted in a hardy, leafy rice that denies weeds sunlight. In addition to improving yields, this reduces the time women must spend weeding, allowing them to devote more attention to the childcare practices that are essential for good nutrition (WARDA 1999).

Insect-resistant crops could have great potential value for poor farmers. So far, however, the development of crops containing genes from the *Bacillus thuringiensis* (*Bt*) bacterium, which produces a natural insecticide, has focused on the crops and cropping environments of North America and on production for developed-country markets. *Bt* crops currently available require knowledge-intensive cultivation[2] and have proved transferable to larger-scale operations in developing countries such as Argentina and Uruguay. Nonetheless, debate abounds about the risks associated with gene-derived pest resistance, such as harm to beneficial species and cross-pollination of wild and weedy relatives, but evidence is so far inconclusive.

Research on crops and problems of relevance to small farmers in developing countries, including biotechnology research, will require expanded adaptive research engaging public and philanthropic institutions, including international agricultural research centers. Additional public resources must be allocated to such efforts. Moreover, the public sector can encourage private-sector research for poor people by converting some of the social benefits to private gains. For example, the state could offer to buy exclusive rights to a newly developed technology and make it available either free or at a nominal charge to small farmers. As in developing technology for the market, the private research agency would bear the risks of failing to develop the technology or having some other research agency do it first. This arrangement is similar to that recently proposed by Harvard University economist Jeffrey Sachs for developing a malaria vaccine for use in Africa (*The Economist* 1999). There is no reason to believe that the social rates of return to agricultural biotechnology research would be less than those for conventional research.

Without investment in biotechnology research oriented to developing-country agriculture, continued expansion of GM crop production in the developed countries may well harm small farmers in the developing world, as imported GM grain and feed crops undercut local production. Some developing-country consumers would benefit, but those consumers who also farm (a very high percentage of consumers in the poorest countries) could experience net losses. Also, the development of GM substitutes for developing-country export crops, such as high-protein rapeseed oil as a substitute for palm oil, could have a devastating impact on the livelihoods of developing-country farmers.

Lessons from conventional breeding. Experience with conventional crop research offers some guideposts for assessing the likely risks and benefits of agricultural biotechnology for developing countries. Risks and benefits may be inherent in a given technology, or they may transcend the technology. The policy environment into which a technology is introduced is critical. For example, International Food Policy Research Institute (IFPRI) research found that in Tamil Nadu, India, adoption of high-yielding grain varieties meant not only increased yields and cheaper, and more abundant food for consumers, but also income gains for small and larger-scale farmers alike, as well as for nonfarm poor rural households. Increased rural incomes contributed to nutrition gains (Hazell and Ramasamy 1991). The benefits were widely shared because the Tamil Nadu state government has pursued active poverty alleviation strategies, including extensive social safety net programs and investment in agriculture, rural development, nutrition, and education, along with a fair measure of equity in access to resources such as land and credit. Where increased inequality followed the adoption of modern crop varieties, this was not because of factors inherent in the technology, but rather a result of policies that did not promote equitable access to resources and development of human capital. Even in these areas, landless rural laborers usually found new job opportunities as a result of increased agricultural productivity, particularly where appropriate physical infrastructure and markets developed.

On the other hand, successful adoption of modern crop varieties depended on access to water, fertilizer, and pesticides. Thus, inequality between well-endowed and resource-poor areas increased because of the properties of the technology itself. Likewise, excessive or improper use of chemical inputs led to adverse environmental impacts in some instances. To some extent, this problem was offset by other characteristics inherent in the technology; by allowing yield gains without expanding cultivated area, the technology kept cultivators from clearing forests and marginal lands.

Applications of agricultural biotechnology in developing countries could address some of these very issues if research focuses on how to reduce the need for inputs and increase the efficiency of input use. This could lead to the development of crops that utilize water more efficiently, fix nitrogen from the air, extract phosphate from the soil more effectively, and resist pests without the use of synthetic pesticides. Such efforts, if successful, would reduce dependence on pesticides, fertilizers, and other inputs, making the technology more readily available to poor farmers.

Introducing agricultural biotechnology into developing countries could help increase productivity, lower unit costs and prices for food, preserve forests and fragile land, reduce poverty, and improve nutrition. Whether it will do so depends on whether the research is relevant to poor people, on the economic and social policy environment, and on the nature of the IPR arrangements governing the technology.

Weighing Risks and Benefits of Biotechnology in Developing Countries

The experience of the industrialized countries. In the industrialized countries, it is generally assumed that the economic benefits of GM crops accrue primarily to the life science companies that develop the new varieties and hold the patents, along with the seed companies that distribute them (increasingly, these firms are integrated as a consequence of mergers and acquisitions). While farmers stand to gain from reduced pest management costs and, in the case of herbicide-tolerant crops, greater efficiency of pesticide use, the potential yield gains may mean reduced prices. Consumers gain through lower prices. There are social and environmental benefits to reduced pesticide use, though these could be offset by potential environmental and health problems.[3]

As GM crops have been commercially available for only about six growing seasons, information is limited on their economic benefits and distribution. Some

Figure 3.8   Distribution of economic surplus generated by the use of Roundup Ready® soybean seed in the United States, 1997

(Total net economic surplus, US$360 million)

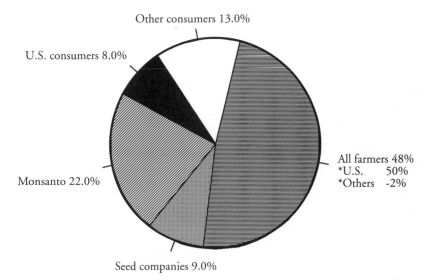

Other consumers 13.0%

U.S. consumers 8.0%

Monsanto 22.0%

All farmers 48%
*U.S.   50%
*Others -2%

Seed companies 9.0%

Source: Falck-Zepeda, Traxler, and Nelson (1999)

recent studies in the United States suggest that the reality may be more complex than conventional wisdom indicates. Falck-Zepeda, Traxler, and Nelson (2000) found that in 1996 U.S. farmers gained the largest share of the benefits from that year's *Bt* cotton crop (59 percent); while the gene developer, Monsanto, received 21 percent; consumers 13 percent; and the germplasm supplier, Delta and Pine Land Company, 5 percent. Falck-Zepeda, Traxler, and Nelson (1999) report that 1997 gains from herbicide-tolerant soybeans favored consumers even more (21 percent), while farmers gained fully half. Agribusiness's share was only 22 percent (Figure 3.8). Another soybean study confirms the global consumer gains and those of agribusiness, but suggests that the price-depressing effects of the yield gains may wipe out any benefits farmers could hope to achieve (Moschini, Lapan, and Sobolevsky 1999). A study of *Bt* maize found that the price premium placed on *Bt* seed was so high that the gains from efficiency and reduced pesticide use may not justify the costs unless farmers face a relatively high probability of European corn borer infestation and their yields are higher than average (Hyde et al. 1999). This literature suggests that, even under monopoly or oligopoly ownership of the technology, farmers and consumers may gain from the technologies and the benefits to consumers may be larger than assumed.

The potential benefits in developing countries. There are many potential benefits for poor people in developing countries. Biotechnology may help achieve the productivity gains needed to feed a growing global population, confer resistance to pests and diseases without costly purchased inputs, heighten the tolerance of crops to adverse weather and soil conditions, improve the nutritional value of some foods, and enhance the durability of products during harvesting or shipping. Bioengineered products may reduce reliance on pesticides, thereby reducing farmers' crop-protection costs and benefiting both the environment and public health. Biotechnology research could aid the development of drought-tolerant maize and insect-resistant cassava, helping small farmers and poor consumers. The development of cereal plants capable of capturing nitrogen from the air could contribute to plant nutrition, could also help small farmers, who often cannot afford fertilizers. Biotechnology may offer cost-effective solutions to the scourge of micronutrient malnutrition, which affects hundreds of millions of poor people in developing countries, through the development of vitamin A and iron-rich crops. For example, *Golden*Rice™, which is rich in beta carotene, a precursor of vitamin A, has been engineered in the laboratory but is not yet grown in farmers' fields. By raising productivity in food production, agricultural biotechnology could help to further reduce the need to cultivate new lands and to conserve biodiversity and protect fragile ecosystems.

Policies must expand and guide research and technology development to solve problems of importance to poor people. Research must focus on crops relevant to small farmers and poor consumers in developing countries, such as bananas, cassava, yams, sweet potatoes, rice, maize, wheat, and millet, along with livestock.

Food safety and biosafety. GM foods are not intrinsically good or bad for human health. Their health effect depends on their specific content. GM foods with higher iron content are likely to benefit iron-deficient consumers. But the transfer of genes from one species to another may also transfer characteristics that cause allergic reactions. Thus, GM foods need to be tested for allergen transfers before they are commercialized. Such testing prevented the commercialization of an allergenic soybean variety containing a Brazil nut gene. GM foods with possible allergy risks must be labeled. Testing for toxicity, digestivity, and the presence of known carcinogens is likewise needed.

Labeling may also be needed to identify content for cultural and religious reasons or simply because consumers want to know the contents of their food and the processes used to produce it so they can make informed choices. While the public sector must design and enforce standards, as well as labeling required to protect public health, other labeling might best be left to the private sector in accordance with consumer demands for information.

Failure to remove antibiotic-resistant marker genes used in research before a GM food is commercialized presents a potential although unproven health risk. Recent legislation in the E.U. requires that these genes be removed before a GM food is deemed safe (Levidow, Carr, and Wield 1999).

Risks and opportunities associated with GM foods should be integrated into the general food-safety regulations of a country. In addition, effective national biosafety regulations should be in place before modern biotechnology is introduced. Aid donors need to help developing countries build the capacity to monitor compliance and enforce these kinds of regulations. In 2000, with the successful negotiation of the Biosafety Protocol to the Convention on Biological Diversity, the international community took some modest steps toward supporting capacity-strengthening in developing countries. Minimal, globally accepted standards need to be put in place with respect to biosafety regimes. The development of a public global regulatory capacity has lagged far behind the pace of economic globalization (Juma and Gupta 1999; Cohen 2000).

The ecological risks that policymakers need to assess include the spread of traits such as herbicide resistance from genetically modified plants to unmodified plants (including weeds), the buildup of resistance in insect populations, unintended harm to nontarget species, and the potential threat to biodiversity posed by widespread monoculture of bioengineered crops. These risks are particularly significant in the centers of origin and diversity of major food crops, which are mainly in developing countries. Applications of technology that can switch specific genetic characteristics off and on offer great promise for the development of seed that will prevent the spread of new traits through cross-pollination. The seed would contain the desired traits, such as pest resistance or drought tolerance, but these would be activated through chemical treatment. Otherwise, the seed would maintain its normal characteristics. Thus, if a farmer planted improved seed, the offspring would not be sterile; rather it would revert to normal seed, without the improved traits. The farmer would have the choice of planting the seed and doing no more, or activating the improved traits by applying the chemical.

Both food-safety and biosafety regulations should reflect international agreements and a given society's acceptable risk levels, including the risks associated with not using biotechnology to achieve desired goals. Poor people should directly participate in debate and decisionmaking about technological change, the risks of that change, and the consequences of inaction or alternative actions.

Thorough testing is necessary to ensure the safety of new crop varieties developed through biotechnology. Questions about environmental safety and health risks must be addressed head-on. Testing of GM crops needs to increase in developing countries; at present, about 90 percent of the testing occurs in developed countries.

Anti-GM activists' destruction of test plots should also cease. Open debate is essential, but physical attacks on research and testing efforts contribute little to the free exchange of ideas or the formulation of policies that will advance food security. Moreover, without testing there can be no clear evidence concerning the safety of GM crops.

Socioeconomic risks. Unless developing countries have policies in place to ensure small farmers access to extension services, productive resources (such as land, water, and credit), markets, and infrastructure, there is considerable risk that agricultural biotechnology could lead to increased inequality of income and wealth, because larger farmers may capture most of the benefits through adoption of the technology, expanded production, and reduced unit costs (Leisinger 1999).

An ex ante assessment of Monsanto's transfer to Mexico of transgenic virus-resistance technology for potatoes examined some of the issues relating to social and economic benefits (Qaim 1999). It found that all classes of potato growers would likely benefit. Because small farmers have higher yield losses from viruses than larger producers, their yield gains and per-unit cost reductions are likely to exceed those of large farmers. This assessment thus found the technology to be biased toward small, rather than large farmers. This bias is reinforced by Monsanto's unwillingness to license the potato leaf roll virus-resistance technology for use with the potato variety that accounts for 69 percent of large farmers' plantings, because this variety is also grown in industrialized countries. Mexican seed distributors would be unlikely to charge a premium for the transgenic seed, which Monsanto transferred without charging royalties, given the competitive nature of the industry in Mexico. The study also found that a targeted government intervention to make transgenic red potatoes available to small and medium-sized farmers, comparable to the government seed distribution program for maize and bean seeds (*Alianza para el Campo*), would enable small farmers to capture 45 percent of the economic benefits from the cultivation of transgenic potatoes. Consumers would benefit from lower prices as a result of higher production. However, as Mexico reduces potato import barriers, the consumer gains are likely to decline (Qaim 1999).

Growing concentration among companies engaged in agricultural biotechnology research may lead to reduced competition, monopoly or oligopoly profits, exploitation of small farmers and consumers, and extraction of special favors from governments. Effective antitrust legislation and enforcement institutions are needed, particularly in small developing countries where one or only a few seed companies operate. As with biosafety, there is an urgent need for global standards regarding industrial concentration.

Finally, developing countries will need to enact and enforce IPR legislation in order to benefit from biotechnology. This legislation must harmonize protection of farmers' rights to access to germplasm and plant breeders' rights to benefit from their innovations.

Trade-related risks. The outcome of the new global agricultural trade negotiations, launched in Geneva in March 2000, could also affect developing countries' social and economic risks related to biotechnology. If the E.U.'s "precautionary principle" is accepted as the basis for new agreements on sanitary and phytosanitary standards and technical barriers to trade, then the E.U. could discriminate against any potential exporters of GM food or feed without scientific evidence of harm. At present, because it is private consumers and retailers who reject GM foods in Europe, the discrimination is not government trade policy and does not violate WTO rules. The Biosafety Protocol permits heightened scrutiny of GM imports, including labeling and segregation of GM and non-GM imports, but not outright bans.

Low-income developing countries that wish to use an agricultural export-led growth strategy will be forced to choose between adopting modern biotechnology in agriculture or maintaining the possibility of GM-free food export to the E.U. They could choose to differentiate and label GM foods and non-GM foods, and if they can manage such a system, they might be able to capture the benefits of modern agricultural biotechnology for domestic consumption while maintaining an export market for GM-free foods. Developing countries may also decide to label GM foods and GM-free foods in their domestic market to enable domestic consumers to choose. Because more productive agriculture is important for both urban and rural poor in low-income developing countries, it is hard to believe they would not utilize appropriate modern biotechnology in agriculture if biosafety regulations can be enacted and enforced.

A large share of the food imported by developing countries originates in the United States. These importing countries must therefore take a position not only on biosafety and food safety, but also on whether they wish to insist on product differentiation and labeling for imported food. Europe and Japan's rejection of GM crops may make such crops cheaper for Asian importers that are willing to purchase them (Anderson, this volume).

For Asian agricultural exporters, trade-related dilemmas are not hypothetical: The E.U. has warned Thailand that it will reject imports of Thai rice containing GM organisms (Petsiri 1999). This could undermine Thailand's rice biotechnology research, which is seeking to develop disease-resistant varieties among other things. In addition, Saudi Arabia has banned imports of Thai tuna because it is usually packed in soy oil, which may be made from GM beans from the United States. Fearing bans in other Middle Eastern countries, Europe, and Japan, Thai canneries have switched to sunflower oil (Paarlberg 2000a; Tanticharoen 2000; Petsiri 1999; Anonymous 2000).

Ethical issues. A major ethical concern is that genetic engineering and "life patents" accelerate the reduction of plants, animals, and microorganisms to mere commercial commodities, bereft of any sacred character, and that humans should not tinker with nature. This is far from a trivial consideration. However, all agricultural activities constitute human intervention in natural systems and processes. Continued human survival depends on precisely such interventions and is likewise a critical ethical concern. Condemning biotechnology for its potential risks without considering the alternative risks of prolonging the human misery caused by hunger, malnutrition, and child death is as unwise and unethical as blindly pursuing this technology without the necessary biosafety.

Modern biotechnology is not a silver bullet for achieving food security. But used in conjunction with traditional knowledge and conventional agricultural research methods, it may be a powerful tool in the fight against poverty. As such, it should be made available to poor farmers and consumers. It has the potential to enhance agricultural productivity in developing countries so as to reduce poverty, improve food security and nutrition, and promote sustainable use of natural resources. Solutions to the problems facing small farmers in developing countries will benefit both farmers and consumers.

The biggest risk of modern biotechnology for developing countries is that technological developments will bypass poor people. A form of what Ismail Serageldin, former chairperson of the CGIAR, calls "scientific apartheid" may well develop in which cutting-edge science is oriented exclusively toward industrialized countries and large-scale farming (Serageldin 1999, 387–89).

Issues for Future Action

To accommodate the different perspectives on modern biotechnology without excluding developing countries from making choices that they consider most appropriate, policy action is required on a number of fronts:

- Expand public investment in agricultural research, including molecular biology-based research where appropriate, aimed at achieving sustainable food security in developing countries.

- Build collaboration, support, and partnerships among NARSs in developing countries and between such national research systems and public- and private-sector research institutions in industrialized nations. The CGIAR could play a key role in facilitating such collaboration, support, and partnership while helping to undertake research of an international public goods nature.

- Strengthen national capabilities for testing GM foods and other agricultural commodities for health and environmental effects and for establishing effective biosafety and regulatory mechanisms.

- Develop IPR regimes in each developing country compatible with international agreements and national circumstances including the maintenance of farmers' rights to replant their own seed.

- Facilitate trade with developing countries irrespective of whether the countries choose to commercialize GM foods and nonfoods in their domestic production and consumption.

Additional efforts are needed to further inform the debate at all levels and in all countries. Such efforts should span the spectrum: from the generation and dissemination of results to the testing of new products and analyses of where modern biotechnology might help solve food, agriculture, and environmental problems and where alternatives are preferable. Education in basic biology with emphasis on improving understanding of the biological aspects related to genetic engineering is also urgently needed.

All parties, including private corporations and advocacy groups, should exercise responsible behavior. Scare campaigns and pressure on decisionmakers to shortcut testing of new products should be replaced by sound testing and evidence-based arguments, debates, and decisions.

Decisionmaking should be left to countries and individuals who are most likely to be affected by the decisions. Self-appointment of spokespersons and representatives of the poor and poor countries should cease, and low-income people and countries should be empowered to make their own choices on the basis of informed debate and their own estimates of risks and benefits.

Notes

1. The Undertaking was approved by the FAO Conference in 1983. The notion of farmers' rights includes the right to save, use, reuse, exchange, share, and market seeds. For more detail see Wright (1997) and various documents available at <http://www.fao.org>.

2. For example, licenses to use *Bt* maize in the United States require farmers to plant a "refuge" of non-*Bt* maize to slow the development of resistance to *Bt* in the targeted pests.

3. For some recent examples see Anonymous 1999; Knutson 1999; and Verzola 1999.

References

ABSF (African Biotechnology Stakeholders Forum). 1999. Re: Biotechnology and Kenya's socio-economic survival. ABSF, Nairobi, Kenya, September, 3. Occasional paper.

Adamu, H. 2000. We'll feed our people as we see fit. *The Washington Post* (September 11): A23.

Alston, J. M., C. Chan-Kang, M. C. Marra, P. G. Pardey, and TJ Wyatt. 2000. *A Meta-analysis of rates of return to agricultural R&D: Ex pede Herculem?* Research Report No. 113. Washington, D.C.: International Food Policy Research Institute.

Alston, J. M., P. G. Pardey, and V. H. Smith, eds. 1999. *Paying for agricultural productivity*. Baltimore: Johns Hopkins University Press.

Anonymous. 1999. Separate place for transgenic products in shop. *Dutch Agrarian Journal* (September 8). Posted to biotech_activists@iatp.org listserver.

———. 2000. Modified oil cited in tuna ban. *Bangkok Post* (March 25).

CGIAR (Consultative Group on International Agricultural Research). 1998. *Shaping the CGIAR's future: Summary of proceedings and decisions*. CGIAR International Centers Week, Washington, D.C., October 26-30, 1998. Washington, D.C.: CGIAR Secretariat.

Cohen, J. I. 2000. Harnessing biotechnology for the poor: Challenges ahead regarding biosafety and capacity building. Background paper prepared for the United Nations Development Programme (UNDP) *Human Development Report 2001*, October.

Environics International, Ltd. 1998. *The Environmental Monitor: 1998 International Report*. Toronto.

European Commission (EC). 2000. The Europeans and biotechnology. *Eurobarometer* 52 (1).

Falck-Zepeda, J. B., G. Traxler, and R. G. Nelson. 1999. Rent creation and distribution from biotechnology innovations: The case of *Bt* cotton and herbicide-tolerant soybeans. Paper presented at the NE-165 conference Transitions in Agbiotech: Economics of Strategy and Policy, Washington, D.C., June 24–25.

———. 2000. Surplus distribution from the introduction of a biotechnology innovation. *American Journal of Agricultural Economics* 82 (2): 360–370.

FAO (Food and Agriculture Organization of the United Nations). 1996. *Investment in agriculture: Evolution and prospects*. World Food Summit Technical Background Document No. 10. Rome.

———. 1998–2000. *State of Food and Agriculture 1998, 1999, and 2000*. Rome.

Gaskell, G., M. W. Bauer, J. Durant, and N. C. Allum. 1999. Worlds apart? The reception of genetically modified foods in Europe and the U.S. *Science* 285 (5426): 384–87.

Hazell, P., and C. Ramasamy, eds. 1991. *The Green Revolution reconsidered*. Baltimore: Johns Hopkins University Press.

Hoban, T. J. 2000. Public perceptions of transgenic plants. In *The handbook of transgenic plants*. New York: Marcel Dekker.

Hyde, J. M., A. Martin, P. V. Preckel, and C. R. Edwards. 1999. The economics of Bt corn: Valuing protection from the European corn borer. *Review of Agricultural Economics* 21 (2): 442–54.

James, C. 2000a. *The global status of commercialized transgenic crops: 1999*. International Service for the Acquisition of Agri-biotechnology Applications Brief 17. Ithaca, N.Y., U.S.A.

———. 2000b. *Preview—Global review of commercialized transgenic crops: 2000*. International Service for the Acquisition of Agri-biotech Applications Brief 21. Ithaca, N.Y., U.S.A.

Juma, C., and A. Gupta. 1999. *Safe use of biotechnology: Biotechnology for developing countries— problems and opportunities.* 2020 Vision Focus 2, Brief 6 of 10. Washington, D.C.: International Food Policy Research Institute.

Knutson, R. 1999. Look at *Bt* benefits with an open mind. *Des Moines Register*, September 14.

Leisinger, K. M. 1999. *Disentangling risk issues.* 2020 Vision Focus 2, Brief 5 of 10. Washington, D.C.: International Food Policy Research Institute.

Levidow, L., S. Carr, and D. Wield. 1999. *Safety of transgenic crops completing the internal market? A study of the implementation of EU Directive 90/220—EU level report.* Prepared under contract no. BIO4CT97-2215, 1997-99, by the Centre for Technology Strategy, The Open University, Milton Keynes, U.K. (November).

Michel, J. H. 1999. *Development co-operation, 1998.* Paris: Organisation for Economic Co-operation and Development.

Monsanto Company. 1999. *Annual report 1998.* <http://www.monsanto.com/monsanto/investor/report/98/financialsection/income.html>. Accessed October 19, 1999.

Moschini, G., H. Lapan, and A. Sobolevsky. 1999. *Roundup Ready® soybeans and welfare effects in the soybean complex.* Department of Economics Staff Paper 324. Ames: Iowa State University (September).

Oxfam. 1999. Genetically modified crops, world trade, and food security. Oxfam GB Position Paper, November, 12–14. Oxford.

Paarlberg, R. L. 2000a. *Governing the GM crop revolution: Policy choices for developing countries.* 2020 Vision for Food, Agriculture, and the Environment Discussion Paper 33. Washington, D.C.: International Food Policy Research Institute.

———. 2000b. Genetically modified crops in developing countries: Promise or peril? *Environment* 42 (1): 19–27.

Pardey, P. G., and J. M. Alston. 1996. Revamping agricultural R&D. 2020 Brief 24. Washington, D.C.: International Food Policy Research Institute.

Petsiri, E. 1999. EU warns Thailand over gene-altered rice exports. *Reuters Business Briefings* (October 12).

Pinstrup-Andersen, P., and M. J. Cohen. 1998. Aid to developing-country agriculture: Investing in poverty reduction and new export opportunities. 2020 Vision Brief 56. Washington, D.C.: International Food Policy Research Institute.

Pinstrup-Andersen, P., M. Lundberg, and J. L. Garrett. 1995. Foreign assistance to agriculture: A winwin proposition. 2020 Vision Food Policy Report. Washington, D.C.: International Food Policy Research Institute.

Pinstrup-Andersen, P., and E. Schiøler. 2001. *Seeds of contention: World hunger and the global controversy over GM crops.* Baltimore: Johns Hopkins University Press.

Qaim, M. 1999. Potential benefits of agricultural biotechnology: An example from the Mexican potato sector. *Review of Agricultural Economics* 21 (2): 390–408.

Reddy, P. C. 2000. When western activism is midguided. Personal communication to Klaus von Grebmer, communications director, International Food Policy Research Institute (October 31). Washington, D.C.

Rockefeller Foundation. 1999. *Annual report 1998.* <http://www.rockfound.org>. Accessed October 19, 1999.

Rosegrant, M. W., M. Agcaoili-Sombilla, and N. D. Perez. 1995. Global food projections to 2020: Implications for investment. 2020 Vision for Food, Agriculture, and the Environment Discussion Paper 5. Washington, D.C.: International Food Policy Research Institute.

Serageldin, I. 1999. Biotechnology and food security in the 21st century. *Science* 285 (16 July): 387–89.

Tanticharoen, M. 2000. Thailand: Biotechnology for farm products and agro-industries. In G. J. Persley and M. M. Lantin eds. *Agricultural biotechnology and the poor.* Washington, D.C.: CGIAR.

The Economist. 1999. Sachs on development: Helping the world's poorest. August 14: 17–20.

Thomson, J. A. 2000. Developing countries can't wait and see. Available at <http://www.cid.harvard.edu/cidbiotech/comments/comments69.htm>. Accessed July 28, 2000.

Verzola, R. S. 1999. The genetic engineering debate. Posted to biotech_activists@iatp.org listserver (November 14).

WARDA (West African Rice Development Association). 1999. *The Spark that lit a flame: Participatory varietal selection.* Bouaké, Côte D'Ivoire.

Wright, B. D. 1997. Crop genetic resource policy: The role of *ex situ* genebanks. *Australian Journal of Agricultural and Resource Economics* 41 (1): 81–115.

Chapter 4

Estimating the Global Economic Effects of GMOS

Kym Anderson, Chantal Pohl Nielsen,
Sherman Robinson, and Karen Thierfelder

Introduction

Virtually all new technologies, even when they unambiguously benefit the vast majority of society, are opposed by at least a few people. The new agricultural biotechnologies that are generating transgenic or genetically modified organisms (GMOs), however, are attracting an exceptionally large degree of opposition to their production and trade. Opponents have raised both environmental and food safety concerns over the development of transgenic or genetically modified crops. The vast majority of opponents at least want to have labels on products that may contain GMOs, while the most extreme of them (particularly in western Europe) want to see GM crops totally excluded from production and consumption in their country.[1] This extreme view contrasts with the more relaxed attitude towards the use of the new biotechnologies in pharmaceuticals, and swamps discussions of the current and prospective positive attributes of GM crops. Also associated with that negative view is the idea that we should not try to measure the economic and other effects of GMOs because too much uncertainty surrounds the technology. We beg to differ with the latter sentiment: without attempts to quantify the economic effects of GMOs, opinion formation and policymaking would be even less well informed because it would have to depend even more on guesswork.

To illustrate the usefulness of quantitative models for informing GMO debates, this chapter draws on recent studies[2] in which we use two existing empirical models of the global economy to examine the possible effects of widespread use of genetically modified (GM) crop varieties in some (non-European) countries in light of different policy or consumer preference responses. Specifically, the standard global, economywide Global Trade Analysis Project (GTAP) model is used to explore the possible effects of an assumed degree of GMO-induced productivity growth for maize and soybean in selected countries. These are more controversial than cotton and rice (see Nielsen and Anderson 2000b) because they are grown extensively in rich countries and are consumed by people there both directly and via animal products. Those maize/soybean results are compared with what they would be if (a) western Europe chose to ban consumption and hence imports of those products from countries adopting GM technology or (b) some western European consumers and intermediate users responded by boycotting imported GM-potential crops. Another study uses a General Algebraic Modeling System (GAMS)-based global computable general equilibrium (CGE) model in which countries can produce both GM and GM-free varieties of maize and soybeans. As in the GTAP analysis, there is an assumed degree of GMO-induced productivity growth for GM varieties. The model is used to explore the impact on production, trade, and the relative price of the GM and non-GM varieties of a preference shift towards GM-free food in western Europe and high-income Asia. The final section discusses areas where future empirical work of this sort might focus.

Estimating Economic Effects of GMO Adoption in the GTAP Model in which Certain Countries Produce Only GM Varieties

The apparent differences in preferences and views on environmental issues and consumers' right to know about food ingredients are unlikely to disappear in the foreseeable future. The extent to which that could lead to trade disputes depends heavily on the directions and magnitudes of the production, trade, and welfare consequences of different responses to the technology by different countries. Theory alone cannot determine the likely direction, let alone the magnitude, of some of the effects of those responses to GMOs. Hence an empirical modeling approach is needed to estimate the economywide impact of assumed GMO-induced productivity growth and any associated policy changes and consumer responses. What follows is a summary of some early attempts at doing that for maize and soybeans.

These quantitative analyses make use of global, economywide CGE models and are based on the same global database, GTAP.[3] The global CGE models capture the vertical and horizontal linkages between all product markets both within the model's individual countries and regions as well as between countries and regions via their separately identified bilateral trade flows. The models are shocked with productivity growth in their sectors producing coarse grain (grain other than wheat and rice, which is primarily maize in the countries considered) and oilseeds (primarily soybeans in the countries considered).

Detailed empirical information about the impact of GMO technology in terms of reduced chemical use, higher yields, and other agronomic improvements is at this stage quite limited (see, for example, OECD 2000 and Nelson et al. 1999). Even so, available empirical evidence (for example, ERS 1999; James 1997 and 1998; and Marra this volume) suggests that cultivating GM crops has general cost-reducing effects.[4] Hence in estimating the economic impact of adopting GM technology in the maize and soybean sectors under different policy and consumer preference assumption, it is assumed that the effect of adopting GM crops can be captured by a Hicks-neutral technology shift, that is, a uniform reduction in each adopting region of all primary factors and intermediate inputs needed to obtain the same level of production. For present purposes using the GTAP model, the GM-adopting sectors are assumed to experience an increase in total factor productivity of 5 percent, thus lowering the supply price of the GM crop to that extent.[5] Assuming sufficiently elastic demand conditions, the cost-reducing technology will lead to increased production and higher returns to the factors of production employed in the GM-adopting sector. Labor, capital, and land consequently will be drawn into the affected sector. As suppliers of inputs and buyers of agricultural products, other sectors will also be affected by the use of genetic engineering in GM-potential sectors through vertical linkages. Input suppliers will initially experience lower demand because the production process in the GM sector has become more efficient. To the extent that the production of GM crops increases, however, the demand for inputs by producers of those crops may actually rise despite the input-reducing technology. Demanders of primary agricultural products such as grains and soybean meal for livestock feed will benefit from lower input prices, which in turn will affect the market competitiveness of livestock products.

The widespread adoption of GM varieties in certain regions will affect international trade flows depending on how traded the crop in question is and whether or not trade is restricted specifically because of the GMOs involved. To the extent that trade is not further restricted and not currently subject to binding quantitative restrictions, world market prices for these products will have a tendency to decline and thus benefit regions that are net importers of these products. For exporters, the lower price may or may not boost their trade volume, depending on price elasticities in foreign markets. Welfare in the exporting countries would go down for non-adopters but could also go down for some adopters if the adverse terms of trade change were to be sufficiently strong.

In modelling the adoption of GMOs in maize and soybean production, Nielsen and Anderson (2001) apply GM-driven productivity growth of 5 percent in coarse grain (excluding wheat and rice) and oilseeds to North America, Mexico, the Southern Cone region of Latin America, China, India, the rest of East Asia (excluding Japan and the East Asian newly independent countries or NICs), and South Africa. Other countries are assumed to refrain from using GM crops in their production systems.

We consider three maize/soybean scenarios. The first is a base case with no policy or consumer reactions to GMOs. The others (scenarios 2 and 3) impose on this base case a policy or consumer response in western Europe. In scenario 2, western Europe not only refrains from using GM crops in its own domestic production systems, but the region is also assumed to reject imports of GM oilseeds and coarse grains from GM-adopting regions. Scenario 3 considers the case in which consumers express their preferences through market mechanisms rather than through government regulation.

Scenario 1: Selected Regions Adopt GM Maize and Soybeans

Table 4.1 reports the results for scenario 1. A 5 percent reduction in overall production costs in these sectors leads to increases in coarse grain production of between 0.4 percent and 2.1 percent, and increases in oilseed production of between 1.1 and 4.6 percent, in the GM-adopting regions. The production responses are generally larger for oilseeds as compared with coarse grain. This is because a larger share of oilseed production as compared with coarse grain production is destined for export markets in all the reported regions, and therefore oilseed production is not limited to the same extent by domestic demand, which is less price-elastic. Increased oilseed production leads to lower market prices and hence cheaper costs of production in the vegetable oils and fats sectors, expanding output there. This expansion is particularly marked in the Southern Cone region of South America, where no less than a quarter of this production is sold on foreign markets (Table 4.1 part a), thereby allowing for a larger production response to the reduced costs of production in this sector. In North America, maize is also used as livestock feed; lower feed prices lead to an expansion of the livestock and meat processing sectors there.

Given large world market shares of oilseeds from North and South America and coarse grain from North America (Table 4.1 part a), increased supply from these regions causes world prices for coarse grain and oilseeds to decline by 4.0 and 4.5 percent, respectively. As a consequence of the more intense competition from abroad, production of coarse grain and oilseeds declines in the nonadopting regions. This is particularly so in western Europe, a major net importer of oilseeds, of which about half comes from North America. Cereal grain imports into western Europe increase only slightly (0.1 percent), but the increased competition and lower price are enough to entail a 4.5 percent decline in western European production. In the

Table 4.1   Scenario 1: Effects of selected regions adopting GM maize and soybean

A. Effects on production, domestic prices, and trade[a]

Commodity	North America	Southern Cone	China	India	Western Europe	Sub-Saharan Africa
Production			(percentage changes)			
Coarse grain	2.1	1.6	1.0	0.4	−4.5	−2.3
Oilseeds	3.6	4.6	1.8	1.1	−11.2	−1.3
Livestock	0.8	−0.0	0.1	0.4	−0.2	−0.1
Meat and dairy	0.5	0.0	0.1	1.3	−0.1	−0.1
Vegetable oils and fats	1.1	4.5	1.4	0.0	−0.9	−1.2
Other foods	0.2	0.1	0.4	1.5	−0.1	0.0
Market prices						
Coarse grain	−5.5	−5.5	−5.6	−6.7	−0.5	−0.4
Oilseeds	−5.5	−5.3	−5.6	−6.5	−1.2	−0.3
Livestock	−1.8	−0.3	−0.4	−1.4	−0.3	−0.3
Meat and dairy	−1.0	−0.2	−0.3	−1.0	−0.2	−0.2
Vegetable oils and fats	−2.4	−3.1	−2.6	−1.0	−0.5	−0.2
Other foods	−0.3	−0.2	−0.5	−1.0	−0.1	−0.2
Exports[b]						
Coarse grain	8.5	13.3	16.8	37.3	−11.5	−20.0
Oilseeds	8.5	10.5	8.2	21.5	−20.5	−26.5
Livestock	8.9	−2.0	−3.3	9.4	−1.1	−1.5
Meat and dairy	4.8	−0.9	−0.9	5.8	−0.5	−0.2
Vegetable oils and fats	5.8	14.3	5.6	−3.8	−4.9	−5.3
Other foods	0.2	0.1	1.6	7.6	−0.6	0.1
Imports[b]						
Coarse grain	−1.6	−4.6	−4.2	−20.5	0.1	11.3
Oilseeds	−2.6	−9.2	−1.6	−8.6	2.5	16.5
Livestock	−2.1	1.3	0.9	−5.2	0.2	0.5
Meat and dairy	−1.9	0.2	0.8	−1.7	−0.0	0.1
Vegetable oils and fats	−3.7	−3.6	−1.7	3.1	1.3	3.4
Other foods	0.0	−0.1	−0.6	−3.1	0.1	−0.1

B. Effects on regional economic welfare

Region/Country	Equivalent variation (EV)	Decomposition of welfare results, contribution of:		
		Allocative efficiency effects	Terms of trade effects	Technical change
	(US$ million pa)		(US$ million)	
North America	2,624	−137	−1,008	3,746
Southern Cone	826	120	−223	923
China	839	113	66	672
India	1,265	182	−9	1,094
Western Europe	2,010	1,755	253	0
Sub-Saharan Africa	−9	−2	−9	0
Other high-income[c]	1,186	554	641	0
Other developing and transition economies	1,120	171	289	673
World	9,861	2,756	0	7,108

Source: Nielsen and Anderson's (2000a) GTAP model results.
a. North America, Mexico, Southern Cone, China, rest of East Asia, India, and South Africa.
b. Includes intra-regional trade.
c. Japan, newly industrialized Asia, Australia, and New Zealand.

GM-adopting developing countries, production of coarse grain and oilseeds expands slightly. The changes in India, however, are relatively small compared with China and the Southern Cone region. This is explained by the domestic market orientation of these sales. That means India's relatively small production increase causes rather substantial declines in domestic prices for these products, which in turn benefits the other agricultural sectors through vertical linkages. For example, 67 percent of inter-mediate demand for coarse grain and 37 percent of intermediate demand for oilseeds in India stems from the livestock sector, according to the GTAP database. Agriculture and food output in non-GM-adopting developing countries, such as Sub-Saharan Africa, decline.

Global economic welfare (as traditionally measured in terms of equivalent variations of income, ignoring any externalities) is boosted in this first scenario by US$9.9 billion per year, two thirds of which is enjoyed by the adopting regions (Table 4.1 part b). It is noteworthy that all regions (both adopting and nonadopting) gain in terms of economic welfare except Sub-Saharan Africa. Most of this gain stems directly from the technology boost. The net-exporting GM-adopters experience worsened terms of trade from increased competition in world markets, but this adverse welfare effect is outweighed by the positive effect of the technological boost. Western Europe gains from the productivity increase in the other regions only in part because of cheaper imports; mostly it gains because increased competition from abroad shifts domestic resources out of relatively highly assisted segments of European Union (E.U.) agriculture. The group of other high-income countries, among which are East Asian nations that are relatively large net importers of the GM-potential crops, benefits equally from lower import prices and a more efficient use of resources in domestic farm production.

Scenario 2: Selected Regions Adopt GM Coarse Grain and Oilseeds plus Western Europe Bans Imports of Those Products from GM-Adopting Regions

In this scenario, western Europe not only refrains from using GM crops in its own domestic production systems, but the region is also assumed to reject imports of GM oilseeds and coarse grain from GM-adopting regions. This assumes that the labeling requirements of the Biosafety Protocol (UNEP 2000) enable western European importers to identify such shipments and that all oilseed and coarse grain exports from GM-adopting regions will be labelled "may contain GMOs." Under those conditions the distinction between GM-inclusive and GM-free products is simplified to one that relates directly to the country of origin,[6] and labeling costs are ignored. This import-ban scenario reflects the most extreme application of the precautionary principle within the framework of the Biosafety Protocol.

A western European ban on the imports of GM coarse grain and oilseeds changes the situation in scenario 1 rather dramatically, especially for the oilseed sector in North America, which has depended highly on the E.U. market. The result of the European ban is not only a decline in total North American oilseed exports by almost 30 percent, but also a production decline of 10 percent, pulling resources such as land out of this sector (Table 4.2). For coarse grain, by contrast, only 18 percent of North American production is exported and just 8 percent of those exports are destined for western Europe. Therefore the ban does not affect North American production and exports of coarse grain to the same extent that it affects soybeans, although the downward pressure on the international price of coarse grain nonetheless dampens the production-enhancing effect of the technological boost significantly. Similar effects are evident in the other GM-adopting regions, except for India—once again because its production of these particular crops is virtually all sold domestically and so is not greatly affected by market developments abroad.

For Sub-Saharan Africa, which by assumption is unable to adopt the new GM technology, access to the western European markets expands when other competitors are excluded. Oilseed exports from this region rise by enough to increase domestic production by 4 percent. Western Europe increases its own production of oilseeds, however, so the aggregate increase in its oilseed imports amounts to less than 1 percent. Its production of coarse grain also increases, but not by as much because of an initial high degree of self-sufficiency. Europe's shift from imported oilseeds and coarse grain to domestically produced products has implications further downstream. Given an imperfect degree of substitution in production between domestic and imported intermediate inputs, the higher prices of domestically produced maize and soybeans mean that livestock feed is slightly more expensive. (Half of intermediate demand for coarse grain in western Europe stems from the livestock sector.) Inputs to other food processing industries, particularly the vegetable oils and fats sector, are also more expensive. As a consequence, production in these downstream sectors declines and competing imports increase.

Aggregate welfare implications of this scenario are substantially different from those of scenario 1. Western Europe now experiences a decline in aggregate economic welfare of US$4.3 billion per year instead of a boost of US$2 billion (compare Tables 4.1 and 4.2 parts b). A closer look at the decomposition of the welfare changes reveals that adverse allocative efficiency effects explain the decline. Most significantly, E.U. resources are forced into producing oilseeds, of which a substantial amount was previously imported. Consumer welfare in western Europe is reduced in this scenario because, assuming that those consumers are assumed to be indifferent between GM-inclusive and GM-free products, the import ban restricts them

Table 4.2   Scenario 2: Effects of selected regions adopting GM maize and soybeans plus western Europe bans imports of those products from GM-adopting regions

A. Effects on production, domestic prices, and trade[a]

Commodity	North America	Southern Cone	China	India	Western Europe	Sub-Saharan Africa
Production			(percentage changes)			
Cereal grain	0.9	0.0	0.8	0.4	5.3	−2.2
Oilseeds	−10.2	−3.6	−0.8	0.8	66.4	4.4
Livestock	1.2	0.3	0.2	0.4	−0.8	0.0
Meat and dairy	0.8	0.3	0.2	1.4	−0.5	−0.0
Vegetable oils and fats	2.4	8.1	1.6	0.1	−3.4	0.0
Other foods	0.3	0.4	0.5	1.6	−0.5	−0.1
Market prices						
Cereal grain	−6.2	−6.0	−5.6	−6.7	0.8	−0.0
Oilseeds	−7.4	−6.8	−6.0	−6.5	5.8	0.4
Livestock	−2.2	−0.7	−0.4	−1.4	0.5	0.1
Meat and dairy	−1.3	−0.4	−0.3	−1.0	0.3	0.1
Vegetable oils and fats	−3.3	−4.0	−2.7	−1.0	2.0	0.0
Other foods	−0.4	−0.3	−0.5	−1.0	0.1	0.0
Exports [b]						
Cereal grain	0.3	−2.9	5.0	23.4	15.9	−13.1
Oilseeds	−28.8	−69.2	−18.4	−8.7	167.2	105.0
Livestock	13.7	4.0	−1.4	12.6	−3.8	−1.8
Meat and dairy	7.5	2.1	0.1	7.1	−1.4	0.3
Vegetable oils and fats	14.4	26.2	7.0	1.3	−15.0	5.8
Other foods	1.5	1.9	2.0	8.0	−1.4	−0.6
Imports [b]						
Cereal grain	−1.9	−5.3	−2.8	−20.0	3.3	13.4
Oilseeds	−5.6	−21.9	3.0	−3.7	0.6	22.5
Livestock	−3.2	0.1	0.1	−5.9	0.9	0.5
Meat and dairy	−2.8	−0.5	0.8	−1.8	−0.2	−0.0
Vegetable oils and fats	−7.7	−5.5	−1.7	4.0	5.5	2.4
Other foods	−0.6	−0.6	−0.8	−2.8	0.1	0.2

B. Effects on regional economic welfare

Region/Country	Equivalent variation (EV)	Decomposition of welfare results, contribution of:		
		Allocative efficiency effects	Terms of trade effects	Technical change
	(US$ million pa)		(US$ million)	
North America	2,299	27	−1,372	3,641
Southern Cone	663	71	−303	893
China	804	74	70	669
India	1,277	190	−3	1,092
Western Europe	−4,334	−4,601	257	0
Sub-Saharan Africa	42	5	38	0
Other high-income[c]	1,371	592	782	0
Other developing and transition economies	1,296	101	531	672
World	3,418	−3,541	0	6,967

Source: Nielsen and Anderson's (2000a) GTAP model results.
a. North America, Mexico, Southern Cone, China, rest of East Asia, India, and South Africa.
b. Includes intra-regional trade.
c. Japan, newly industrialized Asia, Australia, and New Zealand.

from benefiting from lower international prices. To the extent that some western Europeans in fact value a ban on GM products in their domestic markets, such a ban would partially offset the loss in economic welfare.

The key exporters of the GM products, China, North America, and Southern Cone all show a smaller gain in welfare in this scenario compared with the scenario in which there is no European policy response. Net importers of corn and soybeans (for example, "other high-income," which is mostly East Asia), by contrast, are slightly better off in this than in scenario 1. Meanwhile, the countries in Sub-Saharan Africa are affected in a slightly positive instead of a slightly negative way, gaining from better terms of trade. In particular, a higher price is obtained for their oilseed exports to western European markets in this scenario compared with scenario 1.

Two thirds of the global gain from the new GM technology as measured in scenario 1 would be eroded by an import ban imposed by western Europe: It falls from US$9.9 billion per year to just US$3.4 billion, with western Europe bearing almost the entire erosion in economic welfare (assuming as before that consumers are indifferent between GM-free and GM-inclusive foods). The rest of the erosion is borne by the net-exporting adopters (mainly North America and the Southern Cone region). Since the nonadopting regions generally purchase most of their imported coarse grain and oilseeds from the North American region, they benefit even more than in scenario 1 from lower import prices: their welfare is estimated to be greater by almost one fifth with a western European import ban than with no European reaction.

Scenario 3: Selected Regions Adopt GM Maize and Soybeans plus Some Western Europeans' Preferences Shift against GM Maize and Soybeans

As an alternative to a policy response, this scenario analyses the impact of a partial shift in western European preferences away from imported coarse grain and oilseeds and in favor of domestically produced crops.[7] The scenario is implemented as an exogenous 25 percent reduction in final consumer and intermediate demand for all imported oilseeds and coarse grain (that is, not only those which can be identified as coming from GM-adopting regions).[8] This can be interpreted as an illustration of incomplete information being provided about imported products (still assuming that GM crops are not cultivated in western Europe), if a label only states that the product "may contain GMOs." Such a label does not assist western European consumers who want to be able to distinguish between GMO-inclusive and GMO-free products. Thus some European consumers and firms are assumed to completely avoid products produced outside western Europe, shifting demand in favor of domestically produced goods. Western European producers and suppliers are assumed to be able to signal—at no additional cost—that their products are GM-free by, for example, labeling products by country of origin. Because it is assumed that no producers in western Europe adopt GM crops (perhaps as a result of government regulation), such a label would be perceived as a sufficient guarantee of the absence of GMOs.

As the results in Table 4.3 reveal, having consumers express their preferences through market mechanisms rather than through a government-implemented import ban has a much less damaging effect on production in the GM-adopting countries. In particular, instead of declines in oilseed production as in scenario 2 there are slight increases in this scenario, and production responses in coarse grain are slightly larger. Once again the changes are less marked for China and India, which are less affected by international market changes for these products. As expected, domestic oilseed production in western Europe must increase somewhat to accommodate the shift in preferences, but not nearly to the same extent as in the previous scenario. Furthermore, there are minor price reductions for agrifood products in western Europe because (by assumption) the shift in preferences is only partial, and so some consumers and firms do benefit from lower import prices. In other words, in contrast to the previous scenario, a certain link between E.U. prices and world prices is retained here because of only a partial reduction in import demand. The output growth in Sub-Saharan Africa in scenario 2, created by taking the opportunity of serving European consumers and firms while other suppliers were excluded, is replaced in this scenario by declines: Sub-Saharan Africa loses export share to the GM-adopting regions.

The numerical welfare results in this scenario are comparable with those of scenario 1 (the scenario without the import ban or the partial preference shift) for all regions except, of course, western Europe. Furthermore, the estimated decline in economic welfare that western Europe would experience if it banned maize and soybean imports is changed to a slight gain in this scenario (although recall that these welfare measures assume consumers are indifferent to whether a food contains GMOs). The dramatic worsening of resource allocative efficiency in the previous scenario is changed to a slight improvement in this one. This is because production in the lightly assisted oilseeds sector increases at the expense of production in all other (more heavily distorted) agrifood sectors in western Europe.

The welfare gains for North America in this scenario are similar to those of scenario 1. But even scenario 2 gains are large, suggesting considerable flexibility in both domestic and foreign markets in responding to policy and consumer preference changes, plus the dominance of the benefits of the new technology for adopting countries. Given that the preference shift in scenario 3 is based on the assumption that nonadopters outside western Europe cannot guarantee that their exports to this region are GMO-free, Sub-Saharan Africa cannot benefit from the same kind of "preferential" access the region obtained in the previous scenario, where coarse grain

Table 4.3   Scenario 3: Effects of selected regions adopting GM maize and soybeans plus partial shift of western European preferences away from imports of GM products

A. Effects on production, domestic prices, and trade[a]

Commodity	North America	Southern Cone	China	India	Western Europe	Sub-Saharan Africa
Production			*(percentage changes)*			
Coarse grain	1.8	1.3	1.0	0.4	−2.0	−2.6
Oilseeds	1.0	2.8	1.1	1.0	8.7	−1.6
Livestock	0.9	0.0	0.2	0.4	−0.4	−0.1
Meat and dairy	0.6	0.1	0.1	1.3	−0.2	−0.0
Vegetable oils and fats	1.2	5.0	1.4	−0.0	−1.1	−1.2
Other foods	0.2	0.2	0.4	1.5	−0.2	0.1
Market prices						
Coarse grain	−5.7	−5.6	−5.6	−6.7	−0.2	−0.4
Oilseeds	−5.9	−5.6	−5.7	−6.5	0.1	−0.3
Livestock	−1.9	−0.4	−0.4	−1.4	−0.1	−0.3
Meat and dairy	−1.1	−0.2	−0.3	−1.0	−0.1	−0.2
Vegetable oils and fats	−2.6	−3.3	−2.6	−1.0	−0.4	−0.2
Other foods	−0.3	−0.2	−0.5	−1.0	−0.1	−0.2
Exports [b]						
Coarse grain	6.6	9.7	13.9	34.1	−29.7	−24.1
Oilseeds	1.4	−4.5	2.1	14.1	−41.5	−32.4
Livestock	9.8	−0.9	−3.0	10.0	−1.8	−1.2
Meat and dairy	5.3	−0.4	−0.8	6.0	−0.7	0.1
Vegetable oils and fats	6.7	15.8	5.5	−4.0	−5.8	−4.9
Other foods	0.4	0.4	1.7	7.6	−0.7	0.1
Imports [b]						
Coarse grain	−1.7	−4.8	−3.9	−20.4	−23.6	11.5
Oilseeds	−2.9	−9.6	−0.7	−7.4	−17.7	17.3
Livestock	−2.3	1.1	0.8	−5.3	0.4	0.2
Meat and dairy	−2.1	0.1	0.8	−1.7	−0.1	−0.0
Vegetable oils and fats	−4.2	−3.8	−1.5	3.4	1.5	3.4
Other foods	−0.1	−0.2	−0.6	−3.0	0.1	−0.1

B. Effects on regional economic welfare

Region/Country	Equivalent variation (EV)	Decomposition of welfare results, contribution of:		
		Allocative efficiency effects	Terms of trade effects	Technical change
	(US$ million pa)		*(US$ million)*	
North America	2,554	−100	−1,092	3,726
Southern Cone	785	109	−246	917
China	834	106	69	672
India	1,267	184	−9	1,093
Western Europe	715	393	319	0
Sub-Saharan Africa	−5	0	−7	0
Other high-income[c]	1,233	567	674	0
Other developing and transition economies	1,120	168	293	673
World	8,503	1,427	1	7,081

Source: Nielsen and Anderson's (2000a) GTAP model results.
a. North America, Mexico, Southern Cone, China, rest of East Asia, India, and South Africa.
b. Includes intra-regional trade.
c. Japan, newly industrialized Asia, Australia, and New Zealand.

and oilseeds from identifiable GMO-adopting regions were banned completely. Hence Sub-Saharan Africa slips back to a slight loss in this scenario due to a net worsening of its terms of trade and the absence of productivity gains from genetic engineering techniques. Globally, welfare in this case is only a little below that when there is no preference shift: a gain of US$8.5 billion per year compared with US$9.9 billion in scenario 1, with western Europe clearly bearing the bulk of this difference.

Estimating Economic Effects of GMO Adoption in a Global CGE Model with Segmented Markets for GM and Non-GM Varieties in All Countries

An alternative modeling framework is used in a recent analysis by Nielsen, Robinson, and Thierfelder (2001), hereafter the NRT model, which draws on a model developed by Lewis, Robinson, and Thierfelder (1999). The NRT model is expressed in levels and solved using the GAMS modeling language. The model is more aggregated than the GTAP model used in Neilsen and Anderson (2001), with just 7 regions and 10 sectors, but is otherwise similar to the standard GTAP model. The NRT model introduces GM varieties by segmenting the coarse grain and oilseed sectors into GM and non-GM lines of production. In contrast to the Neilsen and Anderson model in which a country produces either GM or non-GM varieties exclusively, the NRT model allows a country to produce both varieties in response to market conditions.

This segregation is introduced based on a notion that there may be a viable market for guaranteed-GMO-free products alongside the new GMO-inclusive varieties if the GMO-critical consumers are willing to pay a price premium. Depending on the strength of opposition toward GM products in important markets and the costs of segregating agricultural markets, developing and developed countries alike may benefit from segregated agricultural markets, which will have different prices. Such a market development would be analogous to the niche markets for organic foods.

In the base data used for this model analysis, it is assumed that all regions initially produce some of both the GM and non-GM varieties of oilseeds and coarse grain (in contrast to the assumption in the preceding scenarios that only a subset of countries can or choose to develop GM crops). The assumed GM shares of production, based on estimates provided in James (1999) and ERS (2000), are just 10 percent in the high-income Asia, Sub-Saharan Africa, and western Europe, and the rest of the world. In low-income Asia, North America, and South America, it is assumed 40 percent of coarse grain and 60 percent of oilseeds (90 percent in South America) contain GMOs. Furthermore, the structures of production in terms of the composition of intermediate input and factor use in the GM and non-GM varieties are initially assumed to be identical, as are the destination structures of exports.

In the NRT model the authors endogenize the decision of producers and consumers to use GM versus non-GM varieties in production and final demand, respectively. The input-output choice is endogenized for four demanders of coarse grain and oilseeds: livestock, meat and dairy, vegetable oils and fats, and other processed food sectors. Intermediate demands for each composite crop (that is, GM plus non-GM) are held fixed as proportions of output. In this way, the initial input-output coefficients remain fixed but, for oilseeds and coarse grain, a choice has been introduced between GM and non-GM varieties. Other intermediate input demands remain in fixed proportions to output. Similarly, final consumption of each composite GM-potential good is also fixed as a share of total demand, with an endogenous choice between GM and non-GM varieties. All other consumption shares remain fixed. The choice between GM and non-GM varieties is determined by a constant elasticity of substitution (CES) function.[9]

Since available estimates of agronomic and hence economic benefits to producers from cultivating GM crops are few and diverse, NRT simply assumes the GM oilseed and GM coarse grain sectors in all regions have a 10 percent higher level of primary factor productivity compared with their non-GM (conventional) counterparts. This shock is different from the shock imposed in the three GTAP scenarios: it is twice the size, but it is applied only to primary factors and not to intermediate input use. This difference in shock size may be interpreted as taking account of market segregation costs in the NRT model, that is, the costs of preserving the identity of non-GM crops "from seed to table" under the assumption that it is this segment of the market that will have to demonstrate its non-GM characteristic.

The NRT model introduces this factor productivity shock in the GM sectors against a variety of base models, which differ in terms of substitution elasticities for GM and non-GM products in two of the most GM-critical regions, western Europe and high-income Asia (mainly Japan). To start with, it is assumed that the elasticity of substitution between GM and non-GM varieties is high and equal in all regions. Then, in order to reflect the fact that citizens in western Europe and high-income Asia are skeptical of the new GM varieties, the elasticities of substitution between the GM and non-GM varieties are gradually lowered so that GM and non-GM varieties are seen as increasingly poorer substitutes in production and consumption in these particular regions. Citizens in all other regions are assumed to be indifferent, and hence the two crops remain highly substitutable in consumption and intermediate use. The results are presented as changes from factor productivity shocks against this range of consumer preferences in the GM-critical regions.

Expected Results

As in the GTAP model scenarios, the more effective GM production process will initially cause labor, land, and capital to leave the GM sectors because lower (cost-driven) GM product prices will result in lower returns to factors of production. To the extent that demand (domestically or abroad) is very responsive to this price reduction, this cost-reducing technology may potentially lead to increased production and hence higher returns to factors. Suppliers of inputs and buyers of agricultural products also will be affected by the use of genetic engineering in GM-potential sectors through vertical (or backward) linkages. To the extent that the production of GM crops increases, demand for inputs by producers of those crops may rise. Demanders of primary agricultural products, for example, livestock producers using grains and oilseeds for livestock feed, will benefit from lower prices, which in turn will affect the market competitiveness of these sectors.

The other sectors of the economy may also be affected through horizontal (or forward) linkages involving postfarm activities. Primary crops and livestock are typically complementary in food processing. Cheaper GM crops could potentially initiate an expansion of food production and create substitution effects. For example, since applying genetic engineering techniques to wheat breeding is apparently more complex compared with maize, the price of wheat will be high relative to other more easily manipulated grains. To the extent that substitutions in production are possible, the food processing industry may shift to the cheaper GM intermediate inputs. Furthermore, widespread use of GM products can be expected to affect the price and allocation of mobile factors of production and also affect the other sectors of the economy.

In terms of price effects, segregating the markets has both a direct and an indirect effect. Resulting directly from the output-enhancing productivity effect, countries adopting GM crops should gain from lower cost-driven prices. The more receptive a country is to the productivity-enhancing technology, the greater the gains. There is also an indirect effect, which comes from demand and will depend on the degree of substitutability between GM and non-GM products. When substitutability is high, the price of non-GM crops will decline along with the prices of GM-crops. The lower the degree of substitutability, the weaker this effect will be, and the larger should be the price wedge between GM and non-GM crops. The net effect of these direct and indirect effects on particular countries is theoretically ambiguous, again underscoring the need for empirical analysis.

The widespread adoption of GM varieties in certain regions will affect international trade flows depending on how heavily the crop in question is traded and preferences for GM versus non-GM goods in foreign markets. World market prices for GM products will have a tendency to decline and thus benefit net importers to the extent that they are indifferent between GM and non-GM products. For exporters, the lower price may expand trade volume, depending on price elasticities and preferences in foreign markets. In markets where citizens are critical of GM ingredients in their food production systems, consumers will not fully benefit from the lower prices on GM crops. Furthermore, resources will be retained in the relatively less productive non-GM sectors in these regions. However, as with organic food production, this would simply reflect consumer preferences and hence would not be welfare-reducing.

Production and Trade Results from the Empirical Analysis

The expected increase in production of the GM crops is borne out in the empirical results for all regions of the NRT model, as a direct consequence of the assumed increase in factor productivity. (In the interests of space, only selected figures showing the results in Nielsen, Robinson, and Thierfelder [2001] are reproduced here.) As a result of the relative decline in productivity in the non-GM sectors, production of conventional coarse grain and oilseeds declines. Attention here focuses on the effects on overall trade and bilateral trade patterns for selected regions should citizens in high-income Asia and western Europe become increasingly critical of GM crops, causing these crops to become correspondingly worse substitutes in consumption and intermediate use in these two regions.

Preference changes in western Europe and high-income Asia affect developing countries—low-income Asia, South America, and Sub-Saharan Africa in the NRT model. The first two regions are initially net exporters of oilseeds and net importers of cereal grains (other than rice and wheat). Low-income Asia is a net importer of both crops. Both South America and low-income Asia adopt GM technology. In both South America (an extensive GM adopter) and Sub-Saharan Africa (a region with a low share of GM varieties in total production), the initial increase in total GM oilseed exports from these regions, given the factor productivity shock, declines as preferences in high-income Asia and western Europe turn against GMOs. (See Figures 4.1 and 4.2, which report the percent change in real exports relative to the base with no productivity shocks and high substitutability between non-GM and GM varieties in all regions.) Exports are directed away from the GM-critical regions and spread evenly over the other importing regions. Of South America's total oilseed exports, 84 percent are initially sold on GM-critical markets as compared with 58 percent of oilseed exports from Sub-Saharan Africa. The adjustment in total GM oilseed exports is therefore relatively larger for South America.

As seen in Figures 4.3 and 4.4, the exports of non-GM oilseeds from these two regions are generally being diverted toward the GM-critical regions and away from other regions. A noteworthy exception is that non-GM oilseed exports to North

Figure 4.1   Changes in exports from South America by destination: GM oilseeds

Percentage change from base 100

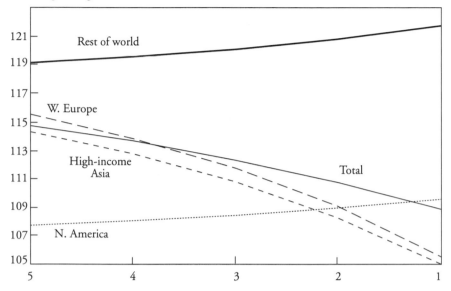

High   GM and non-GM sustainability in Western Europe and high-income Asia   Low

Source: Nielsen, Robinson, and Thierfelder's (2001) GAMs model results.

America also increase marginally as the other high-income countries become more critical of GMOs. Production of non-GM varieties increases mainly to serve the markets in western Europe and high-income Asia as citizens there become increasingly critical of GMOs. Given a high yet imperfect substitutability between the two varieties in noncritical regions such as North America, there is scope for selling both varieties in those markets as well.

Both South America and Sub-Saharan Africa depend on imports for almost one tenth of their total cereal grain absorption. However, in terms of sources, South America depends almost entirely on North America for its imports, while imports into Sub-Saharan Africa come from North America (50 percent), western Europe (16 percent), and the rest of the world (28 percent). Because citizens of South America and Sub-Saharan Africa are assumed to be uncritical of GMO content, total GM cereal grain imports increase as preferences in western Europe and high-income Asia turn against GMOs. This is because GM exports are now increasingly directed to noncritical markets (that is, fewer markets), and so the import price declines even further than the price decline due to the factor productivity shock. Imports of

Figure 4.2   Changes in exports from Sub-Saharan Africa by destination: GM oilseeds

Percentage change from base 100

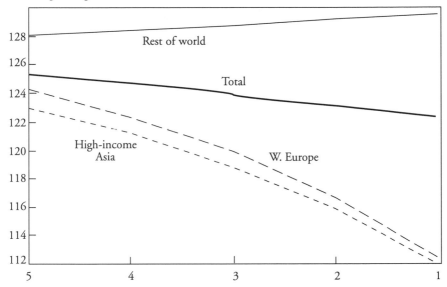

High   GM and non-GM sustainability in Western Europe and high-income Asia   Low

Source: Nielsen, Robinson, and Thierfelder's (2001) GAMs model results.

GM crops from the GM-critical countries of course decline drastically as production of GM crops in these regions declines. For the non-GM varieties, imports from the GM-critical regions increase marginally as substitutability in those regions worsens, and they respond by producing more of the non-GM variety. Given competition from increased supplies of GM crops, prices of non-GM crops also fall, and so South America and Sub-Saharan Africa also face declining prices on non-GM imports from the GM-critical regions as preferences shift.

Low-income Asia is a net importer of both oilseeds and cereal grains. Most of these imports (89 percent of oilseeds and 83 percent of cereal grains) come from North and South America. Total imports of GM crops into this region increase slightly as preferences turn against GMOs in western Europe and high-income Asia. Once again, this is because the redirection of GM export crops means increased supplies on fewer markets and so prices decline even further. The flow of non-GM imports into low-income Asia is relatively unaffected by the preference changes in the GM-critical regions because the bulk of oilseed imports initially comes from the Americas. In terms of bilateral flows, there are marginal increases in non-GM

Figure 4.3   Changes in exports from South America by destination: Non-GM oilseeds

Percentage change from base 100

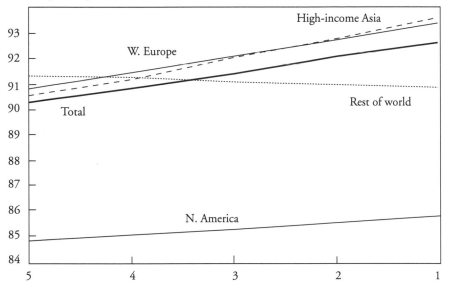

High   GM and non-GM sustainability in Western Europe and high-income Asia   Low

Source: Nielsen, Robinson, and Thierfelder's (2001) GAMs model results.

imports from western Europe since imports from these regions must compete with GM crops in a GM-indifferent market.

Price Wedges between GM and Non-GM Varieties

The bilateral trade results summarized above show that trade diversion is significant. As preferences in high-income Asia and western Europe turn against GM varieties, trade of GM varieties expands in the GM-indifferent markets. At the same time, non-GM exports are redirected toward the GM-critical regions. In other words, markets adjust to accommodate the differences in tastes across countries. The price differential that results between the two crop varieties drives this favorable outcome.

The price wedges that arise as a consequence of the different levels of factor productivity in GM and non-GM crop production are between 4.0 percent and 6.6 percent, varying across crops and regions. Figures 4.5 and 4.6 show how the ratios of non-GM to GM prices develop in different regions as substitutability between the two varieties worsens in GM-critical regions. In GM-critical regions, the non-GM/GM price ratio increases as citizens become increasingly skeptical. This tendency is weaker for cereal grains in western Europe because this region is not as

Figure 4.4   Changes in exports from Sub-Saharan Africa by destination: Non-GM oilseeds

Percentage change from base 100

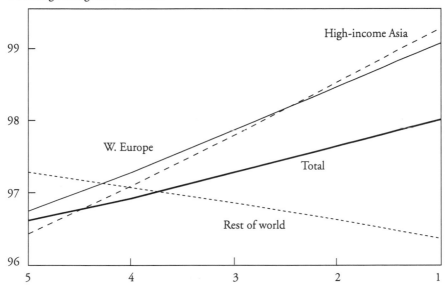

High   GM and non-GM sustainability in Western Europe and high-income Asia   Low

Source: Nielsen, Robinson, and Thierfelder's (2001) GAMs model results.

strongly engaged in international trade in this crop as it is in oilseeds. In North America, the price wedge is generally small, and it declines as GM and non-GM substitutability worsens in the other high-income countries. Given that North America is the world's largest producer and exporter of both crops, when there is high substitutability in all regions, prices of both varieties decline—the GM price declines due to the productivity shock, while the non-GM price declines because of increased competition in GM-indifferent markets. To retain access to GM critical markets, North American production of non-GM varieties increases as citizens of GM-critical regions become increasingly skeptical of GMOs. Production moves from GM toward non-GM varieties in North America in response to trade partners' preference changes, resulting in the declining ratio of non-GM to GM prices in North America, as seen in Figures 4.5 and 4.6.

With the exception of oilseeds in South America (which depends on the GM-critical region for exports), the price wedges in the developing countries are unaffected by the preference changes in western Europe and high-income Asia. Thus it is the productivity differential that determines the price wedge in developing countries, not preference shifts in the GM-critical regions. When develop-

Figure 4.5   Ratio of non-GM to GM prices of oilseeds

Percentage change from base 100

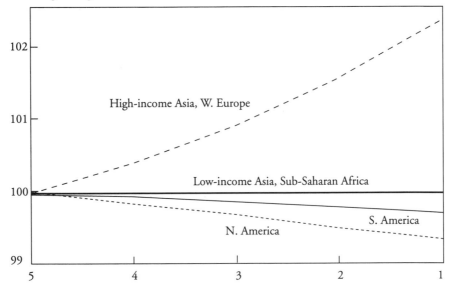

High   GM and non-GM sustainability in Western Europe and high-income Asia   Low

Source: Nielsen, Robinson, and Thierfelder's (2001) GAMs model results.

ing countries are indifferent to the GM content of agricultural products (whether produced domestically or imported) and obtain most of their imports from countries that are extensive adopters of GM crops, they gain substantially from lower import prices.

Economic Welfare Effects by Region

Global economic welfare (that is, absorption) is estimated by the NRT model to increase by US$12 billion per year when GM coarse grain and oilseed production processes experience a 10 percent primary factor productivity increase, given the assumed regional shares of GM and non-GM varieties (see Figure 4.7). As preferences in western Europe and high-income Asia turn against GM varieties, this increase is reduced to US$11 billion. Low-income Asia, North America, and South America are the main beneficiaries of the factor productivity increase. This is because all of them are assumed to be intense adopters of the productivity-increasing crop varieties. North America gains as the major producer and exporter of both crops. The total absorption gain in this region is reduced, but only by 5 percent relative to the high substitutability experiment, as a consequence of changing preferences in its

Figure 4.6   Ratio of non-GM to GM prices of cereal grains

Percentage change from base 100

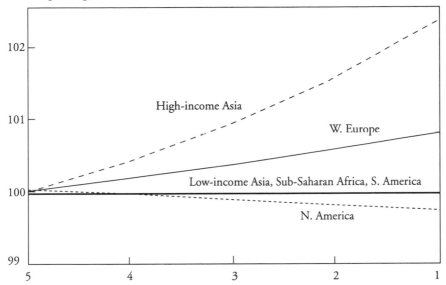

High   GM and non-GM sustainability in Western Europe and high-income Asia   Low

Source: Nielsen, Robinson, and Thierfelder's (2001) GAMs model results.

important export markets in western Europe and high-income Asia. As with the import ban and preference shift scenarios using the GTAP model above, these results also show that the costs of the preference changes are borne mainly by the GM-critical regions themselves, with the gains made in high-income Asia (in terms of lower import prices) almost disappearing. In western Europe, the initial boost in total absorption is cut in half. The increases in total absorption in all the developing-country regions are not affected by the preference changes in the GM-critical regions. Low-income Asia is the major beneficiary in absolute terms because it is a net importer of the two crops, basically indifferent as to GM content, and an adopter of GM technology. Hence the region benefits from substantially lower import prices on GM crops. The increase in total absorption in South America is unaffected by the preference changes in GM-critical regions despite its high dependence on these regions for its exports of oilseeds because bilateral trade flows adjust well; trade diversion offsets the effects of demand shifts in the GM-critical regions. In Sub-Saharan Africa the gains are small in absolute terms, mainly due to the small share of these particular crops in production and trade, but they are also unaffected by preference changes in GM-critical regions.

Figure 4.7   Changes in total absorption for different degrees of substitutability between GM and non-GM crops in high-income Asia and western Europe

Billions of U.S. dollars

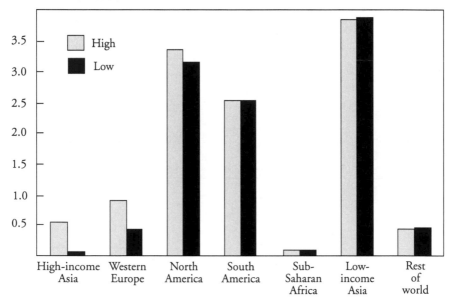

Substitutability between GM and non-GM

Source: Nielsen, Robinson, and Thierfelder's (2001) GAMs model results.

Conclusion

What is to be learned from this analysis? First, the potential economic welfare gains from adopting GMO technology for these crops in even just a subset of producing countries is significant. In the cases in the first scenario using the GTAP model gains amount to an estimated US$9.9 billion per year for coarse grain and oilseeds. Moreover, developing countries would receive a sizeable share and possibly the majority of those gains—as more of them become capable of introducing the new GM technology. The size of these gains, especially for developing countries, is such that policymakers should not ignore them when considering policy responses to appease opponents of GMO technology.

Second, the most extreme use of trade restrictions by western Europe, namely an import ban on GM crops, would be costly to the economic welfare of the region itself—a cost which governments in the region need to weigh against the perceived benefits to voters of adopting the precautionary principle. Imposing a ban prevents

European consumers and intermediate demanders from gaining from lower import prices, farmers would increase domestic production of corn and soybeans at the expense of other farm production, and hence overall allocative efficiency in the region would be worsened. In the case modeled, the GM-adopting regions still enjoy welfare gains due to the dominating positive effect of the assumed productivity boost embodied in the GM crops, but those gains are reduced by the import ban as compared with the scenario in which GM crops are traded freely. Results suggest that countries that do not adopt GM crops and can verify this at the western European borders could gain slightly in gross terms from retaining access to the GMO-free markets when others are excluded. Whether they gain in net terms would depend on the cost of compliance with European regulations.

Third, the results suggest that letting consumers in western Europe who are concerned about GMOs express that preference through the market reduces the welfare gains from the new technology much less than imposing a ban on GMOs in Europe. Developing countries that do not gain access to GM technology, however, may be slightly worse off in terms of economic welfare if they cannot guarantee that their exports entering the western European markets are GMO-free. For these countries, completely segregating GMO-inclusive and GMO-free markets may allow them to reap benefits from selling "conventional" products to GM-critical consumers in industrialized countries.

This leads to the fourth conclusion based on the NRT model results, which indicate how global markets are likely to adjust to such segregation, in the sense that non-GM exports are diverted to the GMO-critical regions while GM exports are diverted to indifferent regions. Price differentials are significant, but tempered by commodity arbitrage. In particular, in certain GMO-favorable regions, the prices of the non-GM varieties also decline because of the high degree of substitutability between the GM and non-GM varieties in domestic use and increased production to supply critical consumers. In the GMO-critical regions, the price differentials reflect minor increases in supply of the non-GM products and marked declines in supply of GMO varieties. An important aspect of these results is that developing countries also respond to these GM preferences and redirect their trade flows among partners accordingly. But this favorable outcome would require the relative price premium on the non-GM products to not only outweigh the productivity growth foregone by not adopting GMOs but also to cover the potentially significant costs of compliance.

The realism of the quantitative results is limited by the lack of empirical data and incomplete knowledge of the effects of GM crops. Unavoidably, the analysis is based on simple assumptions about the productivity impact of introducing GM crops in the agricultural production system, ignoring any externalities. Likewise, the analysis does not consider the costs of segmenting markets and labeling products. More data are needed on the likely nature and size of the productivity gains and any externalities (positive as well as negative) in the various sectors of different countries.

The global models assume perfect competition in all markets, and neither separates out the (relatively tiny) markets for agricultural research and for crop seeds. Furthermore, GMO technology is raising the incentive for vertical integration of firms that produce the biotechnology, the germplasm, the seeds, and some of the chemical inputs such as pesticides. Marketing GM crops separately from conventional crops may alter merger/acquisition incentives for grain-marketing firms in terms of horizontal integration, and in terms of their involvement in the feed-livestock complex. Less likely is that such firms might also vertically integrate into food retailing if enough supermarket chains chose not to stock GM foods. Changes to firm concentration ratios in those sectors could well alter the extent to which they can capture monopolistic rents within the food chain, thereby altering the size of the gains by farmers and final consumers. More complex modeling is needed to estimate the distributional and overall welfare consequences of such possibilities.

Notes

1. Whether import bans to achieve that would be consistent with other obligations members of the World Trade Organization may have is a moot point not discussed here, but see Anderson and Nielsen (2000).

2. Particularly Nielsen and Anderson (2001) and Nielsen, Robinson, and Thierfelder (2001).

3. The GTAP includes a multiregional CGE model based on neoclassical perfectly competitive microeconomic theory and a unique global database for use with this and other CGE models. See Hertel (1997) for comprehensive documentation of the standard GTAP model and McDougall, Elbehri, and Truong (1998) for a description of the GTAP version 4 database, which in its full version comprises 50 sectors and 45 countries/regions and describes the global economic structures and trade flows of 1995.

4. Nelson et al. (1999), for example, suggest that glyphosate-resistant soybeans may generate a total production cost reduction of 5 percent, and their scenarios have *Bt* corn increasing yields by between 1.8 percent and 8.1 percent.

5. Given the absence of sufficiently detailed empirical data on the agronomic and hence economic impact of cultivating GM crops, the 5 percent productivity shock applied here represents an average shock (over both commodities and regions). Changing this shock (for example, doubling it to 10 percent) generates near-linear changes (that is, roughly a doubling) in the effects on price and quantity results reported below.

6. By distinguishing between GMO-inclusive and GMO-free products by country of origin, one concern may be that GM-adopting regions channel their exports to the country or region imposing the import ban (here western Europe) through third countries that are indifferent as to the content of GMOs and that do not adopt GM technology in their own production systems. The possibility of such transshipments is not part of this analysis.

7. See the technical appendix of Nielsen and Anderson (2000a), which describes how the exogenous preference shift is introduced into the GTAP model.

8. The size of this preference shift is arbitrary and simply illustrates the possible direction of effects of this type of preference shift as compared with the import ban scenario.

9. See Nielsen, Robinson, and Thierfelder (2001) for a formal description of how the endogenous choice between GM and non-GM varieties is incorporated into the model.

References

Anderson, K., and C. P. Nielsen. 2000. GMOs, food safety and the environment: What role for trade policy and the WTO? Plenary paper presented at the triennial conference of the International Association of Agricultural Economists, Berlin, August 13–18.

ERS (Economic Research Service of the U.S. Department of Agriculture).1999. Impact of adopting genetically engineered crops in the U.S.: Preliminary results. Washington, D.C., July.

————. 2000. Biotech corn and soybeans: Changing markets and the government's role. <http://www.ers.usda.gov/Emphases/Harmony/issues/biotechmarkets/index.htm>. Accessed July 17, 2001.

Hertel, T. W., ed. 1997. *Global trade analysis: Modeling and applications.* Cambridge and New York: Cambridge University Press.

James, C. 1997. The global status of transgenic crops in 1997. International Service for the Acquisition of Agri-biotech Applications Brief No. 5. Ithaca, N.Y., U.S.A.

————. 1998. *Global review of commercialized transgenic crops: 1998.* International Service for the Acquisition of Agri-biotech Applications Brief No. 8. Ithaca, N.Y., U.S.A.

————. 1999. Preview—Global status of commercialized transgenic crops: 1999. International Service for the Acquisition of Agri-biotech Applications Brief No. 12. Ithaca, N.Y. , U.S.A.

Lewis, J. D., S. Robinson, and K. Thierfelder. 1999. After the negotiations: Assessing the impact of free-trade agreements in Southern Africa. TMD Discussion Paper 46. Washington, D.C.: International Food Policy Research Institute.

McDougall, R. A., A. Elbehri, and T. P. Truong eds. 1998. *Global trade, assistance, and protection: The GTAP 4 database.* Center for Global Trade Analysis, Purdue University, West Lafayette, Ind., U.S.A.

Nelson, G. C., T. Josling, D. Bullock, L. Unnevehr, M. Rosegrant, and L. Hill. 1999. The economics and politics of genetically modified organisms: Implications for WTO 2000. With J. Babinard, C. Cunningham, A. de Pinto, and E. I. Nitsi. Bulletin 809. College of Agricultural, Consumer and Environmental Sciences, University of Illinois at Urbana, Champaign, U.S.A.

Nielsen, C. P., and K. Anderson. 2000a. GMOs, trade policy, and welfare in rich and poor countries. Paper presented at the World Bank workshop on Standards, Regulation, and Trade, Washington, D.C., April 27. (Forthcoming in condensed form in *Quantifying trade effects of technical barriers: Can it be done?* K. Maskus and J. Wilson, eds., Ann Arbor, Mich., U.S.A.: University of Michigan Press.)

————. 2000b. Global market effects of adopting transgenic rice and cotton. Centre for International Economic Studies, University of Adelaide. Mimeo.

————. 2001. Global market effects of alternative European responses to GMOs. *Weltwirtschaftliches*

Archiv [Review of World Economics] 137 (2):320–346. (Available as CIES Discussion Paper 0032, Centre for International Economic Studies, University of Adelaide, July 2000.)

Nielsen, C. P., S. Robinson, and K. Thierfelder. 2001. Genetic engineering and trade: Panacea or dilemma for developing countries. *World Development* 29 (8):1307–24. (Available as TMD Discussion Paper 55, International Food Policy Research Institute, Washington, D.C.)

OECD. (Organisation for Economic Co-operation and Development). 2000. *Modern biotechnology and agricultural markets: A discussion of selected issues.* Directorate for Food, Agriculture and Fisheries; Committee for Agriculture. AGR/CA/APM(2000)5/FINAL, Paris.

UNEP (United Nations Environment Programme). 2000. Cartagena Protocol on Biosafety to the Convention on Biological Diversity. <http://www.biodiv.org/doc/legal/cartagena-protocol-en.doc>. Accessed July 17, 2001.

Chapter 5

Transcending Transgenics—
Are There "Babies in the Bathwater,"
or Is That a Dorsal Fin?

Richard A. Jefferson

Introduction

Most news headlines and assertions of health and environmental concerns about genetically modified (GM) crops center around transgenic technologies. These technologies involve methods of introducing genes into plants by inserting new DNA rather than the more familiar method of introducing genetic material by pollen and egg fusion in a genetic cross.

Modern biotechnologies can do much more than add new genes, and provide single-gene herbicide tolerance and pest resistance in crops like corn, cotton, soybeans, and canola that constitute the lion's share of commercially successful transgenic technologies developed for agriculture to date (see Marra this volume).[1] These innovations have been successful in their target markets, but they were not intended to solve the myriad problems of farmers around the world; except in the minds of the most naïve promoters of the new science, they were never anything other than a simple first generation.

These technologies are still in their early days, with real opportunities for non-scientists (the public, primary producers, and policymakers) to articulate desirable future trajectories and help the scientific community change the way science evolves and interfaces with people's lives. Further, a corresponding opportunity exists for modifying the political and economic landscape—especially in relation to intellectual property rights (IPR)—to encourage fair play and transparency in this pursuit (see Nottenburg, Pardey, and Wright 2001 and this volume).

Crop breeders find transgenic technologies attractive because they make it possible, in principle, to incorporate into plants yield-increasing or nutrient-enhancing traits that would be slow, expensive, or impossible to introduce by conventional means. Most of agriculture is far from the idyllic pursuit of life on the land as envisioned by many urban dwellers; much of it is a hard slog, in a less than benign environment, and typically burdened by debt. Crop production occurs in complex agroecologies, and each farmer's field is different, with challenges that are unpredictable and unique to their circumstances. Rainfall can be excessive (causing waterlogging) or deficient (causing drought if extreme); it varies from year to year and can fall too late or too early in any given year. Most of the world's agricultural soils are either too acidic, too basic, have insufficient nutrients for uptake by plants, or have elevated amounts of salts or metals like aluminum that are toxic to most plants.

Improved crop management practices can alleviate these problems to some extent, but improved crop varieties also have a big role to play. The work of crop breeders is crucial for increasing yields through a stream of improved crop varieties more resistant to drought, waterlogging, and elevated levels of toxic metals or salts; more tolerant to cold; and more robust in their defenses against ever-evolving pests and diseases that overcome previous forms of bred-in resistance. Simply maintaining the historically high yields some now experience is a daunting task. Despite the smugness of those who claim that Malthusian doom has been averted, the natural resource base is dwindling, populations are growing, and the standard of living demanded or desired by burgeoning populations is rising.

The future of crop improvement and plant breeding could be much more exciting and productive than simply servicing the treadmill of current needs. We could make a quantum leap, integrating science with societies, economies, environments, and agricultures. With a new toolkit—both technical and intellectual—breeders could make major contributions to breeding and combining crops and livestock and their associated biota into complex and robust systems. But first, the current vitriol and debate must be transcended so that a shared vision can be devised and ultimately endorsed by many parties.

To understand the furor about transgenics, and to see whether there is a gleaming baby in the turbid bathwater of GM agriculture, we must carefully examine current transgenic technology. It is absolutely critical to appreciate the scientific possibilities—the directions these technologies could take—and to clarify the social and economic forces that are acting on them or that could influence their development.

Defining the Terms Defines the Problem

Language is a very powerful tool, but when abused it is a formidable form of social and psychological manipulation because each word and phrase carries with it a world of context and implied meaning. A productive and respectful discussion about new technologies, trends, and policies demands a linguistic common ground.

Attempts to define the very word "transgenic" illustrate the magnitude of the problem. If we try to define transgenic as a process that involves the introduction of "foreign" DNA, and foreign means from another species, then much of the classical wide-hybridization is transgenic. Of course wide-hybridization is commonly used in conventional plant breeding to broaden the diversity of a crop species, which is generally perceived to be a good thing. The interfertile rice species *Oryza rufipogon*, *Oryza glabberima*, and *Oryza sativa* have been "mined," that is, their respective genomic capabilities to respond to novel challenges have been tapped, and combined for marvelous yield increases by neoclassical plant breeding (Xiao et al. 1998).

If transgenic is defined as a process involving DNA from another genus, the same caveats apply; modern wheat is the fusion of three separate genomes from three distinct species and probably genera, and occurred only a few thousand years ago. Modern triticale is a completely synthetic species created by fusing genomes (by familiar means) that had never before been juxtaposed in nature. Many horticultural crops (berries, for instance) are interspecific hybrids. So where is the line drawn? Many hundreds of plant species, including many crops, are naturally infected by and indeed genetically transformed by the DNA of the naturally occurring soil microbe *Agrobacterium tumefaciens*. The DNA of countless plants actually contains bacterial DNA already, with no human intervention whatsoever.

The DNA sequencing of many genomes has revealed that large numbers of genes and associated sequences are virtually identical—indistinguishable—in organisms ranging from microbes to mushrooms to man (not that big a jump considering some people I've known). The line is further blurred considering that it is now technically feasible for genetic engineers to produce transgenic plants that have only plant DNA introduced into them, with no nonplant DNA sequences. Are these plants transgenic?

When faced with these facts, the debate nonetheless continues in many quarters but shifts its goalposts, and redefines itself as a preference for low versus high technology options, progressing to the issue of whether and to what degree human "intervention" is appropriate in agriculture—a slippery slope considering that all of agriculture is the product of human artifice, intervention, and ingenuity. This trend to object based on the type of technology in question tends to tar transgenics or GM crops—and increasingly any laboratory-based science—with an apparently and implicitly unsavory brush of high technology, at the same time leaving much of modern plant improvement alone. Of course the countless technologies associated with farming, and even more so the processing and provision of food and fiber to consumers, are rarely part of the dialogue.

After all, even the humble hoe or plough, while primitive, invariably derive from sophisticated mining and smelting of ores and alloying, casting, working, and machining of the resulting metals. Many state that the track record for safety or utility of a particular technology renders it acceptable. This is not the whole story, however, as metal-working, besides its very real good in the form of ploughs and construction tools, has been necessary for virtually all weapons as well, from swords and armor to guns and tanks—hardly a benign core technology. Is the issue really track records, or is it just familiarity? Is it the technology, the use of the technology, or more likely the provenance and control of the technology and whether it is perceived to serve a public good. Or are its real benefits preserved for minority interests? Those against swords are rarely against ploughshares, although both depend on similar underlying technologies. Who is using the technology seems to determine much of its acceptability, and this is the crux of the current crisis.

These logical conundra help expose the real interests or misconceptions behind the sometimes vague language and concerns associated with agricultural technologies, and more specifically the interventions of molecular biology. Protests about food safety and environmental concerns could perhaps be better focused on the underlying bone of contention—the control of technology.

"Natural" Is "Good"

Organic, to most people, is equated with natural, and natural is associated with good. The most virulent diseases and plagues that kill millions and devastate landscapes and crops are 100 percent natural, but they are not considered good. Consider smallpox, influenza, polio, HIV, rice blast fungus, plague locusts, and cholera. Consider the deadly natural toxins curare, botulism, diptheria, and so on. Or consider the insidious bacterial agents such as anthrax—a lethal natural candidate for a biological warfare agent.

We must also consider the apparently benign. The wonderful caterpillar-killing, spore-forming bacterium *Bacillus thuringiensis (Bt)*, is used worldwide by the organic agriculture community as a live formulation on many thousands—perhaps millions—of acres to kill myriad lepidopteran organisms, some of them pests. This living soup of trillions of bacteria, each encoding perhaps a few thousand genes of unknown function, is considered "familiar" and "natural" to spray on plants to decimate legions of feeding insect pests. Why is this? Have carefully monitored field trials been done over dozens of years to ensure safety? Have international guidelines for use of the live bacterium been developed and harmonized by supranational bodies, enforced by national legislation? Have stringent quality-control standards been imposed and allergenicity tests mandated? No. Familiarity and accessibility exempt these agricultural practices from such scrutiny: "It doesn't seem to screw things up too badly, anyone can buy a bag of it, and besides—it's natural!" However, as more is learned about these organisms assumed relationships begin to fall apart.

This *Bt* bacterium is closely related to the causative agent of deadly anthrax (*Bacillus anthracis,* a biological warfare agent banned by the United Nations Convention on Biological Weapons) and to food poisoning (*Bacillus cereus*). Some scientists consider these bacteria to be the same species (Helgason et al. 2000). Yet assurances of product and human safety are completely missing in the artisanal applications of these billions of living *Bt* bacteria onto crop plants that are then sold at a premium, since they're organic, in many markets. Are these unacceptable risks? Apparently not. And yet when high technology is used to remove the actual active ingredient—the *Bt* crystal-forming protein toxin—and introduce this into crop plants in a lasting form free of the thousands of other potentially dangerous genes, it is decried by many as a loathsome and unwelcome innovation. Again, is it really the high technology intervention that creates the fear and loathing? Or is it the provenance of the intervention? Authorities fail to regulate countless familiar activities that are far more likely to create problems, such as the potential contamination of organic *Bt* spores with deadly food toxins or lethal pathogens.

The GM debate has been derailed by the very language used. It has little to do with technology. Perhaps if public agencies (departments of agriculture or other entities) rather than large multinational corporations had conducted the first commercial releases of transgenic food crops and their introduction to the food chain the outcry that has dominated the press and industrial and scientific activities would not have reached fever pitch, preventing constructive dialogue.

It seems that the issue must be defined based on whether it impinges on a feeling of acceptability. Acceptability is associated with a comfort-zone that is established by familiarity and by perceived accountability, but is rarely the subject of critical evaluation. Public agencies are rarely more accountable than many in the private sector, which is accountable to the market itself: if the product or process is unacceptable, it doesn't sell (unless the market itself is manipulated). Furthermore, legal and financial liabilities associated with nonperformance or improper performance of products and processes can force adherence to regulatory strictures. And fiduciary and management accountability to shareholders affords an opportunity to scrutinize private-sector behavior. Few of these mechanisms are in place to ensure that the public sector adheres to public-good criteria. Crucially there are few clearly articulated definitions of public good criteria to adhere to, nor frameworks against which to evaluate such behavior.

This is seen in the recent tendency of the public sector to behave in a private-good manner (such as through exclusive or short-sighted patent licensing and by conducting contract research that is not subject to oversight). Ironically, these actions have come in response to demands that the public interest requires the public sector to adhere more closely to supposed private-sector models, especially in control of technology. That said, it really is perception that matters, and this includes the perception that public good is really being provided by public agencies, along with the unspoken corollary in many minds, that the private sector is not concerned with public goods—an unfortunate connection.

Few of even the most ardent critics of "big agriculture" have serious reservations about the value of modest-sized private firms providing farm-level innovations. Small to medium-sized enterprises thus have a potentially enormous role in providing effective R&D and delivery in a package that is acceptable to virtually all observers. It is the "smallness" that engenders trust; the decisionmakers are face-to-face with the outcomes of their decisions and the risks they take are first and foremost on their own heads. The trend in recent years to consolidate and vertically integrate these entities must be examined and the reasons for this action seriously challenged.

If acceptability of the delivery mechanism is paramount, technologies that promote acceptable mechanisms must be encouraged, along with the legal and business instruments that encourage the decentralized innovative process. Technologies are not neutral; barriers to entry, including intellectual property (IP) restrictions, financial capital requirements, context effectiveness, cultural perceptions, market aesthetics, and technological interdependencies, are often intrinsic to particular technologies. And, of course, the design and delivery of new technologies reflect the dominant social and economic forces at work.

In a society characterized by information overload and rapid innovation, even scientists (including myself) are struck by feelings of powerlessness. This issue is at the heart of debates about GM agriculture—not the technology except as an instrument of such disenfranchisement. With this in mind, current and future technologies should be viewed with some detachment: It is important to grasp what they are now, what they involve, what is in the pipeline, and most importantly whether or how technologies can be crafted to cope with the issues at hand—trust, provenance, access, and responsibility to societies and environments.

New Meta-Technologies

Sentinel Plants and Bioindicators

Often, the most robust and sustainable solutions to agricultural problems are initiated and implemented by the very people experiencing the problem—the farmers. These solutions often manifest not in genetic changes but in management changes, such as amended irrigation, fertilization, and plant protection protocols; altered planting regimes; intercropping; and rotations. However, for each of these interventions the managers require sufficient, accurate, and timely information about the challenges and the opportunities for response. One of the greatest untapped opportunities in genetics in agriculture is to increase and improve the information provided to farmers by using the most sensitive biological and chemical sensors known.

These are not silicon devices or expensive neutron probes allied to computers and custom software. They are the plants themselves. Plants have extraordinary capabilities to sense virtually all of the key abiotic and biotic challenges that limit agricultural production and sustainability. However, we don't know how to listen to them well enough, or they don't know how to speak. There are many examples of farm managers planting indicator crops to forewarn of impending diseases or of other stresses. Vineyard managers around the world use rosebushes as sensitive indicators of the fungi that can cause serious loss to grape production; the rose shows symptoms before the vines are damaged, allowing a timely and cost-effective prophylactic regime. Can organisms themselves be used as "instruments"? Can generic methods harness the exquisitely sensitive and specific molecular sensing mechanisms of plants to tell farmers the condition of their fields, their soils, their ecologies, and their crops? Can these be developed to provide timely cues that lend themselves to creative changes in farm management practices? Absolutely.

Envision harnessing the natural ability of a plant to detect trace elements, and converting that detection in the plant to a visual cue that a farmer or agronomist can act upon in a creative manner. Perhaps the plant is engineered to produce a color that is characteristic of the levels of a crucial trace nutrient. A smattering of these plants around a field would then provide a powerful visual signal for farmers to either avoid areas that cannot support the growth of their crops, or to improve the soils with just that cost-effective nutrient and not a wasteful excess of nutrients that are uneconomic, and polluting. Even the most obvious nutrient of all—water—is often not present in absolutely clear quantities. Can reports on water tables, on nitrogen form and concentration, on latent pathogens, even on the crops' own efficiency of using available nutrients be developed? Almost certainly. Can the sensory cues—

colors, shapes, or even smells—be harnessed to allow managers to clearly and unambiguously identify opportunities and challenges? Yes.

As biochemical pathways for pigment synthesis in plants become more clearly known, the opportunities for introducing, modifying, or activating these pathways and their genes in particular plants become correspondingly more realistic. Coupling the production of visible pigments in the correct locations with the intrinsic capability of plants to sense and measure their environment—behaving as biological sensors to indicate particular desired parameters—is also becoming feasible. Methods such as microarray based expression profiling could monitor the transcription of genes that respond to measurement challenges, and isolate and fuse the corresponding promoter to the indicator genes.

If the biological instrument is being used to monitor the presence or level of an abiotic or biotic constraint, the engineering can be readily performed in a noncrop species, to produce what my friend Peter Kenmore at the Food and Agriculture Organization of the United Nations (FAO) likes to call a "sentinel plant," basically a living instrument that relays useful information to farmers about the condition of their crops or cropping systems.[2] The sentinel plants can then be placed in various locations throughout the field, but need not be harvested or consumed. This, of course, leaves the crop unmodified, but allows farmers to use the information to better manage their fields. The sentinel plant is rather similar to the fungal-sensitive rosebush—it doesn't appear in the wine, but makes the farming of the grapes more productive.

If however, the farmer wishes to measure the response to stresses or constraints—for instance, nutrient use efficiency—the crop itself becomes the candidate for bioindicator modification. In this scenario, the effectiveness of nitrogen fixation by soil rhizobia or the health or stress level of the crop can be measured, and farmers can take steps to ameliorate the problems.

The bioindicator approach is also compatible with genetic improvement of the crop. One can set the parameters of a classical plant breeding scheme in which the reporter (or indicator plant's signals) determines the best genetic combinations. After achieving these improvements, the bioindicator (or reporter locus on the plant's genome) could be crossed out, or left in if determined to be benign and acceptable.

Unfortunately, the compelling but simplistic economics of ownership tend to create a culture that imposes solutions in the form of a genetically improved crop (by conventional or nontraditional means), which is sold as seed and requires management regimes to bring the best out of this improved variety. This has been effective in many cases, but it will take creative entrepreneurship and business thinking to secure a revenue stream from a living, self-replicating instrument that costs next to nothing to propagate and very little to actually use, but which could cost a great deal to develop. Revenue from recurrent sales of improved seeds is often seen as the bedrock of capital recovery and hence is crucial to encouraging investment in research to develop new plant biotechnologies.

The combination of high costs and a preoccupation with serving markets in the industrialized word has offered little incentive for scientists to develop these tools, and there are substantial entry barriers presented by intellectual property and financial capital restrictions. Exhortation and inspiration must go hand in hand with improved policy and strategy to foster the inventive spirit that will make innovations possible and deliverable. If the public sector, or small to medium-sized enterprises, were to take the initiative on this issue, progress could be very rapid.

Homologous Allelic Recombination (or Replacement) Technologies (HARTs)

All current methods of plant transformation (transgenesis) are only capable of introducing additional DNA into the genome. They are not capable of removing or specifically altering sequences that are already in place. In genetics terminology, these methods can only introduce a dominant trait. Current methods basically overlay the expression patterns of a transgene on the intrinsic expression of the recipient genome. While techniques such as RNA-mediated gene silencing (broadly encompassing antisense and cosuppression technologies) can effectively "turn off" resident genes of known sequence, this capability is still dominant, and always leaves a "footprint" (that is, new sequences that had not previously been present in the genome). Further, genetic circuitry is so complex that functions are often redundant and silencing one gene does not always silence the trait.

Current commercial transformation techniques for plants typically result in diverse and unpredictable insertion sites into genomes. This situation causes extreme variability in performance of newly introduced traits between lines within the same plant species, making it necessary to generate a large number of primary transgenic events, further involving considerable and expensive effort to rogue these aberrant lines to find only those with stable and acceptable levels of expression of the new gene(s). This logistical requirement makes the process of creating a commercially viable transgenic crop line slower, more cumbersome, and more expensive than it would otherwise be.

Transgenic technology development is still quite primitive, reflecting an inability to understand and harness the natural processes of DNA repair and recombination by which plants routinely and precisely replace or recombine alleles. Alleles are variant forms of the same gene or DNA sequences, and can be considered the cause of intraspecies diversity that plant breeders typically try to optimize.

The most desirable situation for those using genetics to improve crop genomes would be to use homologous recombination to specifically amend the sequence of a particular gene or controlling DNA so that the plant remains in all other ways in its original genetic condition, save for the one subtle change introduced. There would be no need *a priori* for a footprint to be left behind, nor for most of the associated challenges of current trangenics to apply. In short, the desired improvement is brought about with the smallest alteration conceivable, and knowledge about the implications of the change—and the possibility of avoiding unwanted side effects) is maximized.

If a plant's genome were modified with a form of site-directed change that left only a minor allelic variation, it could be sensibly argued that the resulting line was in no way transgenic. The substantial savings in time and money by circumventing the need for adherence to regulatory guidelines developed for conventional transgenics could help lower entry barriers to smaller players in biotechnology, including research and development (R&D) entities in public and private sectors of the developing world. Currently the costs of taking a single product through the regulatory gauntlet imposed by most governments is so high that only comparatively high-margin applications are being pursued, and typically only by large companies. This is a terrible waste of opportunity.

In the baker's yeast *Saccharomyces cerevisiae*, achieving homologous recombination in laboratory conditions is routine. It is also manageable in mammalian cells, with some technical difficulties still to be overcome. Homologous recombination, and its sister technology, site-directed mutagenesis, in which an altered sequence of DNA (or RNA) is used as a template by the natural repair processes to substitute or recombine one allele for another, will almost certainly be developed over the next few years. These technologies, collectively, can be called homologous allelic recombination (or replacement) technologies (HARTs). When they emerge, they will spell the single greatest technical breakthrough since DNA transformation of plants. With HARTs, a modified plant can be, in every way, absolutely identical to its precursor or mother plant with only the most subtle and precise modification.

In fact, until HARTs become available as an experimental tool in plants, much of genomics, the broad catchword used to raise huge amounts of money from unwary investors, is really the "emperor's new sequence." How can scientists formulate a hypothesis about the function of a gene based on information from genomic sequencing or expression patterns and reasonably test that hypothesis? With HARTs, comparative genomics can give rise to precise experimental tests of these hypotheses. Imagine that in comparing sequences around quantitative trait loci of two rice varieties it emerges that a subtle allelic variation—perhaps a DNA sequence change of only a few bases in the gene encoding a regulator—seems to correlate with an important trait. How does one test this? Currently scientists have only correlation—no cause-and-effect relationships—and when moving such alleles around by classical genetics (crossing plants) they get not only babies and the bathwater, but also the bathroom, the whole house, and the neighborhood. Classical genetic crosses, even when followed by exhaustive (and exhausting) back-crosses to clean up and restore the original recurrent genotype, still bring in millions of base pairs of DNA. This encompasses hundreds of variants of genes and nongene sequences, any one of which could be responsible for the observed difference. It is unclear whether critics of transgenesis who use the unfamiliarity of "new" sequences as the lynchpin for their concern know the enormous volume and extent of uncharacterized allelic variation being introduced wholesale by classical plant breeding.

The advent of HARTs in a widely useable fashion would be highly important to anyone wishing to use modern science to improve the performance of agricultural systems through genetics. And it would greatly reduce the entry barrier to diverse innovators. How likely is it to happen and what stands in the way?

A few methods—most of which have been patented, which is not to say unavailable—have achieved a modest frequency of site-directed mutagenesis, site-specific integration (less interesting), or limited forms of homologous recombination. The status quo of site-directed mutagenesis is not yet exciting, but is farthest along (I half-jokingly call the current stage of the technology "site-suggested mutagenesis"). The scientific community's understanding of natural recombination processes is, however, growing rapidly; with the study of *Arabidopsis* biology and genetics, the toolkit to explore such fundamental biological processes is becoming more sophisticated and effective. Modest infusions of private capital into research toward harnessing recombination in plants may well be happening, and clearly private funding of public research—with concomitant control or influence in many cases—is now the norm. It is only a matter of time until HARTs are developed as powerful tools. But this very increase in private interest among the multinationals, the same companies that have been the source of the current generation of field releases, does not necessarily bode well for either the broad availability of the tool or for improved public perception of the craft of modern agricultural genetics. The multinationals need and should have the tools, but should they be the owners, the developers, or the arbiters of their availability?

In a sense, the use of HARTs would be "stealth genetics," undetectable except in its outcomes. When HARTs are achieved, critics doubtless will bemoan the absence of the very footprint (genetic flotsam) that they currently decry. However, these technologies would certainly meet and exceed the requirements and concerns expressed in all the technical criticisms of transgenesis.

Among the intriguing implications of using HARTs are the IP and business challenges associated with an innovation that is virtually undetectable or indistinguishable from other materials, and whose creation may be dependent on process rather than a material difference. The regulatory frameworks currently in place are certainly inadequate to guide the informed deployment of plants (or other organisms) altered by HARTs, unless these are exempt from such oversight.

From a point of democratizing the ability to experiment with information gleaned from genomic analysis, HARTs could be one of this century's great achievements for agricultural research worldwide. But this suite of technologies is vulnerable to being withheld from routine use by onerous or unwise IP terms. Keeping in mind Thomas Jefferson's idea of using a formal grant of intellectual property rights to balance social benefit with private gain, a cogent argument can be made that HARTs for agriculture and medicine would qualify as a unique public good.

Genetic Use Restriction Technologies (GURTs)

The concept of revenue streams through recurrent sales is dogma in the agricultural genetics industries. The track record of hybrid maize is often held up as an example of how the inability to plant-back without losing varietal character has allowed a productive industry to develop based on secure and predictable sales. Citing examples of vegetable seeds that have emerged from the effective use of hybrids, it is persuasively argued that the reliable revenue streams derived from recurrent seed sales have stimulated investment into genetic research to improve the maize crop. The argument hinges on the necessity of recovering the substantial financial investment in high-risk research and the significant delays between the inception of a technological intervention and the delivery of a saleable product.

As a result, methods have been developed to extend the concept of recurrent purchasing to crops that hitherto were not subject to hybrid technologies. In March 1998, U.S. patent number 5,723,765 was granted jointly to the U.S. Department of Agriculture and Delta and Pine Land Company. This patent, called "control of gene expression," soon attracted remarkable attention through an ambitious press campaign conducted by a few concerned activist groups, notably RAFI (Rural Advancement Foundation International, recently renamed the ETC Group), which coined the expression "terminator technology."

The United Nations Convention on Biological Diversity commissioned a substantial review of the technology and its implications (UNEP/CBD/SBSTTA 1999). The Expert Group that prepared the UN report, of which I was author-in-chief, noted that genetic use restriction technologies (GURTs,) could be described as those that could be used to restrict the propagation of the plant itself (V-GURTs, or variety-specific GURTs) and those that would limit the impermissible use of an associated added-value trait (T-GURTs, or trait-specific GURTs). These had very different implications, and needed to be considered separately.

While one of the classes of the technology, V-GURTs, was in principle capable of limiting the germination ability of a second generation of seeds, earning the label terminator, the other class, T-GURTs, could conceivably be an effective tool to put the ability to control transgene expression in the hands of farmers—a necessary step for many socially and environmentally context-dependent applications. However, both technologies were reviled in the press, with the T-GURTs referred to, albeit less evocatively, as "traitor technology." Although the possible use of V-GURTs technology to restrict the potential effects of gene flow in field populations was noted (by making plants carrying the trait or pollinated with the genes encoding the trait unable to germinate), the distinction made by the press was largely nonexistent.

More than the first generation technology (a cumbersome multigene system that had not then, nor has now been reduced to practice) or the principle of recurrent seed purchase (hybrid maize and vegetables and seedless fruit already exemplified that without serious reservations in most quarters), the outrage was largely focused on the anticipated use of this type of technology to further dominate what was being perceived as an already-too-concentrated power base.

The End Run

Rather than struggling to prevent onerous mechanisms designed to ensure recovery of large financial outlays for research and product development, could we rather invent and provide methodologies and policies that would allow technological innovation to be successful without such capital outlays? Could we look at lowering the entry barriers for innovation rather than developing mechanisms that would entrench or at best stifle the status quo?

This approach would identify the underlying reasons that certain technologies are emerging (in this case, the need for recovery of vast sums needed to innovate) and conceive of ways of making those reasons irrelevant (making it cheaper to innovate).

Apomixis—The Germinator

Perhaps the most remarkable example of this positive approach is apomixis, wittily dubbed "the germinator" by Calestous Juma (1999). While some argue that the highest priority for saving the planet is managing population growth through human birth control ("sex without seeds"), others add that a complementary and equally essential innovation will be a revolution in agriculture: apomixis—"seeds without sex." Many plants in nature can reproduce through seeds, but without involving any sexual fusion of sperm and egg cells. This phenomenon, seen prominently in dandelions on most front lawns, allows a genetic makeup that is well adapted for a particular use or environment to breed true and not segregate and squander the optimum condition.

Few agriculturally relevant plants are naturally apomictic. From the thousands of edible plants that could have become the bedrock of modern agriculture, our farmer forebears chose those that seemed to improve over time. Plants that segregated variation were also those that were not apomictic, or not fully so. Today's curious cross-section of flowering plants that serve as our food, fiber, feed, and fuel plants are not capable of the natural process that would allow them to "fix and maintain" the genetic makeup that allows their best performance in a particular environment and to persist with just that makeup. However, many weeds and weedy plants have maintained this capacity, capturing a reproductive strategy that would be perfect for much of the world's agriculture, were it available.

Typically, when most flowering plants reproduce, the pollen, which contains the paternal genome contribution, must fuse with the egg cell containing the maternal genome. That pollen can come from the same plant or another; if it is usually from the same plant, it results in inbreeding. Crops such as rice, wheat, and barley are typically inbred and do not naturally show much hybridity. If, however, the pollination proclivities can be controlled physically or genetically, it is possible, albeit unwieldy, to encourage even these selfing plants to produce hybrids.

The phenomenon of heterosis, often called "hybrid vigor," has been associated with significant increases in productivity in certain crops, most notably maize and rice. More than half of China's rice production is credited to hybrids, which yield substantially more than their inbred parents. Virtually all of the maize production in the United States is from hybrid maize. This phenomenon of heterosis depends on producing plants that have very different (that is, heterozygous) genotypes that can in a sense provide synergism—the resulting whole being greater than the sum of its parts. The problem, of course, is that when a hybrid is produced through normal sexual reproduction, it does not breed true. Thus, bringing a maternal and paternal genome together by genetic crossing produces an ephemeral result that typically must be recreated each generation. For a plant breeding company, this entails extraordinary logistical and cost burdens; for the farmer it requires seasonal seed purchases at prices substantially higher than those of open pollinated or self-pollinated varieties. If one could capture the genetic benefits of heterosis and combine them with the extraordinary logistical benefits of apomixis—being able to "freeze" or fix any genetic combination and have it breed true without requiring pollination of the egg cell—both plant breeding and farming could become much more productive.

The extraordinary progress in the last 10 years in understanding the molecular and cellular events that underlie the sexual process in plants, notably *Arabidopsis*, suggests that the time is ripe to harness apomixis for world agriculture. Excellent reviews of apomixis have been published, most notably that by Grossniklaus, Nogler, and van Dijk (2001) and the current state of apomixis is well reviewed in the companion meeting report from Como (Spillane, Vielle-Calzada, and Grossniklaus 2001).

The Impacts of Apomixis

The impacts of apomixis must guide its development. These impacts range from the development of propagation methods for root and tuber crops such as cassava, potatoes, and yams that could dramatically improve the food security options for the poorest people, to hybrid technologies for new breeds of cereal grain crops. These and other anticipated impacts have been exhaustively reviewed elsewhere (Jefferson 1994; Jefferson and Bicknell 1996). However the most poorly articulated impact, yet possibly the most revolutionary, is not on crops, but on the ability of disenfranchised people to innovate on their own behalf.

The Challenge of Delivery—Pulling All the Pieces Together

Is apomixis really on the horizon? Will the momentum of science in academia, industry, and the international agricultural community eventually produce a useable form of apomixis that achieves even a fraction of its potential, in a timely manner? Ensuring delivery of apomixis to those whose lives will depend on it will require a concerted, strategic, and proactive initiative unprecedented in agriculture, but with parallels in health sciences and engineering.

The suite of ancillary enabling technologies necessary to implement the trait in numerous crops also must be made available, and these technologies must be tuned for the circumstances of the crops, economies, environments, and societies in which they will be applied. Further, they must be delivered with the licenses necessary to practice and in a policy framework that can encourage fair play and equitable access to the fruits of the technology. This is not currently the case.

Targeting the Whole Package

A highly focused, IP-driven initiative is required to proactively provide freedom to operate for all the critical bottleneck technologies. The absence of any one of these tools for a particular crop or group of innovators could halt progress. But wholesale in-licensing of technologies that are on the verge of obsolescence is not the answer.

We need to devlop new technologies that meet stringent guidelines. Almost all of the existing plant biotechnologies have emerged piecemeal from academic observations over the last 20 years, but some are only now emerging with patent protection. The bespoke invention of new enabling technologies has not been done with any vigor or seriousness in international agriculture, even in the private sector, where priorities are shaped by the pressures of coping with low-margin products that have high development costs and long lead times.

Transformation methodology. To be improved, the apomictic trait must be understood, introduced, and modified within many varieties of each species. Many crops of the developing world have abysmal transformation systems often being developed and practiced by niche-scientists with varying skills. We need new approaches that can work in a "platform-independent" manner and freedom to operate on all these methodologies.

Gene control methodology (T-GURTs). Switching apomixis on and off is critical in many applications, but it must be done with cost-effective, environmentally, and socially acceptable compounds, and with the approval of regulatory authorities. These technologies must be readily accessible to allow different forecast implementations of apomixis to be tested and evaluated.

Homologous recombination (HARTs). Apomixis must be precise, stable, penetrant, and ultimately nontransgenic. Regulatory hurdles are not to be underestimated. The tools to test candidates, and ultimately to amend genetic constitution in diverse crops, are simply not available. If candidate loci emerge from ongoing genomics analysis, they must be tested; without HARTs, scientists are in a frustrating position of having access to dominant gain-of-function analyses only. HARTs are the key to making the whole toolbox work in the developing world.

Genotyping and genomic analysis technologies—Diversity Array Technology (DArT). Cost-effective techniques to monitor and target plant breeding opportunities and to evaluate germplasm conservation strategies will be crucial. Molecular markers for analyzing genetic diversity will be essential to using this diversity wisely and to understanding relatedness and distinctness of materials for conservation. In spite of its promise, genomics, at least sequence-based genomics, costs far too much and its throughput is too low to apply to most crops of the developing world. Substantial breakthroughs in cost and throughput are required to allow local-scale investigation and are not married to DNA sequence determination; the transition from DNA sequence to phenotype ultimately requires experimental verification of hypothesis, and this bottleneck remains irrespective of the amount of DNA sequence information to hand. Thus, methods independent of DNA sequence information are really an essential tool to allow rapid, cost-effective introgression and analysis of candidate genetic material into advanced crop and livestock lines. Such methods are on the horizon (Jaccoud et al. 2001), and when combined with apomixis tools (or used to develop them) they will be formidable additions to the plant breeders' arsenal.

Conclusion

Achieving food security and adequate nutrition in a sustainable manner is arguably the greatest challenge of this century for the developing world. The solution lies in galvanizing the capabilities of those whose lives are most affected by these challenges to develop the solutions. Top-down imposition of silver bullets will not work—that is a simple matter of logic. However innovative science and policy can help to craft the meta-technologies to enable those experiencing problems to creatively solve them.

If R&D is too expensive, we must make it cheaper. We must counter the current skew of new technologies toward rich markets and simple problems. If innovative potential is centralized we must decentralize it. We must identify opportunities to engage entrepreneurism in achieving local solutions to the myriad distinct problems in agriculture. Unlike pharmaceutical medicine, which deals predominantly with one genome—the human—agriculture deals with dozens of primary genomes (crops and livestock) and thousands of secondary genomes (pests, beneficials, and so on) in a nonhomeostatic environment (that is, the completely variable agroecosystem). Society needs some different technological and intellectual paradigms to deal with this challenge. This includes creating a new hybrid: Technologies that are accessible and adaptable, disseminated by IP tools that guarantee access, not obstacles.

If HARTs and apomixis, and ideally apomixis by HARTs, can be developed and provided at reasonable costs, then virtually any innovators with a knowledge of their local market and environment can develop nontransgenic products (by current definitions) that will presumably not have to pass through the onerous regulatory regimes. If HARTs become a routine tool, any hypothesis derived from the genomic information that is rapidly accumulating can be cheaply and readily tested, and the product would likely be nontransgenic. Genomic information would indeed become a public good.

If experimental technologies lend themselves to local-scale analysis, and if the tools are dramatically cheaper, diverse and robust private- and public-sector entities can creatively service countless modest-margin markets and create exciting new local-level opportunities.

Notes

1. For a summary of some of the plant and animal biotechnologies currently in the research pipeline, see Pew Initiative on Food and Biotechnology (2001).

2. Kenmore, Director of the Global IPM Facility based at the Food and Agriculture Organization of the United Nations (FAO) is one of the most eloquent exponents of farmer field schools and improved heuristics in integrated pest management, and has had a major impact in IPM adoption in rice and in other crucial crops.

References

Grossniklaus, U., G. A. Nogler, and P. J. van Dijk. 2001. How to avoid sex: The genetic control of gametophytic apomixis. *Plant Cell* 13 (7) (July): 1491–98.

Helgason, E., O. A. Okstad, D. A. Caugant, H. A. Johansen, A. Fouet, M. Mock, I. Hegna, A. B. Kolsto. 2000. *Bacillus anthracis*, *Bacillus cereus*, and *Bacillus thuringiensis*: One species on the basis of genetic evidence. *Applied Environmental Microbiology.* 66 (6): 2627–30.

Jaccoud, D., K. Peng, D. Feinstein, and A. Kilian. 2001. Diversity arrays: A solid state technology for sequence information independent genotyping. *Nucleic Acids Re*search 29 (4.e25): 1–7.

Jefferson, R. A. 1994. Apomixis: A social revolution for agriculture? *Biotechnology and Development Monitor* (June 19): 14–19.

Jefferson, R. A. and Bicknell, R. 1996. The potential impacts of apomixis: A molecular genetics approach. In *The Impact of Plant Molecular Genetics*. B. W. S. Sobral, ed. Boston: Birkhäuser.

Juma, C. 1999. Personal communication, Harvard University.

Nottenburg, C., P. G. Pardey, and B. D. Wright. 2001. Accessing other people's technology. Do non-profit agencies need it? How to obtain it." EPTD Discussion Paper No. 79. Washington, D.C.: International Food Policy Research Institute (September).

Pew Initiative on Food and Biotechnology. 2001. *Harvest on the horizon: Future uses of agricultural biotechnology.* Washington, D.C.

Spillane, C., J. P. Vielle-Calzada, and U. Grossniklaus. 2001. APO2001: A sexy apomixer in como. *Plant Cell* 13 (7) (July): 1480–91.

UNEP/CBD/SBSTTA (United Nations Environment Programme; Convention on Biological Diversity; Subsidiary Body on Scientific, Technical and Technological Advice). 1999. Consequences of the use of the new technology for the control of plant gene expression for the conservation and sustainable use of biological diversity. Paper presented at the fourth meeting of the SBSTTA, Montreal, June 1999. <http://www.biodiv.org/doc/meetings/sbstta/sbstta-04/official/sbstta-04-09-rev1-en.doc>.

Xiao, J., J. Li, S. Grandillo, S. N. Ahn, L. Yuan, S. D. Tanksley, and S. R. McCouch. 1998. Identification of trait-improving quantitative trait loci alleles from a wild rice relative, *Oryza rufipogon*. *Genetics.*150 (2) (October): 899–909.

Comment

Brian Fisher

In listening to the material presented in Part 2, I was reminded of a discussion I had with a French climate negotiator in The Hague in November, 2000, about the differences between the New and Old Worlds. My very good friend from France made the point that some of the people from the New World were a bit outlandish, and he could not quite understand their perspective. I indicated to him that some of my friends from the Old World were a bit outlandish, and I could not understand their perspective either. It's not just a question of being rich or poor; the difference involves the way western Europeans—in particular—observe things on the planet and the way they respond. So we have to ask some fundamental questions about what that means for issues like biotechnology and trade liberalization.

When you look at the common agricultural policy, I think Per Pinstrup-Andersen has been a little too friendly, frankly, to the western Europeans (maybe it's his Danish upbringing). If you go back and look at the Treaty of Rome, the basis of the common agricultural policy, one of the aims is food self-sufficiency and a fundamental tenet underlying this is a willingness to provide almost unprecedented levels of farm support. When we combine a different world view with the existing framework provided by the common agricultural policy it is easy to see why such a gap in approaches to trade liberalization or biotechnology exists between the E.U. on the one hand and, say, the Cairns Group of free trading nations on the other.[1] Such differences are not really about ethics or the environment, they are more about differences in view about trade protection.

So there appears to be a substantial divide between Europe and much of the rest of the world, and I think that it is going to make a big difference to the direction of trade liberalization and the whole question of transgenic agriculture. Kym Anderson and his colleagues raise the question of whether it is possible to effectively segregate those two product streams throughout the system. There's a real question as to whether it is physically and economically possible to do that. In the Anderson et al. model the authors assume that distinct product streams can be maintained and in that case agents cater to niche markets and make some economic rent as a consequence.

The real question—if you farm on the Eyre Peninsula here in South Australia or on the pampas in Argentina—is, "Is it possible to maintain two completely segregated product streams, one containing transgenic product and the other free of transgenic product, from the farm all the way up through the marketing chain?" This segregation would need to include the ability to keep any animal feed separate to ensure that animal products could be classified if required. Practically, it would be both difficult and expensive to guarantee complete segregation, and some serious implications are likely to arise for the new technologies and for trade liberalization. We have an open question for the next round of the World Trade Organization (WTO) and probably for several rounds after that.

I would like to make a couple of technical points for people who do not deal much with general equilibrium models of trade. When you are reading the excellent material by Anderson et al., keep in mind a few points. When modelers do productivity shocks, like the ones illustrated in the Anderson et al. chapter, they tend to simulate large positive benefits. And modelers who do trade liberalization simulations with these types of models typically find small gains from trade liberalization. Research combining productivity shocks with trade liberalization shocks tends to find much larger gains from trade liberalization compared with simulations that exclude productivity effects.

So when comparing trade research analysis it is important to ensure that the simulations you are interested in actually have some basis for comparison. It is not particularly informative to attempt to draw policy conclusions about the benefits of trade reform in two countries if the analysis you have available is done using completely different assumptions about the feedback between reform and productivity growth. Next is an empirical question: "What is the likely level of productivity gains as a consequence of trade reform, market deregulation, or a discovery of a new technology?" It is becoming fairly common for modelers to use productivity shocks of up to 5 percent—a fairly big shock in my experience. I would like to see more empirical work in this area to demonstrate the veracity of the use of such parameters.

Another point to be pretty careful about is that these models can give substantially different results depending on the level of disaggregation of both countries and commodities employed in the simulations. So let's look at the implications of adopting biotechnology, say, for a group of countries like the Cairns Group mentioned above, compared with considering Australia alone. The observation has been made already, I think, that Australia is not a big exporter of maize and soybeans, and as a consequence, you should not take the results directly from a simulation in which the Cairns Group is considered a single aggregated region and assume that they are the results for Australia. Properly interpreting the results from general equilibrium trade models requires substantial common sense and a good understanding of both the characteristics of the commodities and the trade structure of the countries being studied.

The results in Chapter 4 highlight one important feature of this sort of work: Countries that impose trade restrictions and distortions on themselves gain the most from their removal. If you look at the welfare results from the GTAP model presented in the first part of the chapter, for example, it suggests that when the E.U. effectively bans the import of GM products (imposing the biggest distortion), they take the largest welfare loss.

And finally, very quickly moving on to Richard's paper: He makes the fundamental point that countries need to have a strong IP framework in place—one that is legally enforceable, provides certainty, and is not cumbersome. Such a framework is essential to ensuring that the benefits from research can be captured by those making the discoveries, thereby strengthening the incentive to invest venture capital. This brings me back to a point made in Chapter 3 that the public sector could buy research from the private sector and then transfer it to other industries or countries. Jeffrey Sachs has made a related suggestion with respect to vaccines for tropical diseases (Kremer and Sachs 1999). It would be very interesting to see research on whether such a model could feasibly enhance the transfer of gene technology to the developing world.

Note

1. The Cairns Group consists of Argentina, Australia, Bolivia, Brazil, Canada, Chile, Colombia, Costa Rica, Fiji, Guatemala, Indonesia, Malaysia, New Zealand, Paraguay, the Philippines, South Africa, Thailand, and Uruguay.

References

Kremer, M., and J. Sachs. 1999. A cure for indifference. *The Financial Times*, May 5.

Part 3

Intellectual Property
Policies and Practice

Chapter 6

Addressing Freedom-to-Operate Questions for International Agricultural R&D

Carol Nottenburg, Philip G. Pardey, and Brian D. Wright

Introduction

The Green Revolution came about through the unencumbered international trans-fer of germplasm, research results, and know-how. Germplasm found in farmers' fields in Japan and Taiwan found its way to the International Maize and Wheat Improvement Center (CIMMYT) and the International Rice Research Institute (IRRI), some by way of the United States, to form the basis for the high-yielding, semi-dwarf varieties of wheat and rice introduced in the 1960s. No questions were asked about the property rights surrounding the base germplasm, their improved derivatives, or the experimental tools and data used or generated as part of the research. They were available to all, free of charge.

Few of the forms of intellectual property (IP) now prevalent in the biosciences were utilized for agricultural research and development (R&D) when the seeds of the Green Revolution were sown in the 1940s and 1950s. The situation is now much different. A strengthening of IP regimes the world over means that many agricultural technologies are now subject to utility patents, trademarks, contractual claims, or plant breeders' rights, so the unfettered use of these technologies is no longer possi-ble. It is not just privately developed technologies that are now proprietary—the IP developed by public agencies is also increasingly protected.

Access to and use of germplasm, component technologies, and data (including experimental results) are subject to increasingly tighter property protection, calling into question the modus operandi of nonprofit organizations such as the members of the Consultative Group on International Agricultural Research (CGIAR or CG) and similar, often publicly funded, national research agencies the world over. Can the CGIAR members continue to support open access to, and free use of, its research results and the germplasm it holds in trust? How can the CGIAR continue to collect and conserve germplasm and maintain access to the research material, tools, and methods of others when they are increasingly protected in one form or another?

In fact the CGIAR has already begun moving away from the unrestricted use of its in-trust germplasm and research findings. Since 1995, the material transfer agreements included in all the shipments of germplasm held in trust by the CGIAR under a 1994 agreement with the Food and Agriculture Organization of the United Nations (FAO) limit the IP subsequently claimed from the use of this germplasm. The CGIAR's collective attitude to IP is evolving in response to rapid changes in the IP landscape and the organization of the agricultural biotechnology sector. While the latest identifiable CGIAR pronouncement does not clearly delineate a policy regarding patenting by the centers themselves, CIMMYT has declared its intention to take out patents (and other centers have done so), and some centers have entered into licensing arrangements to use the results from CGIAR research (Dalton 2000).[1]

This chapter addresses some of the IP options for the CGIAR, along with their implications, focusing primarily on freedom-to-operate concerns. Through its research and developing-country contacts, the CGIAR has facilitated and accelerated international spillovers of R&D results and improved germplasm. In this way the CG draws from and contributes to the international stock of R&D knowledge and technologies. Though all R&D agencies do this to some extent, a distinguishing feature of the CG is that, by design, it spans the agricultural sciences of the developed and developing worlds and has played an important role in mediating the science and germplasm flows between and within both. In recognition of the current realities surrounding IP, the following discussion broaches both policy and practical issues, mindful of the technology generation and mediation role the CG has played and likely will continue to play.

Forms of Intellectual Property Protection

Intellectual property concerning agricultural technologies and the sciences that generate these technologies has proliferated over the past few decades. By way of background, a brief description of the forms of property protection relevant to agricultural technologies and the seeds and science that give rise to such technologies follows.

Technical Sources of Property Protection

The technical means for conferring property rights over agricultural innovations have expanded in recent years. Hybridization of corn and other crops is a well-established method.[2] Newer methods involve various genetic use restriction technologies (GURTs). Those that confer sterility on seeds saved for reuse are called varietal GURTs (V-GURTs). This technology strategy has been rejected by the CGIAR.[3] Technologies that control the expression of certain traits in saved seeds but otherwise do not affect the performance of the seed are dubbed trait GURTs (T-GURTSs).

Legal Forms of Property Protection

Utility patents on living things. Grants with some form of quasi-monopoly control over things that economists classify as public goods are not new. Utility patents on inventions related to machinery, chemicals, and pharmaceuticals have been around for many years. The authority for the U.S. patent system is enshrined as Article 1, Section 8 of the U.S. Constitution ratified in 1788.[4] Some European countries have had patent protection for far longer, such as the United Kingdom, which has the longest continuous patent tradition in the world, having granted its first patent in 1449.

What is comparatively new is the broadened scope of the protection to include inventions involving living things. In the United States, the first steps in this direction were taken in 1930 with the passage of the Plant Patent Act, which protected asexually reproduced plants—that is, plants like grape vines, fruit trees, strawberries, and ornamentals that are propagated through cuttings and graftings.

Patent scope was further expanded in the early 1970s when General Electric brought a powerful test case on the patentability of a living organism (specifically an oil-eating bacterium). In 1980, the U.S. Supreme Court (in the case of *Diamond v Chakrabarty*) ruled in GE's favor. Although the bacterium was never commercialized, this ushered in a new era for utility patenting of life forms. In 1985, the Board of Patent Appeals ruled in *ex parte Hibberd* that asexually and sexually propagated seeds, plants, and tissue culture could be protected by utility patents. Plants defined by a single recombinant DNA sequence (as distinct from plant varieties per se) are now patentable in the European Union (E.U.), according to a decision of the European Board of Patent Review (Harbison and Wailes 2000).

Plant breeders' rights. The United States introduced a Plant Variety Protection Act in 1970 to strengthen IP protection for nonhybrid varieties (which lack the natural protection against replanting possessed by hybrids). To be granted a plant breeders' right (known as a plant variety protection certification, or PVPC in the United States) an applicant must demonstrate that the variety is new, distinct from other varieties, and genetically uniform and stable through successive generations.[5] Under this scheme, use of plants for further breeding is unrestricted, provided the progeny are distinct from the parents (where distinctness may be, for example in a notorious case, a commercially irrelevant difference in the flower color of soybeans). Thus, in contrast to a utility patent, utility or usefulness is not required for a PVPC. Some forms of plant breeders' rights, consistent with the International Union for the Protection of New Varieties of Plants (UPOV), now exist in most Organisation of Economic Co-operation and Development (OECD) countries. Developing countries are adopting forms of plant variety protection, generally as members of UPOV in compliance with the requirement of the Trade-Related Aspects of Intellectual Property (TRIPs) agreement to grant a sui generis form of protection (that is, unique to a specific field of technology) to plant varieties.[6] Unfortunately, implementing sui generis protection is heterogeneous and institutionally complex (Egelyng 2000).

Material transfer agreements. Since 1995, seeds shipped from CG genebanks are packaged with a Material Transfer Agreement (MTA)—akin to the shrink-wrap user agreements included with a software package—that delineates the assignment of intellectual property rights (IPR) for the seed samples.[7] MTAs also accompany shipments from the breeding programs of the centers and from virtually all public agencies worldwide, as well as genetic and other research materials exchanged among biotechnology labs. The strength of this protection is yet to be established but has the possibility of being as strong as trade secrets.

Bag label contracts. Pioneer Hi-Bred International recently sued some competitors alleging they selected self-pollinated seeds found in bags of Pioneer hybrid corn seed and used them for breeding competitive hybrids. The basis of the suit appears to be the violation of restrictions included in the contract written on the bag label, also akin to the "shrink-wrap" contract for software.

Technology use agreements. These technology agreements between farmers and the technology supplier (for example, Monsanto's *Bacillus thuringiensis [Bt]* or Roundup Ready® [RR] technologies embodied in varieties of corn, cotton, soybeans, canola, and sugarbeets) control the right to plant a given seed on a specific area of land for a certain period of time (one season). In 2000, around half of the U.S. soybean crop, a quarter of the corn acreage, and 61 percent of the cotton area was sown to transgenic crops (NASS 2001). Two thirds of the Canadian crop was transgenic. Argentina and China have sizeable areas under transgenic crops, and plantings are also found in Australia, France, Germany, Mexico, South Africa, and elsewhere (James 2000).

In 2001, the technology fee for a 50-pound bag of RR soybeans in the United States was US$6.50 and for *Bt* cotton it ranged from US$117 to $138.30 per 50-pound bag, depending on the variety or region of sale within the United States.[8] This variation in prices reflects an attempt to price-discriminate among different markets within the United States, perhaps reflecting localized differences in the weed- and pest-control value of these transgenic technologies.

Failure to honor these technology agreements makes the infringer liable for severe penalties, up to 120 times the applicable technology fee plus all legal fees. As of February 1999, Pinkerton investigators working for Monsanto were investigating 525 cases of suspected infringement in the United States (Weiss 1999). About half of these cases have been settled involving payment of tens and even hundreds of thousands of dollars each. The cost of enforcement is expected to be greater.

Trade secrets. Trade secrecy protected under state law has long been a means of asserting property protection over new technologies in the United States and elsewhere. Process innovations are more easily protected by these means than product innovations (because of the possibility of reverse engineering the product to reveal the trade secrets), but trade secrecy has been effectively used to protect some forms of agricultural biotechnology. In particular, parent lines of hybrid corn have been protected under Iowa state trade secrecy laws.

Commercial contracts and licenses. A web of proprietary claims now surrounds the transfer and use of patented biotechnologies, thereby limiting the freedom to operate of public and private agencies alike. Proprietary claims now cover all sorts of biotechnologies:

- parent germplasm;

- trait-specific genes, which control specific input characteristics such as tolerance of abiotic stress, insect, fungal, or viral resistance, herbicide tolerance, cold tolerance, and ripening, and output traits such as increased content of starch, oil, amino acids, proteins, vitamins, and minerals, or decreased content of traits that are harmful (for example, allergens) or contribute to environmental pollution (such as phytates that increase the environmental damage from manure); and

- enabling technologies, including
    — transformation technologies by which a gene that codes for a specific characteristic is inserted into plant cells;
    — promoters, which are used to control expression of the gene in plants;

—selectable markers, which are genes used to determine which plant cells have been successfully transformed to show the desired characteristic; and

—gene silencing or regulating technologies that can be used to suppress or modify gene expression in plants.

Depending on the complexity of the transgenic product, dozens of identifiable proprietary claims can be involved in its development.

The remainder of this chapter focuses on the implications of IP protected by patents—and, relatedly, commercial contracts and licenses—in the United States and other countries of the North on researchers' freedom to operate in other (mainly less-developed) countries of the South, and especially their ability to use technologies developed by private multinational companies. Though for simplicity the discussion focuses on patents and related contracts and licenses, decisions on IP access are shaped by the interactions among all available forms of IP protection and these interactions have important—often different—consequences for public and private research organizations.

Patents as a Form of Intellectual Property

A basic understanding of the nature of IP inherent in a patent is a prerequisite for thinking about the appropriate public R&D role in an increasingly proprietary agricultural science world. Patents protect inventions of tangible things and confer a legally enforceable right on their owners to exclude others from practicing the invention described and claimed in the document. These rights, however, apply for a limited period of time only, in a specific legal jurisdiction, within the scope of the property protection circumscribed by the claims made in the patent.

The details of rights conferred by a patent depend on the nation in which it is awarded; the life of a patent is limited—usually 20 years from date of filing—and the scope of a patent is defined by its specific claims. Patent applications are usually published 18 months after filing. Especially in the United States, the validity of a patent, and its scope, is often unclear until many years after issue, when final legal rulings are issued after a court challenge.

A common misconception is that a patent awarded in one country confers rights across the rest of the world, but this is not so. There is no such thing as an international patent. Patents are awarded by national governments and the protection conferred is limited to the national jurisdiction in which the patent is awarded. Most inventions are patented in just one country, and in many developing countries few inventions are patented. To obtain protection in more than one country, a patent must be awarded in each, the cost of which varies from country to country.

Obtaining protection in all important markets can be very costly—hundreds of thousands of dollars—therefore, many innovations patented in the United States or Europe remain unpatented in other countries where patenting is available.

If an innovation is patented in the United States but not, for example, in Australia, then anyone is free to use it in Australia, but U.S. importation of a product embodying the patented IP, or products resulting from a patented process, might well be subject to legal challenge.[9]

Intellectual Property Rights Proliferation: The Downside

When no prior IP claims on a patented innovation exist, the complementary effect of prior nonpatented research often enhances its value. In effect, the patentee captures value that previous research efforts created. As patents on research tools and products proliferate, the restrictive force of the monopoly conferred by prior patents comes to bear on the next generation of research. Part of this is a natural rescaling as patentees cease to be the beneficiaries of a free ride on prior public and private research (Koo 1998), much as United States hybrid corn companies no longer have elite publicly developed inbred lines available for use as parents of their commercial cultivars.

The diversity of innovations used in modern cultivar development can result in a balkanization of competing claims that can seriously threaten to hinder subsequent innovation. As patenting becomes more prevalent in biotechnology, the number of separate rights needed to produce a new innovation proliferates. Several years ago, it was claimed that more than 40 patents were required to commercialize a new transgenic hybrid corn cultivar. More recently, the prototypic transgenic vitamin A rice incorporates technology based on 70 patents with 32 owners (Kryder, Kowalski, and Krattiger 2000; Gillis 2000). If ownership of these rights is diffuse and uncertain, the multilateral bargaining problem can become difficult if not impossible to resolve. This is the "Tragedy of the Anticommons" noted by Heller and Eisenberg (1998).

Indeed, it is widely reported that some public universities are especially difficult to deal with. Their negotiators are often inexperienced, and the limits on university pay scales make it difficult to attract or keep experienced, effective personnel. Academics are independent agents who engage in invention only as a part-time occupation. Consequently they are typically unfamiliar with the patenting process, and lack the incentive to help the university develop an overall patent portfolio that meets the needs of licensees.

Furthermore, universities face constraints on the types of deals that can be made. For example, in the United States, a university often cannot trade access to one research tool for access to another as easily as could a private corporation. Typically the university, unlike most corporations, has rules obliging it to award a fraction of the value of the invention to employee-innovators. Given that the latter are unlikely to be satisfied with their employer's calculation of their awards unless they are based on actual arms-length financial transactions, exchanges of patent portfolios are problematic for a university.

Although the corporate sector has much greater freedom to maneuver in arranging IPR transactions, trade in IPR markets remains complex. To a significant extent, the high costs of IP transactions have been "solved" by rapid consolidation of biotech suppliers, and consolidation of these with plant breeding and seed distribution, and with plant protection chemical providers (Wright 1999). Between 1995 and 1999, the pace of this concentration of the farm input markets was rapid in Europe and the United States. More recently, the resulting conglomerates have begun to separate their concentrated agriculture-related activities from their more profitable pharmaceutical activities (*The Economist* 2000).

When the necessary rights are held in few hands, bargaining for access becomes more feasible. But even within the private sector, disputes over rights to dynamically evolving technologies have been fierce and extremely costly. Lerner (1995, 470) reports that for every 100 U.S. biotechnology patents, there are six patent suits, an extremely high figure relative to other areas of technology. In the case of one of the earliest applications, use of *Bt* genes in transformation of corn, Barton (1998) lists at least 26 U.S. disputes involving *Bt* as of May 1997. On average, cases that went to trial incurred an estimated average of more than a million dollars of cost, aside from the cost to the judicial system[10] or the cost of complying with the final judgment and conditions of settlement. The willingness of parties to expend such sums shows genuine disagreement over the validity, value, and/or allocation of patent rights indicative of the pervasive uncertainty of the innovation environment. But the prospect of such expenditures poses a barrier to entry, and an incentive for further consolidation in the private sector. Effective and credible defense of IPR in the United States is beyond the financial capacity of most international, nonprofit research institutions, and most start-up private ventures.

When negotiating with the private sector for access to technology, the greatest problem can be refusal to bargain at all. Researchers at the University of California engaged in a project to develop a new tomato variety genetically engineered to express the endogluconase gene to retard softening and enhance shelf life. The germplasm used in this transformation was another tomato variety developed with public support and widely distributed to researchers on the understanding that no patent application had been filed (Shands 2000). When a patent was in fact issued, the corporation owning it reportedly refused to grant, or even bargain for, commercialization rights to the new cultivar (Lemaux 1998), so the entire project had to be abandoned (Wright 1998b).

Erbisch (2000) reports that a research effort that developed a superior turfgrass at Michigan State University encountered similar problems. The cultivar incorporated a gene owned by one corporation and a promoter owned by another. Since neither party was willing to grant a license to the university, the cultivar could not be commercialized.

In another example, the Australian organization Centre for Legumes in Mediterranean Agriculture (CLIMA) obtained permission from another life sciences corporation to use a gene for herbicide tolerance in transformation of a lupin cultivar. After successful completion of this project, CLIMA sought permission to commercialize the transgenic cultivar, but the corporate patentee refused to negotiate a commercial license (Lindner 1999).

A serious consequence of this kind of experience is that researchers—and their funders—become wary of committing long-term research resources to areas where there is some probability that IPR problems will block utilization of the results. Reports claim that tomato producers decided to discontinue support for university development of transgenic cultivars as a result of the case of the California tomato research cited above.

Despite the special disadvantages of the public sector in obtaining freedom to operate, the problem is quite severe in private biotechnology as well. It was recently reported, for example, that Bristol Myers had identified 50 proteins of interest for cancer therapy that it could not work on because of patent holders' demands for unreasonable royalties or refusal to negotiate (Pollack 2001, C2).

Much of the university discussion of protection of IP focuses on the disruption of patterns of intellectual communication essential to the function of the institution. Some expressions of concern along these lines assume a level of free communication of unpatentable knowledge at odds with our own experiences in academic institutions, in a field not famous for their patentable output. Sharing of truly original ideas before claims to authorship are established—via distribution of a working paper, for example—occurs principally among trusted colleagues, if at all. Potentially fruitful collaborative opportunities, including collaborations between academics in universities and their counterparts in international agricultural research centers (IARCs), are lost due to the lack of clearly established rights to credit for ideas. Yet the publication of new ideas and imaginative applications continues, encouraged by the rewards of promotion, tenure, and the respect of one's peers.

Additional concerns include publication delays associated with the need to establish IPR, and embargoes on public presentations to comply with patenting requirements. These delays are likely to be longer than those needed to secure property rights to ideas via publication, so they can be a serious problem, but given that patents very likely speed the development of ideas, their net effect may nevertheless be positive relative to the slower progress of ideas in the absence of IPR.

Recognition of farmers' rights is notable mostly by its lack of progress. Despite a surge of optimism in the past decade regarding the commercial value of biodiversity in situ, current usage of landrace (farmer-developed) germplasm by crop breeders is low in most commercially important crops (Kate 1995; Wright 1998a). For new or minor crops, landraces are used more commonly, though development tends to concentrate on a small fraction of available germplasm. Furthermore, when landraces are used, widespread abuse of the rules of UPOV is alleged to have occurred (RAFI 1998), allowing landraces to be protected as if they were new, distinct cultivars. Problems identified include lack of trials to establish distinctiveness relative to germplasm source, no proof of breeding, and abuse of provisional protection. Many cases of alleged abuse are related to Australia, largely because that country has provided unusually open access to the information necessary as a basis for such allegations. In one prominent example, an attempt by a Western Australian government organization to obtain Australian plant variety protection for two chickpea cultivars obtained from the International Crops Research Institute for Semi-Arid Tropics (ICRISAT) in India, resulted in an international outcry that led to a reversal of the organization's plans, and eventually to a tightening of Australian policy (RAFI 1998; RAFI and HSCA 1998).

Frustration over the lack of compensation for farmer-developed germplasm used for commercial development of private technology is not restricted to farmers of the South. In California, rice varieties have been developed by public-sector breeders supported in part by self-imposed assessments on rice production. The new cultivars are distributed to producers at around the cost of production. Recently, a major agricultural biotechnology corporation used germplasm developed in this way as the basis for a transgenic cultivar incorporating its proprietary herbicide-tolerance gene designed to complement the use of its own patented herbicide (Wright 1998b). If the producers had obtained a PVPC on their cultivar under the United States Plant Variety Protection Act as amended in 1994, perhaps they would have had a claim on the transgenic germplasm as an "essentially derived variety" covered by the PVPC, although the scope of this "essentially derived" characterization has yet to be established. Given the very large sums that biotechnology firms have paid to owners of germplasm in the (admittedly far more lucrative) market for seed corn, it is possible the farmers would have been offered a better deal on the transgenic crop if they owned the base germplasm. On the other hand, maybe the transgenic rice would not have been developed at all.

The average landrace is not very valuable for agriculture. To date, no case is known in which the assertion of farmers' rights over agricultural crops has led to large transfers to those farmers or their governments. But it may have led to some reduction in the selection of cultivars for distribution to farmers and, very likely, decreased the use of landraces in the creation of new cultivars of new or minor crops for use by farmers worldwide. For example, comparing the triennial periods 1991–93 to 1997–99, the number of contributions of breeding lines or varieties to the International Network for Genetic Evaluation of Rice (INGER) fell from 1,212 to 5 for Bangladesh, and from 103 to 37 for China (Egelyng 2000, 11, Figures 1–2). As Henrik Egelyng (2000, 13) notes, "[A]lready the Convention on Biological Diversity (CBD) seems to have severely impacted international germplasm networks, such as INGER, in terms of the number of contributions of rice varieties made by member countries to INGER for testing and dissemination." This is hardly a win/win outcome.

At the moment, access to germplasm owned by corporations of the North with IPR protection may be a far larger problem for breeders (North and South) than is access to landraces in the South. Price (1999, 138) reports the results of a survey of public plant breeding at 21 universities working in 41 crops in the United States. Of 86 respondents, 48 percent indicated they were "having difficulties obtaining genetic stocks from companies." For 45 percent, this had interfered with their research, and for 28 percent with their "ability to release new varieties." A further 23 percent reported that these difficulties interfered with the training of graduate students.

Options for Obtaining Freedom to Operate in Crucial Proprietary Enabling Technology

License IARC Germplasm to Pay for Access to Research Tools

The main valuable outputs of IARCs are germplasm and the associated production-relevant information. In corn seed breeding in the United States, the biotechnology revolution has recently resulted in huge increases in the value of elite privately developed germplasm. Currently, IARCs disseminate both seeds and information gratis, a policy that maximizes efficiency of use unless complementary adaptive investment requires some protection. Charging what the market will bear is against current CG policy for landraces, wild and weedy species, and all other material held as part of the 1994 in-trust agreement with the FAO. For other in-house technology, licensing that precludes use by poor farmers in less-developed countries (LDCs) is presumably unacceptable. If the license terms must be uniform for all licensees, they must be generous to farmers, and so prospective returns from licensing are, at best, meager.

Cross-Licensing

This is a popular solution for deals among biotech oligopolists. Rather than bargain over values of individual innovations, firms exchange rights to a set of patents, with or without compensatory payments (Grindley and Teece 1997; Hall and Ham 1999). Public institutions also find that their ownership of patents can greatly facilitate private-sector collaboration. The experience of the Cooperative Research Centres (CRC) Program in Australia is typical and instructive. "We discovered that research capacity alone was not enough. Research concepts and unpublished data were sometimes interesting for our industry associates, but developing collaborative projects based on them was difficult. The breakthrough came when the CRC for plant science started to take out patents. Patents are property; property is valuable (or so prevailing wisdom then suggested), and therefore it can be traded. It was as if we had suddenly, almost magically, acquired a stack of chips and could get our feet under the card table. It was then that the tactic of progressive engagement started to pay off" (Buller and Taylor 1999). Similarly, when the Crop Development Centre of the University of Saskatchewan developed a commercially viable transgenic flax cultivar, its possession of a U.S. patent on a biolistic transformation process for flax was reportedly important for negotiations to obtain freedom to operate (Stovin and Phillips 2000, 687).

In universities, cross-licensing is often precluded by the nature of contracts for compensation of university innovators. Unlike most corporations, U.S. universities generally grant a substantial share of licensing revenues to their employees who patent valuable innovations, and other universities in OECD countries are following their lead.[11] Many other public and nonprofit institutions have similar rules. The prevalence of similar contracts at CG centers is uncertain at present. In any case, at CG centers, licensing would have to be restricted to property other than landraces they have received and the breeding materials they distribute to national agricultural research systems (NARSs) and others, which they are committed to furnish without charge to the world at large—except perhaps for charges for landraces held on behalf of the countries from which the accessions orginate. Despite these severe constraints, candidates for cross-licensing have already been nominated. The near-isogenic lines of rice germplasm at IRRI, potentially useful in plant breeding, are examples of technology that might be licensed via an MTA. Fischer and Barton (1999) propose an MTA that offers such material at no cost in exchange for access to information about subsequent discoveries (after a lag to allow applications for patents) and zero-cost nonexclusive research licenses to IARCs of the CG and

NARSs in LDCs. Further, they propose that a nonexclusive license for commercialization be granted to the research centers at a reasonable royalty and at zero cost for subsistence agricultural and other uses not in competition with the private sector. Whether such initiatives can be pursued successfully at sufficiently low cost in money and managerial resources is an open question.

For public research organizations that are acting independently, cross-licensing tends to be much more a part of the problem than the solution. As the agricultural biotech industry matures, it is becoming like many other industries where each major participant "holds an IP portfolio, much of which is regularly infringed by competitors. But none . . . usually brings suit . . . because each knows that the defendant would respond with a counterattack based on those of the defendant's patents that it is infringing. Litigation is too much like a nuclear weapon, and the relation becomes one of mutual assured destruction. . . . But . . . there is no reason not to use the portfolio against possible new entrants who might affect the oligopoly rents available to the industry leaders" (Barton 2000, 8). Public or nonprofit breeders might well find themselves, like potential private entrants, shut out by the oligopoly defended by nonlicensing agreements.

Merge or Form a Joint Venture with a Private-Sector Holder of Much Necessary Technology

As Barton (2000, 9) notes, "[M]ergers leading to oligopoly may often be an appropriate mechanism of avoiding a patent fight—the merger is the ultimate cross-license." In agricultural biotech, mergers are a prime private-sector solution to minimize the private cost of transactions in IPR used in research. (See, for example, Marco and Rausser 2000.) They can also lead to the private benefits (and public costs) of monopoly. It is assumed that mergers with private firms (or even public agencies) are not viable options for the CG at this time. However, partnership with the private sector may be possible. Monsanto is marketing transgenic cotton in China in a joint venture with a provincial, public seed-producing organization; their ongoing experience promises to be quite instructive, if not necessarily profitable.

Obtain Research Tools under Research Licenses or Other Agreements Limiting Use to Research Only

This might be attractive for scientists, as it allows them to pursue their projects using state-of-the-art technology. The National Institutes of Health (NIH), which dominates public funding of biotechnology in the United States, urges provision of such licenses gratis, and indeed such licenses are often freely available (NIH 1998a). Furthermore, a research license might generate externalities to the licensee in the form of learning-by-doing and, more generally, by the development of intangible research capacities that might reduce future dependence on proprietary technology.

But a free research license that does not permit commercialization can make a research tool the cuckoo's egg of technology transfer. If the project succeeds, then the bargaining for permission to commercialize (or release to users at no cost) the fruits of the research effort must begin. The fact that the researchers have already incurred the "sunk cost" of all the research expenditures places them in a highly disadvantageous bargaining position. On the other hand, the holder of the IPR, even if it refuses to allow commercialization, gains valuable information about the technology and its downstream applications that it can use for its own purposes. In the extreme, the IPR holder may be able to appropriate the full value of the research output of the licensee, gross of the latter's costs.

In some circumstances the situation might be more favorable to the licensee. If dissemination of successful innovations based on proprietary technology to users in certain markets offers little commercial benefit, a private licensor might be persuaded to license such dissemination gratis to a licensee with noncommercial objectives (for example, elimination of hunger among the poor) if it sees some kind of benefit, such as an enhanced public image, from doing so. This is discussed further below.

Make Common Cause with Other Nonprofits in Pressing for Changes in Public and/or Corporate Policy Regarding Sharing of Technology

The challenges posed by proprietary claims to international collaboration in biotechnology are not unique to agricultural applications and will take time to resolve. They belong to two broad classes. On the one hand are issues of access to innovations useful in biotechnology, which are shared by all other researchers in this general field. On the other hand, problems posed to crop breeders by farmers' rights are similar in nature (but not in degree) to those faced by pharmaceutical researchers interested in access to biodiversity products. These two classes of problems require different approaches.

Access to research tools is a burning issue at the heart of nonprofit research on biotechnology in the United States, the world leader in this area. International agricultural researchers might find the report of the NIH Working Group on Research Tools instructive, if not dismaying (NIH 1998a). The report notes that "although competitive pressures have always given scientists an incentive to withhold new research tools from their rivals, past practices allowed for relatively free exchange, typically without formal agreements and without explicit consideration of commercial rights or potential financial benefits. . . . It seems to be increasingly common, however, for the terms of these agreements to interfere with the widespread dissemination of research tools among scientists, either because owners and users are unable to reach agreement on fair terms or because the negotiations are difficult and cause protracted delays" (NIH 1998a, Executive Summary, 1–2). The summary of problems includes the following observations, among others, which might be familiar to some international agricultural researchers:

- "The value of research tools is difficult to assess and varies greatly from one tool to the next and from one use to the next. Providers and users are likely to differ in their assessments of the value of research tools.

- Case-by-case negotiations for permission to use research tools and materials create significant administrative burdens that delay research.

- Institutions that seek to retain a competitive advantage from their proprietary research tools are generally unwilling to make them freely available. In order to minimize risks of competitive harm, they may seek to limit who has access to the tools, restrict how they are used, and restrict or delay disclosure of research results.

- Differences in the nature and value of research tools and differences in the missions and constraints of owners and users of research tools make it difficult and perhaps undesirable to standardize terms of access to research tools across the broad spectrum of biomedical research" (NIH 1998a, Executive Summary, 1–2).

The Working Group's recommendations include free dissemination of research tools where possible, use of the Uniform Biological Materials Transfer Agreement (UBMTA), and development of guidelines for reasonable terms of licenses and MTAs. It is clear that biotechnology's IP transactions will continue to be problematic, even when all parties are domestic and share NIH funding.

Two members of the working group concluded that "the research and commercialization issues . . . arise as much from the way in which standards of patent law have been applied in the biotechnology area as they do from the terms of MTAs and license agreements" (NIH 1998a, 28, footnote 5). They urged analysis of patenting issues including standards of nonobviousness, appropriate scope of claims, the utility requirement, and the research exemption. Arguably, many academics and other professionals familiar with the current United States situation would agree.

The National Research Council shares concerns similar to those expressed by NIH. In its summary of an ongoing project on "Intellectual Property in the Knowledge-Based Economy," it notes ". . . a growing friction over the assertion and exercise of some IPRs and claims that in some circumstances they may be discouraging research, its communication, and use. The question arises whether in some respects the extension of IPRs has proceeded too far" (National Research Council, Board on Science, Technology, and Economic Policy 1999, 1).

Worldwide, the United States is perceived as the pacesetter in the evolution of IPR; however, the extent of dissatisfaction with the current operation of the patent system within the community of economists, lawyers, and research scientists in the United States is not similarly widely recognized. Clearly, international research institutions have an interest in following the current debate in the United States and Europe. They are probably incapable of influencing the general evolution of IPR, but they can press for inclusion of the interests of international nonprofit research collaborations in measures designed to address the interests of domestic research institutions in the leading countries, including the E.U. and the United States. The CGIAR and FAO are well placed to assist this effort by coordinating advocacy of the interests of international agricultural research institutions in the broader policy deliberations.

One form of pressure is a boycott of companies demanding "unreasonable" terms for key enabling technology. This tactic, recently discussed by Lesser (1999) with respect to plant breeding, would be ludicrous for an organization the size of the CGIAR on its own. But this tactic appears to have been used with some effect by NIH in a protracted struggle with DuPont over the terms of research licensing of a "research tool"—mice genetically engineered with the patented "cre-lox" system (Marshall 1998b). Significantly, the compromise ultimately hammered out excluded not only commercial use but also "use of cre DNA and/or lox DNA in higher plants or agricultural applications" (NIH 1998b, clause 1a). Making common cause with more powerful allies (such as NIH) in applying pressure on holders of IPR might help ensure that in future agreements, any concessions by holders of proprietary rights are extended to international agricultural (nonprofit) research and nonprofit dissemination to noncommercial markets.

Ally with Independent Developers of Research Tools
A quite different approach is to sponsor creation of substitutes to existing proprietary research paths. This is a task beyond the resources of the CG on its own. But promising collaborators do exist. The Center for the Application of Molecular Biotechnology to International Agriculture (CAMBIA) in Australia, for example, aims to generate new research tools for developing-country agriculture, unencumbered by restrictive proprietary claims. The magnitude of the enterprise has been limited by the extent of financial support, the sources of which include licensing revenues from

previously developed biotechnology (notably the β-glucuronidase, GUS, marker) to developed-country corporations.

Increasingly, the technology paths pursued by plant breeders are being influenced by their degree of appropriability by for-profit innovators. It is possible that other paths can be found that score low on appropriability but high on effectiveness. (The discovery of an antibiotic cure for stomach ulcers as a superior alternative to patented pharmaceuticals is an example from the health field.) The CGIAR and other nonprofit collaborators are well placed to pursue such opportunities.

Use Tools Legal in the Host Country, and Allow Recipients of the Newly Developed Cultivars to Handle Intellectual Proprietary Claims in Other Countries

Before discussion of this strategy in detail, it is crucial to emphasize that this is not a passive strategy; rather, it entails the commitment of substantial, high-quality resources for successful implementation.

A survey by Cohen et al. (1998) caused some concern when it revealed that centers are already using research tools and other inputs that are subject to IPR claims. What was not obvious from the survey was how many of these were subject to IPR in the locations in which centers operate. All the centers engaged in agricultural research are in less developed economies. Patents usually are filed in, at most, a select group of countries. Indeed, until recently, few developing countries allowed patents on life forms. In many cases, research tools and genetic material, and especially plant cultivars, may not be covered by patents in the host countries of international centers. Furthermore, international patenting is expensive, and corporations in many, if not most, cases have not obtained patent protection beyond the OECD countries. Where no patents are held, there can be no infringement.

To the extent that CG centers use technologies and cultivars that are not patented where they are made and where they are to be used, they can and should legally proceed without obtaining IPR. Even after compliance with TRIPS, the breeding of new cultivars produced by the CG using cultivars patented in developed countries may be legal under the sui generis protection being adopted in many LDCs. These new cultivars and associated genetic material might not be legally exportable to those countries where they are subject to proprietary claims, but many CG crops are largely consumed domestically, as discussed in detail in Binenbaum et al. (2000). Hence the new world of the World Trade Organization (WTO) might facilitate a kind of indirect market segmentation, in which LDCs get the new technology for free, and proprietary claims are enforced in developed countries. Further, cultivars incorporating genes patented in LDCs may not be subject to effective IP claims if those countries have neither the legal means nor the will to enforce them.

If CG center policies preclude violation of legally valid but practically unenforceable claims, they might consider arranging for their domestic NARS collaborators to address domestic IP concerns.

For the near term, centers are likely to have considerable freedom to operate, if they operate judiciously. Retroactive patenting being impossible, most of the technology useable by the CG over the next half-decade or so is likely unencumbered by relevant IPR, but the above statement cannot be taken as a license to assume freedom to operate in general. Mistakes could result in catastrophic legal liability. To implement a strategy of obtaining IPR only where necessary, it is essential to have access to adequate information on patent rights and appropriate access to expert legal counsel before making research commitments. Such information is not widely available at present on an international basis. Although the CG's Central Advisory Service, housed at the International Service for National Agricultural Research (ISNAR), can offer useful general advice, we are not aware of a comprehensive interactive database that can adequately complement legal expertise in servicing the needs of research strategists in the CGIAR. Such facilities may exist in large life-science corporations for agriculture-oriented internal use.

A very promising initiative to provide such services for third-world research organizations is being pursued by the nonprofit corporation CAMBIA, in Australia, by personnel unusually well informed regarding patents and the negotiation process in all its phases, but this effort is severely hampered by inadequate funding. The aim is to develop interactive software that can help researchers to identify prior IP claims and identify areas of freedom to operate and thus travel more safely through the international IP minefield. This initiative could make further international collaboration more feasible by mitigating the difficulties caused by uncertainty about prior claims to useful biotechnology. Access to personnel with wide experience in international patenting and patent negotiations will be needed to use this strategy to maximum effect. Such expertise is likely to be quite expensive, but without it, this strategy is inoperable or at least hazardous.

A possible drawback to this strategy is that one motivation for developed-country donor support of the CG might be prospective spin-offs of CGIAR research for farmers in their own countries. In the United States, wheat and rice spin-offs have been valuable (Pardey et al. 1996). To the extent that CG technology is subject to IPR claims in donor countries, the technologies will not be available in the countries without appropriate licensing. Although such licensing might still leave donor countries with a major share of the benefits, governments in these countries (especially those that are not home to holders of strong IPR in this area) could be less enthusiastic about such a strategy. Another possible problem is that CG use of unlicensed technology might result in withholding of access to helpful know-how and research tools developed by the IPR holder.

It must be noted that, if this approach is adopted without the assent of IPR holders, the costs could, at least in some cases, be high. They might include loss of fruitful collaborations with the same entities in other areas and possible loss of support from developed-country donors. If biotechnology innovations or products incorporating such biotechnology are exported to countries where patents on the innovations are enforced, the prospect of ruinously costly litigation must be considered. In practice, such South-North trade is not very important for most staple food crops, as demonstrated by analysis of bilateral trade data in Binenbaum et al. (2000).

Persuade the IPR Holder to License Technology Gratis Where the Opportunity Cost Is Low

For many crops other than wheat, maize, some kinds of rice, soybeans, and barley, private (and public) IPR holders might be persuaded to allow IARCs, and NARSs in developing countries, to use proprietary biotechnology without direct compensation given the minimal risk to the significant commercial markets (the focus of the IPR holders' hopes for profits. Foods that are necessities for poor consumers have low income-demand elasticities, and are not likely to be large commercial markets. The markets will not become much more attractive commercially if and when poor consumers' incomes increase. Rather, as consumers gain wealth, they will substitute more desirable foods, including wheat and meat.

Already, there are well-publicized cases of provisions of technology without charge in these noncommercial crops, often under the auspices of the International Service for the Acquisition of Agri-Biotech Applications (ISAAA). Monsanto Corporation has made its technology available to achieve virus resistance in several noncommercial potato cultivars popular among the poor in Mexico (Qaim 1999). It has also supported the incorporation of virus resistance technology in yams in Africa. AstraZeneca and Monsanto have announced they will make technology for the vitamin A rice, currently under development, available gratis for developing countries. (Whether these technologies are proprietary in the recipient countries is, however, unclear.) Corporations might find such collaboration increasingly attractive if international opposition to corporations that market transgenic seeds gathers steam. Technology that helps solve nutritional deficiencies or addresses the health problems of poor consumers could generate especially desirable publicity. Collaboration in technology transfer might be feasible for most other CG crops, especially if the centers have the capacity to use the technology with little assistance from the commercial provider. Potential corporate donors also may want assurances that commercial providers will not suffer blame, loss of reputation, or liability for misuse of their technology.

On the other hand, it is possible that the publicity surrounding recent technology "donations" could lead to excessive optimism regarding corporate generosity with respect to valid IPR claims (see, for example, RAFI 2000, 31). In the cases referenced above, it is difficult to assess the extent to which relevant and valid patents are involved. For example, even though there are reportedly 70 patents on the vitamin A rice technology, according to Kryder, Kowalski, and Krattiger (2000), none is valid in Bangladesh, Iran, Iraq, Malaysia, Myanmar, Nigeria, Saudi Arabia, or Thailand. Though some of the patents are valid in the United States (44 patents) China and Japan (21), and some developing countries such as Indonesia (6), India (5), Viet Nam (9), and the Philippines (1), many (26 of the total of 70) are methods patents that apply to the use of the method and possibly importation of the resulting product as distinct from composition-of-matter patents that restrict production, sale, or importation of the transformed rice seed.

Of course, even if proprietary technology is made available, IARCs must in turn assess the appropriateness of the technology for their organizations. For example, the CGIAR decided against adoption of "terminator" technology that prevents seed-saving for replanting (CG Secretariat 1998, 53). (Whether this was a judicious decision—beyond its political benefits—for LDCs has been questioned by Srinivasan and Thirtle 2000.) Monsanto, which is not the property owner, abandoned commercialization of the technology in October 1999 (Kaiser 1999), though neither property owner—Monsanto's erstwhile takeover target Delta and Pine Land Corporation and the United States Department of Agriculture (USDA)—seems to have followed Monsanto's lead.

Direct Programmatic Research Support from the Private Sector

Rather than cooperate in the piecemeal technology transfer described above, for-profit corporations might be persuaded to give more general support to international agricultural research collaboration. In the genomics field, for example, a consortium of corporations has supported the creation of a public database of genome markers called single-nucleotide polymorphisms (SNPs), in preference to partaking in a competing private-sector initiative (Marshall 1998a). The motivation for this type of expenditure, which does not appear to be conditioned on any claim to property rights, is not clear. But it indicates that the private sector might, on occasion, choose to support public over private research initiatives in areas related to its own endeavors.

A foundation funded by the multinational life science corporation Novartis (now part of Syngenta) is supporting plant biology research at the College of Natural Resources at the University of California, Berkeley (Rausser 1999). This support is conditioned on the right to be the first to negotiate the rights (as distinct from having the right of first refusal) to innovations arising out of research in plant biology that is supported by the donor, and the donor also has rights to appoint a minority of the board that directs research funded by the foundation (Mena and Sanders 1998). But despite prominent expressions of concern (see Press and Washburn 2000 for an eloquent example), the conditions seem surprisingly moderate, given the five-year commitment of US$5 million per year. Knowledgeable observers surmise that a major portion of the return envisaged by Novartis consists of the benefits of intimate access to the intellectual resources of the Berkeley campus.

In a third example, Monsanto Corporation donated technology to transform corn by agrobacterium technology to the University of California. As part of a divestiture of assets ordered by the U.S. Justice Department conditioned under the acquisition of DeKalb, the seed producer, Monsanto, was required to relinquish one of two means of transformation it possessed. Rather than sell to a competitor, under extreme time pressure Monsanto was persuaded to give it to the university, and the university is free to license access to the technology to third parties. The details of this case illustrate the important point that prospective recipients must exercise flexibility and initiative to take advantage of such opportunities. (It is interesting that Monsanto was willing to make this donation soon after the Berkeley-Novartis agreement was announced. Apparently, Monsanto does not view Berkeley as "captured" by Novartis.)

Although, in some cases, donations could be motivated by the prospect of tax deductions in exchange for de facto worthless technology, the above examples suggest that it is conceivable that corporations would be willing to exchange access to technology for close contacts with the innovative activities and expertise of IARCs, without making demands for exclusive proprietary rights to the output. IARCs should consider means of making this kind of transfer easy for the private sector, while clearly establishing the continued independence of their research mission from undue private-sector influence or appropriation. Recently, disturbing (though not conclusive) evidence appeared regarding the bias that can be induced by private funding of research. Thomas Bodenheimer stated that a review of drug trials showed that when the study is funded by the drug owner, the drug was highly rated in 89 percent of cases versus only 61 percent for independent studies (Hilts 2000).[12]

Given the proliferation of IPR associated with crop breeding and related activities, it will be increasingly necessary to obtain freedom to operate from multiple patentees from various countries. Just as CIMMYT is worried about giving its technology away if its value might be appropriated by the holder of a blocking patent on a complementary technology, corporations are concerned about offering their technology with a no-cost license only to find that their largesse has increased the rents accruing to a less generous owner of another essential enabling technology. One way to avoid this is to obtain a joint grant of freedom to operate in certain markets from all holders of relevant IPR.

Such joint agreement is probably infeasible on a case-by-case basis; it would be far better to coordinate a joint commitment by the major biotechnology providers and the CGIAR to provide royalty-free licenses on all IPR in agreed areas of application (distinguished for example by crop, cultivars, regions, or modes of production). Such licenses could perhaps include a provision for royalty payments to come in force should an owner of a complementary technology used in development of a cultivar demand a royalty in the relevant area of application. In negotiating and drafting any such agreement, attention should be paid to the implications of national antitrust laws. This type of negotiation is difficult and costly to all parties, and requires high-quality legal advice. General effective multiparty agreements on technology access are more complex and difficult to achieve than donors imagine.

Institutional Support

Management of IP is a major part of the executive function in private-sector agricultural biotechnology. Indeed, several of the most important U.S. corporations in this field have had lawyers, not scientists or MBAs, as their CEOs. Nonprofit research institutions must maintain the freedom to operate that they need to pursue their missions. Unfortunately this capacity entails the services of high-cost human capital. It is generally judicious to outsource such services. The challenge is to have continuing access to high-quality advice on managing IP issues, including choice of outside counsel for patent prosecution, patent defense, and negotiations with third parties. Ability to operate effectively within the U.S. legal system is likely to be important. In the case of canola in Canada, Phillips and Gustafson (2000, 71, Table 11) report that of the patent attorneys used by six for-profit organizations with active Saskatoon-based IP portfolios, two were in Canada, two in Europe, and six in the United States. By contrast, five public-sector organizations used five patent attorneys in Canada and only one in the United States. Assuming the private sector is the superior guide to optimal patenting strategies, research organizations should expect to contract for legal services in the United States and Europe. To manage such contracting, some internal legal expertise is highly desirable. The Central Advisory Service located at ISNAR could conceivably develop a structure to help nonprofit international researchers (as well as NARSs) manage the contracting of legal services. The need to establish a base of in-house expertise, and the inherent "lumpiness" (indivisibility) of human capital, are factors that favor amalgamation of dispersed centers, such as members of the CG, into a more centralized organization.

Conclusion

The biotechnology revolution has vastly expanded the possibilities for progress in international agricultural research. The fast pace of this revolution in developed countries is in large part a result of the strong incentives given by the introduction of patentability where no prior claims existed. In helping LDCs share the benefits of the new technological possibilities, international agricultural researchers must deal with the proliferation of prior IPR claims seen in the second round of the IPR revolution.

This will not be easy. Maintaining adequate freedom to operate in important technologies will require management that is well informed about the international IP environment and well aware of the need to collaborate creatively on many fronts with other public and nonprofit institutions facing similar challenges.

Notes

1. The CG's genetic resource policy committee stated, "Based on the conviction that their research will continue to be supported by public funds, the centers regard the results of their work as international public goods. Hence full disclosure of research results and products in the public domain is the preferred strategy for preventing misappropriation by others. Consequently, the centers will not assert intellectual property control over derivatives except in those rare cases when it is needed to facilitate technology transfer or otherwise protect the interests of developing nations (CGIAR 1996, 18)." Regarding patents, the committee went on to state, "We recognize that there is an increasing use of patenting in both the private and public sectors. Cells, organelles, genes, or molecular constructs isolated from materials distributed by centers may be protected by recipients only with the agreement of the supplying center. Centers will only give such approval after consultation with the country, or countries, of origin of the germplasm where this is known or can be readily identified. This consultation would include consideration of an appropriate sharing of any benefits, whether bilateral or multilateral, flowing from subsequent commercial development of the protected material, and would require that the original material remains available for the public good (CGIAR 1996, 19).

2. Most saved hybrid seed is not sterile; it simply suffers a loss of performance compared with the original hybrid seed.

3. On October 30, 1998, the CG eschewed the use of terminator gene technology (or more specifically, "any genetic systems designed to prevent seed germination") based on the "recognition of concerns over potential risks of its inadvertent or unintended spread through pollen; the possibilities of the sale or exchange of inviable seed for planting; the importance of farm-saved seed, particularly to resource-poor farmers; potential negative impacts on genetic diversity; and the importance of farmer selection and breeding for sustainable agriculture" (CGIAR 1998, 52).

4. Specifically, Section 8, Clause 8 of the U.S. Constitution states that Congress shall have power "To promote the Progress of Science and useful Arts, by securing for limited Times to Authors and Inventors the exclusive Right to their respective Writings and Discoveries."

5. Distinctiveness is a measure of the differences in the variety's phenotype, or physical traits, compared with all other protected varieties. Uniformity is a measure of similarity among individual plants of the same variety. Stability refers to the degree to which individual plants of a variety remain similar across generations.

6. Alston and Venner (2001) provide convincing evidence that the U.S. PVPA did not stimulate private investment in wheat breeding or an increase in experimental and industry wheat yields as was intended by the Act, despite an increase in the wheat area sown to private varieties from 3 percent in 1970 to 30 percent in the early 1990s. The PVPA apparently served primarily as a marketing tool, which might have increased appropriability of rents on branded cultivars, and this encouraged their diffusion but did not increase their productivity.

7. As described in Barton and Siebeck (1994, 11–12), ". . . MTAs are contractual agreements concluded between two or more parties. As contracts they enjoy the protection of the law in many nations: failure to perform what is promised is a breach of contract which gives one party the right to bring action against the other party, such as suing for damages. Unlike patents or copyrights, MTAs do not rest upon codified legal statutes defining specific rights and obligations. Instead, reflecting freedom of contract, parties to a MTA have wide discretion in setting the terms of their agreement and tailoring them to their specific needs."

8. The cost of the soybean germplasm varies among varieties ranging from US$11.45 to $16.50 per 50-pound bag. Monsanto's technology fee for RR cotton ranged from US$34.70 to $43.20, and for cotton varieties with stacked *Bt* and RR traits it was between US$144 and $188.40 (Monsanto 2001).

9. The nature of patents and the implications of their geographic limitations are pursued in greater detail in Binenbaum et al. (2000).

10. Lerner (1995, 470) estimates that patent litigation in the U.S. Patent and Trademark Office and the federal courts initiated in the year 1991 will lead to total legal expenditures of $1 billion 1991 U.S. dollars, compared with US$3.7 billion spending by firms on basic research in that year. Note that the figure excludes litigation in state courts.

11. There have been recent changes in Japanese patent law that increase the possible rewards for university inventors and relax the grace period for publication (Sumikura 2000). See Phillips and Gustafson (2000, 72, Table 13) for a dramatic contrast between for-profit and public biotech research institutions in Saskatchewan, Canada.

12. Likewise, Barnes and Bero (1998) examined 106 articles reviewing evidence on the effects of passive smoking and, after controlling for various other factors, showed that authors who had a financial affiliation with the tobacco industry were much more likely to conclude that passive smoking is not harmful to health than those without industry affiliations. Similarly, Stelfox et al. (1998) showed that authors who supported the use of a certain kind of drug for treating heart ailments were significantly more likely to have a financial relationship with the drug's maker than those who did not.

References

Alston, J. M., P. G. Pardey, and V. H. Smith. 1999. *Paying for agricultural productivity*. Baltimore: Johns Hopkins University Press.

Alston, J. M., and R. Venner. 2001. The effects of the U.S. Plant Variety Protection Act on wheat genetic improvement. *Research Policy* forthcoming.

Barnes, D. E., and L. A. Bero. 1998. Why review articles on the health effects of passive smoking reach different conclusions. *Journal of the AMA* 279 (19): 1599–70.

Barton, J. H. 1998. The impact of contemporary patent law on plant biotechnology research. In *Intellectual property rights III global genetic resources: Access and property rights*, S. A. Eberhard, H. L. Shands, W. Collins and R. L. Lower, eds. CSAA Miscellaneous Publication, Madison, Wisc., U.S.A.: Crop Science Society of America and American Society of Agronomy.

———. 2000. New international arrangements in intellectual property and competition law. Paper presented at the Swedish International Symposium on Economics, Law and Intellectual Property. Göteborg, Sweden, June 26–30.

Barton, J. H., and W. E. Siebeck. 1994. Material transfer agreements in genetic resources exchange: The case of the international agricultural research centres. In *Issues in Genetic Resources*, International Plant Genetic Resources Institute ed., Rome.

Binenbaum, E., and B. D. Wright. 1998. *On the significance of South-North trade in IARC crops*. A report prepared for the Expert Panel on Proprietary Science and Technology of the Consultative Group on International Agricultural Research, Washington, D.C.

Binenbaum, E., C. Nottenbug, P. G. Pardey, B. D. Wright, and P. Zambrano. 2000. South-North trade, intellectual property jurisdictions, and the freedom to operate in agricultural research on staple crops. EPTD Working paper 70. Washington, D.C.: International Food Policy Research Institute.

Buller, C., and W. Taylor. 1999. Partnerships between public and private: The experience of the Cooperative Research Centre for Plant Science in Australia. *AgBioForum* 2: 17–23.

Cohen, J. I., C. Falconi, J. Komen, and M. Blakeney. 1998. *Proprietary biotechnology inputs and international agricultural research*. International Service for National Agricultural Research Briefing Paper 39, The Hague.

CGIAR (Consultative Group for International Agricultural Research). 1996. *The CGIAR at 25: Into the future*. Report of the CGIAR Genetic Resources Policy Committee. Washington, D.C.: CGIAR Secretariat.

———. 1998. *Shaping the CGIAR's future: Summary of proceedings and decisions*, CGIAR International Centers Week, October 26–30. Washington, D.C.: CGIAR Secretariat.

Contracting Parties to the General Agreement on Tariffs and Trade, Uruguay Round. World Trade Agreement (establishing the WTO and including GATT 1994). 1994. *Annex IC: Agreement on trade-related aspects of intellectual property rights, including trade in counterfeit goods*. Marrakech.

Dalton, R. 2000. Cereal genebank accepts need for patents. *Nature* 404 (April): 534.

Egelyng, H. 2000. *Sui generis* protection of plant varieties in Asian agriculture: A regional regime in the making? Paper presented at the fourth international conference of the Consortium on Agricultural Biotechnology Research, Economics of Agricultural Biotechnology, Ravello, Italy, August 24–28.

Enriquez, J. 1988. Genomics and the world's economy. *Science* 281 (5379): 925–26.

Erbisch, F. H. 2000. Challenges of plant protection: How a semi-public agricultural research institution protects its new plant varieties and markets them. Presented at the workshop on The Impact on Research and Development of *Sui Generis* Approaches to Plant Variety Protection of Rice in Developing Countries, International Rice Research Institute, Los Baños, the Philippines, February 16–18.

FAO (Food and Agriculture Organization of the United Nations). 1983. *International undertaking on plant genetic resources*. Resolution 8/83 of the 22nd session of the FAO conference, Rome, November 5–8, 1983.

Finkel, E. 1999. Australian center develops tools for developing world. *Science* 285 (5433): 1481–83.

Fischer, K. S. 1999. Personal communication, Stanford, Calif., U.S.A.

Fischer, K. S., and J. Barton. 1999. Gene discovery in rice: The exchange of IRRI's biological assets. Stanford Law School, Stanford, Calif., U.S.A. Mimeo.

Ghijsen, H. 1998. Plant variety protection in a developing and demanding world. *Biotechnology and Development Monitor* 36: 3–5.

Gillis, J. 2000. Monsanto offers patent waivers on rice altered to fight illness. *The Washington Post*, August 4: A1.

Grindley, P. C., and D. J. Teece. 1997. Managing intellectual capital: Licensing and cross-licensing in semiconductors and electronics. *California Management Review* 39 (2): 8–41.

Hall, B. H., and R. M. Ham. 1999. The patent paradox revisited: Determinants of patenting in the U.S. semiconductor industry, 1980–94. Department of Economics, University of California, Berkeley, U.S.A. Mimeo.

Harbison, J., and E. Wailes. 2000. Patenting transgenic plants and processes under the European Patent Convention. Paper presented at the fourth international conference of the Consortium on Agricultural Biotechnology Research, Economics of Agricultural Biotechnology, Ravello, Italy, August 24–28.

Heller, M. A., and R. S. Eisenberg. 1998. Can patents deter innovation? The anticommons in biomedical research. *Science* 280 (5364): 698–701.

Hilts, P. J. 2000. U.S. weighs changes in rules on drug research conflicts. *The New York Times*, National Desk, August 16. <http://www.search.NYTimes.com>.

Huffman, W. E., and R. E. Evenson. 1993. *Science for agriculture: A long-term perspective*. Ames, Iowa, U.S.A: Iowa State University Press.

James, C. 2000. *Preview: Global review of commercialized transgenic crops, 2000*. International Service for the Acquisition of Agri-Biotech Applications Brief No. 21. Ithaca, N.Y., U.S.A.

Juma, C. 1989. *The gene hunters: Biotechnology and the scramble for seeds*. African Centre for Technology Studies Research Series No. 1. Princeton, N.J., U.S.A.: Princeton University Press.

Kahin, B. 1998. Memorandum 10/14/99 to participants of step IPR workshop, New Haven, Conn., U.S.A. Office of Science and Technology, The White House, Washington, D.C. Mimeo.

Kaiser, E. 1999. Monsanto vows not to develop "terminator" gene. Reuters, Chicago, October 4.

Kate, K., ten. 1995. Biodiversity prospecting partnerships: The role of providers, collectors and users. *Biotechnology and Development Monitor* 25: 16–21.

Koo, B. 1998. The economics of plant genetic resources: The effects of alternative intellectual property protection systems and advances in biotechnology. Ph.D. dissertation, Department of Agricultural and Resource Economics, University of California, Berkeley, U.S.A. Mimeo.

Kryder, R. D., S. P. Kowalski, and A. F. Krattiger. 2000. *The intellectual and technical property components of pro-vitamin A rice (GoldenRice™): A preliminary freedom-to-operate review.* International Service for the Acquisition of Agri-biotech Applications Brief No. 20. Ithaca, N.Y., U.S.A.

Lehne, R., and G. van Roozendaal. 1995. U.S. government role in biotechnology. *Biotechnology and Development Monitor* 24: 6–8.

Lemaux, P. 1999. Personal Communication, Berkeley, Calif., U.S.A.

Lerner, J. 1995. Patenting in the shadow of competitors. *Journal of Law and Economics* 38 (October): 463–95.

Leskien, D. 1998. The European Directive on Biotechnology. *Biotechnology and Development Monitor* 36: 16–19.

Lesser, W. 1999. "Holding up" the public agbiotech research sector over component technologies. Presentation at the conference Transitions in Agbiotech: Economics of Strategy and Policy, organized by the NE–165 Regional Research Project and sponsored by the Farm Foundation Food Marketing Policy Center, Washington, D.C., June 24–25.

Lianchamroon, W. 1998. Community rights and farmers' rights in Thailand. *Biotechnology and Development Monitor* 36: 9–11.

Lindner, R. 1999. Prospects for public plant breeding in a small country. Paper presented at the International Consortium on Agricultural Biotechnology Research Conference, Rome, June 17–19.

Marco, A. C., and G. C. Rausser. 2000. Mergers and intellectual property in agricultural biotechnology. Paper presented at the Fourth International Conference of the Consortium on Agricultural Biotechnology Research, Economics of Agricultural Biotechnology, Ravello, Italy, August 24–28.

Marshall, E. 1998a. Private help for a public database? *Science* 280 (5364): 667–68.

———. 1998b. NIH, DuPont declare truce in mouse war. *Science* 281 (5381): 1261–62.

Mena, J. and R. Sanders. 1998. Swiss pharmaceutical company Novartis commits $25 million to support biotechnology research at UC Berkeley. Bay Area Coalition for Urban Agriculture. <http://www.bacua.org/news_press8.html>. Accessed December 2000.

Monsanto Company. 2001. Personal communication, St Louis, Mo., U.S.A.

NASS (National Agricultural Statistics Service of the United States Department of Agriculture). 2001. Prospective Plantings. <http://www.usda.mannlib.cornell.edu/reports/nassr/field/pcp-bbp/pspl0301.pdf>. Accessed May 31, 2001.

National Research Council, Board on Science, Technology, and Economic Policy. 1999. Excerpt from summary sheet (dated 8/16/99) for the conference on Intellectual Property in the Knowledge-based Economy, University of California, Berkeley, U.S.A., October 19, 1999.

NIH (National Institutes of Health). 1998a. Report of the National Institutes of Health Working Group on Research Tools. Presented to the Advisory Committee to the Director, June 4. Mimeo.

———. 1998b. Memorandum of understanding: DuPont Pharmaceuticals Company and Public

Health Service, United States Department of Heath and Human Services. July. Also known as the NIH/DuPont Cre-lox memorandum of understanding. <http://ott.od.nih.gov/new-pages/cre%2Dlox.htm>. Accessed October 2001.

Nijar, G. S. 1998. Community intellectual rights protect indigenous knowledge. *Biotechnology and Development Monitor* 36: 11–12.

Pardey, P. G., J. M. Alston, J. E. Christian, and S. Fan. 1996. *Hidden Harvest: U.S. Benefits from International Research Aid.* Food Policy Report. Washington, D.C.: International Food Policy Research Institute.

Phillips, P. W. B., and J. Gustafson. 2000. Patent strategies in the biotechnology industry and implications for technology diffusion. Paper presented at the fourth international conference of the International Consortium on Agricultural Biotechnology Research, Economics of Agricultural Biotechnology, Ravello, Italy, August 24–28.

Pollack, A. 2001. Bristol-Myers and Athersys make deal on gene patents. *The New York Times.* January 8: C2. <http://www.search.NYTimes.com>

Powledge, F. 1995. Who owns rice and beans? Patents on plant germplasm. *Bioscience* 45 (7): 440–45.

Press, E., and J. Washburn. 2000. The kept university. *The Atlantic Monthly* 285 (3): 39–54.

Price, S. C. 1999. Public and private plant breeding. *Nature Biotechnology* 17 (10): 938.

Qaim, M. 1999. Modern biotechnology for small-scale farmers in developing countries: Contradiction or promising option? Paper presented at the international conference of the Consortium on Agricultural Biotechnology Research, Rome, June 17–19.

RAFI (Rural Advancement Foundation International). 1994. *Conserving indigenous knowledge.* New York: United Nations Development Program.

———. 1998. Plant breeders' wrongs righted in Australia? RAFI News Release, November 10.

———. 2000. In search of higher ground: The intellectual property challenge to public agricultural research and human rights and 28 alternative initiatives, *Occasional Paper Series* 6 (1) (September).

RAFI (Rural Advancement Foundation International) and HSCA (Heritage Seed Curators Australia). 1998. Plant breeders' wrongs: An inquiry into the potential for plant piracy through international intellectual property conventions. A report by RAFI in partnership with HSCA, September 16.

Rausser, G. 1999. Public/private alliances. *AgBioForum* 2 (1): 5–10.

Ronald, P. C. 1998. Genetic resource recognition fund. *AgBiotech News and Information* 10 (1): 19N–21N.

Shands, H. 2000. Personal communication, Washington, D.C.

Srinivasan, C. S., and C. Thirtle. 2000. Impact of terminator technologies in developing countries: A framework for economic analysis. Paper presented at the fourth international conference of the International Consortium on Agricultural Biotechnology Research, Ravello, Italy, August 24–28.

Stelfox, H. T., G. Chua, K. O'Rourke, and A. S. Detsky. 1998. Conflict of interest in the debate over calcium-channel antagonists. *The New England Journal of Medicine* 338 (January): 101–10.

Stovin, D. T., and P. W. B. Phillips. 2000. Establishing effective intellectual property rights and reducing barriers to entry in Canadian agricultural biotechnology research. Paper presented at the fourth international conference of the International Consortium on Agricultural Biotechnology Research, Ravello, Italy, August 24–28.

Sumikura, K. 2000. Personal communications, The University of Tokyo.

Swaminathan, M. S. 1998. Farmers' rights and plant genetic resources. *Biotechnology and Development Monitor* 36: 6–9.

The Economist. 2000. Life sciences: Green and dying. November 18: 77.

van Wijk, J. 1995. Plant breeders' rights create winners and losers. *Biotechnology and Development Monitor* 23: 15–19.

Weiss, R. 1999. Seeds of discord. Monsanto's gene police raise alarm on farmers' rights, rural tradition. *The Washington Post*, February 3: A01.

Wright, B. D. 1997. Crop genetic resource policy: The role of *ex situ* genebanks. *Australian Journal of Agricultural and Resource Economics* 41 (1): 81–115.

———. 1998a. Valuing farmers' rights. In *Agricultural values of plant genetic resources*, R. E. Evenson, D. Gollin, and V. Santaniello eds. Wallingford, U.K.: CAB International.

———. 1998b. Public germplasm development at a crossroads: Biotechnology and intellectual property. *California Agriculture* 52 (6): 8–13.

———. 1999. IPR challenges and international research collaborations in agricultural biotechnology. Paper presented at the conference, Agricultural Biotechnology in Developing Countries: Towards Optimizing the Benefits for the Poor, *Zentrum fur Entwicklungsforschung* (ZEF) [Centre for Development Research], Bonn, Germany, November 16.

Chapter 7

Public Good and Private Greed: Realizing Public Benefits from Privatized Global Agrifood Research

Peter W. B. Phillips and Dan Dierker

Introduction

Increasing productivity and economic growth have become prime objectives for most governments since the later part of the twentieth century. Increasing the size of the pie is now believed to be as, if not more, important than how the pie is distributed among different groups in society. Taking their lead from economists such as Paul Romer (1990), governments have increasingly tried new or different policies to increase the number of "recipes" available to the economy to accelerate growth. In this headlong rush to grow, government frequently have ignored the public interest.

Governments have made two major changes to support increased research, development, and commercialization in the agrifood world. In the first instance, virtually all governments have moved to extend private intellectual property rights (IPR) to plant innovations in order to encourage greater private research and commercialization. While the United States had granted patents to asexually reproduced plants in 1930 and some European states granted plant breeders rights in the 1930s and 1940s, the International Union for the Protection of New Varieties of Plants (UPOV), negotiated in 1962, was the first international agreement on property rights for new plant varieties. It granted plant breeders exclusive rights to new varieties for 20 years, with some exemptions. Since then those rights have been expanded domestically—the United States granted its first patent on a sexually reproduced plant in 1985—and through international agreement with revisions to UPOV in 1972, 1978, and 1991 and development of the Trade-Related Aspects of Intellectual Property (TRIPs) Agreement in the World Trade Organization (WTO) in 1995. In less than 40 years, we have gone from few intellectual property rights to an extensive system of binding, actionable national and international rules. Meanwhile, many governments have changed their policies allowing universities and public agencies to patent and exploit their innovations (for example, the Bayh-Dole Act) and providing incentives to public researchers to collaborate more extensively with private partners (for example, Agriculture and Agri-food Canada's [AAFC] Matching Investors' Initiative).

This public policy has been successful in accelerating privately managed development and commercialization of agricultural innovations, but creating monopoly rights for new innovations has changed the incentives for public versus private research. It has also shifted some of the benefits of innovation to private hands. As a result, both public and private research programs face new challenges. At the research stage, generating basic knowledge—a true public good—appears to have slowed, which will, over time, dampen private investment. At the development stage, many researchers are finding they have less the freedom to operate, slowing some types of research (Nottenburg et al. this volume). Finally, at the commercialization stage, the shortage of independent, verifiable research on the health, safety, and economic impacts of these new technologies impedes consumer acceptance. If new technologies are not used, there is no public (or for that matter, private) benefit.

This chapter reviews the problems of this new world and examines strategies to help decisionmakers promote the public good through the creation and diffusion of this new technology.

Background

It is incorrect to suggest that private property rights in the agricultural sector began with the recent extension of patents and plant breeders' rights. For thousands of years innovators have relied upon trade secrets, steep costs for imitators, and natural barriers to exploitation to enable them to capture a portion of the benefits from their innovations. Although many agrifood research programs continue to use these traditional methods (Phillips 2000; Phillips and Gustafson 2000), the rapid extension of private IPR in the agricultural industry after 1980 triggered a massive acceleration of private investment into agricultural applications, accompanied by a rapid expansion in the patenting of new innovations and products. Both the private and public sectors have moved aggressively to protect their innovations and intellectual property (IP) through patents. In Canada, for instance, patenting activity across all

Table 7.1   Patenting activity in key crops

Crop	Total issued	U.S. patents Number issued since 1985	Number issued since 1985 as share of total
		(count)	*(percent)*
Apples	26,723	23,091	86
Rice	13,487	9,192	68
Corn	10,511	7,096	68
Cotton	5,563	3,462	62
Wheat	2,136	1,519	71
Soybeans	1,980	1,504	76
Potatoes	1,674	1,155	69
Tomatoes	959	737	77
Barley	909	717	79
Flax	400	292	73
Canola/rapeseed	350	324	93
Peas	326	285	87
Alfalfa	290	226	78
Sugar Beets	234	151	65
Squash	231	163	71
Legumes	253	183	72
Papayas	62	48	77
Total	66,088	50,145	

Source: U.S. Patent and Trademark Office (2000).

sectors increased 2.9 percent per year on average in the 1990s while biotechnology patent applications increased 12.2 percent per annum (Rafiquzzaman and Smith 2000).

Extending private property rights has radically altered the research world. Whereas before 1980 only asexually reproduced plants (such as apples) were protected under U.S. patent law, now all plants with novel, useful, and nonobvious traits are patentable in the United States and other countries as well. A quick search of the U.S. patent database (see Table 7.1) shows the extent of patenting related to a number of major food and industrial crops or products. Apples, rice, and corn each have more than 10,000 patents that make claims related to those products. Some claims relate to technologies to develop new varieties, some relate to product traits that those crops could have, and others relate to the methods used to process those crops or to products that contain elements of those crops. Similarly there are more than 5,500 patents related to cotton, around 2,000 patents for wheat and soybeans, almost 1,000 each for tomatoes and barley, and between 60 and 400 patents per crop for a wide variety of other agriculturally useful plants. On average, more than 75 percent of the patents issued to these crops were filed after January 1985, with the highest percentage being 93 percent for canola/rapeseed and the lowest being 65 percent for sugar beets. Because patents are granted by nations, for each patent application in the United States an application could be filed in any—in the extreme, every—other country with a patent system. This is further complicated by the fact that the decisions of the various national patent systems can and often do differ based on their interpretation of prior art and their specific statutes.

From one perspective, this is good news. It suggests that the rate of innovation (at least the rate of innovations destined for commercialization) has accelerated. While the Green Revolution accelerated growth in the yields of major food crops in the 1960s and 1970s, that growth slowed in the 1980s and remained relatively steady until this new wave of research began to be commercialized.

This apparent success masks three potential problems. First, there may not be enough basic research to sustain the development of new technologies, so that, in essence, the current strategies may kill the golden-egg-laying goose of innovation. Second, conflicting and poorly constructed property rights systems and strategies in both the public and private sectors may be limiting the exploitation of new technologies. Third, the rapid increase in integrated public-private research has reduced the number of independent researchers who can assure consumers of the efficacy and safety of the new products. Without answers, consumers are wary of using the technology, which reduces the social benefit.

Research Incentives and Priorities

Basic, know-why research is the foundation for most of the innovation in the agrifood sector. The search for scientific knowledge (the principles and laws of nature, plant physiology, plant molecular biology, theoretical and applied genetics, genomics, and biochemistry) has historically been undertaken in publicly funded universities and public research institutes. Phillips (2000) estimated that between 1981 and 1996 public researchers discovered more than 94 percent of the basic knowledge related to canola. As public research funding has shifted toward patentable research or into collaborations with private companies, some evidence (discussed below) indicates that this basic, know-why research has suffered. Phillips (2000) observed that in the canola area, all of the universities, AAFC, and the National Research Council (NRC) have actively moved their organizations to protect and exploit their IP by setting up IP offices and then by patenting and licensing their innovations.

Two specific policy changes supported this move. First, faculty and research scientists are now rewarded for their commercial innovations both directly, with a share of the financial returns, and indirectly, with patents providing credit toward merit increases and promotion. Second, many of the public institutions have begun to sell their services on a fee-for-service basis. Many of the faculty and research scientists at all of the universities working on canola have entered into contractual relationships with private companies (University of Alberta with Alberta Wheat Pool; University of Calgary with DowAgrosciences; University of Manitoba with Rhône-Poulenc, Union Grain Growers, and Saskatchewan Wheat Pool; and University of Saskatchewan with Saskatchewan Wheat Pool) while AAFC has undertaken extensive fee-for-service variety development work for Monsanto, AgrEvo, and others.

The evidence suggests that these shifts have diminished the output of know-why research from these public institutions (Phillips 2000). After engaging in commercial arrangements, AAFC and the five key Canadian universities' share of academic publications declined. Even more disconcerting, the quality of the work being published publicly (based on the number of citations) in most Canadian institutions has dropped relative to the rest of the institutions doing research. The research being published by AAFC and the five traditional canola-research universities has a lower citation rate than the average in the period after they began to work in collaboration with industry, whereas they had above-average citation rates earlier. The National Research Council, which has seen a rise in its share of total publications and a sharp rise in its citation rate, engages in less fee-for-service work, instead favoring extensive collaborations on precommercial and noncompetitive topics where both cash and intellectual capital are exchanged.

Much of the effort not reflected in publication is devoted to patentable research. It could be argued that this should not be a problem, because information in patents becomes public. Practically, however, about 70 percent of the information contained in patents does not appear in any trade journal for at least five years after the patent has been granted, and at least 50 percent of this information is never published in mainstream technical journals (Industry Canada 2000). This diversion of output to the proprietary route slows the dissemination of information, and the cost and difficulty of accessing full patent information at times may make the results of the research inaccessible to many academics.

Patent Strategies

Patent strategies in the public and private sector may reduce the use of new innovations. The massive rise in demand for new patents in the agrifood area, which has become a deluge with the rise in patents filed for genomics, has stressed patent systems worldwide. There were 299,400 patent applications in the United States in 2000, in addition to the more than 2.7 million patents already granted. With only 4,900 patent examiners, on average each examiner has only about 30 hours to review and decide upon each patent (authors' calculations using U.S. Patent and Trademark Office [PTO] data). If you have ever looked at some of the patent claims, you will immediately see the problem. Even relatively straightforward patent applications often involve 20 to 30 claims, cite 50 to 100 sources acknowledging prior art, and in cases involving genes can stretch to more than 200 pages. In the face of this mountain of work, the United States and many other patent systems tend to side with the patent applicant and grant a broad patent claim, even if it might result in unsubstantiated claims or overlapping rights. Clearly, with more than 10,000 patents related to some products, significant potential for overlap exists in those claims. The PTO leaves it to the marketplace and/or the courts to decide who owns what. This has led to a sharp rise in the business of patent searching, patent matching, and litigation.

Although companies can exploit monopoly rights to their IP excessively, and there are some suspected cases of that (Lindner 1999), the more insidious problem is that the sheer number of patents and the potential for overlapping patent rights have raised the cost of acquiring the freedom to operate to develop or commercialize new products using patented technologies.

Three recent cases illustrate the point. The development and commercialization of the *Bacillus thuringiensis* (*Bt*) gene in cotton and corn has generated significant litigation. A recent patent search showed that 81 separate research organizations (59 private and 22 public) owned a total of 388 patents (345 private and 43 public) for the *Bt* gene and its use in various crops (U.S. PTO search 2000). In the first instance this has led to three major lawsuits that involve four large multinationals and to date have cost millions of dollars to litigate. This litigation has led to settlements totaling more than $175 million and, by some estimates, has destroyed more than $1 billion of shareholder value, a significant share of the total value generated from the *Bt* technology so far. Second, the core of the Roundup Ready® (RR) technology involves 11 specific patented technologies that originally were owned by four major companies. The difficulties of negotiating rights to use those patents may be one of the contributing reasons for the spate of mergers in this area that has reduced the number of companies to two (Goodhue et al. 1999). Third, the much-heralded development of vitamin-A-enhanced *Golden*Rice™ hit a snag when the Swiss developers looked at securing the rights to commercialize their development. The International Service for the Aquisition of Agri-Biotech Applications (ISAAA) produced a freedom-to-operate study that showed that researchers needed to acquire rights to approximately 70 patented technologies (including *the Agrobacterium tumefaciens* transformation system, the 35S growth promoter, the beta-carotene gene, and polymerace chain reaction [PCR]), more than 40 of which were privately owned (ISAAA 2000). When the developers became aware of this problem, they sought bids from private companies willing to invest to acquire the freedom to operate, thus limiting the influence of the International Rice Research Institute (IRRI), their original partner. In exchange for making the technology available free of charge to poor farmers in countries facing high levels of anemia and vitamin A deficiency, AstraZeneca acquired worldwide rights to the innovation, which had cost millions of dollars to develop. The Rural Advancement Foundation International (RAFI) countered with a study claiming that many of the 70 patents were duplicates and that actually only about a dozen major patents existed that were recognized in the target countries for the technologies (RAFI 2000a and 2000b).[1] Regardless, resolving the legal entanglements of patents in each of these cases has been both expensive and uncertain.

The public sector often contributes to this confusion through its own patent strategies. Ignoring the possibility that many of the patents being filed have little or no appropriable value in the market and perhaps should simply be released freely into the public domain through publication, there are three recent practices of public institutions that impede commercialization of their innovations. In the first instance, many public institutions act proprietarily with their innovations. In Canada, each of the more than 60 colleges and universities has its own commercialization offices, and each of the major federal labs or research agencies manages its own IP. As a result, these institutions' public commercialization efforts are fragmented, economies of scale are lost, and their bargaining power relative to the large private biotechnology companies has been reduced. Second, Phillips and Gustafson (2000) surveyed the key research enterprises in Saskatoon, Canada, in spring 2000 and discovered that most public institutions explicitly and formally agreed to distribute a significant share (10 percent to 50 percent) of any royalties or licensing fees to the inventors, while private firms used their greater flexibility to decouple compensation to the inventors from the exploitation of the technology (that is, they offered lump-sum payments, stock options, and career advancement). While that may seem just on the part of the public sector, it poses real problems for commercialization of innovations. In the search for freedom to operate, virtually all biotechnology programs actively pursue cross-licensing of patents, which usually involves a mutual exchange of access to patented processes or materials without any financial exchange. The public sector may have made cross-licensing more difficult by linking incentives to specific patents. For example, suppose a public lab had a technology that was useful but the cost of licensing it was too great for it to be used by others. One option would be for the public organization to identify another technology that it could use in its work and try to cross-license the two pieces, in effect, bartering the two technologies. Two larger, diversified research organizations could find technologies to barter via cross-licensing, but the technology coming into the public organization might not be used by the inventor of the outgoing innovation but by another researcher in the institution. In this case, there are no royalties, and so the inventor in the public institution either accepts the deal for the "good of the team" or attempts to block it. In short, public institutions have added a complication by tying researcher incentives and compensation to specific innovations. Third,

many public institutions have a stated preference and policy to license their innovations widely, rather than to a single entity, in order to achieve the greatest public
good. The problem is that many new technologies require some further investment
in development in order to commercialize them. Private investors realize that competition reduces their ability to recoup their expenses for further development.

Market-Making Knowledge and Information

Perhaps the biggest impediment to realizing any public good from these innovations
is limited adoption and commercialization. Consumers have a wide range of questions and concerns about the potential impact of genetically modified foods and
crops: Will the new crops will hurt the environment? Are they safe to consume? Will
they disadvantage certain vulnerable groups in society? These questions require
research, but who does the research is as much a part of the answer as the results
themselves. Regulators already have seen and reviewed evidence on these and other
issues, but the data has for the most part been developed by or funded by private
interests, tainting it in the minds of many consumers. Increasingly there are fewer
and fewer true "public" scientists and academics. Granting councils, universities, and
public programs have encouraged almost all of them to partner with private interests, creating potential conflicts of interest. This is also true for social scientists who
are encouraged to find private funding for their programs.

As a result of this regulatory capture, there is virtually no one left who can comment without raising the question of conflict of interest. If consumers can't trust the
regulators (Gaskell et al. 1999) or public sector scientists, they rely on public interest groups, the retail chains, or their own judgement (Einsiedel, Finlay, and Arko
2000). Hence the rise in interest worldwide in credible labeling for genetically modified (GM) foods. Phillips and McNeill (2000) conclude that the global market is
dividing into GM and non-GM areas that cut across geographic boundaries and
through product markets. Even that is not the end of the problem. Incomplete testing technologies, rudimentary identity preservation systems, and inadequate verification of market information limit the potential for the two markets to coexist.

The result has been a slowing rate of adoption of GM crops and signs that private investment in agricultural biotechnology may decline. A number of the large,
so-called "life science companies" have announced plans to divest their agricultural
biotechnology operations: Upjohn Pharmacea reduced its stake in Monsanto in
2000 to 85 percent and has plans to go to a minority interest shortly; the newly
merged Aventis (AgrEvo and Rhone Poulenc) will spin off its merged agbio division
as Agreva; and following the merger of Novartis and AtraZeneca, the new venture
has spun off its agbio division under the name Syngenta. Given that none of the
divested units would have internally generated enough funds to continue its current

rate of R&D, the units will soon come under the scrutiny of the financial markets, which have indicated that they find some of the investments less than attractive.

In summary, the public good of innovations in the agrifood world is in jeopardy because of distorted public research priorities, problems with the structure and use of legally sanctioned patent systems, and inadequate research and verification of information to support market adoption.

A Model for Examining Public Good and Private Greed

The debate in the IP literature about what type of incentive formal IP institutions generate in the private sector may be largely spurious. Innovations occurred long before Great Britain adopted the Statute of Monopolies, never mind the TRIPs requirement that signatory nations adopt legislative protection for trade secrets. The western European guilds, during the Middle Ages, seemed well able to accomplish some exclusion. Government involvement in research and development is also a relatively recent phenomenon. It was not government operated or funded laboratories that developed the wheel, the pulley, the inclined plane, maize, wheat, or the cross and long bows. The better question may well be whether formal IP protection increases the overall rate of technological change and the associated increase in social welfare.

The following model (Figure 7.1) would suggest that the adoption of patent and copyright protection is on the whole welfare-enhancing but that it can seriously limit socially optimal levels of research and commercialization. We use a two-sector model—research and product markets—and assume profit-maximizing research companies. In this model, the profits (Π) available to the innovator in the product market are for simplicity assumed to equal zero where there is no patent and copy-

Figure 7.1   A simple model for research with and without IPR

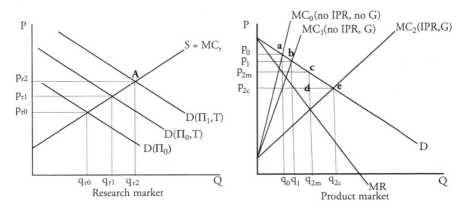

right protection in place, that is with D in the product market and D_1 in the research market. Trade secrets can be abstracted because anything that can be kept secret without legal authority can be kept secret with legal authority. Governments directly demand some level of research (G), subject to a tax constraint (T). Both firms and government pursue research in order to lower marginal cost in the product market, depicted here as pivoting the marginal cost curves (MC) in the product market downward.

In the absence of IPR and government research, the private sector demands research along the demand curve D_0, in the research market, which results in q_{r0} research being done at the price p_{r0} at the equilibrium of D_0 and the research supply curve, S, assuming the competitive supply of research is equal to the marginal cost of doing research, MC_r. This transforms, in the products market, to marginal cost curve MC_0. Along MC_0, q_0 of the product is supplied at price p_0. Allowing government as well as firms to demand research will shift the demand for research out to D_1 with a corresponding increase in the amount of research q_{r1} at the price p_{r1}, which corresponds to marginal cost curve MC_1 in the product market. In equilibrium q_1 will be supplied at the price p_1. If society chooses to adopt patent and copyright protection, firms can price as monopolists in the product market and earn profits equal to the area bounded by p_{2m}, c, d, and p_{2c}. Assuming that government research does not crowd out, or only partially crowds out, private research, this will prompt the rational firm to demand more research, shifting the research demand curve to D_2, where the market will demand research quantity q_{r2} at price p_{r2}. This extra research will lower the marginal cost in the product market to MC_2, with the firm monopolist pricing at price p_{2m} while supplying quantity q_{2m}. Thus, adopting IPR creates a *Pareto* improvement in the product market, as q_{2m} is greater than q_1 while p_{2m} is less than p_1.[2]

Although the model shows that the adoption of IPR can be *Pareto*-improving, a number of points bear notice. First, adoption of IPR is a second-best solution as the results were generated by constraining government. Second, if there are increasing returns to scale in research from spillovers, as Romer (1990) suggests as a possibility, average cost will lie above marginal cost, and the monopoly rents may not be large enough to induce the optimal level of research. Third, this model can be used to illustrate a number of the points made earlier about public research priorities. If too little basic research is undertaken, the marginal cost or supply curve for research rises, increasing the cost of all research and ultimately choking off private investment. Similarly, if the public sector demands more applied research, it squeezes out private research as it reduces the returns remaining in the product market. Fourth, the model reveals the dead-weight loss resulting from the monopoly—the triangle cde. This is, of course, the result of private firms using the monopoly power that legislated institutions grant them, thus leaving unsatisfied demand ($q_{2c} - q_{2m}$) at the marginal cost of production (p_{2c}). Finally, if the demand curve in the products market is sufficiently elastic, the profits available to a monopolist will not be sufficient to induce the private sector to shift the demand in the research sector up. Only after property-right protection was granted to open pollinated crops in most of the developed world did private firms perform any significant amount of research on open pollinated crops. This is consistent with the argument that if research results are non-appropriable, then private firms will not invest. A good or a process that is essentially freely available must, in competitive markets, by definition, have a nearly perfectly elastic demand curve. Thus, the rationale for the observation, "One common and important argument is that the extent of market failure and the degree of private underinvestment will be greater in more basic research, whose benefits are by definition less appropriable that those of more-applied or near-market research" (Alston and Pardey 1999, 14). From a policy perspective, less developed countries should consider the implications of final market demand that is unresponsive to price changes when considering what sort of IP regime to adopt, if any.

It is worth noting that the welfare-enhancing effect of IPR is at least partially offset by the difficulties of acquiring freedom to operate. Freedom to operate is the ability of one entity to use the IP of another entity to come up with either an advancement on the original IP or some new invention or creation. Constraints on using other technologies raises the marginal cost of doing research, reducing the amount of research undertaken. One would expect a larger increase in welfare under an IPR regime that incorporates freedom-to-operate provisions. Figure 7.2 illustrates this point. IPR_2 in the figure incorporates freedom-to-operate provisions, while IPR_1 (the situation modeled in Figure 7.1) does not. The area bounded by p_{3m}, b,

Figure 7.2   A simple model for research with IPR and freedom-to-operate provisions

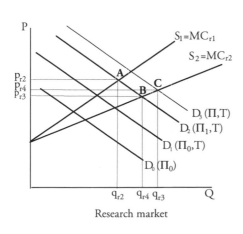 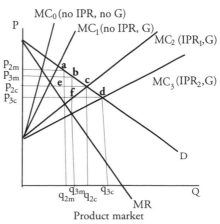

Research market   Product market

f and p_{3c} is larger than the area bounded by p_{2m}, a, e, and p_{2c}. Thus, as well as the shift to $S_2 = MC_2$ the move from point A, which is the same as point A in Figure 7.1, to point B in the research market, the anticipated extra profits will shift $D_2(P_1,T)$ to $D_3(P_2,T)$, point C in Figure 7.2. In Figure 7.2, the P's, T's and G's have the same meaning as in Figure 7.1.

These models suggest several hypotheses that should be testable empirically. The first is that the social welfare gained from research will increase in the following order: neither government research spending nor IPR; government research spending but no IPR; and both government research spending and IPR. Second, the returns to research will increase with the amount of research done—that is, the supply curve in the product market will continue to shift or pivot downward. Coupling the first and second hypothesis leads to a third: returns to research increase with the adoption of IPR protection.

Existing studies on the rates of return to agricultural research seem to support all of these hypotheses. The 1998 study by Alston et al., in the words of Alston and Pardey (1999, 10):

> . . . documented and discussed the results of more that 290 studies of the social and private rates of return to agricultural research. The overwhelming conclusion was that estimated real rates of return to agricultural research have been very high, typically well in excess of 20 percent per year.

Malla, Gray, and Phillips (1999, 40), however, observed that "the increase in private research and development efforts did not actually yield as much net benefit as one would expect when witnessing a large amount of private investment flowing into an otherwise public funded research area." This suggests that, while the third hypothesis above appears from the empirical work to hold true, it requires the caveat that firms and government have the potential to over-invest in research. Received economic theory would hold, however, that in a market economy with IPR protection, a tendency to over-invest would be remedied quickly by the bankruptcy or change in investment strategy of the firm undertaking the research—if the research is complementary or similar to work being done by government.

Finally, if the new technology or new products affect the environment, human health, or social outcomes, significant potential would exist for product demand to change, either by a shift inward or possibly by a rotation (that is, flattening) of the demand curve were consumers to choose product alternatives not involving the technology. Clearly, demand shifts sharply reduce profits in the product market, inducing a decline in the demand for research.

Although an effective IPR regime can be welfare-enhancing, the fiscal and transactional costs of establishing and managing an IPR system can be prohibitive, especially in developing countries with other institutional problems (for example, ineffective judicial systems). In addition, it is likely that freedom to operate, even in the developed world, is curtailed either by opportunistic behavior or by transactions costs. Should this be the case, then even countries with effective IP regimes will not fully benefit from the potential gains of innovation. [3]

Potential Strategies for Optimizing Public Benefits of Research

The public sector has to take some of the blame and holds most of the answers to resolving the three classes of problems related to the extension of IPR in the agrifood world. The public sector created the property-rights regimes, it funds a major share of research and development in the sector (for some products the lion's share), and it controls the public risk analysis structure that assesses, manages, and communicates with citizens and consumers about the risks and benefits of new technologies. Following are some of the options the public sector, either alone or in partnership with the private sector, could consider to remedy each of the identified problems.

Research Incentives and Priorities

The public sector will need to re-examine its priorities and incentive structures to see if it can renew research into basic, know-why knowledge development. This is the one true public good that nobody seems to be nurturing. The push to commercialize has drawn many basic researchers toward applied research, where all the rewards from this new system lie. A new balance needs to be set between private greed and public good in the development of public research objectives. Malla (2000) argues that this would logically entail more public basic research and, in those markets with well developed private-sector participants, a reduction in public applied research (which potentially crowds out private research or results in excess research and lower social returns). In small product markets, however, the state may have a larger role to play because the potential rewards may not be large enough to attract private capital. Public applied research or directed, public market-making efforts may be required.

In practical terms, this requires rebalancing the incentives. Researchers need to see that public-good research will pay as well for them as commercializable research. That may require reweighting the benefits from peer-reviewed research relative to patentable research in public universities, a decoupling of public-sector compensation from patents, and an increase in the funds available for public research to backfill for foregone private capital. The spirit of curiosity-based inquiry needs to be rekindled.

Even so, the public sector may continue to have reasons to collaborate with private interests. There is no doubt that the rapid development of herbicide-tolerant, transgenic canola in Canada was possible only because the private companies (for example, AgrEvo) were able to partner with the public research agencies. AgrEvo worked with the NRC to develop species-specific enabling technologies and with AAFC to express their proprietary genes in elite germplasm, which had been developed by AAFC breeders. These two examples indicate where public benefits of collaboration may accrue. In the case of technology, many of the refinements that can be developed will cost more than any single firm may be able to afford, yet offer significant social benefits when numerous companies use the technology in a product area. In those cases, collaborations tend to have demonstrable social value. Similarly plant-breeding skills, especially for small-area crops, are often hard to develop and maintain in a private setting. In this case, AAFC was able to facilitate the introduction of this new technology, which benefits both producer and consumer.

An earlier work (Phillips 2000) suggested that the AAFC and NRC stories may have a deeper meaning for priority setting. The fact that the quantity and quality of the NRC output rose both absolutely and relatively to the total sector effort while AAFC output and quality fell relatively over the same period suggests that the strategies the two institutions were pursuing may have different outcomes. Since 1989, the NRC has done significant work with others: half its published work has been through collaborations with others, of which 90 percent was via joint-venture collaborations with groups of private companies that involve the pooling of money, staff, and IP. In contrast, AAFC tends to do a significantly larger share of its work in-house (79 percent of its publications) or with single companies via fee-for-service work, which in many cases has not led to any contribution other than money. In the NRC case, the greater exchange of nonfinancial information appears to support the development of more valuable, basic, know-why knowledge. This difference of operation may help to explain why the NRC has seen a significant rise in its volume and quality of know-why work, while AAFC has seen a fall in both. Other public institutions could take a lesson from their experiences.

Patent Systems and Strategies

The patent system and the public use of patents both warrant consideration. Acting alone, or in concert, governments could improve the operations of the patent-granting system. Monopolistic exploitation can and should be manageable with the current tools. The public sector, however, should reexamine how it uses the system to protect and commercialize its own innovations. Finally, there are a number of approaches the public sector, in partnership with the private sector, could implement to reduce the transaction costs for patent systems.

The various national patent systems have already begun to converge, partly through international agreement (for example, UPOV, TRIPs, and the Patent Convention Treaty) and partly through their use by innovators. Nevertheless, the system is far from perfect. As a first step, the international agencies could further reduce the cost of acquiring effective property protection for innovations by collaborating more on assessing patent claims. While arguably it will be difficult to get every country to agree on what should be patentable (for example, multicellular organisms), it should be possible to collaborate on the assessment of prior art. Just as the food and environmental safety regulators are cooperating to develop a common understanding of the biology of plant platforms and of the molecular characterization of GM traits, it should be possible to build an international understanding of the state of the art around specific technology platforms or species (Phillips and Buckingham 2001). Almost of necessity this will involve drawing upon the expertise of hands-on public and private scientists, who are often concentrated in discrete places in the world (Phillips and Khachatourians 2001). Such specialization could both accelerate decisions and reduce the possibility of accepting claims that pirate traditional knowledge, overlap others' rights, or are not replicable. That would help reduce the transaction costs of acquiring and using patents.

The public sector already has a number of tools for reducing the monopolistic exploitation of patents. Most countries have measures either within their patent legislation or their competition laws that prohibit anticompetitive behavior by withholding licenses to use a patent, by not working a patent, by tying use of the patent to other processes, or by cross-licensing or patent pooling that can lead to anticompetitive outcomes. A number of remedies exist including compulsory licensing for dormant, insufficiently exploited, or blocking patents; revocation of patents for egregious behavior; or voiding, nullifying, or changing a contract that is anticompetitive. Over and above that, if the foregone consumer surplus from exploiting the technology competitively (area cde in Figure 7.1) exceeds the monopolistic rents, in a mutually satisfactory transaction, the public sector could buy out the patent right and make the innovation generally available. Many developing countries have a different set of choices to make. As RAFI (2000a and 2000b) and Binenbaum et al. (2000) note, many key technologies are only incompletely patented worldwide, hence many developing countries can ignore patent concerns and adopt and use others' technology with impunity. That strategy, however, is fraught with problems if the country ever hopes to export any product or derivative that has used unlicensed technology, as many countries have laws that allow injunctions or civil cases against trade in unlicensed IP. Clearly, more work needs to be done to determine the feasibility of that option, although Binenbaum et al. (2000) represent a start in that direction.

The public sector should explore options to more effectively exploit their own innovations that have commercial possibilities. The fragmented, unfocused, and, at times, misguided efforts to exploit public innovations often destroy the public good of their work without generating a commensurate private return. As discussed earlier, public institutions need to be much clearer about why they want to patent in the first place. If they have a modest innovation and are simply seeking a financial return, they may be disappointed, because few patents earn significant financial returns. If they seek to spur local economic development through local commercialization of an innovation, they may need to rethink their desire to see their innovations widely disseminated. Most innovations require significant investments to adapt them to the market, which often require exclusive licensing arrangements. If they seek to create a "toolkit" as a basis to bargain for freedom to operate, they may need to pool innovations from a much larger group than their own institutions. Groups of complementary researchers should consider pooling their IP, even if that would require inter-university, public-private, or international arrangements. Furthermore, for that strategy to work, it may be necessary to sever the link between compensation for the inventor and commercialization of the innovation.

The public sector could do more to reduce the search, negotiation, and enforcement costs of patents. Putting various national patent databases on the Internet is a start (for example, Canada, the European Union, Japan, the United States, and the World Intellectual Property Organization), but the patents are still difficult to search conclusively, information about who owns or represents the invention is often not available, and the concordance of rights between jurisdictions is still being developed. Transparent markets for these technologies are still a long way off. Many law firms, patent agents, and institutions such as ISAAA and Dow's Advanced-AgriTraits Inc. are attempting to provide marketplaces for certain technologies, but they are still limited. In the absence of markets, price transparency is missing and many firms are forced to cross-license to gain access to technologies, potentially excluding those without anything to license and imposing all the costs of trying to match wants through barter. While negotiations are often specific to the technologies, greater transparency of the terms and conditions would help to make technology markets more effective. Similarly, the public sector could provide facilitation and mediation to assist smaller firms and less significant technologies to enforce their rights and to resolve any disputes.

Finally, the public sector needs to remember that markets function better when information is readily available. Most public research programs are as tight-lipped about their technologies, contracts, and returns as many private companies, if not more so. Many of these institutions have undertaken expensive and valuable freedom-to-operate studies that could shed light on the structure and imperfections in many technology markets. Although they might suffer some loss of bargaining power, society as a whole may gain from greater market transparency of the technologies and their uses. In almost every instance, greater transparency reduces unequal bargaining powers and reduces the spread between bid and ask prices, increasing the aggregate consumer and producer benefits of new technologies (often at the expense of those who have preferential access to market knowledge).

Market Making Knowledge and Information

Perhaps the single most important thing the public sector could do to increase the public benefits of new agrifood innovations would be to restore public confidence and trust in the risk analysis systems used around the world. Consumers appear to harbor significant doubts about the system, which seems to be captured by private interests. Restoring confidence in the regulatory system clearly involves going beyond doing more and different kinds of research, but that would be a start. The public sector needs to recommit to sustaining public-interest type research in the agrifood system. It will not be enough, given the appearance of capture, for private companies to do this research. It may, however, be enough for government to require private firms to provide their research results for the purpose of attempting replication, while allowing access to the data to public interest groups for the same purpose. This will involve providing funds to public researchers to investigate questions that have no direct private commercial value, such as whether or not a particular gene can outcross, without human intervention, to a related species in a field setting. Public researchers need to be encouraged to ask the questions that no one else will ask. Well-trained and funded researchers often surprise the critics, producing both important, relevant research results to address public concerns but also, in the process, inventing new technologies and products with significant private commercial value.

Implications and Further Research

Twenty years after the first patent for an organism, the public sector should pause and reconsider its role in the rush to develop and use new life-science developments in the agrifood world. The potential for the new technologies developed in the past generation is almost limitless, but problems also exist. The public sector, by reorienting its research and policies toward supporting private interests and away from traditional public concerns, has created a situation that could seriously limit the public good from that effort. Inadequate basic research, inappropriate patent systems, and strategies and gaps in market-making research and information threaten the further expansion of agrifood innovation and development.

The next step is to investigate the evidence and identify actionable policy outcomes. Numerous studies indicate large welfare gains from agricultural research; surveying researchers in both the public and private sectors could determine whether or not researchers are constrained in the pursuit of their research agendas because of failures in the freedom-to-operate provisions of patent legislation. The merger mania in the industry witnessed over the past decade or so could well be based on attempts to economize on the transactions costs of obtaining access to IP.

Properly constructed, a survey should be able determine whether the researchers believe overly broad patenting to be a problem. It should be able to ascertain if they believe there is a tendency for patent holders to refuse to bargain in good faith. It will have to determine the researcher's sense of the extent to which search, litigation, and monitoring costs affect their decisions respecting the nature and direction of their research and whether or not to patent the results of that research. It must be capable of assessing their perceptions of any current or perceived future problems with accessing germplasm or traditional lore in the developing world. It will also need to be able to garner from researchers and patent holders whether they feel the uncertainty over the race to the patent office in a first-to-register jurisdiction is greater or less than the uncertainty of ownership inherent in a first-to-invent juris-diction. It would be an added bonus if such a survey could ascertain the reasons for the mergers. Finally, the survey must indicate the extent to which potential liability for negative externalities associated with patented material affects the decision to patent.

Notes

1. See also Nottenburg et al. this volume.

2. A *Pareto* improvement, according to Varian (1996), is a change in circumstances where at least one economic agent is made better off, while no other agent is made worse off.

3. One conclusion, prevalent in the popular press, holds that governments are afraid of oppor-tunistic behavior by property rights holders, in particular multinational corporations, and by gov-ernments of the developed nations; that is, they fear that through an overly broad patent claim or the patenting of some local tradition, custom, germplasm, or some such thing—particularly if a first-to-register rather than first-to-invent policy is adopted—the patent holder using monopoly pricing will price the patented good or process beyond the resources of the poor in the developing world. Fear also exists that if government in the developing world use measures such as forced licensing to weaken the property-right holder's ability to extract rents—legal under Article 31 of TRIPs—governments of the developed world will involve them in international trade disputes.

References

Alston, J. M., and P. G. Pardey. 1999. The economics of agricultural R&D policy. In *Paying for agri-cultural productivity*, J. M. Alston, P. G. Pardey, and V. H. Smith eds. Baltimore: Johns Hop-kins University Press.

Binenbaum E., C. Nottenburg, P. G. Pardey, B. D. Wright, and P. Zambrano. 2000. South-North Trade, intellectual property jurisdictions, and freedom to operate in agricultural research on staple crops. Environment and Production Technology Discussion Paper No. 70. Washington, D.C.: International Food Policy Research Institute. <http://www.ifpri.org>. Accessed August 20, 2001.

Einsiedel, E. F., K. Finlay, and J. Arko. 2000. Meeting consumers' needs for information on biotechnology. Paper prepared for the Canadian Biotechnology Advisory Committee. <http://www.cbac_cccb.gc.ca>. Accessed August 20, 2001.

Gaskell, G., M. W. Bauer, J. Durant, and N. O. Allum. 1999. Worlds apart? The reception of genetically modified foods in Europe and the U.S. *Science* 285 (July 16): 384–87. <http://www.sciencemag.org/cgi/content/full/285/5426/384>. Accessed September 18, 2000.

Goodhue, R., G. Rausser, S. Scotchmer, and L. Simon. 1999. Biotechnology, intellectual property and value differentiation in agriculture. Paper presented at the NE–165 conference, Transitions in Agbiotech: Economics of Strategy and Policy. Washington, D.C., June 24–25.

Industry Canada. 2000. A guide to patents. Canadian Intellectual Property Office. <http://strategis.ic.gc.ca/sc_mrksv/cipo/patents/pt_main-e.html> via a link to <http://www.strategis.pc.gc.ca/sc_mrksv/cipo/patents/patc2000.pdf>. Accessed August 20, 2001.

ISAAA. 2000. *Summary–The intellectual and technical components of pro-vitamin A rice: A preliminary freedom to operate review.* International Service for the Acquisition of Agri-biotech Applications Brief No. 20. Ithaca, N.Y. , U.S.A. <http://www.isaaa.org>. Accessed August 20, 2001.

Lindner, R. 1999. Prospects for public plant breeding in a small country. In *The shape of the coming agricultural biotechnology transformation.* Proceedings of the fourth international conference of the Consortium of Agricultural Biotechnology Research. Rome: University of Rome, *Tor Vergata.*

Malla, S. 2000. Searching for genes: Public and private spillovers in agricultural research. Ph.D. thesis, University of Saskatchewan.

Malla, S., R. Gray, and P. W. B. Phillips. 1999. The effectiveness of the research funding in the canola industry: An interim report for the agricultural development fund of Saskatchewan Agriculture and Food. Department of Agricultural Economics, University of Saskatchewan, Saskatoon.

Phillips, P. W. B. 2000. Intellectual property rights and public research in Canada. In V. Santaniello, R. Evenson, D. Zilberman, and G. Carlson, eds. *Agriculture and intellectual property rights: Economic institutional and implementation issues in biotechnology.* Wallingford, U.K.: CAB International.

Phillips, P. W. B., and D. Buckingham. 2001. Hot potato, hot potato: Regulating products of biotechnology by the international community. *Journal of World Trade.* 35 (1): 1–31.

Phillips, P. W. B., and J. Gustafson. 2000. Patent strategies in the biotechnology industry and implications for technology diffusion. In *The shape of the coming agricultural biotechnology transformation.* Proceedings of the fourth international conference of the Consortium of Agricultural Biotechnology Research. Rome: University of Rome, *Tor Vergata.*

Phillips, P. W. B., and G. G. Khachatourians. 2001. *The Biotechnology revolution in global agriculture: Invention, innovation and investment in the canola sector.* Wallingford, U.K.: CAB International.

Phillips, P. W. B., and H. McNeill. 2000. Labeling for GM foods: Theory and practice. In *The shape of the coming agricultural biotechnology transformation.* Proceedings of the fourth international conference of the Consortium of Agricultural Biotechnology Research. Rome: University of Rome, *Tor Vergata.*

RAFI (Rural Advancement Foundation International). 2000a. Golden Rice and Trojan trade reps. RAFI Communiqué 65, September/October. <http://www.rafi.org>. Accessed August 20, 2001.

———. 2000b. Golden Rice and the search for higher ground. Update on Trojan trade reps, October 12. <http://www.rafi.org>. Accessed August 20, 2001.

Rafiquzzaman, M., and K. Smith. 2000. Special report: Innovative activity in Canada by technological field. Monthly Economic Indicators. <http://www.strategis.ic.gc.ca/pics/ra/spc0300e.pdf>. Accessed August 20, 2001.

Romer, P. 1990. Endogenous technological change, *Journal of Political Economy.* 98 (5:2): S71–S102.

U.S. Patent and Trademark Office. Quick search of U.S. patent database. Available at <http://www.delphion.com/>. Accessed December 20, 2000.

Varian, H. 1996. *Intermediate microeconomics: A modern approach.* 4th ed. New York: W. W. Norton.

Comment

Ron Duncan

Nottenburg, Pardey, and Wright clearly demonstrate substantial problems in the operation of the intellectual property rights (IPR) policy regime. These problems relate mainly to the issue of freedom of entry of innovators. The IPR concept itself is not in question, but rather the design and management of the policy regime. The IPR regime is now well established, and improving its operation will take considerable imagination and effort.

Phillips and Dierker also demonstrate the problems in the IPR policy regime, but various parts of their chapter are not helpful in clearly thinking through the issues. They see an IP right as the conferring of a monopoly, and thus analyze the IPR market as being imperfectly competitive. Monopoly positions may exist, but they do not arise from IPR per se; rather they arise through the way the policy regime has allowed the market to develop.

An IP right should be recognized as just that—a private property right. In a market economy, if all factors not in perfectly elastic supply do not have clearly defined private-property rights (unless they are public goods), production will be suboptimal. To make matters clear, instead of thinking of an innovation over which there is a property right, think of land. If a secure property right to the land is in place, the land will be put to its most efficient use, it will be protected, and more will be created, for example, by increasing the fertility of existing land or by creating land where none existed before (such as landfill). Without secure property rights, the land will suffer open-access problems of overexploitation and lack of investment.

We do not think of landowners or holders of leases over land as being monopolists. There is some rent, because land is not in perfectly elastic supply. Similarly, holders of IPR can be thought of as earning some rent, but this is subject to being competed away as there is (or should be) freedom of entry for competitive new ideas. Without IPR, investment in new ideas will be suboptimal. Of course, basic research leading to what Phillips and Dierker call "know-why" knowledge is a different matter. It is a public good and therefore should not be subject to private-property rights, and being non-rival and nonexcludable it does not suffer problems of open access.

The imperfectly competitive model of Figures 7.1 and 7.2 presented by Phillips and Dierker does not appropriately represent the IPR market. Holders of IPR do not have a monopoly position. Inventors enjoy freedom of entry (except for the freedom-to-operate problems in the existing IPR regime). In addition, the way in which the supply curves are drawn, originating from the origin, is a very restrictive functional form that gives predetermined results on the incidence of the benefits from shifts of the supply curve (see Duncan and Tisdell 1971 and Sarhangi et al. 1977).

Phillips and Dierker have several concerns about the research system itself, following the introduction of the IPR regime. First, they argue that the amount of basic research being carried out now is too low, and to support this they show that basic research in Canada has fallen; but that is not the same as showing that basic research is too low.

Second, because basic research is too low, particularly in public research organizations, public quality-control over new products coming forward to consumers is deteriorating. Phillips and Dierker argue for more government involvement in ensuring health and safety with new products, but this argument ignores the role of competition. Policy advisers should not jump to the conclusion that regulation is the answer to problems of quality or health and safety. In fact, the "Great March of Regulation" over the past 40 years has proven extremely costly to society in terms of activities conforming to regulations, the supervision of activities, and the legal costs related to regulation. So long as there is freedom of entry, competition between firms will ensure quality of products and services. The goal should be better balance between competition and regulation.

Finally, Phillips and Dierker are not in favor of incentive mechanisms in universities that allow researchers to share directly in the benefits flowing from their innovations; rather, they prefer a pooling system. But pooling gives rise to "free rider" problems, and for that reason researchers should receive at least some direct benefit from their work.

References

Duncan, R. C., and C. Tisdell. 1971. Research and technical progress: The return to producers. *Economic Record* 47 (117): 124–29.

Sarhangi, R. F., R. C. Duncan, J. Logan, and P. Hagan. 1977. Who benefits from agricultural research: Comment. *Review of Marketing and Agricultural Economics*, December, 179–85.

Comment

Bob Lindner

In my view, it is appropriate that the first session to address specific issues relating to agricultural biotechnology be about intellectual property policies and practice. Elsewhere I have predicted that the long-term prospects for agricultural biotechnology will depend more on the resolution of IPR issues than on such issues as consumer acceptance, farmer adoption, or the environmental impact of GMOs that currently seem to preoccupy much of the policy debate. This prediction is based partly on the belief that consumer acceptance will improve dramatically once industry finds ways to enable market segmentation and price differentials between GM and non-GM foods to emerge and to deliver consumers a significant part of the benefits from first-generation GM crops, and subsequently more direct and substantial net benefits through the successful introduction of much heralded second and third generation GMOs. Only time will tell whether this prediction is bold or merely courageous. What is clear is that development of a substantial and sustainable market for GMOs is a necessary, but not sufficient, condition for agricultural biotechnology to eventually fulfill its early promise.

For the transgenic revolution to continue, not only must scientific discovery continue to create value but private investors must also have the incentive to continue investing in further technology development. In the longer run, I believe that the key question will not be whether value will be created from agricultural biotechnology, but whether private investors can appropriate enough of the value created to profit from continued investment in technology development. Intellectual property rights are key to investors' capturing value from investment in ongoing development of agricultural biotechnology; these rights are also key to the distribution of value created by investments in agricultural biotechnology, a crucial policy issue in the context of international developments.

This is a fascinating area of study. Interactions involving advances in scientific knowledge, changes in the legal framework for IPR, and competitive forces in the market are driving economic outcomes from agricultural biotechnology. Extended property rights have created the foundation for new markets, but it is the opportunities arising from scientific discoveries that have provided powerful incentives for firms to enter these markets, while it is the competitive forces unleashed by these developments that will transform agricultural production, often in unexpected ways. Hence to understand and address the policy issues relating to how IPR might affect future investment in agricultural biotechnology, we need to understand three different disciplines: the science of molecular biology, the law relating to IPR, and the economics of commercialization of new technologies, including in particular monitoring the use of proprietary technology, detecting infringements, and enforcing rights—issues that until now have received relatively little attention.

The history of other revolutionary technologies demonstrates how intellectual property rights can influence the evolution of radically new technologies and the distribution of benefits from such technologies. For instance, important insights into the possibility that patent gridlock (the so-called "tragedy of the anticommons") will stall the development of a new technology can be gleaned from case histories of the development of the incandescent light bulb, the fuel combustion engine, airplanes, radio, semiconductors, and computers. These innovations are examples of cumulative technologies where patents of wide scope on basic inventions were granted, and where the potential for patent blockages to impede technological progress existed. In some cases, institutionalized cross-licensing arrangements emerged sooner rather than later, but in other cases progress languished until basic patents expired. Whether this scenario will unfold for the life sciences industry is currently a topic of intense debate.

Part 4

Biotechnology Impacts: The Economic Evidence

Chapter 8

Agricultural Biotechnology: A Critical Review of the Impact Evidence to Date

Michele C. Marra

Introduction

It has been less than 10 years since the first transgenic crop was approved for commercial release. The Flavr-Savr™ tomato, genetically engineered to delay softening so the tomato could ripen on the vine and retain its "fresh picked" flavor, was introduced commercially in the United States in 1994. It was a scientific success, but a colossal business failure. Although the tomatoes achieved the delayed-softening and taste-retention objectives of their developers, yields were poor, mechanical handling equipment turned most of them into mush before they got to market, and consumers weren't willing to pay enough of a premium over conventional fresh tomatoes to cover costs. The seeds of the biotechnology protests started with the Flavr-Savr™, too, when Jeremy Rifkin managed to persuade Campbell's Soup not to use biotech tomatoes in its products (Kasler and Lau 2000).

Nevertheless, seven years later farmers in several countries where the transgenic crops have been approved for planting are devoting significant portions of acreage to them. Their costs and benefits at the farm level have been documented in ex ante economic studies, farmer testimonials in the farm press, and reports issued by national departments of agriculture. A few studies have attempted to measure the the impacts among producers and consumers and other participants in the marketing chain by aggregating up from the farm-level studies. Specific information is still sketchy for many of the events,[1] and the reported economic impacts vary widely in both size and magnitude, even within the same location and for the same event in some cases.

This chapter critically examines evidence of economic impacts reported to date to categorize the types of evidence by potential biases and provide a range of values for some of the impacts based on the available results from public research.

The Current Status of Event Introduction and Farmer Adoption

Event Introduction

By early 2001, more than 187 crop events involving nine basic phenotypic (physical) characteristics have been deregulated or approved for planting, feed, or food use in at least one of 13 individual countries plus the countries of the European Union (E.U.). Successfully modified traits important for the major agricultural crops include delayed ripening, herbicide tolerance, insect resistance, modified color or oil, male sterility/fertility restoration, and virus resistance (AGBIOS Inc. 2001). Table 8.1 lists the major agricultural crops by modified trait, country approving at least one event within the trait, and type of approval as of February 2001. The majority of the approved events have been for food uses and over a fifth involved approvals for food or livestock feed uses without planting approval, implying that livestock and feed producers in the relevant country must import the feed. Most of the approvals have been issued in Canada and the United States, with very few issued so far in developing countries.

Approval processes and intellectual property rights (IPR) laws vary across jurisdictions and, in many instances, are still being developed for these unique products, so it is not surprising that only a handful of countries have issued approvals to date. The lists of modified traits and events for which applications are pending in at least one country are lengthening, however (AGBIOS 2001).

Adoption

In those countries where planting approval has been granted and seed is available in sufficient quantities, farmers are generally adopting the new technologies fairly rapidly (Table 8.2). So far, U.S. farmers have been the keenest adopters of transgenic crops, both in terms of absolute acreage planted and the share of the sum of harvested acres of those crops for which at least one transgenic planting approval exists. The proportion of transgenic acreage in Canada and the United States declined notably from 1999 to 2000, though it appears to have recovered in 2001, principally because of a substantial increase in the share of U.S. soybean acreage planted to trans-

Table 8.1   Major transgenic crops by trait, country, and approval type

Crop	Trait	Country	Approval type Unconfined planting	Feed use	Food use
Canola	Herbicide-tolerant	Australia			✔
		Canada	✔	✔	✔
		European Union			
		Japan	✔	✔	✔
		United States	✔	✔	✔
	Herbicide-tolerant and male sterility/fertility restoration	Canada	✔	✔	✔
		European Union			
		Japan	✔	✔	✔
		United States	✔	✔	✔
	Oil content	Canada	✔	✔	✔
		United States	✔	✔	✔
Carnations	Delayed ripening	Australia	✔		
		European Union	✔		
	Flower color	Australia	✔		
		European Union			
Chicory	Herbicide-tolerant and male sterility	European Union	✔		
Corn	Herbicide-tolerant	Argentina	✔	✔	✔
		Australia			✔
		Canada	✔	✔	✔
		European Union		✔	✔
		Japan	✔	✔	✔
		United States	✔	✔	✔
	Herbicide-tolerant and male sterility	Canada	✔	✔	✔
		United States	✔	✔	✔
	Insect-resistant	Argentina	✔	✔	✔
		Australia			✔
		Canada	✔	✔	✔
		European Union	✔	✔	✔
		Japan	✔	✔	✔
		South Africa	✔	✔	✔
		Switzerland		✔	✔
		United States	✔	✔	✔
	Insect-resistant and herbicide-tolerant	Argentina	✔	✔	✔
		Canada	✔	✔	✔
		Denmark			✔
		European Union	✔	✔	✔
		Japan	✔	✔	✔
		The Netherlands		✔	✔
Corn		Switzerland		✔	✔
		United Kingdom		✔	✔
		United States	✔	✔	✔
Cotton	Herbicide-tolerant	Argentina	✔		
		Australia	✔		✔
		Canada	✔	✔	✔
		Japan	✔	✔	✔
		United States	✔	✔	✔
	Herbicide-tolerant and insect-resistant	Japan	✔	✔	✔
		United States	✔	✔	✔

Table 8.1   Major transgenic crops by trait, country, and approval type (continued)

Crop	Trait	Country	Approval type Unconfined planting	Feed use	Food use
	Insect-resistant	Argentina	✔	✔	✔
		Australia	✔	✔	✔
		Canada		✔	✔
		China	✔	✔	✔
		Japan	✔	✔	✔
		Mexico	✔	✔	✔
		South Africa	✔	✔	✔
		United States	✔	✔	✔
Melon	Delayed ripening	United States	✔		✔
Papaya	Viral-resistant	United States	✔		✔
Potato	Insect-resistant	Canada	✔	✔	✔
		Japan			✔
		United States	✔	✔	✔
	Insect-resistant and viral-resistant	Canada	✔	✔	✔
		United States	✔	✔	✔
Rice	Herbicide-tolerant	United States	✔	✔	✔
Soybeans	Herbicide-tolerant	Argentina	✔	✔	✔
		Australia			✔
		Brazil	✔	✔	✔
		Canada	✔	✔	✔
		European Union			
		Japan	✔	✔	✔
		Korea			✔
		Mexico	✔	✔	✔
		The Netherlands		✔	✔
		Russia			✔
		Switzerland		✔	✔
		United States	✔	✔	✔
Soybeans		Uruguay	✔	✔	✔
	Oil content	Australia			✔
		Canada	✔	✔	✔
		Japan	✔	✔	
		United States	✔	✔	✔
Squash	Viral-resistant	Canada			✔
		United States	✔		✔
Sugar Beets	Herbicide-tolerant	Canada			✔
		Japan		✔	✔
		United States	✔	✔	✔
Tobacco	Herbicide-tolerant	European Union			
Tomatoes	Delayed ripening	Canada			✔
		Japan	✔		✔
		Mexico	✔	✔	✔
		United States	✔		✔
Wheat	Herbicide-tolerant	Canada	✔	✔	✔
Total			66	64	81

Source: Adapted from AGBIOS Inc. (2001), using data from "Crops and Traits," "Genetic Elements," and "Regulatory Approvals."
Note: United States data presented here as "Food use" and "Feed use" correspond with the AGBIOS "Food/Feed" entries, with the exception of tomatoes, papayas, and squash, which are listed here under "Food use" only because the Food and Drug Administration (2001) has approved these technologies and crops as "Human Food" only.

genic varieties and continuing growth in the cotton acreage sown to transgenics (NASS 2001).

Table 8.3 lists the percentage of crop acreage planted to transgenic crops by U.S. state in 2001. Herbicide-tolerant soybeans—mostly Roundup Ready® (RR)—are now planted on about two thirds of the soybean acreage throughout the United States. About one quarter of the corn acreage in the United States was planted to transgenic varieties in 2001, of which most were insect resistant with a small percentage (6 percent) being herbicide-tolerant or combining herbicide tolerance with insect resistance. Transgenic cotton was adopted on a majority of cotton acreage in most southeastern U.S. states in 2001 and over a quarter of California's cotton acreage. An important reason for different adoption rates across geographic regions has been the lag in getting the genetic trait into varieties appropriate for the different regions. This is especially true for cotton in Texas. The cotton varietal laws in California have hindered adoption there, but some transgenic varieties are now becoming available.

These astounding early adoption rates provide indirect evidence of potentially large, positive farm-level returns for many of these crops, at least for a significant number of farmers. For many purposes, more explicit evidence is needed on the farm-level gross and net benefits from these technologies. As is discussed below, farm-level impacts are difficult to estimate, and typical approaches are susceptible to bias.

Other measures of benefits, going beyond the farm level, are of interest for some purposes, and estimates of these benefits often depend on measures of impacts at the farm level; an additional reason for wanting to obtain unbiased and precise estimates. For instance, when estimating aggregative welfare measures, a small mistake in estimating the underlying farm-level impacts can result in over- or underestimating the shift in product supply, which in turn can result in a distorted measure of the change in industrywide profit or economic welfare. One cannot accurately predict future demand for a particular transgenic variety using incorrect estimates of impacts at the farm level. Because many transgenic varieties have environmental as well as pecuniary implications, an error in predicting future demand at the farm level can result in mismeasurement (and mismanagement) of the environmental impact.

Clearly, it is important to get the farm-level impacts right, and a critical examination of the economic impact evidence to date is a useful exercise at this early stage of the innovation process.

Types Of Farm-Level Economic Impacts

Yield

Many transgenic technologies in crops are designed to reduce yield losses from pests. These are generally the ones that insert genes that code for pesticides, such as

Table 8.2   Transgenic acreage

Country	Year	Total transgenic acres	Total harvested area of crops with at least one approved event	Share
		(million acres)		*(percentage)*
Argentina	1996	0.3	23.4	1.3
	1997	3.5	26.4	13.1
	1998	10.6	27.2	39.0
	1999	16.6	28.2	58.7
	2000	24.7	29.4	84.1
Australia	1996	<0.2	0.8	—
	1997	0.2	0.9	26.5
	1998	0.2	0.9	26.2
	1999	0.2	1.1	22.4
	2000	0.5	1.2	41.1
Canada	1996	0.2	41.3	0.6
	1997	3.2	43.2	7.4
	1998	6.9	42.6	16.2
	1999	9.9	42.2	23.4
	2000	7.4	42.0	17.6
China	1998	0.5	11.0	4.5
	1999	0.7	9.2	8.1
	2000	1.2	10.0	12.4
United States	1996	10.7	158.1	6.7
	1997	25.2	165.1	15.2
	1998	60.4	166.4	36.3
	1999	78.5	166.1	47.3
	2000	69.6	169.6	41.0
	2001	82.3	167.8	49.0

Sources: For Australia, Argentina, Canada, and China, "Total transgenic acres" are from James (1997, 1998, 1999, and 2000b) and "Total area of crops" is from FAO (2000). For United States the share of acreage sown to transgenic crops for 1996–99 is from ERS (2001) and for 2000 and 2001, from NASS (2001). Corresponding total crop acreages were obtained from NASS (2001).
Note: Data represent transgenic acreages of crops with at least one approved event. For Australia and China, the data represent area under cotton; for Argentina, the area under soybeans, maize, and cotton; for Canada, the area under canola, maize, potatoes, soybeans, and wheat; and for the United States, the area planted to cotton, maize, and soybeans.

the *Bacillus thuringiensis* [*Bt*] crops (corn, cotton, potatoes, and soybeans). These crops can be thought of as pesticide-inherent crops. The pesticide kills pests that eat the plant, thus providing an effective and virtually complete pest control mechanism, at least in the short run. If these particular pests are present but are not in sufficient numbers to significantly affect yield, or if the pests affect yield but are cheap to control by other means, then the producer of pesticide-inherent crops may not experience a net benefit. If the pests are prevalent to an economically damaging extent in the area, however, then this complete control can result in significant yield increases. These pesticide-inherent crops may reduce yield risk, as well. Most farmers are averse to yield variability (as evidenced by crop-insurance purchases and by

Table 8.3   Transgenic crops by state and U.S. total, percentage of planted crop acres, 2001

Crop	State	Herbicide-resistant	Insect-resistant	Stacked gene	All transgenic varieties
			(percent)		
Corn	Illinois	3	12	1	16
	Indiana	6	6		12
	Iowa	6	25	1	32
	Kansas	11	26	1	38
	Michigan	7	8	2	17
	Minnesota	7	25	4	36
	Missouri	8	23	1	32
	Nebraska	8	24	2	34
	Ohio	4	7		11
	South Dakota	14	30	3	47
	Wisconsin	6	11	1	18
	Other Corn States	8	11	1	20
	United States	*7*	*18*	*1*	*26*
Cotton	Arizona	29	21	28	78
	California	27	11	2	40
	Georgia	43	13	29	85
	Louisiana	14	30	47	91
	Mississippi	15	10	61	86
	North Carolina	37	9	38	84
	Texas	35	8	6	49
	Other Cotton States	33	18	33	84
	United States	*32*	*13*	*24*	*69*
Soybeans	Arizona	60			60
	Illinois	64			64
	Indiana	78			78
	Iowa	73			73
	Kansas	80			80
	Michigan	59			59
	Minnesota	63			63
	Mississippi	63			63
	Missouri	69			69
	Nebraska	76			76
	North Dakota	49			49
	Ohio	64			64
	South Dakota	80			80
	Wisconsin	63			63
	Other Soybean States	64			64
	United States	*68*			*68*

Source: NASS (2001).

researcher measures of farmers' past attitudes toward risk), so many farmers would
be willing to pay for reduced variability.

Pest-Control Costs

Direct cost reduction. Many studies show that pesticide-inherent crops reduce the
number of sprays required to control pests. If reduced pest-control costs outweigh
the additional cost of the seed, then farmers gain. Herbicide-tolerant crops also can
significantly reduce savings in weed-control costs. RR cotton is a good example.
Before the introduction of this herbicide-tolerant crop, there were no cotton herbicides that could be sprayed over the top of the cotton crop to control weeds (Carpenter and Gianessi 2001). Now, post emergence, over-the-top sprays are substituted
for more expensive preplant incorporated applications of herbicides and mechanical cultivation to control weeds. Also, fewer weed-control field operations may be
needed, which can result in significant savings.

Indirect effects. Three indirect economic effects can result from the adoption of
transgenic crops. First, as farmers widely adopt these crops area demand for conventional counterparts and competing pesticides and herbicides may decrease, which
may lower prices for the transgenic systems (Gianessi and Carpenter 2000). All
farmers, including nonadopters of the transgenic varieties, will benefit from reduced
pesticide and herbicide prices. Second, field operations are saved with the transgenic
crops; this may release resources for other crops at crucial times during the growing
season, allowing the farmer to better manage those crops. For instance, the timing
of soybean planting can have a major effect on weed control: If planting is delayed,
weeds can begin to compete before the soybean canopy closes, causing lower soybean
yields, higher weed-control costs, or both. Growers that plant herbicide-tolerant cotton on part of the farm have more time to plant their soybeans during the planting
period.

Farmers may also benefit from increased flexibility. Many chemical alternatives
to the herbicide-tolerant crops (for example, conventional cotton treated with a
weed-control system that includes the relatively new herbicide, Staple®) present
carry-over problems so that farmers cannot plant certain crops the next growing season. Herbicide-tolerant crops, used in conjunction with short-lived herbicides, eliminate this constraint in many cases. Farmers may also be able to strip-crop or practice
conservation tillage more easily with transgenic crops (Fernandez-Cornejo et al.
1999).

Pest Susceptibility to Substitute Pesticides

Conventional farming operations. For a particular pesticide, whether inherent in the
plant or not, pest resistance can develop with use over time, reducing pest control

and, therefore, the comparative yield gains or cost savings. This has been a concern of scientists and policymakers and has resulted in rules to help slow the development of resistance. For *Bt* cotton in the United States, farmers must plant either 20 percent of their cotton land to a conventional variety using conventional pest control or approximately 4 percent to a conventional variety with no pest control.[2] Also, in order to preserve pest susceptibility to *Bt* in cotton, restrictions limit how much *Bt* corn can be planted in a county with significant cotton acreage. Because the transgenic crop is more profitable, or presumably would not have been planted, these requirements reduce farmers' net benefits in the short run.

A major group of conventional insecticides for southeastern U.S. cotton, the pyrethroids, has been developing serious resistance problems in the bollworm/budworm complex of insects in some areas of the Deep South. Adoption of the *Bt* varieties is slowing development of the insects' resistance to conventional pesticides. This preserves pesticide choices for farmers for a longer period, a farm-level and regional benefit from adoption of the transgenic varieties (Marra, Hubbell, and Carlson 1997).

Organic farming operations. Bt is an approved foliar insecticide for organic farming operations in the United States. Assuming refuge requirements do not completely halt resistance development to a particular *Bt* protein, adoption of transgenic *Bt* crops in a particular area increases the chances that foliar *Bt* will become a less effective insecticide for organic producers. Because organic producers have fewer pesticide options, the development of resistance will be costly for them in terms of lower yields and, perhaps, lower prices from decreases in quality.

Farm-Level Environmental Effects

Farmer and worker health. So far, the pesticide-inherent varieties have contained biological insecticides, which are safer for humans and wildlife than their conventional counterparts (Gianessi and Carpenter 1999). Also, the pesticide-inherent crops involve no spray drift problems, special handling requirements, or reentry intervals. This can increase farmer and worker welfare in two ways. First, reduced health concerns, these crops eliminate the inconvenience of complying with spray drift rules, purchasing and donning special safety clothing, and waiting to reenter the field after conventional application. Second, restricting pesticide applications to days and times when drift will not occur is costly, and pest control may not be timely or as effective. With pesticide-inherent crops, control is continuous throughout the growing season.

Most of the herbicide-tolerant crops are tolerant of glyphosate, one of the safest in the arsenal of currently available herbicides.

> Glyphosate has a half-life in the environment of 47 days, compared with 60–90 days for the herbicides it commonly replaces. The herbicides that

glyphosate replaces are 3.4 to 16.8 times more toxic, according to a chronic risk indicator based on the EPA [Environmental Protection Agency] reference dose for humans (Economic Research Service 2000, 17).

Therefore, farmers and workers may experience fewer herbicide-related health effects when using this type of compound.

Wildlife and water-quality effects. As well as caring about their own and their workers' health and safety, farmers also care about the environment (Beach and Carlson 1993). Since transgenic crops are more environmentally benign than conventional crop/pesticide systems, farmer welfare should benefit from the favorable environmental impact of these crops compared with other crops that require conventional chemical pesticides. Glyphosate, for instance, binds to the soil and does not leach into groundwater or run off into surface water. As mentioned above, *Bt* is an approved pest-control substance for organic farmers.

Pesticide-inherent crops kill only pests that feed on the crop, therefore beneficial insects—those that feed on crop pests—are not harmed by this mode of pesticide delivery. This can enhance indirectly the effectiveness of the pesticide.

A caveat. Concern about the gene insertion process itself still looms large, particularly in Europe at this writing, and this health concern could have a dampening effect on demand for transgenic crops, thus affecting the returns to farmers through lower prices and/or higher costs of identity preservation in the supply chain. The recent recall by Frito-Lay, Inc. of consumer products potentially containing transgenic (Starlink®) corn is an example of the potential consequences of this concern. The proportion of U.S. corn acreage planted to transgenic varieties in 2000 fell by about a quarter from its 1999 level, but stabilized at this lower level in 2001.

Sources of Bias in the Evidence

Field Trials

Over the 10-year period, 1986–95, 3,647 annual field trials for transgenic crops were conducted in 34 countries (James 1996). The number of field trials conducted annually around the world has increased exponentially, so it is likely that at least as many have been conducted since 1995 as were conducted before then. The traditional objective of field trials has been to quantify differences among the experimental treatments—very often different varieties (in variety trials) and, less often, different pest-control regimes or different cultural practices (fertilizer rates, tillage, irrigation, and so on). The effects measured almost always include yield and, in the case of trials of pest control or cultural practices, differences in input use. Sometimes economic comparisons (complete or not) accompany the physical evidence. Most

Table 8.4   Potential bias in measured economic impact by field trial type and transgene trait

Type of field trial	Transgene trait	
	Herbicide-tolerant	Pesticide-inherent
Direction of potential bias in the measured economic impact		
Simple variety		
Currently used conventional versus transgenic	downward	downward
Conventional transgenic parent versus transgenic	upward	upward
Pesticide use trials	uncertain	downward
On-farm, side-by-side comparisons	None if farmer-chosen inputs, otherwise downward	none

Source: Developed by author.

of the transgenic crop field trials have been variety trials reporting yield only, although some also provide some information on differences in pesticide use.

Biases can be introduced into the resulting measures of farm-level impacts of the transgenic varieties in several ways (Table 8.4). Yield differences measured by variety trials typically hold everything else constant. The choice of varieties to be compared may also mean that the measured yield differences would be biased if used to represent the expected farm-level yield impacts. One class of variety trials compares the transgenic variety to its conventional parent, which generally is not among the set of conventional varieties farmers have chosen to grow in the area (because other varieties provide higher yields and/or greater net benefits). So, although this yield difference directly measures the change in yield provided by the transgene, it will overestimate the farm-level impact of adopting the transgenic variety.

Economic impacts calculated from side-by-side variety trials of pesticide-inherent transgenic and conventional varieties (for example, *Bt* crops) can be biased by the halo effect. The insect suppression of the *Bt* crop may spill over onto the conventional treatment, providing another source of pest control, which may increase the yield relative to what it would be if the conventional crop were grown in isolation. The measured yield difference between the conventional and transgenic variety may be biased downward as a result.

Biases can be introduced into the measures of economic impact by the type of field trials that measure differences in pesticide use, as well. Agricultural scientists typically manage pests in field trials to maximize yield, not profit. Therefore, the pest-control regimes tested in the field trials may not reflect what a profit-maximizing farmer would use. The direction of this bias is difficult to predict if the transgenic crops tested are herbicide-tolerant. In the case of pesticide-inherent crops, the measured difference in pesticide use, thus the economic impact, may be underestimated.

Alston, Norton, and Pardey (1998) discuss the importance of defining the relevant counterfactual when evaluating the impact of a particular technology. The correct comparison, to ensure that farm-level impacts are measured accurately, is one where the set of practices and input mixes that would minimize costs (or maximize profits) is employed under each technology. The current conventional crop/pesticide system is the relevant counterfactual to compare with the new technology. This comparison is made most directly on farms where partial adoption, for purposes of estimating the on-farm impact, has occurred. Although experiments set up on farms where farmers control the cultural practices for both technologies can be used to measure the impact, biases may still be introduced if some of the decisions are left to the researchers, and these decisions differ from those farmers would make.

A remaining source of potential bias arises when farmers alone make all the decisions. If farmers assign fields other than randomly between the technologies (that is, taking into account the recent cropping history, the natural fertility, or pest incidence, or other factors that determine the relative profitability of the alternatives), the comparison may be distorted. For instance, farmers might plant herbicide-tolerant varieties on heavily weed-infested fields to "clean them up" and traditional varieties on cleaner fields. The advantage of the herbicide-tolerant variety in weed-infested conditions would be masked in a simple comparison that would implicitly assume the fields were identical. Furthermore, the dynamic benefits from the cleanup would be left out of a simple assessment. So, too, a downward bias in measuring economic impact could result if pesticide-inherent crops are grown in remote fields where pest control is generally more difficult, or if they are grown primarily in fields with heavier infestations of both target and nontarget pests.

Farmer Surveys

Two general types of farmer surveying methods gather evidence on the economic impact of transgenic crops: area-frame surveys by the U.S. Department of Agriculture (USDA) and whole-farm surveys by individual researchers or by marketing research firms. Each method has advantages and disadvantages.

Field-Level Surveys. The USDA and other national departments of agriculture acquire data about production practices, costs, and returns periodically using a combination of area-frame and list-frame sampling techniques. The area-frame sampling technique uses various types of geographic representations of land area to divide land area into small segments (about one square mile). Then a random sample of these segments is chosen for further study. Usually, field investigators personally interview the operator of the land in a chosen segment (NASS no date). During the personal interview, a further randomization takes place to choose one field about which to ask detailed questions about production practices, costs, returns, or other desired information. For example, on the 1999 Agricultural Resource Management Study (ARMS) Upland Cotton Production Practices Report, the only farm-level questions about production practices, costs, or returns are "How many acres of cotton did this operation plant this year?" and "What is the total number of upland cotton fields that were planted this year?" (NASS 1999, 2). The rest of the production questions pertain to the randomly selected field.

One survey question asks the type of seed used in the field (genetically modified, herbicide-resistant *Bt* variety for insect resistance, variety with both insect and herbicide resistance, or other). If the farmer reported "other," there is no way to tell whether the field is part of a farm where transgenic technology has not been adopted at all or if it just happens to be a field on a farm where there is partial adoption (either true partial adoption or a required refuge field where conventional cotton is grown). Since there have been demonstrated differences between adopters and nonadopters of almost all new agricultural technologies or techniques that can also influence yield, production practices, production costs, or returns, the economic impact due solely to the technology cannot be known from this type of survey. For example, the difference in yield between the transgenic crop and the conventional crop cannot be calculated on each farm under the same management and general growing conditions. It can only be calculated as an average of all selected fields planted with the transgenic crop against the average of all fields not planted with the transgenic crop.

USDA National Agricultural Statistics Service (NASS) surveys have a large sample size, are conducted in person (producing a high response rate), and are generally conducted over a number of years with largely the same questions asked each time, so they are the only source of long-term, national, public information about these technologies. Several marketing firms have conducted surveys for the companies producing the technologies, but this information is not available in the public domain.

Farm-Level Surveys. The only way to hold constant the other factors that can influence the difference between the two technologies is to ask adopting farmers about the transgenic acres and the nontransgenic acres on their farm. They are the optimizers, both in their choice of whether or not to adopt and in the input choices and production method for each technology. As noted above, this also means that optimizing farmers will choose to allocate their transgenic and nontransgenic acres according to the relative advantages of the alternatives within their farm, which means that each variety will do better on average than if the varieties had been assigned at random among acres. Hence, a comparison of commercial performance of varietal technologies, even within a farm, would tend to understate the impact of adoption of the new technology, which presumably has been applied where it does comparatively better.

Table 8.5   Comparing means of different groups of respondent farmers and farms:
The case of *Bt* cotton impacts in the southeast, 1996

| | Group comparison | | |
| | Adopters who planted both: | Adopters' *Bt* acres versus | All farms: All *Bt* acres |
Indicator/state	*Bt* versus conventional acres	nonadopters' conventional acres	versus all conventional acres
Yield difference	*(pounds lint per acre)*		
Alabama	166	230	206
Georgia	84	216	158
North Carolina	−3.2	−11	−14
South Carolina	119	113	109
Insecticide cost difference	*(dollars per acre)*		
Alabama	3.10	−2.34	−0.87
Georgia	−29.67	−34.81	−28.07
North Carolina	−27.49	−16.95	−17.68
South Carolina	−31.12	−20.51	−23.93
Spray number difference	*(number of insecticide applications per acre)*		
Alabama	0.31	−0.06	1.81
Georgia	−2.68	−1.26	1.70
North Carolina	−2.38	−2.11	2.51
South Carolina	−2.46	−2.47	0.46

Source: Marra, Hubbell, and Carlson (1997).

Table 8.5 illustrates the role of optimizing behavior. These data are taken from a 1996 farm-level survey by North Carolina State University and the University of Georgia. A total of 1,000 cotton farmers from the four southeastern states (Alabama, Georgia, North Carolina, and South Carolina) were surveyed by mail, with a follow-up mailing and some telephone follow-up. The proportion of regional cotton acreage in each state was used to stratify the sample. The usable response rate was 36 percent (Marra, Hubbell, and Carlson 1997).

Economic impacts of transgenic crops, in terms of differences in yield, insecticide cost and pesticide use differences, are calculated three ways in Table 8.5. The first column of numbers represents differences between the two technologies (*Bt* cotton and conventional cotton) calculated within an adopting farmer's farm. The last column represents differences calculated as if the data came from a field-level survey, similar to the NASS surveys described above. Notice the disparity between the two estimates in every category. There are two contributing factors. Farmers who do not adopt the technology are either: (a) less educated with smaller farms and generally lower yields (which would make the difference in yields larger in the "all farms" column and the pesticide use differences smaller), or (b) operating farms with higher yields and less pest pressure to begin with (which would make the difference in yields smaller in the "all farms" column and the pesticide use differences larger) (Marra, Hubbell, Carlson 2001 and Ervin et al. 2000). Therefore, although we cannot assign any particular bias to the numbers calculated from field-level surveys, we can say they are likely to be different compared with the impacts calculated from within-farm comparisons.

Comparing the difference in the number of insecticide applications per acre across the columns highlights this point. In the within-farm comparison, there is either a very slight increase or a significant decrease in insecticide sprays on the transgenic acres, while the "all farms" column shows a consistent increase in insecticide sprays. The estimates in the middle column also illustrate the degree to which grouping of observations or survey methods can change the estimates. Given that these types of comparisons are quoted in the popular press and used by other researchers and interest groups, errors of this magnitude can cause grave concern (Wolfenbarger and Phifer 2000). It is important to get these numbers right.

The calculations in Table 8.5 are examples of the great differences one can encounter when the underlying survey methodology differs. These comparisons should be made over a number of crop years before confidence can be placed in any systematic biases found in the estimates. Estimates over time from the same source are not available, but in some cases for some transgenic crops, we can begin to make the first, tentative estimates of some of the economic impacts at the farm level based on information from a combination of field trials that mimic farmer production practices; on-farm, side-by-side comparisons; and farmer or consultant surveys. This empirical evidence is the subject of the next section.

Empirical Evidence of Farm-Level Impacts

A search of the relevant academic journals, Internet searches, and inquiries of researchers who work in this area produced a number of estimates of several measures of farm-level impacts associated with commercially available transgenic crops.[3] Some ex ante estimates were discovered, as well. Estimates of yield differences, revenue differences, pesticide cost differences, pesticide use differences and net returns to transgenic crops were collected directly where available or, where possible, imputed from the reported information. Sources examined fall into one of the following categories: the various types of field trials listed in Table 8.4, farmer and consultant surveys, studies reporting ex ante estimates of economic impacts, or field-level surveys.[4]

Estimates known to be erroneous based on the reasoning above were first eliminated from consideration. Then, for groups of studies in which enough estimates remained for a particular combination of impact measure, location, and transgene type, the mean and a range of the estimates are reported in Tables 8.6 and 8.7, by crop/event.

Most of the impact measures to date have been for *Bt* cotton, *Bt* corn, and RR soybeans. The range of yield differences between *Bt* and conventional cotton appears quite large, mostly because of the wide range of pest incidence in the years since the commercial introduction of *Bt* cotton. Across the U.S. Cotton Belt, a much higher incidence of the bollworm/budworm complex that *Bt* cotton is designed to control occurred in 1997 than in 1996, for example. Even so, in 9 of the 11 states, average yields for *Bt* cotton exceeded those of conventional cotton. There is also evidence of reduced pesticide use with *Bt* cotton—on average, a reduction of between 1.3 and 3 pesticide sprays per season. Nine of 10 states report a reduction in average pesticide costs (Arkansas is the exception), while in all states where data permit comparisons, *Bt* cotton was more profitable than its conventional counterpart. The mean profit advantage ranges from about $20 to almost $100 per acre, including the costs of the technology fee. The most prevalent impact measure so far for *Bt* corn is the yield difference.[5] In most locations and years, however, the incidence of European corn borer is not thought to be significant enough to control with pesticides, so the yield difference is sufficient to calculate total additional monetary benefits. In the states where a range could be reported, all show an unambiguous yield increase with *Bt* corn, although one estimate (Illinois 1998) is below the break even yield increase to cover the additional technology cost (assuming US$2.00 per bushel for the corn and an US$8.00 per acre technology fee). Studies estimating the impact of *Bt* corn across the Corn Belt give yield increases ranging from 5.3 to 14.9 bushels per acre. The mean yield increases are all in the profitable range, with results for some states (Illinois and Minnesota) indicating substantial profitability from early adoption of *Bt* corn. If identity preservation does not become an issue, or if the costs of segregation are comparatively minor, then *Bt* corn should continue to be profitable.

Studies from Illinois and North Carolina show positive mean yield differences for RR soybeans, with yield gains of up to 6.83 bushels per acre in North Carolina in 1997. However, most of the available evidence for RR soybeans shows a slight drop in yields, the greatest of which is a loss of 5.7 bushels per acre in Nebraska in 1997. The only profit estimates available so far indicate a net return averaging $14 per acre to using RR soybeans in North Carolina. The results for RR soybeans are a good example of where the results from variety trials are insufficient to draw conclusions about the profitability of using transgenic versus conventional crop varieties. Although more research is required to be definitive, the widespread adoption of this technology clearly indicates that the production costs are sufficiently lower to make RR soybeans profitable for the vast majority of growing conditions and farm types throughout the United States.

Table 8.6 Summary of farm-level impact evidence for Bt cotton

	Differences in:															
	Yield				Pesticide cost				Pesticide use				Profit			
State	No. of estimates	Mean	Min.	Max.	No. of estimates	Mean	Min.	Max.	No. of estimates	Mean	Min.	Max.	No. of estimates	Mean	Min.	Max.
	(count)	(pounds lint per acre)			(count)	(dollars per acre)			(count)	(sprays per acre)			(count)	(dollars per acre)		
BT COTTON																
Alabama	4	143.5	38.0	231.5	2	-32.4	3.1	-68.0	2	-1.3	0.3	-3.0	2	77.6	38.7	116.5
Arizona	8	116.7	-331.5	917.0	9	17.1	97.0	-24.6	3	-2.2	-1.8	-2.5	10	57.5	-104.0	465.0
Georgia	3	75.2	38.0	104.0	3	-23.4	27.5	-68.0	3	-2.7	-2.5	-3.0	3	92.0	38.7	169.2
Louisiana	2	-7.5	-37.0	22.0	2	-20.0	-15.4	-24.6	2	-2.4	-2.2	-2.5	2	16.5	-3.1	36.0
Mississippi	8	22.6	-73.0	92.0	8	-5.1	13.8	-24.6	4	-2.4	-1.3	-3.3	6	34.5	-3.1	79.5
North Carolina	8	41.6	-35.7	182.5	2	-14.3	-1.2	-27.5	2	-2.4	-2.4	-2.5	8	20.5	-25.3	95.1
Oklahoma	4	168.0	123.0	203.0					4	-3.4	-2.3	-6.5	4	53.8	25.5	85.5
South Carolina	2	90.5	62.0	119.0	2	-16.2	-1.2	-31.1	2	-2.5	-2.5	-2.5	4	51.8	17.1	80.1
Tennessee	2	-79.0	-243.0	85.0	1	-5.6			1	-1.8			2	67.5	60.7	74.3
Texas	3	116.6	81.0	177.5									1	46.0		
Virginia	1	62.0			1	-1.2			1	-2.5			1	41.7		
China	1	325.0			1	-7.1							1	66.0		
Mexico	1	182.0			1	36.0							1	173.0		
RR COTTON																
Arkansas	1	-150											1	17.1		
Tennessee	1	-243			1	-145.3							1	74.3		
BT/RR COTTON																
Arkansas	2	292.8	-331.5	917.0	2	79.5	-269.0	159.0					2	243.0	21.0	465.0

Source: Compiled by author.

Table 8.7   Summary of farm-level impact evidence for other technologies and crops

Transgene type	State			Yield				Profit	
		No. of estimates	Mean	Min.	Max.	No. of estimates	Mean	Min.	Max.
		(count)	*(bushels per acre)*			*(count)*	*(dollars per acre)*		
Bt corn	Corn Belt	6	10.8	5.3	17.0	1	60.1		
	Illinois	4	16.3	1.5	30.0	1	23.4		
	Iowa	5	7.1	2.9	12.2				
	Kansas	3	7.8	3.7	12.0				
	Minnesota	1	18.2	18.2	18.2				
	Nebraska	2	7.4	4.2	10.5				
	South Dakota	2	10.3	7.7	12.9				
	United States	5	6.7	3.3	12.0	3	4.8	−1.8	18.0
RR Canola	Australia	2	24.49	7.62	41.36				
	Canada	3	−1.9	−2.7	−1.0	2	11.3	−1.9	24.5
			(tons per acre)						
VR Potatoes	Mexico	6	23.7	6.7	43.0	6	288.8	69.6	559.4
			(bushels per acre)						
RR Soybeans	Illinois	5	1.3	−0.3	1.8				
	Iowa	3	−3.4	−4.0	−2.8				
	Kansas	1	−3.0	−3.0	−3.0				
	Michigan	3	−2.2	−2.5	−1.7				
	Minnesota	3	−4.4	−4.6	−4.2				
	Nebraska	3	−4.4	−5.8	−2.1				
	North Carolina	4	2.7	−2.3	6.8	2	14.0	6.0	22.1
	Ohio	3	−2.3	−3.1	−1.7				
	South Dakota	3	−3.8	−5.0	−2.4				
	Wisconsin	3	−1.2	−2.0	0.1				
			(tons per acre)						
IR Sweet Potatoes	Kenya	2	12.1	7.8	16.3	2	65.5	42.3	88.6
VR Sweet Potatoes	Kenya	2	16.6	14.7	18.5	2	88.7	76.2	101.1
Bt Irish	Illinois					3	15.5	−4.6	37.2
Potatoes	United States					3	22.4	−1.8	51.0

Source: Compiled by author.

Aggregate Impacts

A few studies have attempted to estimate the aggregate economic impact of a particular transgenic crop (or group of crops) and the distribution of the impact on the different sectors involved. Each of these has had to employ some measure of farm-level effects. Most of the studies present their results in terms of total welfare effects and the distribution of those effects under various scenarios, or assumptions, regarding parameters they view important. Moschini, Lapan, and Sobolevsky (1999) model the global welfare effects of RR soybeans. They develop a three-region world model that includes a monopolist technology seller as well as consumers and producers. They assume the technology results in a US$20 per hectare increase in profit at the farm level, based on conditions in Iowa in 1997–98. Using the methodology outlined in Alston, Norton, and Pardey (1998), they estimate changes in consumer, producer, and total surplus for the United States, South America, and the rest of the world (ROW), and the surplus accruing to the monopolist. Moschini, Lapan, and Sobolevsky (MLS) generally find large increases in total social welfare from the technology, but mostly negative producer surplus changes in all regions. They examine the sensitivity of the results to the supply shift assumptions and find that halving or doubling of the profit change for any region can have a large impact on the size and distribution of the welfare changes.

Falck-Zepeda, Traxler, and Nelson (1999) model the change in welfare effects from adoption of Bt cotton and RR soybeans using a two-region general framework (United States and ROW) similar in structure to the MLS model (except that the farm-level benefit is allowed to vary among U.S. states creating several subregions) and based on the Alston, Norton, and Pardey paradigm. Falck-Zepeda, Traxler, and Nelson (FTN) use confidential market survey data, as well as published agronomic and farmer survey data to estimate their supply shifts in the United States and assume that the ROW either experiences the same or half of the efficiency gains as the United States. FTN find that, for the 1996 and 1997 crop, Bt cotton adoption generated large increases in global social surplus and significant increases in U.S. producer surplus at the expense of ROW producers. For RR soybeans in 1997, FTN find again, large global surplus increases and large U.S. producer surplus increases with relatively small decreases in producer surplus in ROW.

Pray et al. (1999) consider the impact of Bt cotton in China. They collected farm-level data on the net benefits of the Bt varieties (Appendix Table 8A.1) and, using the same basic modeling approach as MLS and FTN, estimate the distribution of benefits among farmers, seed companies, and research institutes/companies. They find significant aggregate net benefits to farmers and much smaller benefits to the seed companies and research institutes/companies. Pray et al. also present the only quantified farm-level nonpecuniary benefits I have found. They report that only 4 percent of farmers planting the Bt varieties suffered any effects of pesticide poisoning, compared with 33 percent of those who did not plant Bt cotton.

Some ex ante studies of the potential for transgenic crops in developing countries have been undertaken. One is a study of virus- and weevil-resistant sweet potatoes in Kenya (Qaim 1999) and another is a study of virus-resistant potatoes in Mexico (Qaim 1998). The farm-level benefits used in both studies are based on a consensus of expert opinion. The aggregate net benefits are calculated using the Alston, Norton, and Pardey method for estimating changes in regional producer surplus and consumer surplus resulting from technical change. Qaim finds that central and eastern Kenyan producers would benefit much less than western producers and that the benefits accruing to all groups are greater for the weevil-resistance technology compared with the virus- resistance technology. In the Mexican case study, producers were divided into small, medium, and large farmers, and the benefits were measured with and without the potential for trade. Qaim reports that trade reduced the benefits to this small-country producer and that some trait and distribution assumption combinations favored small farms, while others favored the larger farms. In all cases, Qaim estomates a large net gain to all sectors and farm sizes.

All of the above studies of the aggregated effects of transgenic crop adoption were completed before the controversy over the safety of GM food grew to the point that identity preservation became an issue. Fulton and Keyowski (2000), in a theoretical modeling exercise, point to the importance of farmer heterogeneity in modeling the distribution of benefits when the transgenic and traditional markets are segregated.

Burton et al. (2000), using the same methodology as the other aggregate studies, considered the effects of various identity preservation schemes on the total and distributional aspects of the benefits from adoption of GM canola. Based on Fulton and Keyowski, they assume that adoption of GM canola decreased marginal costs at the farm level by 8.5 percent. They divide the world into consumers and producers of GM and non-GM canola and estimate the distribution of total surplus accruing to each group under various assumptions about the form of technical change, the incidence of identity preservation costs, and the impact of a technology fee. They find that, under most scenarios, consumers of the non-GM canola lose, while consumers of GM canola gain. Changes in producer surplus vary widely, depending on the assumptions listed above, but producers of the non-GM canola seem to fare better in most cases than the producers of the GM canola.

Conclusion

It is worth emphasizing again that estimates of farm-level impact summarized in Tables 8.6 and 8.7 are for a small number of locations and years. As more useful data become available for economic comparisons, estimates of this type can be viewed with more confidence. It is fair to say only three things at this point with much confidence:

- Growing transgenic cotton is likely to result in reduced pesticide use in most years in most states, and it is more likely than not to be a relatively profitable enterprise in most of the U.S. Cotton Belt.

- *Bt* corn will provide a small but significant yield increase in most years across the Corn Belt, and in some years and some places the increase will be substantial.

- Although there is some evidence of a small yield loss in the RR soybean varieties, in most years and locations savings in pesticide costs and, possibly, tillage costs will more than offset the lost revenue from the yield discrepancy.

There are still many farm-level impacts, the value of which no one has attempted to measure thus far. The most important of these, in my view, is the "convenience factor" for the RR crops: farmers report that even if there is a slight "yield drag" with RR soybeans, the reduced herbicide costs and the extra time available to attend to their higher-value crops are more than sufficient compensation. Farmers are optimizers and they generally make good decisions given the information they have available to them at the time. The impressive rates of adoption for many of these transgenic crops are strong evidence of their relative value. Only time will tell if consumer concerns will slow this pace significantly and permanently, but if these concerns can be addressed satisfactorily, then many of the first-generation transgenic crops are a win-win situation for farmers. They can expect higher profits and environmentally safer growing conditions. If identity preservation becomes a fact of life, then these farm-level benefits are much more open to question to the extent that either adopting farmers have to pay the costs of segregation or transgenic varieties incur significant price discounts.

Policymakers and consumers will benefit from better estimates of the farm-level benefits because they are part of the cost of regulation. Additional studies are warranted to estimate the potential pecuniary benefits more precisely by using on-farm results based on farmer decisions, especially in light of new developments at the final product level for some crops. It is time also for an initial attempt to quantify the non-pecuniary benefits.

Appendix Table 8A.1 Ranges of benefits by crop, geographic area, and study

Event	State/ Region/Country[a]	Reference	Study type[b]	Period	Yield	Herbicide cost	No. of herbicide sprays	Insecticide cost	No. of insecticide sprays	Profit
						Evidence (Transgenic–Conventional) per acre				
					(bushels)	(U.S. dollars)	(count)	(U.S. dollars)	(count)	(U.S. dollars)
CORN										
Bt	Iowa	Rice and Pilcher 1998	A	1997	7.6					
		Gianessi and Carpenter 1999	A	1997–98	2.9–12.2					
	Illinois	Gianessi and Carpenter 1999	A	1997–98	1.5–17.4					23.37
		European Commission 2000	A	1998	16.33					
		The Economist 2000	B	1998	30					
	Kansas	Gianessi and Carpenter 1999	A	1997–98	3.7–12					
		Sloderbeck, Buschman, Dumler, and Higgins 1999	A	1997–98 avg.	7.7					
	Minnesota	Rice and Pilcher 1998	A	1997	18.2					
	Nebraska	Gianessi and Carpenter 1999	A	1997–98	4.2–10.5					
	South Dakota	Gianessi and Carpenter 1999	A	1997–98	7.7–12.9					
	U.S. Heartland	Hart 1999	F	1997					0.06	
	U.S. Corn Belt	European Commission 2000	A	1997	14.9					
	United States	Gianessi and Carpenter 1999	A	1997–98	4.6–9.4					
	U.S. Corn Belt		A	1997	10.8–17					
			A	1998	7					
RR	U.S. Heartland	Hart 1999	F	1997			0.3			
COTTON						(pounds lint)				
Bt	Alabama	Jones et al. 1996	A	1994–95	138.5–231.5					
		Marra, Hubbell, and Carlson 1997	B	1996	165.9			3.1	0.31	116.48
		Mullins and Mills 1999	A	1998	38			–67.99	–3	38.74
	Arkansas	Bryant, Robertson, and Lorenz 1999	A	1996–97				4.38–11.29		–26.95–86.74
		Bryant, Robertson, and Lorenz 1998	A	1997	–24					–25

Region	Study		Year					
	Mullins, and Mills 1999	C	1998	22		-15.43	-2.2	36.03
	Benson and Hendrix 1999	A	1998	-37		-24.63	-2.54	-3.12
Bt/RR	Bryant, Allen, Bourland, and Earnest 1999	A	1998	917	62	97		465
	Bryant, Allen, Bourland, and Earnest 1999	A	1998	-331.5	-366	97		21
Bt/RR	Bryant, Allen, Bourland, and Earnest 1999	A	1998	917	62	97		465
Bt	Bryant, Robertson, and Lorenz 1999	A	1998			-10.22		64.52
	Capps, Allen, Earnest, Tugwell, and Kharbouti 1999	A	1998	452				
	Mullins, and Mills 1999	C	1998	85		-5.57	-1.8	60.7
China	Pray, Ma, Huang, and Qiao 1999	B	1999	325		-71		66.3
Georgia	Marra, Hubbell, and Carlson 1997	B	1996	83.55		-29.67	-2.68	169.24
	Stark 1997	C	1996	104		27.5	-2.5	68
	Mullins and Mills 1999	A	1998	38		-67.99	-3	38.74
Louisiana	Mullins and Mills 1999	C	1998	22		-15.43	-2.2	36.03
	Benson and Hendrix 1999	C	1998	-37		-24.63	-2.54	-3.12
Mexico	Magana et al. 1999	A	1998	182		36		173
Mississippi	Wier, Mullins, and Mills 1998	A	1995	92		-22.7		79.5
	Cooke and Freeland 1998	A	1996	-73 to 0		0-0.67		
	Wier, Mullins, and Mills 1998	A	1996-97	46-84		1.87-5.19		24.71-50.73
	Gibson et al. 1997	A	1996	47		13.84		16.23
	Layton, Stewart, Williams, and Long 1998	A	1997-98				-3.34 to -1.34	
	Mullins and Mills 1999	C	1998	22		-15.43	-2.2	36.03
	Benson and Hendrix 1999	C	1998	-37		-24.63	-2.54	-3.12
North Central	Jones et al. 1996	A	1994-95	63.5-182.5				
	Bacheler, Mott, and Morrison 1998	D	1996					7.49-8.96
	Marra, Hubbell, and Carlson 1997	B	1996	-3.21		-27.48	-2.38	3.54
	Mullins and Mills 1999	C	1998	62		-1.19	-2.5	41.71

Appendix Table 8A.1 Ranges of benefits by crop, geographic area, and study (continued)

Event	State/Region/Country[a]	Reference	Study type[b]	Period	Yield	Evidence (Transgenic–Conventional) per acre				
						Herbicide cost	No. of herbicide sprays	Insecticide cost	No. of insecticide sprays	Profit
					(bushels)	(U.S.dollars)	(count)	(U.S.dollars)	(count)	(U.S.dollars)
	Oklahoma	Karner, Goodson, and Hutson 2000	E	1996–99	120–203				−6.5 to −2.3	25.46–85.53
	South Carolina	Marra, Hubbell, and Carlson 1997	B	1996	119			−31.12	−2.47	80.06
		ReJesus, Greene, Hammig, and Curtis 1997	A	1996						68.44
		Mullins and Mills 1999	A	1998	62–85			−5.57 to −1.19	−2.5 to −1.8	41.71–60.7
	Texas	Jones et al. 1996	A	1994–95	91.4–177.5					45.99–52.72
		Speed and Ferreira 1998	A	1996–97	80.6–81	2.11–9.09				41.71
	Virginia	Mullins and Mills 1999	A	1998	62			−1.19	−2.5	
	Cotton Belt	Hart 1999	F	1997				−0.92 to −3.03		
RR	Mississippi Portal	Hart 1999	F	1997		−1.32				17.12
Bt	South Carolina	ReJesus Greene, Hammig, and Curtis 1997	A	1996						
RR	Arkansas	Bryant, Allen, Bourlan, and Earnest 1999	A	1998	−150	2		0		−104
	Tenessee	Slinsky, Edens, Larson, and Hayes 1998	A	1996	−243	−145.3				74.26
Bt/Rr	Arkansas	Bryant, Allen, Bourland, and Earnest 1999	A	1998	−331.5	−366		97		21
SOYBEANS										
Ht	U.S. Heartland	Bryant, Allen, Bourland, and Earnest 1999	F	1997			−0.54			
	Mississippi Portal		F	1997			−0.53			
	North Carolina		F	1997			0.07			
Ht	Pacific Garden	Hart 1999	F	1997			−1.1			
QE	United States	McVey, Pautsch, and Baumel 1995	F	ex ante						0.49/bu– 0.11/bu
RR	Illinois	European Commission 2000	A	1997	1.71					
	Iowa		A	1997	−3.42					
	Kansas		A	1997	−2.96					
	Minnesota		A	1997	−4.16					
	Mississippi	Couvillion, Kari, Hudson, and Allen 2000	F	1997–98		−6.69–4.24				−4.24–6.69
	North Central	Harley 1999	B	1996–97	3.24–6.83					

	Location	Study	Type	Year	Value (hundredweight)	
		Dunphy and York 2000	A	1999	-2.3	
		Coble 1997	A	1994–96 avg.		6
	South Dakota	Dunphy, Heiniger, and York 2000	A	1996–98 avg.		22
	Wisconsin	European Commission 2000	A	1997	-4.16	22
			A	1997	-1.59	
	United States	Moschini, Lapan, and Sobolevsky 1999	E	ex ante	2.25	20
	Michigan	European Commission 2000	A	1997	-1.71	
	Nebraska		A	1997	-5.75	
	Ohio		A	1997	-1.71	
CANOLA						
RR	Australia	Pioneer Hybrid 2000	A	1999	7.82–41.36	-84.97 to 95.51
	Alberta, Canada	European Commission 2000	A	1998	-2 to -1	
	Saskatchewan, Canada		A	1999	-2.7	-16.83
					-10	
IRISH POTATOES						
Bt	United States	Gianessi and Carpenter 1999	F	1997–98		-1.81 to 18
	Illinois		F	1996–98		-4.63 to 37.24
	N.W. United States		F	1998		51
Virus-resistant PVX-PVY	Mexico	Qaim 1998	E	ex ante	6.68–10.72	69.6–139.84
Virus-resistant PVX-PVY-PLRV			E	ex ante	34.98–42.98	390.9–559.38
SWEET POTATOES						
Virus-Resistant	Kenya	Qaim 1998	E	ex-ante	7.8–16.33	42.31–101.12

Source: Compiled by author.

Note: Under "study type," A denotes field trial-conventional versus transgenic varieties; B denotes farmer survey-side-by-side comparisons; C denotes field trial-side-by-side, on-farm comparisons; D denotes paired field comparisons; E denotes expert opinion; F denotes other means of comparison.

Notes

The author thanks Alice Kassens, Bailey Norwood, and Patricia Zambrano for some original sleuthing, and Julian Alston and Philip Pardey for substantial input that improved the paper significantly.

1. An event is a specific gene insertion in a particular crop that results in a desired expressed trait in the crop. For example, insertion of the *Bt* cry1A(c) protein into various cotton varieties is considered to be one event.

2. With pesticide-inherent crops, some pests with resistance may survive. Providing a portion of the field where susceptible pests can survive and mate with the resistant pests slows the rate of resistance buildup.

3. Several studies, including York and Culpepper (1999) and Wilcut et al. (1999) report only percentage changes, which cannot be compared directly with measures from the studies presented here.

4. All of the data collected are presented in Appendix 8A. Though the estimates in the appendix are not an exhaustive list (particularly in light of the large number of unpublished field trials and market surveys that are not accessible in the public domain), they should be sufficient to begin to make some inferences about farm-level impacts.

5. An interesting and well-done study by Hyde et al. (2000) of the potential value of *Bt* corn in the Corn Belt gives ranges of values under various probabilities of European corn borer infestation (presumably corresponding to different sections of the Corn Belt) and risk attitudes, but they are not specific enough for the purposes of this discussion.

References

AGBIOS Inc. (Agricultural and Biotechnology Strategies [Canada] Inc.). 2001. Global status of approved genetically modified plants. (June). <http://www.agbios.com/_Synopsis.asp>. Accessed July, 2001.

Alston, J. M., G. Norton, and P. G. Pardey. 1998. *Science under scarcity: Principles and practice for agricultural research evaluation and priority setting.* Wallingford, U.K.: CAB International.

Bacheler, J. S., D. W. Mott, and D. E. Morrison. 1998. Large-scale evaluation of Bollgard resistance to multiple pests in North Carolina under grower conditions. In *Proceedings of the Beltwide Cotton Conference*, Vol. 2, 961–64. Memphis, Tenn., U.S.A.: National Cotton Council.

Beach, E., and G. Carlson. 1993. A hedonic analysis of herbicides: Do user safety and water quality matter? *American Journal of Agricultural Economics* 75: 612–23.

Benson, M. A., and W. H. Hendrix III. 1999. Economics of a tracer/karate Z conventional cotton program vs. *Bt* cotton. In *Proceedings of the Beltwide Cotton Conference*, Vol. 2, 1143–45. Memphis, Tenn., U.S.A.: National Cotton Council.

Bryant, K., C. T. Allen, F. M. Bourland, and L. D. Earnest. 1999. Cost and return comparisons of RR and Bollgard cotton varieties. In *Proceedings of the Beltwide Cotton Conference*, Vol. 1, 236–38. Memphis, Tenn., U.S.A.: National Cotton Council.

Bryant, K. J., W. C. Robertson, and G. M. Lorenz III. 1998. Economic evaluation of Bollgard Cotton in Arkansas: 1997. In *Proceedings of the Beltwide Cotton Conference*, Vol. 1, 388–89. Memphis, Tenn., U.S.A.: National Cotton Council.

————. 1999. Economic evaluation of Bollgard cotton in Arkansas. In *Proceedings of the Beltwide*

Cotton Conference, Vol. 1, 349–50. Memphis, Tenn., U.S.A.: National Cotton Council.

Burton, M., S. James, B. Lindner, and J. Pluske. 2000. A way forward for Frankenstein foods. Paper presented at *The Economics of Agricultural Biotechnology*, Fourth Conference of the International Consortium on Agricultural Biotechnology Research, Ravello, Italy, August 24–28.

Capps, C. D., C. Allen, L. Earnest, P. Tugwell, and M. Kharbouti. 1999. Performance of Bollgard cotton with and without insecticides. In *Proceedings of the Beltwide Cotton Conference*, Vol. 2, 1239–41. Memphis, Tenn., U.S.A.: National Cotton Council.

Carpenter, J. E., and L.P. Gianessi. 2001. *Agricultural biotechnology: Updated benefit estimates.* Washington, D.C.: National Center for Food and Agricultural Policy.

Coble, H. 1997. Unpublished field trials, North Carolina State University, Raleigh, N.C., U.S.A. Mimeo.

Cooke, F. T., and T. B. Freeland. 1998. Some economic considerations for *Bt* cotton planting in the Yazoo-Mississippi Delta. In *Proceedings of the Beltwide Cotton Conference*, Vol. 1, 383–84. Memphis, Tenn., U.S.A.: National Cotton Council.

Couvillion, W., F. Kari, D. Hudson, and A. Allen. 2000. *A preliminary economic assessment of Roundup Ready soybeans in Mississippi.* Mississippi State University Research Report 2000–005, Mississippi State.

Dunphy, J., and A. York. 2000. Progress report to North Carolina Soybean Producers' Association Inc. Raleigh. Available at <http://www.ncsoy.org/Research/1999/99-06/99-06.htm>. Accessed September 25, 2001.

Dunphy, J., R. Heiniger, and A. York. 2000. Progress report to North Carolina Soybean Producers' Association Inc. Raleigh. Available at <http://www.ncsoy.org/Research_/2000_Annual_Reports/2000_annual_reports.htm>. Accessed September 25, 2001.

ERS (Economic Research Service of the U.S. Department of Agriculture). 2000. Genetically engineered crops: Has adoption reduced pesticide use? Agricultural Outlook, Washington, D.C.

———. 2001. Agricultural biotechnology: Adoption of biotechnology and its production. <http://www.ers.usda.gov/Briefing/biotechnology/chapter1.htm> linked to "Excel spreadsheet" at http://www.ers.usda.gov/Briefing/biotechnology/data/gmoacres1.xls. Acessed August, 2001 (May 31).

Ervin, D. E., S. Batie, R. Welsh, C. Carpentier, J. I. Fern, N. J. Richman, and M. A. Schulz. 2000. Transgenic crops: An environmental assessment. Policy Studies Report No. 15. Arlington, Va., U.S.A.: Henry A. Wallace Center for Agricultural and Environmental Policy, Winrock International.

European Commission. 2000. Economic impacts of genetically modified crops on the agri-food sector. <http://europa.eu.int/comm/ dgo61/publi/gmo/fullrep>. Accessed December 26, 2000.

Falck -Zepeda, J., G. Traxler, and R. Nelson. 1999. Rent creation and distribution from biotechnology innovations: The case of *Bt* cotton and herbicide-tolerant soybeans. Paper presented at Transitions in Agbiotech: Economics of Strategy and Policy, NE–165 conference, June 24–25, Washington, D.C.

FAO (Food and Agriculture Organization of the United Nations). 2000. FAOSTAT Agriculture Data. <http://www.apps.fao.org/page/collections>. Accessed November 28, 2000.

FDA (Food and Drug Administration). 2001. List of completed consultations on bioengineered foods. <http://www.cfsan.fda.gov/~lrd/biocon.html>. Accessed June 2001.

Fernandez-Cornejo, J., C. Klotz-Ingram, and S. Sans. 1999. Farm-level effects of adopting genetically engineered crops in the U.S.A. Selected paper presented at Transitions in Agbiotech: Economics of Strategy and Policy NE–165 Conference, June 24–25, Washington, D.C.

Fulton, M., and L. Keyowski. 2000. The impact of technological innovation on producer returns: The case of genetically modified canola. Storrs, Conn., U.S.A.: Food Marketing Policy Center, University of Connecticut.

Gianessi, L., and J. Carpenter. 1999. Agricultural biotechnology: Insect control benefits. Washington, D.C.: National Center for Food and Agricultural Policy.

————. 2000. Agricultural biotechnology: Benefits of transgenic soybeans. Washington, D.C.: National Center for Food and Agricultural Policy.

Gibson, J. W., D. Laughlin, R. Luttrell, D. Parker, J. Reed, and A. Harris. 1997. Comparison of costs and returns associated with Heliothis resistant *Bt* cotton to nonresistant varieties. In *Proceedings of the Beltwide Cotton Conference*, Vol. 1, 244–47. Memphis, Tenn., U.S.A.: National Cotton Council.

Harley, K. 1999. Unpublished survey data. North Carolina State University, Raleigh, N.C., U.S.A.

Hart, K., 1999. Biotech crops do not improve yield or cut pesticide costs, USDA Finds. *Pesticide and Toxic Chemical News*, July 1, 11–13.

Hyde, J., M. Martin, P. Preckel, C. R. Edwards. 2000. The economics of *Bt* corn: Valuing protection from the European corn borer. *Review of Agricultural Economics* 21 (2): 442–54.

James, C. 1996. *Global review of the field testing and commercializatiuon of transgenic plants*. International Service for the Acquisition of Agri-Biotech Application Brief No. 1. Ithaca, N.Y., U.S.A.

————. 1997. *Global status of transgenic crops in 1997*. International Service for the Acquisition of Agri-Biotech Application Brief No. 5. Ithaca, N.Y., U.S.A.

————. 1998. *Global review of commercialized transgenic crops: 1998*. International Service for the Acquisition of Agri-biotech Applications Brief No. 8. Ithaca, N.Y., U.S.A.

————. 1999. *Global review of commercialized transgenic crops*. International Service for the Acquisition of Agri-Biotech Applications Brief No. 12. Ithaca, N.Y., U.S.A.

————. 2000a. *Global status of commercialized transgenic crops, 1999*. International Service for the Acquisition of Agri-Biotech Applications Brief No. 17. Ithaca, N.Y., U.S.A.

————. 2000b. *Preview: Global review of commercialized transgenic crops, 2000*. International Service for the Acquisition of Agri-Biotech Applications Brief No. 21. Ithaca, N.Y., U.S.A.

James, C., and A. F. Krattiger. 1996. *Global review of field testing and commercialization of transgenic plants, 1986 to 1995: The first decade of crop biotechnology*. International Service for the Acquisition of Agri-Biotech Applications Brief No. 1. Ithaca, N.Y., U.S.A.

Jones, K, T. Kerby, H. Collins, T. Wofford, M. Bates, J. Presley, J. Burgess, B. Bueler, and R. Deaton. 1996. Performance of NuCOTN with Bollgard. In *Proceedings of the Beltwide Cotton Conference*, Vol. 1, 46–48. Memphis, Tenn., U.S.A.: National Cotton Council.

Karner, M, J. Goodson, A. Hutson. 2000. *Bt Cotton technology in Oklahoma: An overview*. OSU Current Report No. 7465. Stillwater: Oklahoma State University.

Kasler, D., and E. Lau. 2000. At Calgene, a harvest of uncertainty. Promise and peril: The future of biotechnology. *The Sacramento Bee*, May 7, 2000. <http://www.sacbee.com/news/projects/ biotechnology/>. Accessed November 13, 2000.

Layton, M. B., S. D. Stewart, M. R. Williams, and J. S. Long. 1999. Performance of *Bt* cotton in Mississippi, 1998. *Proceedings of the Beltwide Cotton Conference*, Vol. 2, 942–45. Memphis, Tenn., U.S.A.: National Cotton Council.

———. 1998. Performance of *Bt* cotton in Mississippi, 1997. In *Proceedings of the Beltwide Cotton Conference*, Vol. 2, 970–75. Memphis, Tenn., U.S.A.: National Cotton Council.

Magana-Magana, J. E., J. G. Garcia, A. J. O. Rodriguez, and J. M. O. Garcia. 1999. Comparative analysis of producing transgenic cotton varieties versus no transgenic variety in Delicias, Chihuahua, Mexico. In *Proceedings of the Beltwide Cotton Conference*, Vol. 1, 255–56. Memphis, Tenn., U.S.A.: National Cotton Council.

Marra, M. C., B. Hubbell, and G. A. Carlson. 1997. Unpublished survey data. North Carolina State University, Raleigh, N.C., U.S.A.

———. 2001. Information quality, technology depreciation, and *Bt* cotton adoption in the Southeast. *Journal of Agricultural and Resource Economics* 26 (1): 158–75.

McVey, M., G. Pautsch, and P. Baumel. 1995. Estimated domestic producer and end user benefits from genetically modifying U.S. soybeans. *Journal of Production Agriculture*. Vol. 8(2): 209–14.

Moschini, G., H. Lapan, and A. Sobolevsky. 1999. Trading technology as well as final products: Roundup Ready soybeans and welfare effects in the soybean complex. *The shape of the coming agricultural biotechnology transformation: Strategic investment and policy approaches from an economic perspective*. Rome, Italy.

Mullins, J. W., and J. M. Mills. 1999. Economics of Bollgard versus non-Bollgard cotton in 1998. In *Proceedings of the Beltwide Cotton Conference*, Vol. 2, 958–61. Memphis, Tenn., U.S.A.: National Cotton Council.

NASS (National Agricultural Statistics Service of the United States Department of Agriculture). 1999. *Agricultural resource management study: Upland cotton production practices report for 1999* (survey instrument). Washington, D.C.: U.S. Government Printing Office.

———. 2001. Crop production—acreage—supplement (PCP-BB). (Acreage, June 1996–2001, text and pdf files). <http://www.usda.mannlib.cornell.edu/reports/nassr/field/pcp-bba/>. Accessed July, 2001.

———. No date. NASS surveys: The foundation of estimates. <http://www/usda.gov/nass/nass-info/estimate.htm>.

Pioneer Hybrid International, Inc. 2000. Products and info: Canola. <http://www.pioneer.com/ australia/canola/44c71results>.

Pray, C. E., D. Ma, J. Huang, and F. Qiao. 1999. Impact of *Bt* cotton in China. Draft manuscript. Rutgers University, New Brunswick, N.J., U.S.A. Mimeo.

Qaim, M. 1998. *Transgenic virus resistant potatoes in Mexico: Potential social implications of North-South biotechnology transfer*. International Service for the Acquisition of Agri-Biotech Applications Brief No. 7. Ithaca, N.Y., U.S.A.

———. 1999. *The effects of Genetically Modified Orphan Commodities: Projections for Sweet Potato Production in Kenya*. International Service for the Acquisition of Agri-Biotech Applications Brief

No. 13. Ithaca, N.Y., U.S.A. and *Zentrum fur Entwicklungsforschung* (ZEF) [Centre for Development Research], Bonn, Germany.

ReJesus, R. M., J. K. Greene, M. D. Hammig and C. Curtis. 1997. Economic analysis of insect management strategies for transgenic *Bt* cotton production in South Carolina. In *Proceedings of the Beltwide Cotton Conference*, Vol. 1, 247–51. Memphis, Tenn., U.S.A.: National Cotton Council.

Rice, M., and C. D. Pilcher. 1998. Potential benefits and limitations of transgenic *Bt* corn for management of the European corn borer (Lepidoptera crambidae). *American Entomologist* 44 (1): 75–78.

Slinsky, S. P., E. R. Edens, J. A. Larson, and R. M. Hayes. 1998. Evaluation of cost and returns for Roundup Ready cotton. In *Proceedings of the Beltwide Cotton Conference*, Vol. 1, 340–43. Memphis, Tenn., U.S.A.: National Cotton Council.

Sloderbeck, P., L. Buschman, T. Dumler, and R. Higgins. 1999. *Bt* corn and Non-*Bt* corn refuges: How do the economics pencil out? Report, Kansas State University, Manhattan Kans., U.S.A. Mimeo.

Speed, T. R., and K. L. Ferreira. 1998. Performance of PM 2326RR and PM 2200RR on the Texas High Plains: A two-year summary. In *Proceedings of the Beltwide Cotton Conference*, Vol. 1, 565–66. Memphis, Tenn., U.S.A.: National Cotton Council.

Stark, Jr. C. R.1997. Economics of transgenic cotton: Some indications based on Georgia producers. In *Proceedings of the Beltwide Cotton Conference*, Vol. 1, 251–53. Memphis, Tenn., U.S.A.: National Cotton Council.

The Economist. 2000. Genetically modified crops: To plant or not to plant. January 14. <http://www.thecampaign.org/newsupdates/_januaryj.htm>. Accessed October 21, 2000.

Wier, A.T., J. W. Mullins and J. M. Mills. 1998. Bollgard cotton: Update and economic comparisons including new varieties. In *Proceedings of the Beltwide Cotton Conference*, Vol. 2, National Cotton Council, Memphis, TN, 1039–40.

Wilcut, J., S. Askew, B. Brecke, D. Bridges, S. Brown, J. Chandler, R. Hayes, J. Kendig, D. Miller, R. Nichols, and C. Snipes. 1999. A beltwide evaluation of weed management in transgenic and non-transgenic cotton. In *Proceedings of the Beltwide Cotton Conference*, Vol. 1, 746–47. Memphis, Tenn., U.S.A.: National Cotton Council.

Wolfenbarger, L., and P. Phifer. 2000. The ecological risks and benefits of genetically engineered plants. *Science* 290 (5499): 2088–93.

York, A., and A. Culpepper. 1999. Economics of weed management systems in BXN, Roundup Ready, and conventional cotton. In *Proceedings of the Beltwide Cotton Conference*, Vol. 1, 744–45. Memphis, Tenn., U.S.A.: National Cotton Council.

Chapter 9

The Economics of Herbicide-Tolerant Wheat and Bifurcation of World Markets

Richard Gray

Introduction

The biotechnology revolution in agriculture has begun. Biotechnology has spawned new crops with novel characteristics. Some of these crops have new product characteristics, such as crops with more desirable fatty acids in the oil or more desirable amino acids in the proteins. The most successful agricultural biotech products have been the development of new input traits that have reduced in the cost of production by changing the input mix required for production. Two prominent examples are the *Bt* (*Bacillus thuringiensis*) gene that introduces a naturally occurring insecticide found in a bacteria to a number of crops, most notably corn, and the creation of herbicide-tolerant field crops resistant to low-cost, broad-spectrum herbicides. In the past two years the majority of corn, soybean, and canola varieties grown in the Americas have at least one of these input traits, heralding the commercial success of these innovations.

As already discussed in previous chapters, the introduction of genetically modified organisms (GMOs) has created a great deal of controversy. Consumers are worried about unforeseen long-term health impacts from the consumption of GMOs. Environmentalists are concerned about adverse impacts on natural ecosystems. Although many farmers have adopted genetically modified (GM) crops, many farmers are concerned about long-term agronomic effects as well as potential adverse price effects. As a result of these concerns some governments have blocked the introduction of GMOs. The European Union (E.U.) has currently blocked trade and placed a three-year moratorium on the approval of GMOs. Many consumers in other countries want labeling of GM food products, and legislation has been introduced in a number of countries including Australia, Japan, and Korea. Some countries have introduced GM varieties in some crops but have blocked the introduction in other crops. Other countries have put regulatory approval of GM crops on hold while they await more information. At this point it remains unclear how the markets for GM products will develop.

This chapter examines some of the economic consequences of the potential introduction of herbicide-tolerant (HT) wheat in Canada. Both GM and non-GM HT wheat now exist in Canadian research plots. The non-GM HT wheat, which was created by mutagenesis—a process that causes mutation—is in cooperative registration trials, and could be ready for release as early as 2002. These two forms of HT wheat could create different reactions in the marketplace. At this point there are explicit rules against the import of many GM products into the E.U. Similar rules do not yet exist for products of mutagenesis. While this situation may change so that both commodity forms are accepted by consumers, the status quo for each of these products is a useful comparison.

The analysis presented in this chapter will not provide robust conclusions about the desirability of HT wheat; rather it presents a framework to identify important questions that must be addressed before a reasonable assessment can be made. This process involves identifying the private benefits and cost of producing HT wheat, the nonprivate production costs, the segregation costs, and the private and external consumer benefits and costs. The size of these benefits and costs will depend on the extent of production and consumption of these products in the marketplace. The analysis will demonstrate that a partial assessment of these costs and benefits may be a misleading indication of the overall desirability of HT wheat.

Herbicide Tolerance and Genetic Modification

Genetic modification is a complex term to define. The generally accepted definition of GMO is any plant that has recombinant DNA, that is, where DNA has been extracted from one organism and recombined with the DNA of another. This is accomplished by identifying a single gene from the thousands of genes in an organism, manipulating it in the laboratory, and then transferring or introducing it into a host plant cell, and later recovering a complete, new organism (Lemaux 2000). The scientific community has a very broad conception of genetic modification that differs from the narrower, more accepted definitions stated above. Figure 9.1 depicts

Figure 9.1   Scientific view of genetic modification

Selective crossbreeding

Biotechnology
transgenic techniques

rDNA

mutagenesis

hybridization techniques

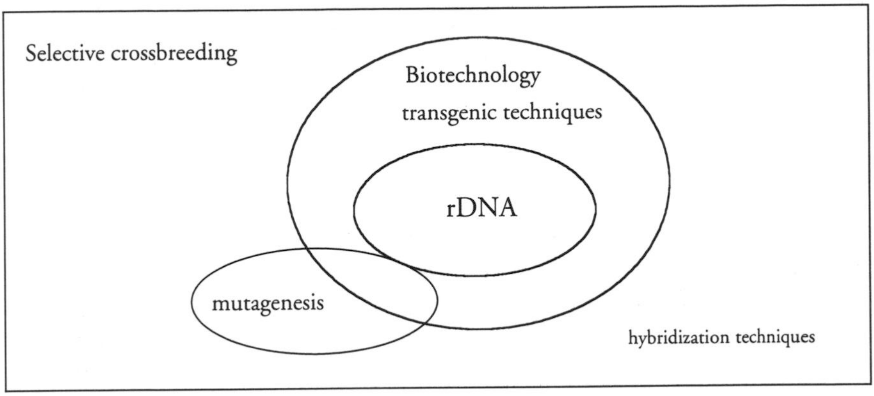

Source: Devised by author.

the scientific community's view that many processes can bring about genetic modification. Many traditional methods exist, including selective cross-breeding and hybridization techniques. Other forms of genetic modification include interspecies and intergeneric protoplast fusion, in vitro gene transfer techniques, somaclonal selection, haploid doubling, and mutagenesis (McHughen 2000). Virtually all agricultural crops have been genetically modified over time. For this reason, the scientific community prefers alternative terminology including "genetically engineered," "genetically transformed," "rDNA technology," "gene splicing," or—simply— "transgenics" (Stevens 2000).

Herbicide tolerance refers to a genetic trait introduced to a crop, enabling it to tolerate a particular herbicide. The most common HT trait inserted into plants is tolerance to the chemical glyphosate most commonly sold under the brand name of Roundup®. The Roundup Ready® (RR) trait was developed by Monsanto and provides plants with resistance to glyphosate herbicides. The development of the HT technology provides potential benefits in terms of increased crop yields and reduced cost of production (Mayer and Furtan 1999; Marra this volume). From an economic perspective these traits are most useful when the crop is given resistance to wide-spectrum, low-cost herbicides.

Herbicide tolerance has been achieved in crops using numerous methods, some transgenic or GM, others using mutagenesis (McHughen 2000). While the latter are HT, they are not transgenic or considered GM by the E.U. regulators at this point, though it is unclear whether this distinction will remain in the long run. While mutagenesis does not involve the transfer of genes from one species to another, it does involve a process of chemical or radioactive treatment of genetic material creating mutations. This mutated material is then selected for the desired traits. Given there is little control over the nature or the number of mutations that occur in DNA, some scientists find this process potentially more dangerous than the more precise, transgenic GM technologies. To date, despite these scientific views, transgenic rather than mutagenic products have been the targets of adverse consumer reaction and regulatory control.

Canada has some experience with HT crops. A GM HT flax variety named Triffid was the first GM crop to receive regulatory approval in Canada (McHughen 2000). The industry feared losing the E.U. market, which made up over 90 percent of export sales. Working with industry, the Flax Council of Canada took action to remove this variety from the market before it was grown commercially. Despite the registration of the variety over five years ago, the Canadian flax industry remains GMO-free today. Canola was the second crop where GM varieties were developed in Canada and developed very differently. The rapid adoption rate of HT canola in western Canada indicates that farmers have seen its benefits. HT canola is one of the most rapidly adopted technologies in the history of western Canadian agriculture. Its market share in Canada reached 70 percent of total canola production in 1999 (Fulton and Keyowski 1999).

General Framework for Identifying Costs and Benefits

The genetic modification of crops is a new technology with many potential costs and benefits. These impacts accrue at different stages in the marketing chain including variety sales, farm production, marketing, and consumption. Moreover, the parallel links in the non-GM marketing chain can be positively or negatively affected by the introduction of a GM crop. In addition to the effects on the domestic marketing chains, other countries are also affected through trade and research and development costs. Finally, there are important environmental costs and benefits that tend to exist outside of the marketplace.

Figure 9.2 illustrates the potential gain from introducing an HT crop assuming costless segregation and no nonmarket externalities. If GM and non-GM HT wheat could be costlessly segregated into different markets and heterogeneous producers and consumers were evenly distributed worldwide, the market equilibrium could be depicted as in Figure 9.2 whereby some producers receive marginal benefits per unit through growing the GM product. Those with the greatest benefit would be willing to grow the GM product at the greatest price discount. On the demand side, some consumers may be willing to pay a slight price premium for HT wheat, perhaps because it is associated with less toxic herbicides.

Figure 9.2   Economic surplus gains with costless segregation and no externalities

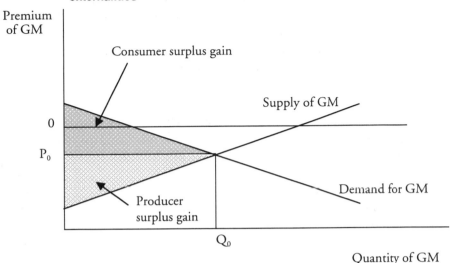

Source: Devised by author.

The consumer willing to pay the greatest premium (or least discount) would form the intercept on the GM demand curve. As the quantity available increased, the market would expand to those consumers with a larger and larger aversion to GM products. The market would clear at some discount P_0 and corresponding quantity Q_0. The total surplus gain would be equal to the area above the supply curve and below the demand curve. In this case an economic surplus will be generated with certainty, as long as the GM product is adopted and sold in a competitive marketplace and there are no negative externalities associated with production or consumption. If the technology can be delivered to producers at an attractive cost to adopt, gains in total economic surplus will be unambiguous. In this case the regulators' role is simple: allow the market to work.

Externalities

The benefits created in the GM marketplace will be a good measure of overall benefits only if no externalities exist; however, the presence of externalities is at the heart of the GM debate.

Potential externalities associated with HT production and consumption occur in several forms (Gray, Hobbs, and Haggui 2000). First is the potential cost imposed on non-GM producers and consumers in an unsegregated market. These costs are not incurred by the GM producers and consumers and are therefore external to this market. For instance, a producer's independent decision to grow GM wheat could lower the price for all non-GM producers when the product is not costlessly segregated. These external costs are potentially very important for HT wheat but require further quantification (and will be discussed in more detail later in the chapter).

The second type of externality would be associated with food safety and health costs. While no scientific evidence indicates that GM HT products either increase or reduce health costs, the costs of any adverse health consequences from GM food consumption would be borne by taxpayers and are therefore not reflected in the consumer demand function (Gray and Malla 1998). As a result, the external portion of potential health costs (or savings) would have to be subtracted from (or added to) consumer welfare gains.

A third type of externality is related to the agronomic and potential segregation costs imposed on non-GM wheat producers. For instance, if the production of GM wheat destroys the ability of a neighboring producer to sell organic products to the United Kingdom, the cost associated with the loss of the organic market would have to be incorporated. Perhaps more importantly, if an HT crop is spread to neighbors who have to incur additional costs to eliminate the "new weed" these costs should also be considered. These externalities are potentially important, especially in the longer run, as trace quantities of the HT crop can survive and quickly multiply under conventional herbicide treatment until they reach an economic threshold when they will be dealt with. This has already become an issue with HT canola. Wheat is less prone to spreading than canola, but the herbicide required to eliminate volunteer HT wheat would be more costly. These additional agronomic costs for non-HT wheat producers would have to be added to the overall cost of the technology.

A related agronomic externality is the development of herbicide resistance in weed populations. If a herbicide-resistant weed develops on one farm, the additional cost of controlling these weeds will spill over to other farmers. This is a problem in both conventional and GM crops, and as a result a calculation of the net effect of a switch to GM varieties would have to made. The introduction of HT wheat should give producers additional types of herbicides to combat weeds, which should reduce the potential build of resistance. Therefore this reduced herbicide resistance should be a positive benefit shared by HT and non-HT producers. These additional benefits for neighboring production systems need to be incorporated in an overall evaluation.

A fourth type of externality is the impact on natural ecosystems. Concerns have been raised that HT products could become superweeds taking over natural ecosystems. These fears are largely unfounded with herbicide tolerance because HT wheat should not gain any advantage to compete in an environment where herbicides are not used.[1] Outcrossing of HT wheat with a weedy relative is also a remote possibility. If this were to occur it would affect agricultural systems far more than natural ecosystems where herbicides are not used.

On balance the most important externalities for HT wheat would appear to be market impacts on nonsegregated, non-GM products. HT crops should lower overall external agronomic costs while posing little threat to the environment. As we learn more about these external costs and benefits, they need to be incorporated in the analysis.

Markets With Costly Segregation

Markets are not costlessly segregated, especially in the case of HT wheat where many sources of product mixing exist, and it is difficult to distinguish between HT and non-HT products without expensive testing. This is especially true when the tolerance for mixed product is very low. Experience in other GM grains suggests that the cost of maintaining greater that 99 percent non-GM purity would be expensive and would cost up to US$40 per tonne to maintain (Symthe and Phillips forthcoming). This difficulty in maintaining purity was highlighted with Starlink® corn, which found its way to the grocery shelf despite regulations to limit sales to the feed market.

In the case of HT GM wheat it is unlikely that voluntary segregation will be economically feasible. Mayer and Furtan (1999) estimated the gains to HT Canola producers to be about US$6 per tonne. If one doubles these benefits to create an upper bound of cost savings of US$12 per tonne for HT wheat, then at price discounts of US$12 per tonne or greater, very little HT wheat would be grown in a segregated market. A segregation system could only be feasible if the marketing clearing discount for GM was greater than the private segregation costs, allowing the conversion of an apparently GM product into a proven non-GM product. Given the relatively small per-tonne benefits from growing HT wheat relative to segregation costs, it seems unlikely that segregation could be maintained except for possibly small niche markets that do not have access to foreign non-GM supplies.

Figure 9.3 depicts consumer surplus effects with costly segregation. For simplicity it is assumed that the total demand for wheat is perfectly inelastic at Q_T and the demand for GM wheat is a function of the discount to non-GM wheat prior to GM introduction. Here it is assumed that GM wheat trades at a price discount of P_0 in the world market and can be segregated at a cost of $0 - P_1$, per unit. Consumers to the left of Q_0 enjoy a surplus gain in this new market. Consumers between Q_0 and Q_1 continue to consume GM product because non-GM product is now more expensive. Consumers to the right of Q_1 consume non-GM product but are worse off because they must now incur a segregation cost to do so. The net effect on

Figure 9.3   Consumer surplus effects with costly segregation

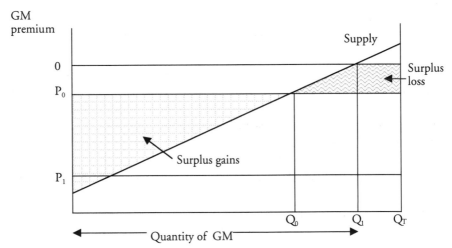

Source: Devised by author.

Figure 9.4   Producer surplus effects with costly segregation

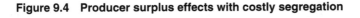

Source: Devised by author.

consumers with costly segregation is ambiguous, depending on the relative gains of those who receive a GM product at a lower cost, and those incur costs because of the segregation costs.

Figure 9.4 depicts the effect on producer surplus when product segregation is costly. The quantity of GM produced is equal to Q_1, which corresponds to the point where the price of the nonsegregated products are the same. However, all producers to the right of Q_0 incur a surplus loss as they now receive the price P_0 for their product, between Q_0 and Q_1 they grow GM but do not receive sufficient remuneration for doing so. Between Q_1 and Q_T producers grow non-GM products but receive the lower GM price. The overall impact on producers will hinge on the heterogeneity of producers and the discount for GM products and the GM-related cost savings.

If segregation is not feasible or too costly relative to gains, then countries will decide to become either a GM or non-GM country. If they become a GM country, both GM and non-GM markets will clear at the GM price. If they forego GM status, they will forego both the potential gains and losses.

The distributional impacts of the decision to become a GM country are important. Those producers that can best take advantage of the technology will be better off than those that see no benefit in the HT system. Consumers choosing an HT product in a costlessly segregated market will benefit while those choosing a non-HT product will lose. Given that compensation will not be paid to the losers, little can be said about overall welfare. The problem of the regulator in this case is to evaluate the gains to consumers and producers and decide whether to become a GM country or not. This involves the market effects that are depicted in Figures 9.3 and 9.4, as well as nonmarket or external impacts. The regulator may also be constrained by existing institutions. For instance, in most countries only food and environmental safety requirements have to be met for varietal registration; the loss of markets cannot be considered. Trade laws may also prevent blocking trade for nonphytosanitary reasons.

The Operation of a Bifurcated World Wheat Market

As outlined earlier, it is unlikely that segregation systems will develop at a cost low enough to maintain parallel GM and non-GM product streams. A far more likely scenario is that segregation will be controlled at international borders, as countries choose to be either GM or non-GM in production, processing, and consumption. These bifurcated markets have already begun to emerge with other GM products. The E.U. made a conscious decision not to use GM canola while Canada, the United States, and other countries have continued to produce GM products and no longer have access to the E.U. market. The national decisions to be GM or non-GM will ultimately affect the discount for GM products, which in turn affects the costs and benefits for other countries. The discount for GM wheat will depend on which countries decide to produce, process, and consume GM wheat. These effects are illustrated in Figure 9.5. The price intercept on the demand curve represents the price of non-GM wheat, that is, no discount for the first unit. The downward slope

Figure 9.5   The world market for GM wheat

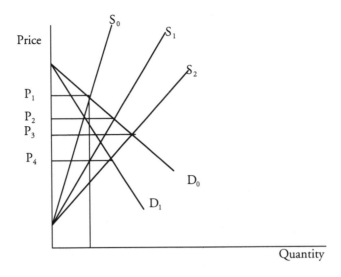

Source: Devised by author.

on the demand curve implies that as the supply of GM wheat increases the limited market for the product will result in GM wheat trading at some discount to non-GM wheat.

If only one country decides to produce GM wheat while several are willing to process and consume it, then a very small discount for GM wheat will result, depicted as P_1 in Figure 9.5. A small discount will tend to attract other countries to produce GM wheat. This will increase the supply of the GM wheat, from S_0 to S_1, in turn increasing the discount and the price from P_1 to P_2. Additional increases in adoption could increase the supply to S_2 and decrease the price of GM wheat to P_3. If the supply increases were accompanied by additional import restrictions, demand could be reduced to D_1 and the GM price could decrease to P_4. The independent nature of these decisions leaves the eventual outcome extremely unclear, however the interdependence of the payoff functions suggests that these moves could be made strategically. This adds to the complexity of predicting the behavior of a given country and whether the decision to become GM is, ultimately, in its domestic interest.

The discount for GM versus non-GM wheat will be set in a world market where individual decisions could have dramatic effects, further complicating the regulator's decision. Not only must they estimate the potential domestic supply and demand curve for GM products and the domestic nonmarket costs and benefits, they must estimate how the world market for these products will evolve.

Conclusion

The effects of the introduction of GM HT products are complex, with many potential externalities associated with their introduction. While HT tolerance may lower production cost and be adopted by producers voluntarily, this is not a test of overall viability. Many potential externalities are also associated with production. A preliminary assessment suggests that environmental, agronomic, and health externalities are likely to be small and in some cases positive. The key externality appears to be associated with information. Losses from the costs of segregation in some cases will exceed the cost savings of the technologies themselves. Two separate product streams are unlikely to develop within countries; rather, the result will be a bifurcated international wheat market where countries produce, process, and consume either GM or non-GM wheat.

In countries that decide to produce and consume GM wheat, producers will receive a lower GM price for their products, and consumers will not have non-GM products available unless they pay additional costs. This suggests that, in each country, some will gain while others lose. Because the price of GM and non-GM products will be determined by every country's decision, assessing the benefits and costs of GM adoption requires an assessment of producer costs and consumer preferences in each country, as well as speculation about which countries will become GM. These prices will in turn influence the decisions countries make, and their gains and losses.

Note

1. This could, however, be a problem with other traits such as the *Bt* gene or the drought resistance that could give such crops an additional advantage in the wild.

References

Agriculture and Agri-Food Canada. 2000. *Economic impacts of genetically modified crops on the agrifood sector.* Ottawa, Ontario: Agriculture and Agri-Food Canada.

Canadian Canola Growers Association. 1999. Producer's perspective on biotechnology. <http://www.canola-council.org/orgs/ growerbiotech.htm>. Accessed December 15, 2000.

Canadian Food Inspection Agency (CFIA). 2000. Regulation of Biotechnology in Canada. <http://www.cfia-acia.agr.ca>. Accessed January 5, 2001.

Carlson, G., M. Marra, and B. Hubbell. 1997. Transgenic technology for crop protection. *Choices* (Third Quarter): 31–36.

ERS (Economic Research Service of the U.S. Department of Agriculture). 2000. Impacts of adopting genetically modified crops in the United States. <http://www.ers.usda.gov>. Accessed January 7, 2001.

Feldmann, M., M. Morris, and D. Hoisington, 2000. Genetically modified organisms: Why all the controversy? *Choices* (First quarter): 8–12.

Fernandez-Cornejo, J., and W. McBride. 2000. Genetically engineered crops for management in U.S. agriculture. <http://www.ers.usda.org>. Accessed December 13, 2000.

Fulton, M., and L. Keyowski. 1999. The producer benefits of herbicide-resistant canola. *AgBioForum* 2 (2): 85–93.

Gray, R., and S. Malla. 1998. A note on evaluating agricultural policy in the presence of health care cost externalities. *Canadian Journal of Agricultural Economics* 46: 246–57.

Gray, R., J. Hobbs, and F. Haggui. 2000. *The identification, classification and assessment of the potential magnitude of non-market externalities associated with GMO production, marketing, and consumption.* A report prepared for Agriculture and Agri-Food Canada. Saskatoon.

Heap, I. M. 1999. *The occurrence of herbicide-resistant weeds worldwide.* <http://www. weed-science.com/>. Accessed June 12, 2000.

Lemaux, P. 2000. *From food biotechnology to GMOs: The role of genetics in food production.* <http://www.plantbio.berkeley.edu/~outreach/jpctalk.htm>. Accessed May 10, 2000.

Marra, M, G. Carlson, and B. Hubbell. 1998. Economic impacts of the first crop biotechnologies. <http://www.ag.econ.ncsu.edu/>. Accessed June 17, 2000.

Mayer, H., and W. H. Furtan. 1999. Economics of transgenic herbicide-tolerant canola: The case of western Canada. *Food Policy* (24): 431–42.

McHughen, A. 2000. *Pandora's picnic basket: The potential and hazards of genetically modified foods.* New York: Oxford University.

Moss, C. B., and A. Schmitz. 2001. Vertical integration and trade policy: The case of sugar. *Agribusiness: An International Journal* (forthcoming).

Powell, D. 1999. Seminal paper of agriculture biotechnology: A summary of the science. <http://www.plant.uguelph.ca>. Accessed June 17, 2000.

Royal Society. 1998. Genetically modified plants for food use. <http://www.royalsoc.ac.uk>. Accessed June 16, 2000.

Schmitz, T., A. Schmitz, and C. Dumas.1997. Gains from trade, inefficiency of government programs, and the net economic effects of trading. *Journal of Political Economy* 105 (3): 637–47, (June).

Stevens, J. 2000. Environmental impacts of transgenic crops. Draft manuscript, Centre for Studies in Agriculture Law and the Environment, University of Saskatchewan, Saskatoon. Mimeo.

Smyth, S. and P. W. B. Phillips. (Forthcoming). Competitors co-operating: Establishing a supply chain to manage genetically modified canola. *International Food and Agribusiness Management Review* (special issue).

Chapter 10

Potential Impacts of Biotechnology-Assisted Selection on Plant Breeding Programs in Developing Countries

Michael L. Morris, Jean-Marcel Ribaut,
Mireille Khairallah, and Kate A. Dreher

Introduction

Recent advances in molecular biology, quantitative genetics, genomics, bioinformatics, and related fields have led to the development of new biotechnology-based research tools with many potential applications to plant breeding. One tool of particular interest is DNA-based molecular markers. In addition to providing a means of characterizing genetic resources, uniquely identifying individual germplasm samples, mapping plant genomes, and tagging specific genes, molecular markers can accelerate crop genetic improvement research by enabling breeders quickly and reliably to identify plants carrying the allele or alleles associated with a desired trait (an allele is one of several alternative forms of a gene). Conventional selection methods do not offer nearly the same degree of precision. With conventional selection, breeders make controlled crosses in large populations of plants and use phenotypic screening techniques combined with statistical analysis to search for progeny that exhibit the desired trait.

The theoretical basis for marker-assisted selection (MAS) is well established. Numerous published studies have shown that using molecular markers can increase the efficiency of many types of breeding projects in a wide range of crops (for example, see Ragot 1995; Ribaut et al. 1997; Moreau et al. 2000). Less well established, however, are the practical and economic benefits of MAS, especially for the small and medium-sized breeding programs found in many developing countries. Establishing laboratory facilities for molecular breeding requires large initial investment and high recurrent expenditures; therefore, MAS may be attractive mainly to large breeding programs that can handle high levels of throughput. If biotechnology-assisted plant breeding is characterized by important economies of scale, then breeding programs in many developing countries may have difficulty implementing molecular marker technologies, impeding millions of farmers who rely on those programs for improved crop varieties.

This chapter examines the economics of MAS methods, discusses the potential benefits of molecular marker technologies for plant breeding programs, highlights obstacles that may slow successful implementation of molecular marker technologies in developing countries, and discusses possible avenues for overcoming those obstacles.

Use of Molecular Markers in Plant Breeding

Since ancient times, farmers have altered the characteristics of their crops by selectively saving and replanting seeds collected from high-yielding, healthy, well-adapted plants. Without rigorous selection methods, however, farmer breeding tended to be slow and unpredictable. With the advent of science-based selection strategies based on Mendelian principles of inheritance, genetic improvement began to be realized at a rapid rate. "Conventional" plant breeding methods have evolved considerably since their emergence around the beginning of the twentieth century, but they continue to revolve around three basic steps: (a) generation of a population of plants with desirable traits, (b) evaluation of the population and selection of superior individuals, and (c) recombination of the superior individuals to generate a new population for subsequent cycles of selection and improvement.

Conventional breeding methods have produced impressive results in improving the yield and quality of many commercially important crops, but it is not clear that historical rates of genetic gains can be sustained using conventional breeding methods alone. Evidence suggests that yield growth in major cereals is slowing in some countries (Pingali and Heisey 1999). Should these trends continue, genetic gains generated through conventional breeding will fall behind the rate of growth in demand for several leading food crops. This would disrupt grain markets in industrialized countries, and subsistence farmers in developing countries could suffer. To ensure that productivity growth keeps pace with rising demand for food, new breeding tools will be required.

Many experts predict that the new tools needed to reinvigorate plant breeding will come from the rapidly evolving field of biotechnology. Kaeppler (2000) distinguishes three areas in which biotechnology is likely to have a significant impact:

- Genome management (use of molecular markers for quantitative trait improvement, introgression of new germplasm into breeding lines, genetic diversity analysis, parental selection)

- Genetic diversity enhancement (introduction of new genes, directed mutagenesis and optimization of gene expression, gene discovery)

- Intellectual property protection (use of DNA fingerprinting to identify improved cultivars, breeding lines, and germplasm constructs)

This chapter focuses on the first of these three areas of potential impact—genome management.[1] Genome management in plant breeding increasingly involves the use of molecular markers, short pieces of DNA that correspond to particular sequences of DNA in the plant genome located within or close to genes that code for traits of interest. Using molecular markers, breeders can perform laboratory analyses on small samples of plant tissue to detect the presence of desirable alleles in individual plants. If the presence of the desirable alleles can be detected using markers, costly and time consuming phenotypic evaluation becomes unnecessary.

Use of MAS need not fundamentally change a plant breeder's selection strategy. A basic objective of any crop genetic improvement scheme is to identify within a differentiated population of plants elite individuals that can pass on their desirable characteristics to their progeny. Since observable differences in the physical characteristics of plants are usually caused by nonobservable differences in the plants' genetic makeup, what breeders are trying to do when they make selections in the field is choose individual plants that contain favorable alleles in desirable combinations. Conventional breeders must rely on phenotypic evaluation, which does not always accurately indicate the underlying information present in a plant's genome. Environmental influences and genetic interactions can obscure the presence or absence of specific alleles, making it difficult for breeders to identify the plants they really seek. Even when a plant's phenotype provides reliable evidence about the plant's underlying genetic characteristics, phenotypic evaluation can be difficult, costly, or time-consuming. Molecular markers solve this problem by allowing plants with the desirable allele to be identified quickly, reliably, and cost-effectively.

Many different types of DNA-based marker assays are available for use in plant breeding. The most popular of these include restriction fragment length polymorphisms (RFLPs), amplified fragment length polymorphisms (AFLPs), simple sequence repeats (SSRs) (also known as microsatellites), and single nucleotide polymorphisms (SNPs). Information about the use of molecular markers in plant breeding is abundantly available, so no attempt will be made here to describe how each type of marker works (for reviews, see Mohan et al. 1997; Hoisington, Listman, and Morris 1998; Ribaut and Hoisington 1998; and Crouch 2000).

Each type of molecular marker has distinctive advantages and disadvantages. Generally speaking, the suitability of a particular type of marker for a specific breeding application will depend on (a) the distribution of the marker within the genome, (b) the difficulty of performing the assay, and (c) cost. Relatively little effort has been made to evaluate the cost-effectiveness of marker technologies: as with any new technology, research protocols have changed frequently, making meaningful cost evaluation difficult. But now that standardized MAS methods are being used in more and more breeding programs, cost issues are attracting closer scrutiny.

Economics of Marker-Assisted Plant Breeding

What do we know about the economics of marker-assisted plant breeding? Is capacity to conduct marker-assisted breeding expensive to establish compared with capacity to carry out conventional breeding? And once research capacity is in place, do MAS methods offer significant cost savings compared with conventional selection methods?

Little information is publicly available about the economics of marker-assisted plant breeding because protocols (and hence costs) are still evolving and large-scale commercial use of MAS technology remains concentrated in the private sector, which has little incentive to disclose information about research costs.

While much remains to be learned about the economics of biotechnology-assisted plant breeding, information is starting to emerge. The following sections review the available evidence regarding (a) the cost of establishing and maintaining biotechnology research capacity and (b) the cost-effectiveness of MAS relative to conventional selection.

Establishing Biotechnology Research Capacity

In order for MAS to be a viable option for a plant breeding program, adequately equipped laboratory facilities and appropriately trained scientists must be available. Thus, the first decision facing research managers is whether to invest in biotechnology research capacity. This decision has been analyzed by Maredia, Byerlee, and

Figure 10.1 Biotechnology research production metafunction

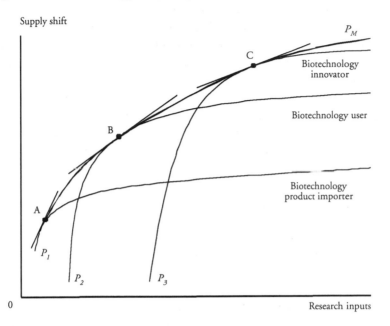

Source: Adapted from Byerlee and Traxler (1996).

Maredia (1999). These authors argue that since developing-country agriculture is unlikely to attract socially optimal levels of private investment (given its non-commercial nature), the appropriate model to use in developing countries is a public investment decision model. In such a model, the desirability of investing in biotechnology research capacity depends on whether the investment is expected to generate social benefits equal to or exceeding the social benefits that would be generated by alternative investments of the same magnitude.

The optimal amount of research investment can be conceived with the help of a research production function relating research inputs to research outputs. From a country perspective, the national research production function can be thought of as a meta-function comprising the frontier of many smaller functions, each representing a different level of research capacity distinguished by complexity and scope (Figure 10.1) (Brennan 1989; Byerlee and Traxler 1996; Maredia, Byerlee, and Maredia 1999). Movement along the meta-function—accomplished by adding discrete subprograms—is associated with changes in focus and increases in capacity of the national research program.

For a national plant breeding program, adding new biotechnology-based sub-programs is equivalent to taking a series of discrete steps associated with increasing complexity and cost. These steps have the effect of moving the program from one level of research capacity to the next. In highly stylized form, these levels can be characterized as follows:

1. *Biotechnology product user.* The research program imports germplasm products developed using biotechnology and tests them for potential immediate release or incorporates them into its existing conventional crop improvement schemes (usually by crossing them with local germplasm).

2. *Biotechnology tools user.* The research program imports biotechnology tools to improve current crop-improvement practices, if necessary adapting the tools to local circumstances.

3. *Biotechnology methods innovator.* The research program establishes full capacity needed to develop novel biotechnology tools and products.

Moving from one level of research capacity to the next often requires "lumpy" investments that are not readily divisible (for example, investments in expensive laboratory equipment, along with appropriately trained staff). This causes discontinuities in the production meta-function. Therefore, the practical decision facing research managers who want to establish capacity to conduct biotechnology research is not to identify the optimal amount of divisible investment, but rather to select from among different levels of biotechnology research capacity characterized by increasing complexity and cost (A or B or C in Figure 10.1). The choice is based on whether increasing the level of research capacity is expected to generate enough additional benefits to justify the additional expenditure. For most plant breeding programs, benefits consist of value-added to crop production enterprises, so the incentives to invest in additional research capacity will tend to increase with the size of the area planted to crops expected to benefit from the research, as well as their value.

The stylized biotechnology research production meta-function depicted in Figure 10.1 closely resembles that faced by managers of established conventional plant breeding programs who are considering investing in molecular marker research capacity. For a conventional plant breeding program, becoming a molecular marker "product user" need not necessarily involve significant additional investment; germplasm products developed using markers can easily be incorporated into the program's pool of source materials, and desirable genes/traits can then be moved around using conventional crossing procedures. But becoming a molecular marker "tools user" and eventually a molecular marker "methods innovator" require considerable additional investment in laboratory facilities, research materials, and staff training. Listed in increasing order of expense, these higher levels of molecular marker research capacity might include, for example, the ability to perform automated, high-throughput MAS on a routine basis (needed to capture economies of scale), the ability to carry out genetic engineering (needed to fully exploit the power of existing molecular markers), and the ability to carry out structural and functional genomics studies (needed to develop new markers).

What amount of investment is required to move from one level of biotechnology research capacity to the next level? Few public organizations in developing countries have established biotechnology research facilities, so little empirical evidence is available from which to estimate the cost of building and equipping a biotechnology laboratory for use in plant breeding. Approximately two dozen developing countries have established (or are currently establishing) the capacity to use imported biotechnology tools for crop genetic improvement purposes, and only a handful of these have established fully equipped biotechnology research facilities. Based on data from a small sample of developing countries, Maredia, Byerlee, and Maredia (1999) estimate that the cost of building a medium-sized laboratory capable of supporting molecular marker work ranges from US$150,000 to US$200,000 (cost of facilities, equipment, and basic laboratory supplies only). The same authors estimate that the cost of establishing a medium-sized laboratory capable of supporting genetic transformation work is approximately twice as high (US$300,000 to US$400,000). Significant additional investments will be needed to train qualified biotechnology researchers, as well as competent managers needed to operate a biotechnology research laboratory. Maredia, Byerlee, and Maredia estimate that training costs are likely to double the investment requirements.

Evidence from members of the Consultative Group for International Agricultural Research (CGIAR) suggests that these estimates are probably conservative. The relatively small number of CGIAR centers that have scaled up their throughput capacity in order to use molecular markers routinely have all invested at least US$1 million in biotechnology research facilities (TAC 2000).

It is important to note that this scale of investment can provide the capacity to perform biotechnology research using imported materials and procedures, but it will not be sufficient to establish the capacity needed to conduct basic research, including the development of new molecular markers. Marker development work, which often involves laborious and time-consuming basic research in structural and functional genomics, requires sophisticated equipment not available in most laboratories. Because of its complexity, cost, and specialized nature, basic research is often undertaken collaboratively. For example, the well-publicized public effort to sequence the rice genome involved an international consortium of research organizations that between them were able to mobilize large numbers of scientists and to support them with vast arrays of costly machinery and formidable computing capacity. Similar biotechnology research consortia have been convened (although at a smaller scale) to work on crops of interest mainly to developing countries, for example through the USAID-supported Collaborative Research Support Programs (CRSPs), through regional networks organized by CGIAR centers, and by philanthropic organizations such as the Rockefeller and McKnight Foundations.

Once biotechnology research capacity has been established, maintaining that capacity requires significant annual outlays to purchase chemicals, replace disposable laboratory supplies, and operate and service equipment. Once again, it is not easy to generalize about recurrent costs, since these will vary depending on the level of research capacity, but biotechnology laboratories at some public U.S. universities currently have annual operating budgets exceeding US$1 million. In the private sector, the sums are often far greater, especially among the industry leaders. Data are not readily available, but private investment in agricultural biotechnology research in the United States is currently estimated at US$500 million per year, of which a significant proportion goes for operation and maintenance of existing research facilities (Pray 2000).

In summary, the investments required to establish and maintain biotechnology research capacity are substantial, and developing countries that wish to take full advantage of biotechnology-based crop improvement technologies will have to invest at a different order of magnitude than in conventional plant breeding research.

Costs and Benefits of Marker-Assisted Selection

Assuming that an initial investment has been made and that biotechnology research capacity is in place, how is the typical plant breeding program likely to be affected? More specifically, how is the cost of crop genetic improvement research likely to change?

Information about the cost of using MAS for specific breeding projects is gradually starting to emerge from empirical case studies. For example, researchers at the International Maize and Wheat Improvement Center (CIMMYT) recently examined the costs and benefits of using MAS for a common application in maize breeding (for details, see Dreher et al. 2000 and 2001). A central finding of the CIMMYT case study was that costs and benefits of MAS projects are likely to vary depending on the crop being improved, the breeding objective being pursued, the skill of the breeder, the capacity of the research organization, the location where the work is done, the cost of key inputs, and many other factors.

Despite the risks in extrapolating from the results of a single case study, the findings of the CIMMYT study suggest some general conclusions regarding the cost-effectiveness of molecular markers in crop genetic improvement. Broadly speaking, two types of benefits from MAS can be distinguished: cost savings and time savings.

Cost Savings

For certain applications, MAS methods can directly substitute for conventional selection methods, and for these applications the relative cost-effectiveness of the two methods can be determined simply by comparing the screening cost per sample.[2] Generally speaking, as the cost of phenotypic screening rises, markers are more likely to represent a cost-effective alternative. For applications in which phenotypic screening is easy and cheap (for example, visual scoring of leaf color), MAS will not offer any obvious cost advantage. But for applications in which phenotypic screening is difficult or expensive (for example, assessing root damage caused by nematodes), MAS will often be preferable.

Although detailed empirical analysis is required to determine cost-efficiency rankings for specific cases, Dreher et al. (2000, 2001) identify a number of breeding applications for which MAS methods are likely to offer significant cost savings compared with conventional selection methods (Table 10.1).

Time Savings

Plant breeders must worry about controlling costs, but they also must be concerned about getting products out quickly. For this reason, in assessing the desirability of MAS relative to conventional selection, breeders must also consider the time requirements of alternative breeding strategies. Even if MAS costs more than conventional selection (as it does in some, although not all cases), breeders who use molecular markers may be able to generate a desired output more quickly. Accelerating the release of improved varieties can bring significant benefits, so the length of a breeding cycle is an important consideration in addition to cost (Brennan 1989; Pandey and Rajatasereekul 1999; Koo and Wright 2000).

For breeding applications in which MAS offers cost savings *and* time savings, the advantages of MAS compared with conventional breeding are unambiguous. With many applications, however, MAS methods cost more to implement than conventional selection methods but also reduce the time needed to accomplish a breeding objective. This commonly happens, for example, with inbred line conversion schemes based on backcrossing procedures; in such schemes, MAS methods often can be used to derive converted inbred lines containing one or more incorporated genes in much less time than would be possible using conventional selection methods alone.

In applications that involve a trade-off between time and money, under what circumstances is the higher cost of MAS relative to conventional breeding justified? The choice of plant breeding method can be viewed as an investment decision and can be evaluated using conventional investment criteria (Sanders and Lynam 1982). Using data from the CIMMYT case study, Morris et al. (2001) explored the rela-

Table 10.1   Plant breeding applications for which marker-assisted selection (MAS) is likely to be cost-effective compared with conventional selection

Plant breeding application	Potential advantages of marker-assisted selection (MAS)
Selection for traits controlled by multiple genes	MAS may allow breeders to identify the presence of multiple alleles related to a single trait. With conventional methods, it is often necessary to conduct separate trials to screen for individual alleles (assuming that individual alleles exert a detectable influence on the expression of the trait).
Simultaneous selection for several traits	MAS may allow breeders to select for several traits simultaneously. With conventional methods, it is often necessary to conduct separate trials to screen for individual traits.
Selection for traits expressed only in certain seasons	MAS may allow breeders at any time of the year to screen for traits that are expressed only during certain growing seasons. Using molecular markers, breeders can screen in the summer for the presence of alleles associated with traits that are expressed only in the winter, and vice versa.
Selection for traits expressed only in certain locations	MAS may allow breeders in any location to screen for traits whose expression depends on geographical considerations. Using molecular markers, breeders in one location can screen for the presence of alleles associated with traits that are expressed only in other locations.
Early detection	MAS may allow breeders to screen for the presence of the allele or alleles associated with a desirable trait well before the trait is expressed and can be detected phenotypically. This can be particularly important in species that grow slowly, for example tree crops.
Detecting the presence of recessive genes	MAS may allow breeders directly to identify heterozygous plants that carry an allele of interest whose presence cannot be detected phenotypically. With conventional methods, it would be necessary to carry out additional cycles of selfing to infer the presence of the allele.

Source: Compiled by authors.

tionship between time and money as it relates to crop genetic improvement research by developing a simple model of a plant breeding program and using it to compare the returns to alternative inbred line conversion schemes based, respectively, on conventional selection and MAS. Two criteria were used to evaluate these alternatives: the net present value (NPV) of the discounted streams of costs and benefits, and the internal rate of return (IRR) to the investment.

Figure 10.2 depicts the stylized "variety life cycle" assumed by the model. The stream of costs and benefits associated with development, release, and farmers' adoption of an improved variety can be divided into three stages: (a) a research stage during which the variety is developed, (b) a release stage during which the variety is evaluated and registered for release, and during which commercial seed is produced, and (c) and an adoption stage during which the variety is grown by farmers. During the first two stages, net benefits are negative, because costs are incurred without

Figure 10.2 Stylized economic model of a plant breeding program

Net annual benefits (US$)

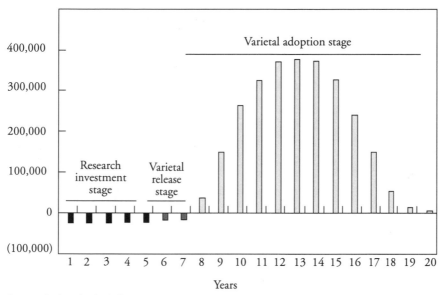

Source: Authors' calculations.

any benefits being realized. During the third stage, net benefits turn positive as farmers adopt the variety; net benefits increase until the peak adoption level is achieved and then decline when the variety is replaced by newer varieties.

The model was used to estimate the NPV and the IRR of conventional and marker-assisted inbred line conversion schemes. Research cost data were taken from the CIMMYT case study. Plausible values were used for key parameters relating to the varietal release and adoption stages (for details, see Morris et al. 2001). Figure 10.3 shows the streams of net benefits generated by each of the two breeding schemes.

NPVs were calculated by summing the stream of net benefits associated with each breeding scheme over the life of the variety (n years):

$$NPV = \sum_{t=1}^{n}(GB_t - VR_t - RC_t) \qquad (10.1)$$

where GB = gross benefits (calculated as area planted to the variety x incremental benefits associated with adoption); VR = varietal release expenses (cost of evaluation trials, registration procedures, seed multiplication, advertising and promotion, and so on), and RC = research investment costs. IRRs were conventionally calculated by solving for the discount rate at which the NPV equals zero.

Figure 10.3 Net benefits flow, conventional versus marker-assisted line conversion scheme

Net annual benefits (US$)

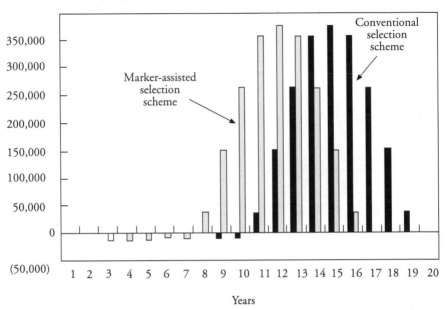

Years

Source: Authors' calculations.

The profitability rankings of the two breeding schemes—MAS and conventional—differ depending on the measure of project worth that is used. The MAS scheme generates the highest NPV, whereas the conventional breeding scheme generates the highest IRR on investment.[3] From an economic perspective, the relative attractiveness of conventional versus MAS methods will depend on the availability of research investment capital. If investment capital is abundantly available, then it makes sense to choose MAS, since MAS generates the largest NPV. If investment capital is constrained, however, then it makes sense to choose conventional selection, which generates the largest IRR.

This finding is consistent with what has been happening in the plant breeding industry. Private firms, which can raise investment capital by drawing on corporate cash reserves, floating shares in the stock market, or borrowing in commercial credit markets, have invested aggressively in biotechnology, including molecular marker technologies. Private firms can increase the net benefits (profits) generated by their breeding programs by investing in technologies that allow them to bring new products into the market faster, even if these technologies require large up-front expenditures.[4] In contrast, public research organizations, which face capital constraints in that they are required to operate within their budget allocation, have been much slower to invest in biotechnology, including molecular marker technologies. Public research organizations can maximize the returns to their limited investment resources by sticking to lower-cost conventional selection methods, even though this means that breeding projects will take longer to complete.[5]

Projected Developments in Marker Technology

The evidence presented in the previous section regarding the cost of establishing and maintaining biotechnology research capacity and of using molecular markers for specific plant breeding applications provides useful insights about the current cost of the technology and helps explain recent investment patterns in the public and private plant breeding industries. The empirical results should be interpreted with caution, however, because the cost structure of biotechnology-assisted plant breeding is certain to change with future advances in knowledge. Although it is impossible to predict exactly where molecular marker technology is headed, some general trends can be anticipated based on research underway in three key fields: structural genomics, functional genomics, and bioinformatics.

Structural genomics. Many research laboratories are currently conducting genomic mapping experiments that will speed the development of MAS technology and increase its practical utility for crop genetic improvement (Lee 1995). Unfortunately, even though quantitative trait loci (QTL) have been identified for many traits of interest, individual QTL frequently express a reduced amount of phenotypic variance, and they often interact strongly with environmental factors. As a result, to date relatively few concrete MAS results have been published that would justify the initial enthusiasm (Mohan et al. 1997; Ribaut and Hoisington 1998). The situation is expected to change, however, as more genomic information becomes available and additional markers are developed. The cost of developing markers is still prohibitive for many breeding programs, so the projected advances in mapping should make the technology more widely accessible by greatly reducing the cost of MAS schemes.

Functional genomics. Following the recent development of genomic technologies that provide functional information, gene characterization work has received a significant boost during the past few years. One such technology, microarrays, has matured to the point that the expression of thousands of genes can be monitored through a single hybridization using small quantities of RNA derived from relatively small amounts of plant tissue (Schena et al. 1995 and 1996). With further advances in functional genomics, it should soon be possible to identify hundreds if not thousands of genes that determine a plant's response to specific environmental factors. This will be extremely useful in breeding for particular target environments—especially environments characterized by abiotic stresses such as drought, heat, and cold. Since it will probably be impossible to manipulate all of the relevant genes simultaneously, once the overall set of genes has been characterized, it will be important to identify the key genes that regulate the activity of the others. Once the key regulatory genes have been identified, the next step will be to determine how elite alleles of those key genes can be efficiently manipulated to improve a given variety.

Bioinformatics. Rapid proliferation of genomic knowledge will generate demand for expanded data archiving capacity, as well as new statistical analysis techniques capable of handling vast amounts of data. DeRisi, Iyer, and Brown (1997, 685) correctly point out that "...perhaps the greatest challenge now is to develop efficient methods for organizing, distributing, interpreting, and extracting insights from the large volumes of data these experiments [in structural and functional genomics] will provide." As the focus of research attention shifts from the level of entire plants to the level of individual genes, the number of data points that must be tracked, archived, and analyzed increases exponentially. Powerful new computing systems will be needed to deal with the sheer volume of data being generated, as will innovative statistical analysis procedures capable of extracting meaningful information from molecular data. Development of these crucial research support tools will require multi-talented bioinformatics specialists skilled in quantitative genetics theory, statistical analysis, and software development.

These projected advances in genomics and bioinformatics, as well as projected advances in other related fields, are likely to affect crop improvement research significantly. As genomic knowledge accumulates and research procedures are refined, plant breeders will be able to design new, more efficient breeding schemes. Armed with molecular technologies that allow them to track individual alleles across successive generations of progeny, breeders are likely to focus increasingly on custom assembly of known favorable alleles to produce desired plant types. By accelerating the rate at which favorable combinations of alleles can be assembled within the same germplasm background, they will be able to reduce the time spent bringing in desirable traits from source materials that otherwise have few desirable characteristics ("good by bad" crossing) and move more quickly to schemes involving only elite lines that perform well under the target environment conditions ("good by good" crossing) (Ribaut and Betrán 1999). Another promising new avenue consists of combining varietal pedigree information, molecular data generated through DNA fingerprinting, and information obtained from field evaluation of elite germplasm. Using data from all three sources, breeders will be able to identify and trace favorable alleles already accumulated in the germplasm through conventional breeding.

In summary, plant breeding in the future will become less of an art and more of a science, less empirical and more knowledge-based. Field evaluation of experimental materials in diverse environments will always be crucially important, but breeding strategies and crossing schemes increasingly will be designed with the help of detailed genomic knowledge managed in computerized databases, rather than relying on experiential knowledge residing inside the heads of experienced breeders.

Potential Impacts on the Plant-Breeding Industry

How will the global plant breeding industry be affected by these projected developments in biotechnology, and especially by anticipated improvements in MAS methods? Will molecular marker technology be widely accessible—available not only to the private firms that target mainly commercial producers, but also to the public breeding programs on which most subsistence farmers rely? Or will it be captured disproportionately by certain breeding programs, possibly further widening the gap between the "haves" and "have-nots"?

For most breeding programs, the accessibility of a new technology depends first and foremost on its affordability. Because the cost of establishing biotechnology research capacity is high, many small and medium-sized plant-breeding programs will not be able to make the significant investments needed, at least not in the near term. Even if a breeding program is able to support the initial investment needed to establish biotechnology research capacity (possibly with help from external donors), fully exploiting that capacity will usually require significant additional annual outlays to cover maintenance and operating costs. Expenditures of this magnitude will be difficult to justify, especially for minor crops grown on limited areas, since the benefits are likely to be modest.

The situation regarding biotechnology is analogous to that prevailing in the conventional plant breeding industry, where economically justifiable levels of investment in research capacity also vary with the size of the expected benefits. In a recent review of public crop improvement research in developing countries, Traxler and Pingali (1999) distinguish three categories of national breeding programs based on increasing levels of research capacity. Stage 1 breeding programs screen imported varieties for local release. Stage 2 breeding programs perform test crosses and develop new varieties adapted specifically to local production conditions. Stage 3 breeding programs develop source materials for their own breeding programs, perform test crosses, and develop new varieties adapted specifically to local production conditions. According to Traxler and Pingali, by the mid-1990s only four developing countries had established Stage 3 capacity for wheat breeding research, and only about 10 developing countries had established Stage 3 capacity for rice breeding research.

Traxler and Pingali argue that the scarcity of Stage 3 programs is economically rational, since for most small and medium-sized developing countries the most efficient breeding strategy is to import germplasm and technology developed by Stage 1 programs, CGIAR centers, and research organizations in industrialized countries.

The stratified organization of today's conventional plant breeding industry provides clues about the likely organization of tomorrow's biotechnology-based plant breeding industry. Since biotechnology research is more expensive than conventional breeding research, the projected advances in biotechnology-assisted breeding methods are likely to lead to even greater concentration in global plant breeding research capacity—particularly the capacity to perform basic research. This suggests that the knowledge-intensive plant breeding of the future will be performed most efficiently by a small number of large, well-funded organizations possessing technical research capacity, genomic knowledge, and access to proprietary germplasm. Recent trends in the global plant breeding industry suggest that these organizations will be mainly private firms, rather than public organizations.

Not everyone is comfortable with the prospect of a global plant breeding industry dominated by a few large breeding programs, many of them profit-oriented private firms. The concern is that these breeding programs will concentrate on commercial markets in which farmers are able and willing to pay for improved varieties, while noncommercial markets will be neglected—including markets for many food crops grown by small-scale, subsistence-oriented farmers in developing countries. In order to prevent this, measures may be needed to ensure that the benefits of biotechnology-based breeding technologies reach noncommercial markets that are unlikely to attract the attention of the large breeding programs.

Key Challenges for Developing Countries

What can be done to ensure that developing countries have an appropriate level of biotechnology research capacity? The optimal position along the biotechnology research production function will differ from country to country. Yet regardless of whether a country seeks to become a biotechnology innovator or merely an importer and user of biotechnology products and methods developed elsewhere, it will have to overcome three key challenges: (a) building human capital, (b) financing investment costs, and (c) managing intellectual property (IP).

Building human capital. The first key challenge facing developing countries is to build the human capital needed to conduct biotechnology research. Biotechnology researchers must be well-trained in molecular biology, genetics, and plant breeding, fields in which formal academic training tends to be expensive. Relatively few universities in developing countries offer graduate degrees in biotechnology-related fields, so scientists often must acquire their training overseas. With the total cost of training a doctoral student in Japan, North America, and western Europe approaching US$250,000, many developing countries will be hard-pressed to finance human capital development. More affordable training opportunities are sometimes available elsewhere—including the courses being offered by some CGIAR centers and by many universities in the North—but these cannot satisfy the entire demand.

Financing investment costs. The second key challenge facing developing countries is to finance the cost of establishing and maintaining biotechnology research facilities. Building and maintaining the physical infrastructure needed to carry out biotechnology research requires substantial investment. Public plant breeding programs will often have difficulty supporting these costs, which are usually significantly higher than the cost of expanding an existing conventional breeding program (Maredia, Byerlee, and Maredia 1999). In recent years, many development assistance agencies have helped public research organizations finance the construction of biotechnology research facilities, but it is not clear that these agencies are willing to support future operation and maintenance costs. Public organizations will therefore have to implement cost-recovery mechanisms to help defray recurrent costs. One option currently being explored by public research institutes in South Africa, Thailand, and a number of other countries is to offer custom breeding services to private companies on a commercial basis.

Managing intellectual property. The third key challenge facing developing countries is to develop the capacity to manage intellectual property. With the current trend toward privatization of agricultural research, intellectual property rights (IPR) are becoming increasingly important in influencing access to vital technologies, including many technologies needed to carry out MAS. Many countries now allow IP protection to be extended not only to laboratory equipment, materials, and methods used for plant breeding research, but also in some cases to germplasm and genomic information. Critics argue that the scope of this protection is often too broad and that many existing laws will eventually be revised or struck down, but for now they remain in place. In this context, accessing IP owned by others and protecting one's own IP requires expertise in IP management, something that many public research organizations lack.

Access Strategies for Developing Countries

Relatively few developing countries will be able to justify the large expenditures needed to become innovators capable of developing new molecular markers. For most developing countries, the economically rational strategy to benefit from molecular markers will be to import germplasm products developed elsewhere using marker technology, or to import and use the technology itself. In cases where useful marker technology is already available, developing countries can pursue a number of access strategies. These strategies, many of which are explored by Nottenberg, Pardey, and Wright (this volume), include

- using publicly available technology—the easiest and cheapest option, given the considerable amount of technology that is publicly available;

- inventing around existing proprietary technology—a slower and more costly option requiring local biotechnology research capacity;

- negotiating commercial licenses—possible only when commercial licenses are available and affordable;

- soliciting technology donations—possibly effective when commercial applications of the technology are limited or when prospective donors are motivated by public relations considerations; and

- securing IPR that can be offered as bargaining chips in exchange for IP owned by others—rarely an option because few research organizations in developing countries own proprietary technology that is of interest to others.

Summary

Recent advances in biotechnology have led to the development of molecular marker-based selection tools that can increase the speed of crop genetic improvement and in some cases reduce the cost. These tools have already made plant breeding more efficient and will continue to do so. With projected future refinements to the technology, eventually it should be possible to use molecular markers to assemble specific combinations of known favorable alleles to produce desired plant types virtually on a custom basis.

Marker-assisted selection methods show great promise for the plant breeding industry, but unless appropriate policies are implemented to ensure that key technologies are made widely available, the benefits are likely to be distributed unequally. Currently, the high costs associated with establishing and maintaining biotechnology research capacity mean that advanced molecular marker technologies are attractive mainly to large research organizations with the ability to mobilize significant investment capital. These tend to be profit-oriented private firms, whose primary motivation is to use biotechnology for research targeted at major commercial crops.

Looking ahead, unless the cost of developing new markers falls significantly, relatively few plant breeding programs in developing countries will be able to justify the substantial investment needed to become innovators in molecular marker technology. For most programs, the most efficient way to harness the power of molecular markers will be to import and use technology developed elsewhere. This strategy will be particularly attractive with crops of major global importance, including many cereals (maize, rice, wheat, sorghum, barley), oilseeds (soybeans, canola, sunflower, safflower), and pulses (beans, peas, lentils). A large amount of marker-related research has been done in industrialized countries on most of these crops, and relatively low-cost technology is already available for immediate use.

More problematic, at least in the short run, will be crops that have not attracted the attention of breeding programs in industrialized countries, including dozens of minor food crops grown mainly by subsistence farmers in developing countries. For these "orphan crops," it is not clear who will do the basic research needed to develop new molecular markers, especially markers for traits that may primarily interest noncommercial producers. Organizations that possess the requisite research capacity are unlikely to invest—private firms recognize the difficulty of appropriating economic benefits, and public research organizations in industrialized countries do not find these crops relevant. The most promising avenue for progress for orphan crops will be through international consortia supported at least in part with public funds. The CGIAR centers could also play an important facilitating role in helping to mobilize resources from the public and private sectors (Morris and Hoisington 2000).

Fortunately, cost considerations may prove less of an obstacle in the future. Continuing advances in genomics are likely to dramatically lower the cost of developing new markers in all species, making work even on minor crops economically justifiable. Recently announced progress in sequencing the genomes of model species such as *Arabidopsis* and rice should boost molecular marker development efforts across the board, because once the genes in a given species have been identified, it should be possible to use many of them as markers in other species. Falling costs thus can be expected to make molecular marker technologies more widely accessible in the years to come, even to plant breeding programs in developing countries for whom these valuable research tools have until now remained largely out of reach.

Notes

The authors wish to thank David Hoisington and Prabhu Pingali of CIMMYT for contributing useful comments.

1. This chapter does not address genetic engineering, so no attempt is made to examine the many regulatory issues associated with transgenics (such as human health and safety, animal health and safety, environmental impacts, and ethics).

2. Comparing the cost-effectiveness of MAS relative to conventional selection is complicated because the two are not always perfect substitutes. Using molecular markers, breeders can often obtain more information than with conventional phenotypic screening methods; based on the additional information, they may decide to modify their entire breeding strategy in ways that make direct cost comparisons difficult. For example, marker-assisted breeding schemes often produce fewer improved plants than conventional breeding schemes, but much more is known about the genetic constitution of these plants. Scale factors also complicate cost comparisons because the cost of using markers tends to be sensitive to the number of samples being analyzed.

3. Similar results have been reported by Brennan (1989) based on a study of public wheat breeding programs in Australia.

4. Another factor that has motivated private firms to invest heavily in biotechnology is related to IPR. The rapid evolution of IPR regimes in many countries has created a climate of uncertainty that, if anything, has encouraged overinvestment; fearing that they may be left behind, many firms have invested in biotechnology with little appreciation of whether or not their investment is likely to pay off.

5. Accelerated release of improved varieties by public breeding programs also results in increased benefits (for example, higher incomes for farmers, lower food prices for consumers), but since public breeding programs generally do not sell their products commercially, these "social benefits" usually are not appropriated through increased returns. This does not mean that these social benefits are small. Pandey and Rajatasereekul (1999) estimate that the economic benefits from shortening by two years the average length of the breeding cycle for a rice variety in Thailand is on the order of US$18 million over the useful life of a variety.

References

Brennan, J. P. 1989. An analysis of economic potential of some innovations in a wheat breeding programme. *Australian Journal of Agricultural Economics* 33 (1): 48–55.

Byerlee, D., and G. Traxler. 1996. The role of technology spillovers and economies of size in the efficient design of agricultural research systems. Paper prepared for the conference, Global Agricultural Science Policy to the 21st Century, Melbourne, Australia, 26–28 August.

Crouch, J. H. 2000. Molecular marker-assisted breeding: A perspective for small to medium-sized plant breeding companies. Paper prepared for Asian Seed 2000, the seventh annual conference of the Asia and Pacific Seed Association, Bangalore, India, 25–28 September.

DeRisi, J. L., V. R. Iyer, and P.O. Brown. 1997 Exploring the metabolic and genetic control of gene expression on a genomic scale. *Science* 278: 680–86.

Dreher, K., M. Khairallah, J-M. Ribaut, and M. L. Morris. 2001. Money matters (I): Costs of field and laboratory procedures associated with conventional and marker-assisted maize breeding at CIMMYT. Mexico City. In preparation.

Dreher, K., M. L. Morris, J-M. Ribaut, M. Khairallah, S. Pandey, and G. Srinivasan. 2000. Is marker-assisted selection cost-effective compared to conventional plant breeding methods? The case of quality protein maize. Paper presented at the fourth annual conference of the International Consortium for Agricultural Biotechnology Research, Ravello, Italy, August 24–28.

Hoisington, D., G. M. Listman, and M. L. Morris. 1998. Maize varietal development: Applied biotechnology. In *Maize seed industries in developing countries,* M. L. Morris ed. Boulder, Colo., U.S.A.: Lynne Rienner and CIMMYT.

Kaeppler, S. 2000. Role of biotechnology in maize improvement. Lecture notes prepared for presentation at the Advanced Maize Breeding Course, CIMMYT, Mexico City, September.

Koo, B., and B. Wright. 2000. Optimal timing of evaluation of genebank accessions and the effects of biotechnology. *American Journal of Agricultural Economics* 82 (4): 797–811.

Lee, M. 1995. DNA markers and plant breeding programs. *Advances in Agronomy* 55: 265–344.

Maredia, M., D. Byerlee, and K. Maredia. 1999. Investment strategies for biotechnology in emerging research systems. Paper presented at the third annual conference of the International Consortium on Agricultural Biotechnology Research, Rome, Italy, June 17–19.

Mohan, M., S. Nair, A. Bhagwat, T. G. Krishna, M. Yano, C. R. Bhatia, and T. Sasaki. 1997. Genome mapping, molecular markers and marker-assisted selection in crop plants. *Molecular Breeding* 3: 87–103.

Moreau, L., S. Lemarie, A. Charcosset, and A. Gallais. 2000. Economic efficiency on one cycle of marker-assisted selection. *Crop Science* 40: 329–37.

Morris, M. L., and D. A. Hoisington. 2000. Bringing the benefits of biotechnology to the poor: The role of the CGIAR Centers. In *Agricultural biotechnology in developing countries: Towards optimizing the benefits for the poor,* eds. M. Qaim, A. Krattiger, and J. von Braun. Dordrecht, the Netherlands: Kluwer.

Morris, M. L., K. Dreher, J-M. Ribaut, and M. Khairallah. 2001. Money matters (II): Costs of maize inbred line conversion schemes at CIMMYT using conventional and marker-assisted selection. Mexico City. In preparation.

Pandey, S., and S. Rajatasereekul. 1999. Economics of plant breeding: The value of shorter breeding cycles for rice in Northeast Thailand. *Field Crops Research* 64: 187–97.

Pingali, P. L., and P. W. Heisey. 1999. Cereal crop productivity in developing countries: Past trends and future prospects. CIMMYT Economics Program Working Paper 99/03. Mexico City: CIMMYT.

Pray, C. 2000. Personal communication. Rutgers University, August.

Ragot, M. 1995. Marker-assisted backcrossing: A practical example. In *Techniques et utilisations des marqueurs moléculaires,* A. Berville and M. Tersac eds. Paris: *Institut National de la Recherche Agronomique.*

Ribaut, J-M., and J. Betrán. 1999. Single large-scale marker-assisted selection (SLS-MAS). *Molecular Breeding* 5: 531–41.

Ribaut, J-M., and D. Hoisington. 1998. Marker-assisted selection: New tools and strategies. *Trends in Plant Science* 3 (6): 236–39.

Ribaut, J-M., X. Hu, D. Hoisington, and D. González de León. 1997. Use of STSs as rapid and reliable preselection tools in a marker-assisted selection-backcross scheme. *Plant Molecular Biology Reporter* 15: 154–62.

Sanders, J. H., and J. K. Lynam. 1982. Definition of the relevant constraints for research resource allocation in crop breeding programs. *Agricultural Administration* 9 (4): 273–84.

Schena, M. D., D. Shalon, R.W. Davis, and P. O. Brown. 1995 Quantitative monitoring of gene expression patterns with complementary DNA microarray. *Science* 270: 467–70.

Schena, M. D., D. Shalon, R. Heller, A. Chai, P. O. Brown, and R. W. Davis. 1996. Parallel human genome analysis: Microarray-based expression monitoring of 1,000 genes. *Proceedings of the National Academy of Science (U.S.A.)* 93: 10614–19.

Technical Advisory Committee (TAC), Consultative Group for International Agricultural Research. 2000. *Review of CGIAR plant breeding programs.* Washington, D.C.: CGIAR.

Traxler, G., and P. L. Pingali. 1999. *International collaboration in crop improvement research: Current status and future prospects.* CIMMYT Economics Program Working Paper 99/11. Mexico City: CIMMYT.

Part 5

Regional Perspectives on Biotechnology Policies

Chapter 11

Agricultural Biotechnology in Latin America and the Caribbean

Eduardo J. Trigo, Greg Traxler, Carl Pray, and Ruben Echeverría

Introduction

Agricultural biotechnology development is critical for Latin America and the Caribbean. Agriculture is a key sector for every country in the region—in the value of agricultural exports or its importance in addressing poverty. Biotechnology can contribute to the region's economy through cost reductions that enhance competitiveness in international commodity markets and by adding value to agricultural products. Today, the region has a number of world-class research groups and institutions, and commercial utilization has led to a genetically modified (GM) crop area second only to North America's. These trends are uneven throughout the region, with large differences even between neighboring countries that share common ecologies and a longstanding tradition of scientific and technical cooperation. This chapter summarizes the current picture as background for a discussion of the challenges and policy options that need to be addressed in order for the region to tap biotechnology's potential benefits.

Current Status Of Agricultural Biotechnologies in the Region

Overall the biotechnology sector in Latin America and the Caribbean (LAC) has considerable scientific potential for improving agricultural productivity and enhancing consumer products. Scientific capacity is concentrated in the region's large countries, particularly in a few respected institutions in Argentina, Brazil, and Mexico.

Similarly, commercial use of genetically modified organisms (GMOs) is significant in only a couple of countries, and impending field trials do not indicate a change in this pattern in the immediate future. Biotechnology capacity is still in the early stages for most countries; marshaling the technical expertise to implement functional biosafety and patenting systems will require a sustained effort and the commitment of significant additional resources. A similar disparity exists in the private sector: Argentina, Brazil, and Mexico have excellent potential, while seed markets in other countries are impeded by size and lack of infrastructure.

Biotechnology Research Capacity and Utilization

Despite lack of comprehensive data on the institutional, human, and financial resources being invested in biotech activities, it is possible to compile a serviceable picture from a variety of sources. A recent study by the International Service for National Agricultural Research (ISNAR) provides an institutional map of research capacity (Cohen, Komen, and Verastegui 2001). The study covered some 292 institutions in 13 countries—Argentina, Brazil, Chile, Colombia, Costa Rica, Ecuador, Guatemala, Jamaica, Paraguay, Peru, Trinidad and Tobago, Uruguay, and Venezuela—with 85 institutions participating. Survey responses from Argentina, Brazil, Chile, and Colombia represent 76 percent of the total, indicating the relative importance of the biotechnology capacity in these four countries relative to the other countries in the survey.

The institutional distribution of biotechnology research is different from the distribution of agricultural research in general. The majority of agricultural biotech R&D is conducted in public universities (44 percent), followed by public research and development (R&D) centers (26 percent) and private firms (20 percent). This is in line with figures reported in other studies (IICA 1992; Jaffé 1993; Trigo 2000).

The institutional distribution of one of the most applied areas of biotech research—field trials of GM varieties—is dominated by the private sector, particularly by multinational input firms. Seventy-five percent of the trials in Argentina, Brazil, and Mexico have been conducted by multinational firms. In some countries, particularly in Mexico, local input firms play a major role. The large Mexican company Savia, which operates internationally and has controlling interests in the vegetable seed company Seminis and the biotech firm DNA Plant Biotechnology (DNAP) in the United States, is active in a number of Latin American countries. Local agricultural processing firms, including those in the sugar and paper industries, also play a role, particularly in Brazil. The government plays a minor role in Argentina and Brazil and a somewhat larger role in Mexico. For the region as a whole, public institutions conducted just 9 percent of the trials, a share similar to that of the public sector in U.S. trials. The institutional structure of agricultural biotech research is quite different from other agricultural research in Latin America, which is concentrated in public R&D centers, with limited research carried out at universities and the private firms (Echeverría, Trigo, and Byerlee 1996).

Although biotechnology research investments in Latin America are insignificant compared with those of other countries to date, by the region's standards, the resources dedicated to biotechnology research are considerable. Table 11.1 shows estimates of expenditure and number of scientists derived from the ISNAR survey (Cohen, Komen, and Verastegui 2001). The expenditures are underestimated because a number of the institutes did not report their expenditure or may not have included all research costs. For example, in contrast to the US$3.4 million expenditure in Brazil reported in the ISNAR study, Dias Avila et al. (2001) indicate that Embrapa alone spent some US$14 million on biotech research in 2000. In addition *Fundaçao do Amparo à Pesquisa do Estado de Sao Pāulo* [the Sao Pāulo Research Foundation] (FAPESP) was spending at least US$15 million over three years on agricultural biotech research. Nevertheless, Table 11.1 provides at least a lower bound estimate of research expenditure in the region, with Colombia showing the largest expenditure, in part because the International Center for Tropical Agriculture (CIAT) invested US$1,600,000 in 1999, followed by Brazil, Argentina, Chile, and Peru. Peru's expenditure is explained by the contribution of another international organization, the International Potato Center (CIP), which invested US$1,470,000—98 percent of the total. While Mexico was not included in the Cohen, Komen, and Verastegui (2001) survey, an earlier survey by Falconi (1999b) indicated Mexican investment in biotech on the scale of investment by Argentina, Brazil, and Mexico. In addition, the International Maize and Wheat Improvement Center (CIMMYT) invests about US$3 million annually in biotech. Two small countries with noteworthy investments in biotech are Costa Rica (at least US$500,000 annually) and Cuba, for which data are not available.

Brazil had the most scientists working in the field of biotechnology with 435, followed by Argentina with 257, Colombia with 251, and Mexico with 238. Mexico had the highest proportion of researchers with doctoral degrees although Brazil had the most researchers with doctorate and masters degrees. In Argentina, 21.8 percent (56) of the country's biotechnologists held doctorates, and 22.2 percent (57) held masters degrees. While the data are incomplete, it seems the academic qualifications of biotechnologists in other countries such as Costa Rica, Peru, and Venezuela are consistent with the overall level of scientific development in these countries. In Ecuador and Guatemala there was less expertise: in both countries about 60 percent of the total number of scientists involved in biotechnology research were trained only to bachelor-degree level.

Table 11.1   Financial and human resources for biotechnology R&D, 1999

| Country | Survey responses | Financial resources [a] | | Number of scientists | | | |
		Country total	Institute average	Ph.D.	M.Sc.	B.Sc.	Total
	(count)	(U.S. dollars[a])		(count)			
Argentina	13	2,945,000	226,538	56	57	144	257
Brazil	16	3,363,255	210,203	150	102	183	435
Chile	7	2,154,716	307,817	35	22	36	93
Colombia	17	5,808,614	263,038	44	55	152	251
Costa Rica	4	453,245	113,311	8	9	12	29
Ecuador	2	160,000	80,000	1	2	6	9
Guatemala	2	55,600	27,800	1	3	6	10
Mexico[b]	n.a	n.a	n.a.	127	49	62	238
Peru	3	1,496,338	13,169	10	5	19	34
Venezuela	6	214,475	35,746	18	11	13	42
TOTAL		16,651,243		450	315	633	1,398

Sources: Falconi (1999a) for Mexico, and Cohen, Komen, and Verastegui (2001) for all other countries.
Note: n.a. indicates date were unavailable.
a. Exchange rates as at December 29, 1999.
b. Mexico data are for 1997.

Section A in Table 11.2 indicates the types of biotechnology research being performed. Cell biology techniques appear the most frequently used in the 13-country sample, with about 29 percent of the total number of applications reported, followed by genetic marker techniques at 27 percent, diagnostic techniques at 20 percent, genetic engineering techniques at 14 percent, and lastly microbial techniques at 10 percent. Cell biology techniques generally require smaller amounts of financial and human capital, so it is not surprising that they are the most commonly used, while genetic engineering techniques that are more demanding of resources are among the least used. Somewhat surprising, however, is that molecular marker techniques are used almost as extensively as cell biology techniques.

Production constraints receiving the most attention were plant production (27 percent), followed by genetic resources (25 percent) and plant health (25 percent). The combined interest in animal production and health also reflects the importance of livestock in most countries of the region (16 percent). The interest in food production, pharmaceutical applications, and uses in various other industries (5 and 2 percent respectively) reflects an emerging industrial demand for innovation, quality, and competitiveness in some Latin American economies (Table 11.2 section B).

There is a diverse array of biotechnology applications among crop and livestock species, ranging from fruit trees and forestry species at 20 percent to animals and microorganisms with 5 percent (Table 11.2 section C). The research performed in each country is represented in almost every species category with, perhaps, some regional specialization toward wheat and cereals in Southern Cone countries— Argentina, Bolivia, Brazil, Chile, Paraguay, and Uruguay—and potatoes, roots, and tubers in Andean/tropical countries—Colombia, Ecuador, and Peru. Within each country, Argentina concentrates its efforts on cereals and oilseeds, cattle, and other livestock (57 percent of responses); Brazil emphasizes horticulture, legumes, cattle, and other livestock (63 percent); in Chile horticulture-legumes-berries and fruit and forest research represent 57 percent of the total effort; and in Colombia, there is a much wider and more even distribution aside from the importance given to industrial crops (21 percent).

National and International Biotechnology Programs

Much of the capacity reported in the previous section has evolved within special programs to support the development of scientists at the regional, subregional, and country levels. In general these programs have concentrated on creating or consolidating the local R&D base, with biotechnology support a component of the overall funding for R&D, including infrastructure and human resource development. In most cases the bulk of these efforts were funded through loan projects from either the Inter-American Development Bank (IDB) or the World Bank (Table 11.3). In recent years many projects were designed to support general R&D activities, usually within the framework of competitive funding schemes.[2] Although no comprehensive data are available, partial evidence from some countries (Argentina, Brazil, Chile, and Venezuela) indicates that biotechnology-related research has captured a significant share of the total funding through these mechanisms. In Argentina, of the more than 1,100 projects approved by *Fondo para la Investigación Científica y Tecnológica* [National Fund for the Promotion of Science and Technology] (FONCYT) in 1997 and 1998, almost 30 percent can be categorized under biotechnology.

Another important development is the inclusion of significant funding—both as soft loans and competitive grants—for the development of links between public scientific institutions and the food and agriculture sector and for technological modernization and innovation within individual firms. The most recent projects implemented in Argentina, Brazil, Chile, Uruguay, and Venezuela involve cofunding to allow public and private R&D institutions to establish business units to improve their technological services capacities, promote joint public-private ventures, and direct funding for R&D and innovation initiatives undertaken by commercial firms. In Argentina, both general and agricultural biotechnology-related projects appear prominently among those funded since the inception of these new initiatives, all of which have been developed with funding from the IDB and represent critical sup-

Table 11.2   Biotechnology techniques and research focus in selected Latin America and the Caribbean countries, circa 2000

Description	Argentina	Brazil	Chile	Colombia	Costa Rica	Ecuador	Guatemala	Jamaica	Paraguay	Peru	Trinidad and Tobago	Uruguay	Venezuela	Total
A. BIOTECHNOLOGY TECHNIQUES						*(number of applications of technique)*								
Cell biology techniques														**259**
Micropropagation	13	9	13	39	8	5	3		2	11			11	114
Anther culture	3	2	3	9		1				1			2	21
Embryo rescue	4	1	4	6	1								3	19
Protoplast fusion		1		2										3
In vitro germplasm conservation and exchange	5	3	3	14	4	2				1			10	42
In vitro insemination		2		1										3
Embryo manipulation and exchange	3	5		1									2	11
Animal cell cloning		3		1										4
Other—cell biology	3	3	5	21	3	1							6	42
Genetic engineering techniques														**124**
Agrobacterium mediated	11	12	6	7	4					7			4	51
Microprojectile bombardment	4	11	7	6	3	1							5	37
Electroporation		7	1	1		1							4	14
Microinjection		4		1										5
Other—genetic engineering	7	5	2	2	1									17
Genetic marker techniques														**239**
RFLP	7	9	3	10		2				2			2	35
RAPD	15	24	11	14	2	6				4			5	81
Microsatellite markers	13	10	8	12	3	1				4				51
AFLP	13	6	7	8	1	1				4				40
Others	6	9	10	4		1							2	32
Diagnostic techniques														**176**
ELISA	6	12	3	13		2			2	2			3	43
Monoclonal antibodies	1	5	2	4		1			2	1			1	17
Nucleic acid probes	1	5	1	1						1			4	13
PCR	10	29	12	11		1				1			4	68
Other		5	5	20	2	2							1	35
Microbial Techniques														**90**
Design–delivery biocontrol agents	1	3	2	7			5							18
Design–delivery of biofertilizers	2	2		2									1	7
Fermentation, food processing	2	4		17		1								24
Animal growth hormones	2	2												4
Rumen manipulation		1												1
Design–delivery of r vaccines	5			1										6
Other—microbiology	6	1	2	17	2	1							1	30
Total	143	195	110	252	34	30	8		6	39			71	888

port for research along with technology transfer efforts. These funding mechanisms do not necessarily replace private venture capital for start-up activities, but represent an important step toward facilitating linkages between scientific research and technological capacities.[3]

International cooperation programs have played a significant role in the development of biotechnology generally and agbiotech specifically, particularly in smaller

Table 11.2   Biotechnology techniques and research focus in selected Latin America and the Caribbean countries, circa 2000 (continued)

Description	Argentina	Brazil	Chile	Colombia	Costa Rica	Ecuador	Guatemala	Jamaica	Paraguay	Peru	Trinidad and Tobago	Uruguay	Venezuela	Total
B. PRODUCTION CONSTRAINT OR NEED TARGETED														
Plant production[a]	26	16	20	39	12	2	2		2	7			12	138
Plant health[b]	20	30	15	35		3	5		1	8			9	126
Animal production[c]	10	15	3	4		3								35
Animal health[d]	23	2	4	14		2								45
Genetic resources[e]	22	23	24	21	14	9				2			9	124
Food/pharmaceutical needs[f]		8	1	10	2		2			1				24
Genomics	1	2												3
Other		3	4	4		1								12
Total	102	99	71	127	28	20	9		3	18			30	507
C. CROP/LIVESTOCK BREEDING														
Cereals[g]	25	13	11	14		1	1						7	72
Roots and tubers[h]	10	10	6	23	7	13				11			9	89
Horticultural plants[i]	16	37	18	31	3		5			9			4	123
Fruit trees and forestry species	13	14	29	39	9	2			3	12			18	139
Medicinal, tropical, and native plants	6	6	8	13	8	2	2						14	59
Industrial crops[j]	3	5	1	42	5		1			1			14	72
Bovine, beef, and dairy	27	13	6	15										61
Other livestock[k]	18	19	2	12										51
Other livestock and organisms[l]	5	7	2	9	3	9	3							38
Total	123	124	83	198	35	27	12		3	33			66	704

Source: Cohen, Komen, and Verastegui (2001).
Notes: RFLP denotes restriction fragment length polymorphism; RAPD, random amplified DNA polymorphism; AFLP, amplified fragment length polymorphism; PCR, polymerace chain reaction; and ELISA, enzyme linked inmmuno sorbent essay.
a. Plant breeding, cloning, productivity, abiotic stress, other.
b. Protection, diseases, diagnostics, other.
c. Reproduction, productivity, other.
d. Protection, variability, selection, vaccines, diagnostics, other.
e. Characterization, variability, selection, conservation.
f. Nutritional quality, functional food, drugs, enzymes.
g. Wheat, barley, maize, and other cereals.
h. Potatoes, roots, and tubers.
i. Oilseeds, legumes, berries, and ornamental plants.
j. Coffee, sugarcane, tobacco, palm, and so on.
k. Swine, goats, sheep, horses, and poultry.
l. Aquatic animals, dogs, birds, insects, and so on.

countries. The most relevant programs include the Regional Biotechnology Program of the United Nations, funded by the United Nations Development Program (UNDP), the United Nations Education, Scientific, and Cultural Organization

Table 11.3   Government programs supporting biotechnology in selected Latin American and Caribbean countries, 1980–2000

Country	Names and dates	Executing agency	Objectives	Investment level
				(millions US$)[a]
Argentina	*Programa Nacional de Biotecnología*	Department of Science and Technology (SeCyT)	Promotion and funding of biotechnology R&D	3.8
	Programa de Modernización Tecnológica I (IDB 1993)	Department of Economic Planning and Programming and Department of Science and Technology	Support for general science and technology research and for increased private-sector participation in R&D activities, through loans and risk-sharing mechanisms.	91.0
	Programa de Modernización Tecnológica II (IDB 1999)	*Agencia Nacional de Promoción Científica y Tecnológica (ANPCyT)*	Support for science and technology research in general and grants for private sector involvement in R&D activities	280.0
Brazil	*Programa Nacional de Biotecnología* (1981)	National Research Council (CNPq) and National Fund for the Promotion of Scientific and Technological Research (FINEP)	Funding of biotechnology R&D	3.3
	PADCT/*Biotecnología* (World Bank 1984)	Ministry for Science and Technology	Human resources and infrastructure in biotechnology-related scientific fields	12.9
	Biotechnology Parks	Ministry for Science and Technology	Infrastructure and services for start-up firms	n.a.
	Genome Project	Sao Paulo Science and Technology Foundation (FAPESP)	Infrastructure and research by universities, research institutes, and private firms	30.0+
	Science and Technology Promotion Program (IDB 1991)	Ministry of Science and Technology (CNPq)	Grants for scientific and technological research in R&D public- and private- sector institutions. Support for risk- sharing initiatives in the private sector	100.0
	Science and Technology Reform Support (World Bank 1997)	Ministry of Science and Technology	Improve the quality of advanced research and training and promote cooperative R&D between public and private institutions and private investments in R&D	360.0
Chile	National Biotechnology Committee (1983)	National Council for Scientific and Technological Research (CONICYT)	Human resources development/ Promotion and Coordination of R&D	n.a.
	Programa de Ciencia y Tecnología (IDB 1994)	CONICYT and the *Coorporación de Fomento* (CORFO)	Promotion of science and technology research in general and private sector involvement in R&D activities through risk sharing mechanisms	94.0
	Programa de Desarrollo e Innovación Tecnológica (IDB 2000)	Economics Ministry	Promotion of public and private R&D for improving the competitiveness of production sectors, with special emphasis on the use of biotechnological approaches	200.0
Colombia	Biotechnology Program (1984)	*Instituto Colombiano para el Desarrollo de la Ciencia y la Tecnología* (COLCIENCIAS)	Planning, coordination and funding of R&D	n.a.
	Programa de Desarrollo Científico y Tecnológico (IDB 1995)	COLCIENCIAS	General support for scientific and technological research and technological innovation in strategic sectors	100.0

(UNESCO), and the United Nations Industrial Development Organization (UNIDO). This set of programs pioneered the process of diffusion of basic techniques among significant numbers of research institutions in the region. It also facilitated the creation of a number of "national biotechnology commissions" to coordinate national efforts throughout the region.

Other initiatives aimed at developing basic research capacities are the Biotechnology for Latin America and the Caribbean of the United Nations University (UNU/BIOLAC) and the agricultural biotechnology network of the Food and

Table 11.3   Government programs supporting biotechnology in selected Latin American and Caribbean countries, 1980–2000 (continued)

Country	Names and dates	Executing agency	Objectives	Investment
				(millions US$)[a]
Mexico	*Programa Nacional de Desarrollo Científico y Tecnológico* (PRONDETYC 1984)	*Consejo Nacional de Ciencia y Tecnología* (CONACYT)	Funding support for biotechnology research in universities and other public research centers	n.a.
	Apoyo al Desarrollo Científico y Tecnológico (IDB 1993)	CONACYT	Infrastructure and funding support for science and technology research and direct funding for precompetitive R&D in small and medium-sized private enterprises	150.0
Uruguay	*Programa de Desarrollo Científico y Tecnológico* (IDB 1991)	CONICYT	General support for R&D (human resources, infrastructure and R&D expenditures)	35.0
Venezuela	*Programa Nacional de Ingeniería Genética y Biotecnología* (1986)	*Consejo Nacional de Investigaciones Científicas y Tecnológicas* (CONICYT)	Funding of R&D	0.5
	Programa Nuevas Tecnologías (IDB 1992)	CONICYT	General support for R&D (human resources, infrastructure, and R&D expenditures)	30.0
	Segundo Programa de Ciencia y Tecnología (IDB 1999)	CONICYT	Support for science and technology research and promotion of private sector involvement in R&D activities, through a grants program	200.0

Sources: Developed by the authors from Jaffé (1993), Inter-American Development Bank and World Bank official documents, such as Annual Reports, project and loan documents.
Notes: Data are not an exhaustive list of initiatives; n.a. indicates not available; IDB denotes Inter-American Development Bank.
a. For the IDB and World Bank supported programs, investments reported are for the projects as a whole, not the biotechnology components in particular.

Agriculture Organization of the United Nations (FAO), REDBIO. Both initiatives represent important coordination and exchange mechanisms for Latin American researchers and research centers.

At the subregional level several programs foster cooperative research of common interest to the participating countries, stimulating the sharing of information and technology transfer. The most important is the *Centro Argentino Brasileño de Biotecnología* [Argentine-Brazilian Center for Biotechnology] (CABBIO), in operation since 1985 and funding about 70 projects, many of them in agricultural and food-related areas. CABBIO began as a binational initiative involving Argentina and Brazil, but later expanded to include all the MERCOSUR [Common Market of the South] countries with the addition of Chile, Paraguay, and Uruguay. Human resource development and technology transfer are the two most important outputs of CABBIO to date, but there are significant R&D results in a number of areas that are rapidly maturing into the product development stage.

The Cooperative Agricultural Research Program for the Southern Cone (PRO-CISUR), linking the Southern Cone countries, also has a significant impact on participating national programs with the support of the countries involved and various international assistance organizations. Another noteworthy cooperation effort is

CamBioTec, a Canadian initiative funded by the Canadian International Development Agency (CIDA) and the International Development Research Centre (IDRC) to facilitate business ventures in Latin America by promoting biosafety regulations and public awareness, and by establishing links between public and private Latin American and Canadian R&D capacities.

Finally, the biotechnology programs and activities of the International Agricultural Research Centers (IARCs), particularly CIAT, CIP, and CIMMYT and the Tropical Agricultural Research and Education Center (CATIE), have also lent critical support for the development of biotechnology through the diffusion of strategic technologies and the development of human resources. The IARCs have developed an extensive network of research collaboration with advanced public and private research institutes in industrialized and developing countries. Their primary focus is building capacity through research into tropical crops and animal species. The 16 IARCs together invest around US$25 million annually on biotechnology, representing around 7.7 percent of the Consultative Group on International Agricultural Reseach's (CGIAR's) total budget. Of the US$25 million, about 27 percent is related directly to livestock (primarily animal health), with about 15 percent of the total going to genetic engineering (Morris and Hoisington 2000). Appendix Table 11A.1 summarizes the biotechnology-related activities that are carried out by CIMMYT, CIAT, and CIP, along with their collaborative relationships with other institutions.

The Output of Latin American Biotech Research

Biotechnology research conducted in Latin America has produced new knowledge, new tools, and new technology; however, the major advances in technology used by farmers—GM soybeans, corn, and cotton—have been developed by U.S. and European companies.

The FAPESP genome program in Brazil, mentioned above, has achieved the most success in terms of basic biotechnology research. In July 2000 it was the first group to completely sequence a plant pathogen—*Xylella fastidiosa*, the pathogen that causes citrus variegated chlorosis, an important citrus disease. Since then FAPESP has completed sequencing the organism that causes citrus canker, *Xanthomonas citri*. In April 2001 scientists supported by FAPESP and local sugar cooperatives finished sequencing the sugarcane genome and another FAPESP-industry consortium is commencing work on the Eucalyptus genome (Rohter 2001). Brazilian researchers have also developed technologies to improve their research efficiency and to provide the freedom to commercialize their transgenic crops (Avila et al. 2001).

Three GMOs—Roundup Ready® (RR) soybeans, *Bacillus thuringiensis (Bt)* maize, and *Bt* cotton—have been commercialized in LAC. More than 95 percent of the GMO area in the region is sown to RR soybeans (Table 11.4). By the 1999

Table 11.4   Area under commercial production of GM crops, 1999

Country	Soybeans	Corn	Cotton
		(hectares)	
Argentina	6,400,000	260,000	10,000
Brazil	1,000,000		
Chile		20,000[a]	
Mexico	500	47,000	20,000
Uruguay	5,000		
Total	7,405,500	327,000	30,000

growing season, more than 6 million hectares, 80 percent of soybean area, were planted to herbicide-tolerant soybeans in Argentina, and an estimated 1 million hectares were being grown in Brazil. Small areas of RR soybeans have been introduced in Mexico and Uruguay. *Bt* maize provides resistance to certain Lepidopteran insects, the European corn borer in the United States, and the sugarcane borer in Argentina. *Bt* maize holds significant potential and has been introduced in Argentina and Mexico but has been planted to a total of only 327,000 hectares. *Bt* cotton has been grown in Argentina and Mexico, but on relatively small areas.

Field trials on new GM crops provide another measure of the output of applied biotech research. More than 800 GMO field trials were conducted in the region from 1987 to 2000 (Table 11.5 section A), comprising about one fifth of the world field trials conducted outside the United States. These tests have been concentrated in Argentina, Brazil, and Mexico, which together account for 84 percent of LAC trials; Argentina, Brazil, and Mexico rank fourth, sixth, and ninth respectively worldwide. During 1998–99 only two countries, the United States and Canada, conducted more field trials than Argentina or Brazil.

Regional field tests have been conducted on a total of 24 different GMO crops; however herbicide-tolerance (HT) and insect-resistance (IR) traits have been the primary focus in the main commercial crops of maize, soybeans, cotton, and sunflowers (Table 11.5 section B). These four crops constitute 80 percent of all trials, while herbicide tolerance and insect resistance (in all crops) also account for 80 percent of all trials. The product quality (PQ) trials that have been conducted to date are dominated by delayed ripening in tomatoes in Mexico. Trials of disease (DR) and virus-resistant (VR) crops are becoming more frequent.

Challenges for Accessing the Benefits of Biotechnology

The application of biotechnological approaches to agriculture offers significant potential benefits, but a number of important issues have yet to be addressed. These

Table 11.5   GM field trials in the LAC region, by year and by trait, 1987–2000

	1987	1988	1989	1990	1991	1992	1993	1994	1995	1996[a]	1997[a]	1998[a]	1999[a]	2000[a]	Total	Share of Total
A. APPROVED TRIALS BY YEAR								(count)								(percent)
Argentina					3	7	9	18	32	38	67	71	76	0	321	37
Belize					4	1									5	1
Bolivia					3	1		1	1			2			8	1
Brazil											25	88	110	24	247	28
Chile	1					4	7	6	21				16		55	6
Colombia														7	7	1
Costa Rica					1	4		2	10						17	2
Cuba				1	1	2	4	5	5						18	2
Guatemala			1					1	1						3	0
Mexico		1				4	6	7	10	27	36	31	23	21	166	19
Peru								2							2	0
Uruguay												29			29	3
LAC Total	1	1	1	1	8	26	27	42	80	65	128	221	225	52	878	
World Total[b]	1	10	37	48	74	156	222	351	476	532	681	815	813	514	4,730	
LAC Share								(percent)								
of World[a]	100	10	3	2	11	17	12	12	17	12	19	27	28	10	19	

B. APPROVED TRIALS BY TRAIT							(count)								
	HT	IR	HT/IR	PQ	VR	DR	MG	AP	UN	HT/AP	HT/DR	HT/MG	HT/VR	VR/IR	Other	Total
Argentina	104	106	58	15	7	22	1	4		1	1			1	1	321
Belize	3	2														5
Bolivia	2	2		1			1	2								8
Brazil	112	95	10		6											223
Chile	21	6	6	14	3	1	1					2	1			55
Colombia		2		1	1				3							7
Costa Rica	11	4		1	1				1							18
Cuba		10			6	1	1								2	20
Guatemala				2	1											3
Mexico	30	52	10	36	26	1	10	2								167
Peru									2							2
Uruguay	19	10														29
LAC Total	302	289	84	70	51	25	14	8	6	1	1	2	1	1	3	858
LAC share							(percent)								
of world	35	34	10	8	6	3	2	1	1	0	0	0	0	0	0	

Sources: For Argentina, CONABIA (2001); for Brazil, CTNBio (2001); for Peru, Guislain (2001); for Mexico, SAGAR (2001); for Chile, Hinrichsen (2000) and James and Kratigger (1996); for Colombia, Artunuaga-Salas (2001); for Belize, Bolivia, Costa Rica, Cuba, and Guatemala, James and Kratigger (1996); and for Uruguay, Blanco (1998). World data compiled from Courtmanche, Pray, and Govindasamy (2001).

Notes: HT denotes herbicide tolerance; IR, insect resistance; PQ, product quality; VR, virus resistance; DR, disease resistance; MG, marker genes; AP, agronomic properties; and UN, unidentified.

a. For trials by year, data are incomplete for some countries for some years; for trials by trait, not all countries include 2000 data.

b. Data excludes the United States, but includes regional totals for Latin America and the Caribbean.

c. Field trial data measures the number of applications approved by the appropriate government entity for field tests of GM crops worldwide. One application may include approvals for more than one location.

Figure 11.1 Discovery and development process of a transgenic crop variety

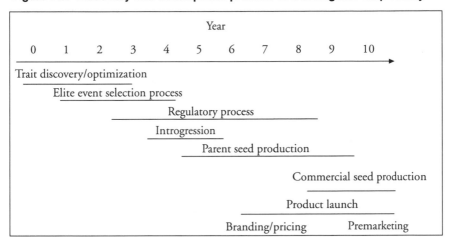

Source: Convent (2000).

issues relate to the organization of technology and innovation systems, the scientific basis of biotechnology and its interface with traditional agricultural research, and, as in the rest of the world, issues related to delivery mechanisms, biosafety and consumer acceptance, and proprietary rights.

Chronic Underinvestment

The novel character of biotechnology and the long timeframe required to get products to markets make the biotechnology industry an expensive endeavor (Figure 11.1). No comprehensive figures exist on biotechnology-related investments in LAC, but a brief look at general agricultural research investments indicates that the region's biotech environment is characterized not only by a serious underinvestment problem, but also abnormally high year-to-year fluctuations in research budgets.[4]

According to Mateo et al. (1999), in 1995 LAC countries invested less than 0.45 percent of their agricultural gross domestic product in agricultural R&D—equivalent to only about one tenth of Australia's, one sixth of Israel's, and one fifth of Canada's relative investments. Between the early 1980s and 1990s, investments in the region fell by 10 percent in real terms. In 1992–93, investments in research were estimated at US$588 million (current value); that figure grew to about US$1 billion in 1997, only to fall to less than US$640 million in 1998–99 (Mateo et al. 1999).[5]

There is a high concentration of investments in a small number of countries: Argentina and Brazil account for almost 75 percent of total investments, and if

Colombia, Peru, and Venezuela are included, the figure grows to over 85 percent. On average, over 85 percent of the budgets go to researchers' salaries, which makes it difficult to undertake an effective research program.

At present nothing indicates that this pattern of investment will change substantially. Fiscal adjustment programs continue to tighten public and private research budgets. As mentioned above, a number of externally funded initiatives are setting the stage for closer cooperation between the public and private sectors in the form of R&D joint ventures, but these are relatively small given the task, and there are no venture-capital mechanisms to help diffuse and accelerate these initiatives.

Private research investment in LAC is also below that of other regions. While private R&D in Australia, Canada, and the United States has increased significantly, in LAC it still represents a very small share of total investments. Essentially its evolution has followed the same course as public funding, with the exception of plant breeding research in some cereals and oilseeds in Argentina, Brazil, and Mexico (cereals and oilseeds), and some tropical crops in Brazil, Central America, and Colombia (such as coffee and sugarcane).[6] This investment behavior probably reflects the fact that potential markets of sufficient size to support significant R&D in LAC are limited. Large potential markets exist for only a few crops in Argentina, Brazil, and Mexico. Together these three countries account for more than 80 percent of the total cropped area in LAC and more than 85 percent of the area under the main commercial crops of maize, soybeans, and cotton. These three countries contain 12 crop areas of more than a million hectares within their boundaries (maize in all three countries, soybeans and wheat in Argentina and Brazil, beans in Brazil and Mexico, cassava and rice in Brazil, and sunflowers in Argentina). The only other LAC country containing more than a million hectares sown to a single crop is Paraguay (soybeans). Commercial seed markets are also underdeveloped in the region; again, the three largest countries dominate commercial sales.

The Scientific Organization of R&D Processes

Biotechnology should not be considered in isolation from traditional agricultural research technologies. In theory, biotechnology transforms and expands the scope of technological possibility, but at its present level of development it should be viewed as a set of tools to complement traditional research approaches, making them more effective.

The nature of this complementarity is evident in areas such as crop breeding and epidemiology. In crop breeding, biotechnological approaches such as genomics and modern genetic engineering can make breeding more efficient and define technological alternatives outside the envelope of technological possibilities available just a few years ago, even in terms of designing completely new products. But once the new technologies are available the need remains to backcross the new GM varieties into the broad germplasm of existing commercial varieties, and undertake large-scale field evaluations to adapt the new products to local ecological conditions and cultural practices. This step still needs to be done through conventional crop breeding and agronomic work, and through public-private collaborations akin to those supporting agricultural technology development systems. Even in cases where the private sector leads the process, public involvement will still be necessary as part of the approval process and the development of appropriate data to support the approval of the new materials.

The critical issue, however, is not so much the public-private involvement but the nature of the scientific environment in which technology development takes place. Traditional agricultural R&D has a "vertical" structure, where the development of the basic knowledge and its applications to technology generation are closely interrelated, usually undertaken within the same organization. But biotechnology development, also has a "horizontal" nature, being applicable across a broad range of areas such as health, the environment, industry, and agriculture. Biotechnology capacities are generic, and the appropriate institutional environment includes basic science departments of universities and advanced research institutions, not necessarily linked to the technology delivery systems of the region.

A Credible Capacity for Biosafety Oversight

Modern biotechnology offers a wide array of benefits for agricultural development as well as for consumers; however, the novel characteristics of some of its components—particularly GMOs—creates concerns regarding their safety for human health and the environment. Table 11.6 summarizes current biosafety regulations in LAC countries. The overall picture is extremely weak. Only a few countries (Argentina Brazil, Costa Rica, Cuba, and Mexico) have operational systems, and the remaining countries (Bolivia, Chile, Colombia, Paraguay, Peru, and Uruguay) have only partial systems in place or none at all. Even some of the more advanced systems require assessment and strengthening. An ISNAR study of Argentina—probably the most advanced country in commercial use of GMOs—has concluded that the existing mechanisms need improvement in at least four areas: (a) roles and responsibilities at the administrative, technical, and political levels of the evaluation and approval process, (b) scope and depth of the scientific base available to support decisionmaking, (c) efficiency and transparency of the review processes, and (d) public awareness and acceptance (Burachik and Traynor 2001, 23).

Intellectual Property Rights

The growing importance of enforceable property rights, covering both the tools and the products of research, requires the public sector to reexamine its role in agricultural research and development activities, including management and funding

Table 11.6 Summary of biosafety regulations in Latin America and the Caribbean

Country	Existence of formal mechanism	Level of the norm	Coverage	Comments	Operational experience
Argentina	Yes	Ministerial Resolution (1992)	Plants and microorganisms for veterinary use (norm concerning animals is under consideration; there have been voluntary evaluations about animals)	Advisory Commission including evaluation of health and environmental issues and commercial risks of introduction of GMOs	More than 300 field trials including commercial releases in maize, soybeans, cotton, sunflowers, potatoes, canola, wheat, rice, and sugar beets; commercial releases in soybeans, maize, and cotton
Chile	Yes	Ministerial Resolution (1993)	Plants only	Advisory mechanism based on adaptation of seeds law with emphasis on "winter nursery," now extended to cover local releases	Field trials conducted in maize, soybeans, tomatoes, canola, wheat, tobacco, and sugar beets
Uruguay	Yes	National Decree (2000)	Plants only	Advisory mechanism based on adaptation of seeds law with emphasis on "winter nursery," now extended to cover local releases (covers field experiments only, not laboratory experimentation)	Field trials conducted in several species; commercial releases approved in soybeans and maize
Paraguay	Yes	Ministerial Resolution (1997)	Plants only	Advisory mechanisms for executive decisions	No operational experience
Brazil	Yes	Law (National Biosafety Law No. 8974 of 1995)	Wide coverage including plants, animals, and microorganisms of health, agriculture, and the environment	Executive mechanism including sanctions against infractors	Large number of field trials; no commercial approvals in maize, soybeans, cotton, potatoes, sugarcane, fruits, tobacco, and rice
Bolivia	Yes	National Decree (1997)	Plants only	Advisory mechanisms for executive decisions	Limited experience with field trials in cotton and potatoes; no commercial releases
Peru	Yes	Law (1999)	Wide coverage (plants, animals and microorganisms)	Advisory mechanism as part of the biodiversity protection law; specific procedures applicable for the agricultural sector are still under review	
Colombia	Yes	Ministerial Resolution (1998)	Plants only	Advisory mechanism, for field evaluations only, not laboratory work	Limited experience with field trials in flowers and cotton; no commercial releases

Table 11.6 Summary of biosafety regulations in Latin America and the Caribbean (continued)

Country	Existence of formal mechanism	Level of the norm	Coverage	Comments	Operational experience
Venezuela	Approved, in process of organization	The Biological Diversity Law, passed on May 2000, includes a chapter on biosafety, which served as the basis for the system been set in place[a]	Covers all GMOs and derivatives	The system is based on an Advisory Commission on Biosafety, which will operate in the Ministry of the Environment; monitoring and control functions to be implemented by the different sectoral ministries (agriculture, health, and so on)	
English-speaking Caribbean	There is no regionwide framework			Some countries (Jamaica, Trinidad and Tobago) have regulations for the import of GM plants; coverage is for laboratory and field trials; in Jamaica they are being applied to papaya	
Cuba	Yes	Decree Law #190 on Biological Safety (1999)	Wide application (plants, animals, and microorganisms)	Follows the guidelines of the Convention on Biological Diversity	Field trials approved in potatoes, canola, vegetables, sugarcane, and tobacco; no commercial releases
Costa Rica	Yes	National Technology Advisory Committee on Biosafety (Crop Protection Law N°7664) (1997)	Only plants	Normative emphasis in "winter nurseries"	Field trials in maize, soybeans cotton, and wheat
Mexico	Yes	Mexican Federal Norm (1995)	Wide coverage (plants, animal, microorganisms)	Resolutions of obligatory applications	Field trials approved in maize, soybeans, cotton, tomatoes, vegetables, canola, wheat, fruits, tobacco, rice, alfalfa, and others
Ecuador, Dominican Republic, Panama, Nicaragua, Honduras, El Salvador, Guatemala	Do not report any formal mechanism in operation				

Sources: Compiled by the authors based on information from ISNAR Biotechnology Service (IBS), regulatory agencies' websites, and personal information and communications with regulatory authorities.

a. In operation from the second semester of 2001.

Table 11.7   Agricultural biotechnology property protection in Latin America and the Caribbean, circa 2000

Country	Discovery	Biological process	Plants[b]	Plant varieties[c]	Animals (breeds)	Micro-organism	Genes
Argentina	✗	✓	✓	✓	✓	✓	✓
Chile	✗	✓	—	✓	✓	✓	—
Brazil	✗	—	✗	✓	✗d	✓	—
Uruguay	✗	✗	✗	✓	✗	✓	✗
Paraguay	✗	✗	✗	✗	✗	✓	—
Bolivia[a]	✗	✗	✗	✓	✗	✓	—
Peru[a]	✗	✗	✗	✓	✗	—	—
Ecuador[a]	✗	✗	✗	✓	✗	—	—
Colombia[a]	✗	✗	✗	✓	✗	—	—
Venezuela[a]	✗	✗	✗	✓	✗	—	—
Mexico	✗	✗	✓	✓	✗	✓	—
Costa Rica	✗	✗	✗	✗	✗	—	—

Sources: Compiled by authors from ISNAR (2000), IICA (2000), Lele, Lesser, and Horstkotte-Wesseler (1999).
Note: ✓ indicates protection is possible; ✗ indicates protection is not possible; and — indicates unknown.
a. Legislation is under the scope of Decision 344 of the Cartagena Agreement.
b. Genetic modification.
c. UPOV 1978 and/or 1991.
d. Possible in the case of animal breeds.

mechanisms. With property rights now enforceable in areas previously in the public domain, the legitimacy of public subsidies to research is called into question particularly in the context of significant ongoing underfunding in most public research institutions. If the process is left to market forces, research will focus disproportionately on areas where intellectual property rights (IPR) are effective and profitable, leading to a monopolization of key technologies/areas where high technology fees might be extracted. The public-sector role needs to evolve beyond sourcing R&D to encompass "market regulation" to avert monopolistic behavior that could exclude the less commercially attractive sectors from the benefits of the technology.

Table 11.7 presents the status of IP legislation for countries where information is available. The Dominican Republic, English-speaking Caribbean, El Salvador, Guatemala, Honduras, Nicaragua, and Panama do not report any formal IPR system for plants or other commodities. Even where legislation is available, its coverage is unclear, and it could be said that no country fully complies with the Trade-Related aspects of Intellectual Property (TRIPs) agreement. Salazar et al. (2000) note that these are new and complex issues only beginning to be discussed and defined.

The situation is somewhat different regarding the protection of plant species because plant breeders' rights have a longer history in the region. Argentina, Chile, and Uruguay have had legislation in this area for about 20 years, though it has been fully implemented only since the mid-1980s. Brazil, Mexico, and the Andean Pact countries have also adopted legislation since then. A recent study by Amsterdam University and the Interamerican Institute for Cooperation on Agriculture (IICA) indicates the direct impact is minor, but local breeding programs have been strengthened, especially in open pollinated species, and local industry has gained access to advanced varieties, particularly fruits and flowers (Banchero, Correa, and Bergel 1999).

IPR issues are also poorly understood and managed by research organizations. The Salazar et al. (2000) study, which covers five countries of the region, shows that 33 percent of the cases where researchers were using protected technologies had no information on the means of protection, and most respondents were unaware of the territory implications of patents or the potential consequences for their research. Most of the formal agreements reported fell into the category of material transfer agreements (MTAs), allowing the use of the technologies for research but restricting their use by third parties in the event of commercialization of resulting products. The majority of the research centers (70 percent), however, did not anticipate problems from the dissemination of final products from their biotechnology research, even though they had high expectations for protecting these products: of the 50 expected products reported, 74 percent were expected to be protected either by patents or by plant variety protection.

Technology Delivery Infrastructure

R&D capacities are insufficient to exploit the potential benefits of biotechnology, given that most of the relevant products are "embodied" (meaning they need to be packaged either as seeds or other physical imputs, such as vaccines and diagnostic kits). Consequently, the capacity to develop prototypes and scale them to industrial production and marketing is a critical factor in developing a biotechnology sector.

The sector review undertaken by ISNAR reports that about 35 firms in Argentina, 45 in Brazil, 30 in Chile, and 25 in Mexico are involved in manufacturing or service activities in the biotechnology area.[7] Tissue culture and micropropagation applications are the more diffused technologies in use; there is also important utilization of animal and plant health products, but not the more advanced technologies. As a whole, the weakness of private-sector developments at this level substantially limits future development of the system. The roots of the problem do not appear to be linked to scientific capacity but to other restrictions affecting the creation of start-up companies or the factors affecting private investments in R&D. The weakness of local capital markets and the absence of risk and venture capital mechanisms in most of the countries is clearly a key constraint and a potential area of future intervention.

The need for identity preservation and segregation of GMOs within the food supply is a critical aspect for the future development of the technology, not because of the present consumer protection aspects but because such identification is essential to justify and protect investments. As second and third generation biotechnologies appear (and product quality traits become available), it is the producers who are interested in identifying the GMO origin of the product. In either case (environmental and consumer protection or product differentiation opportunities), exploiting potential benefits—lower production costs or the new quality characteristics of the products—will depend on the capacity to credibly segregate GM from non-GM crops. In most Latin American countries, the logistical and marketing systems, particularly in grains, oilseeds, and other staples, have developed to exploit economies of scale in situations where identity preservation of individual lots brought no aggregate value. In the case of the new GM varieties, segregation becomes the critical issue for adoption and diffusion; only through segregation can the markets adjust their price signals in favor of the new products—if, in fact, consumers are willing to pay a higher price for the quality characteristics offered. The needed private investments for new marketing infrastructure will become available only with institutional innovations in the present contractual and market regulatory systems.

Policy and Institutional Options

Despite a restrictive R&D investment environment the Latin American and the Caribbean region has significant capacity in the agricultural biotechnology area covering a range of production constraints, crops, and livestock species. But in terms of actual commercial applications, biotechnology is still at an early stage of development, concentrated in basic cell biology, diagnostic techniques, and genetic engineering applications in a small number of countries, most within temperate climates.

Multinational corporations outside the region have instigated the majority of the events. As with all novel technologies, initial diffusion patterns tend to reflect the science base and market sizes; to date, most scientific efforts in the field apply to temperate agriculture. How will the technology evolve in coming years, and what policies can countries in the region adopt to position themselves to take advantage of these technologies to improve agricultural and food production and productivity?

It is important to consider the following points in developing a national agricultural biotechnology strategy:

- Agricultural biotechnology is an integral part of agricultural research and technology development—not a separate strategy.

- Universities and nonagricultural advanced research centers are as important as the traditional agricultural research institutions in building required scientific research capacities.

- For plant biotechnology to advance in the region, the capacity to deliver seeds to farmers is critical. This will require substantial public-sector investment in improving germplasm collection and conservation, conventional plant breeding, and creating conditions favorable to private-sector investment in seed development.

- Innovative regional and/or subregional collaborative mechanisms, both in R&D as well as in other activities, can maximize economies of scale that emerge both from complexities of the science and laborious biosafety assurance processes involved.

- The private sector plays a central role in the development of biotechnology. Furthermore, most technologies and events relevant to the region's agricultural conditions are now proprietary, making public-private interaction and active IPR management strategies essential elements for any effort in agricultural biotechnology.

- The capacity to modernize the institutional and physical infrastructures that support product and input markets are as important to the delivery of the new technologies as the creation of enhanced R&D capacity.

Table 11.8 identifies a range of policy instruments needing development and support. The table is organized as a continuum, from the minimum instruments that any country should have if it wants to incorporate biotechnological approaches to its technology development systems, to a situation where it is a full player in the industry.

At the bottom of the scale, the overriding issues are related to establishing technological acquisition capacities; most technology and investments relate to this effort will come from abroad, largely from private multinational concerns. Countries with weak NARSs and no seed distribution systems in place are probably not even exploiting the benefits from conventional approaches so biotechnology offers very limited opportunities. The public-sector role is to support the development of basic capacities in the NARSs; biotechnology opportunities are essentially limited to tissue culture and micropropagation applications for improved planting materi-

Table 11.8   Public-sector roles and policy options for biotechnology development

Public-sector role/ policy objectives	Capacities required	Policy instruments
COUNTRY CHARACTERISTICS		

1. Limited capacity

Small countries with very weak national agricultural research systems and under-developed seed distribution systems, unable to provide new varieties at the farm level on a continuing basis (Dominican Republic, Honduras, Nicaragua, Panama, Paraguay, and most of the English-speaking Caribbean)

Focus is on the development of conventional capacities, and accessing traditional cellular approaches (mainly tissue culture and micropropagation technologies)	Applied and adaptive research capacities in agronomy and conventional breeding	Support for national agricultural research system infrastructure and human resources development
	Tissue culture and micropropagation facilities in strategic crops	Seed-related legislation
	Institutional framework for seed market development	Regional and/or subregional biosafety/ risk evaluation support mechanisms
	Minimum biosafety and IPR frameworks and management capacities	Regional and/or subregional IPR information/management support mechanisms

2. Modest capacity

Countries with active seed markets and NARSs with limited applied research capacities and crop breeding programs providing germplasm at farm level in some crops (Bolivia, Ecuador, El Salvador, and Guatemala)

Creating the environment for accessing potential spillover benefits from existing research and development investments	An intellectual property protection framework (at minimum plant breeders rights)	Intellectual property protection legislation
	Biosafety regulatory capacities	Regional or subregional biosafety regulations and enforcement capacities
	Complementary scientific and technical capacities to orient and support a technology acquisition strategy, including strategy and priority formulation and a working plant breeding program able to incorporate desirable traits into commercial varieties	Regional and/or subregional biosafety/ risk evaluation support mechanisms
		Regional and/or subregional IPR information/management support mechanisms
	An operational seed market with institutional and logistical systems capable of differentiating throughout the production chain	Support to national agricultural research systems and science and technology institutions for infrastructure and human resource development
		Institutional and/or project funding support for research in areas related to technology and biosafety evaluation
		Seed legislation
		Legislation supporting/permitting new input supplier-producer-processor coordination (integration mechanism)
		Quality, certification, and identity preservation systems
		Public investments and credit support for private participation in development of logistical infrastructure

Table 11.8   (continued)

Public-sector role/ policy objectives	Capacities required	Policy instruments

COUNTRY CHARACTERISTICS

3. *Medium capacity*
    Country with one or more strong science institutions and national agricultural research institutes with applied research capacities and breeding programs, and active private seed markets (Chile, Colombia, Costa Rica, Uruguay, and Venezuela).

Improving public goods production and strengthening/ building capacities for technology acquisition and exploitation in plant and animal health related R&D and targeted transgenic research in tropical and "important" crops	Scientific and technological capacities to apply – Cellular and molecular approaches in areas related to genetic resources conservation and evaluation, epidemiology, and pest and diseases control, and so on – Molecular marker technologies and genetic engineering approaches to incorporate (transform) already existing gene constructs into new crops National commodity programs with strong applied breeding capabilities Private sector involvement in product development and commercialization, both in seeds and other agricultural technological input sectors	Support to national agricultural research systems and science and technology institutions for infrastructure and human resources development Funding support for research projects that integrate capacities from different institutions including those abroad Mechanisms for facilitating public/private joint ventures in biotechnology-related R&D projects Public funding for private sector R&D projects (cofinancing, subsidized loans, tax credits for R&D) Promotion of risk and venture capital mechanism

4. *Comprehensive capacity*
    Countries with a wide science base and large public-sector research programs and well developed agricultural inputs and services sectors (Argentina, Brazil, and Mexico).

Promotion and support for basic and strategic research directed to improving the efficiency and scope of technology development activities as a whole	Basic and strategic transgenic and genomic research capacities in both the public and private sectors National commodity programs with comprehensive breeding capacities (wide scope of crops and prebreeding research)	Support to national agricultural research systems and science and technology institutions for infrastructure and human resources development Single and multi-institute project funding mechanism

Source: Devised by authors.

Note: The inclusion of countries in the first or second categories is indicative only. In assigning categories, judgment was made based on the typical situation for each country; exceptions will occur.

als, probably in a small number of export crops and through ad hoc institutional arrangements.

A second group of countries—including countries where NARSs have limited but operational capacities, basically crop breeding, and seed distribution systems able to reach farmers with improved materials on a regular basis—are potential beneficiaries of spillovers. The policy objective for these countries is to establish conditions for technology transfer/acquisition, including the regulatory environment necessary—that is a transparent IPR regime (mandated by the trade agreements signed by most countries) and an operative biosafety mechanism. Without these capacities, no country will be able to take advantage of the benefits of the new technologies, because it is unlikely that private or public entities offering technological capabilities will enter into technology transfer agreements. Lack of IPR protection will endanger the possibilities of recuperating the investment costs, or lack of a biosafety mechanism will preclude the safe movement and environmental release of new biotechnologies. Beyond these aspects, the absence of a seed system assuring a minimum seed turnover at the farm level will make it impossible for innovative traits to be effectively incorporated in production processes. The actions to establish these conditions are essentially the same as those needed to promote conventional technologies; however, biosafety and IPR-related capabilities present some differences that should be considered.

Biosafety regulations and risk evaluation approaches require not only specific normative, administrative, and enforcement capacities but also a substantive level of scientific expertise (scientific information and judgment)—different capacities from those required to use technologies for product development. For many of the countries, this means a potentially critical conflict of interest, because they lack a pool of scientific capacities (people and institutions) large enough to fully separate the regulatory function from the R&D process—avoiding the inevitable conflict and loss of transparency that follows if the same people and institutions involved in developing a technology provide the expertise to evaluate the risk and assess the biosafety implications. Under these circumstances, regional or subregional mechanisms could pool resources, thereby offering support to biosafety regulatory institutions nationally. IPR presents similar problems, although they are not related to potential conflicts of interest, but to the costs of maintaining appropriate databases and advisory capacities for research institutions. If several countries join in exploiting those capacities they can achieve significant economies of scale.

A third group of countries with more developed research and agricultural services systems can take advantage of the new technologies to improve public-good production. These initiatives will be greatly influenced by the strength of existing R&D capacities, as well as public-sector promotion of private-sector involvement, by lowering the risks and reducing levels of investment needed (through increased public research), promoting public/private R&D joint ventures or directly subsidizing private research, and promoting venture capital mechanisms to fencourage start-up companies to exploit promising R&D results.

A final group of countries with a comprehensive capacity will require all the previously discussed components, along with efforts to promote technology development in strategic areas through support to basic science. The nature of policy instruments evolves together with the complexity of the various roles envisaged for the public sector as (a) research becomes less "vertically" specialized, both in an institutional and sector sense, in favor of general scientific components, and (b) policies emphasize incentives to private-sector research and input industry participation.

It is difficult to relate roles and countries in this region, except in a general way. The large majority of countries lack even the basic capacities. Consequently, efforts should focus on creating the conditions of the basic enabling environment for countries like Bolivia, the Dominican Republic, Ecuador, El Salvador, most of English-speaking Caribbean, Guatemala, Honduras, Nicaragua, and Panama. A small group of countries—Chile, Colombia, Costa Rica, Uruguay, and to a lesser extent, Venezuela—enjoys the confluence of a relatively strong scientific and institutional system and dynamic agricultural export markets. Within these countries there are some signs that the public sectors are starting to broaden their roles while a local private sector is beginning to develop at least in terms of the more traditional biotechnologies (tissue culture and plant propagation, immunology technologies and diagnostic kits, and so on). Only Argentina, Brazil, Cuba, and Mexico go beyond the intermediate level potentially to become full players in the development of the technology and, eventually as sources of spillover benefits for the rest of the countries in the region.

Appendix Table 11A.1   Biotechnology R&D capacity at CIMMYT, CIAT, and CIP

Mandate crop	Research activities	Techniques involved	Collaborating institutes
CIMMYT			
Maize	Resistance to maize stem borers	RFLP, RAPD, AFLP Agrobacterium-mediated transformation microprojectile bombardment	
	Resistance to rootworm	RFLP, RAPD, AFLP	
	Resistance to Fusarium ear rot	RFLP, RAPD, AFLP	
	Resistance to maize streak virus	RFLP, RAPD, AFLP	
	Resistance to mosaic virus	RFLP, RAPD, AFLP	
	Tolerance to drought	RFLP, RAPD, AFLP	
	Tolerance to acid soils	RFLP, RAPD, AFLP	
	Nutrient-enriched maize	RFLP, RAPD, AFLP	
	Apomixis	RFLP, RAPD, AFLP, Wide hybridization	*Institut de Recherche pour le Développement*, IRD (France) Pioneer Hi-Bred (United States) Groupe Limagrain (France) Novartis Seeds (United States)
Wheat	Resistance to leaf rust	RFLP, RAPD, AFLP	
	Resistance to stripe rust	RFLP, RAPD, AFLP	
	Resistance to Fusarium head blight	RFLP, RAPD, AFLP	Japan International Research Center for Agricultural Sciences
	Resistance to barley yellow dwarf virus	RFLP, RAPD, AFLP	
	Resistance to Septoria diseases	RFLP, RAPD, AFLP	
	Resistance to karnal bunt	RFLP, RAPD, AFLP	
	Tolerance to drought	RFLP, RAPD, AFLP	
	Tolerance to aluminum toxic soils	RFLP, RAPD, AFLP	
	High yielding wheat	RFLP, RAPD, AFLP	
CIAT			
Beans	Resistance to bacterial blight	Embryo rescue	
	Tolerance to low phosphorous	Genetic markers	University of Michigan (United States)
	Tolerance to golden mosaic virus	Genetic markers	CORPOICA (Colombia) Novartis (United States) Plantek (Japan)
Cassava	Mapping resistance genes to mosaic disease	Microsatellite markers	International Institute of Tropical Agriculture, IITA Clemson University (United States)
	Mapping resistance genes to whitefly	Microsatellite markers AFLP	University of Florida (United States)
	Genetic resistance to bacterial blight	RFLP	IRD, Montpellier (France)
	Resistance to stem borer	Agrobacterium-mediated transformation	CORPOICA (Colombia)
	Production of clean planting material	Micropropagation	University of Louvain (Belgium)
	Long-term conservation	In vitro conservation	Rutgers University (United States) *Instituto Internacional de Estudios Avonzados*, DEA (Venezuela) *Empresa Polar* (Venezuela)
	Root physiological deterioration	Microsatellite markers PCR	*Corporación* BIOTEC (Colombia)

Appendix Table 11A.1   (continued)

Mandate crop	Research activities	Techniques involved	Collaborating institutes
Rice	Resistance to hoja blanca virus	Agrobacterium-mediated transformation Microprojectile bombardment	Bath University (United Kingdom)
	Improving grain quality and yield	RFLP	Cornell University
	Resistance to blast	RFLP Microsatellite markers	Purdue University Paradigm Co. (United States)
CIP			
Potatoes	Resistance to potato tuber moth	Agrobacterium-mediated transformation	Michigan State University Unicrop (Finland)
	Resistance to potato viruses	Agrobacterium-mediated transformation	John Innes Centre (United Kingdom)
	Resistance to late blight	Agrobacterium-mediated transformation RFLP, RAPD, AFLP Microsatellite markers	Max Planck Institute (Germany) *Centre de Recherche Public* (Luxembourg) Molecular Plant and Protein Biotechnology (Germany) Federal Institute for Plant Research (Germany) IRD (France) University of California United States Department of Agriculture Oregon State University Clemson University (United States) Smart Plant International (United States)
	Diagnostic kits for viruses and viroids	ELISA Monoclonal antibodies Nucleic acid probes PCR	
	Reduction of natural toxicants	Agrobacterium-mediated transformation	U.S. Department of Agriculture
Sweet potatoes	Resistance to weevils	Agrobacterium-mediated transformation RFLP, RAPD, AFLP Microsatellite markers	Laval University (Canada)
	Resistance to viruses	Agrobacterium-mediated transformation RFLP, RAPD, AFLP Microsatellite markers	North Carolina State University Austrian Research Centers
	Improvement of flour quality	Agrobacterium-mediated transformation	IACR Long Ashton (United Kingdom)
Potatoes and sweet potatoes	Germplasm DNA fingerprinting	RAPD, AFLP Microsatellite markers	Scottish Crop Research Institute University of Wisconsin Cornell University
Roots and tubers	Germplasm conservation	In vitro conservation	University of Wisconsin

Source: Cohen, Komen, and Verastegui (2001).
Note: RFLP denotes restriction fragment length polymorphism; RAPD, random amplified DNA polymorphism; AFLP, amplified fragment length polymorphism; PCR, polymerace chain reaction; and ELISA, enzyme linked inmmuno sorbent essay. CIMMYT is *Centro Internacional de Mejoramiento de Maíz y Trigo* [International Maize and Wheat Improvement Center]; CIAT is *Centro Internacional de Agricultura Tropical* [International Center for Tropical Agriculture]; CIP is *Centro Internacional de la Papa* [International Potato Center].

Notes

1. The sources used to identify the institutions include the most reliable national and regional biodirectories available, such as REDBIO—FAO (all countries), CamBioTec (Argentina, Chile, Colombia, and Cuba), *Foro Argentina de Biotecnologia* (Argentina), *Fundaçao Osvaldo Cruz* and Embrapa (Brazil), *Instituto de Investigaciones Agropecuarias* (INIA) (Chile), *Colciencias* (Colombia), and *BioMundi* (Cuba).

2. Notable initiatives include CONICYT in Venezuela, the National Fund for Scientific and Technological Research (FONDECYT), the National Fund for Technological Development (FONTEC), and the National Fund for Development Promotion (FONDEF) in Chile; the National

Council for Scientific and Technological Research (CONICYT) in Uruguay; the National Fund for Science and Technology (FONCYT) and the Argentinean Fund for Technology Development (FONTAR) in Argentina.

3. In Argentina, FONTAR has funded projects with biotechnology firms and provided support for the establishment of biotechnology-based service units at the national agricultural research institute, INTA, in areas related to genetic and sanitary quality assurance of planting materials in fruit trees (citrus, prunes, olives, grapes) and horticultural crops (garlic, potatoes, and so on), livestock improvement and animal health (diagnostic kits, vaccine development, embryo transfer), and forestry (improved planting materials) among other areas.

4. The figures discussed in this section exclude resources coming into agricultural research from outside agriculture, such as the general science and technology budgets. These types of funds have been on the rise in recent years and represent an important source of support, especially for biotechnology-related research activities. However, their magnitude does not materially change the situation and trends highlighted here.

5. These figures exclude Mexico.

6. According to a recent ERS report (Shoemaker et al. 2001), private investments in agricultural research in the United States nearly tripled in real terms from 1960 to 1995 to about US$3.5 billion, representing almost 60 percent of total expenditures. For LAC, no estimate places private research above 15 percent of total expenditures (Ardila 1999; Trigo 2000).

7. Other sources reported in Trigo (1999) also identify a very small number of firms operating in countries such as Colombia, Costa Rica, Uruguay, and Venezuela. Cuba is also commercializing a relatively important number of biotechnology products including recombinant animal vaccines, plant antibodies, and transgenic crops, as well as tissue culture and micropropagation commercial scale applications (ISNAR 2000).

References

Ardila, J. 1999. Scenarios for agriculture in Latin America and the Caribbean: An approach from a technical change perspective. Paper presented at the executive committee meeting of the Inter-American Institute for Cooperation on Agriculture, San José, Costa Rica, April 22–23.

Artunuaga-Salas, R. 2001. Personal communication. *Instituto Colombiano Agropecuario* (ICA), Colombia.

Avila, A. F. D., T. R. Quirino, E. Contini, and E. L. R. Filho. 2001. Social and economic impact ex-ante evaluation of Embrapa's biotechnology research products. Paper submitted to the fifth international conference of the International Consortium on Agricultural Biotechnology Research, Ravello, Italy, June 15–18, 2001.

Banchero, C., C. Correa, and S. Bergel. 1999. Diffusion of biotechnology in Argentina and Brazil: The case of transgenic plants. Paper presented at an Argentina-Brazil seminar, Rio de Janeiro, June 10–11, 1999.

Blanco, G. 1998. Personal communication. *Instituto Nacional de Semillas* (INASE), Uruguay.

Burachik, M. S., and P. L. Traynor. 2001. *Analysis of a national biosafety system: Regulatory policies and procedures in Argentina.* The Hague, the Netherlands: International Service for National Agricultural Research (in press).

Cohen, J. I., J. Komen, and J. Verastegui. 2001. Plant biotechnology research in Latin American countries: Overview, strategies, and development policies. Paper presented at the fourth Latin American plant biotechnology meeting (REDBIO2001), Goiana, Brazil, June 4–8, 2001.

CTNBio (*Comissão Técnica Nacional de Biossegurança*) [Biosafety National Technical Commission], Brazil. 2001. "OGM" website: <http://www.ctnbio.gov.br/ctnbio/Sistema/LIBERA-COESogm.asp>. Accessed September 2001.

CONABIA (*Comisión Nacional Asesora de Biotecnología Agropecuaria*) [National Advisory Committee on Agricultural Biosafety]. 2001 *Genetically engineered crops: Releases in Argentina.* <http://siiap.sagyp.mecon.ar/http-hsi/english/conabia/liuk.htm>. Accessed September 2001.

Convent, B. 2000. The role of the private sector in providing biotechnology access to the poor. In *Agricultural biotechnology in developing countries: Towards optimizing the benefits for the poor,* M. Qaim, A. F. Krattiger, and J. von Braun eds. Dordrecht, the Netherlands: Kluwer Academic Publishers.

Courtmanche, A., C. E. Pray, and R. Govindasamy. 2001. The importance of intellectual property rights in the international spread of private sector agricultural biotechnology. Report to the World Intellectual Property Organization. New Brunswick, N.J., U.S.A.: Rutgers University Department of Agricultural, Food, and Resource Economics. Mimeo.

Díaz, R. 2000. Personal communication. *Instituto de Investigaciones Agropecuarias* (INIA) [Agricultural Research Institute] Uruguay, July 11.

Echeverría, R. G., E. J. Trigo, and D. Byerlee. 1996. *Institutional change and effective financing of agricultural research in Latin America.* World Bank Technical Paper No. 330. Washington D.C.

Falconi, C. A. 1999a. *Agricultural biotechnology research capacity in four developing countries.* ISNAR Briefing Paper No. 42. The Hague, the Netherlands: International Service for National Agricultural Research.

_____. 1999b. Agricultural biotechnology research indicators and managerial considerations in four developing countries. In *Managing agricultural biotechnology: Addressing research program needs and policy implications,* J. I. Cohen ed. Oxon, U.K.: CABI Publishing.

Guislain, M. 2001. Personal communication. International Potato Center.

Hinrichsen, P. 2000. Personal communication. *Instituto de Investigaciones Agropecuarias* (INIA), Chile.

IICA (Inter-American Institute for Cooperation on Agriculture). 1992. Formulation of policies for the development of biotechnology in Latin America and the Caribbean. Program II: Technology Generation and Transfer. San José, Costa Rica.

———. 1993. Technical requirements for agrobiotechnology research and development. Miscellaneous publication series, San José, Costa Rica.

———. 2000. *El Impacto de las Nuevas Biotecnologías en el Desarrollo Sostenible de la Agricultura de América Latina y el Caribe: El caso de las Plantas Transgénicas.* [Impact of New Biotechnologies on Sustainable Development in Latin America and the Caribbean] *Serie Documentos Técnicos, Area de Ciencia, Tecnología y Recursos Naturales,* San José, Costa Rica.

ISNAR (International Service for National Agricultural Research). 2000. Implications of developments in agricultural biotechnology in Latin America and the Caribbean for IDB lending. Background report submitted to the Inter-American Development Bank (contract No. EMD.0.072.00-F). The Hague, the Netherlands.

Jaffé, W. 1993. *Commercial agrobiotechnology in Latin America and the Caribbean.* San José, Costa Rica: Inter-American Institute for Cooperation on Agriculture.

Jaffé, W., and D. Infante. 1996. *Oportunidades y Desafíos de la Biotecnología para la Agricultura y Agroindustria de América Latina y el Caribe.* [Biotechnological Opportunities and Challanges for

Latin American and Caribbean Agriculture and Agro-industry]. Washington, D.C.: Inter-American Development Bank.

Jaffé, W., and J. van Wijk. 1995. *The impact of plant breeders' rights in developing countries*. The Hague, the Netherlands: Directorate General for Development Cooperation.

James, C. 2000. *The global status of commercialized transgenic crops: 1999*. International Service for the Acquisition of Agri-biotechnology Applications Brief 17. Ithaca, N.Y., U.S.A.

James, C. and A. Kratigger. 1996. *Global review of the field testing and commercialization of transgenic plants—1986 to 1995*. International Service for the Acquisition of Agri-biotechnology Applications Brief No. 1. Ithaca, N.Y., U.S.A.

Lele, U., W. Lesser, and G. Horstkotte-Wesseler eds. 1999. *Intellectual property rights in agriculture: The World Bank's role in assisting borrower and member countries*. Washington D.C.: World Bank.

Mateo, N., E. Alarcón, J. Ardila, and E. Moscardi. 1999. Agricultural research in Latin America and the Caribbean and the financing paradox. Preliminary paper prepared for the roundtable, Toward a Better Use of LAC Institutional Infrastructure in Support of Agricultural Technological Research and Development, Montevideo, Uruguay, September 2–3.

Morris, M. L., and D. Hoisington. 2000. Bringing the benefits of biotechnology to the poor: The role of the CGIAR centers. In *Agricultural biotechnology in developing countries: Towards optimizing the benefits for the poor*, M. Qaim, A. F. Krattiger and J. von Braun eds. Dordrecht, the Netherlands: Kluwer Academic Publishers.

REDBIO/FAO [Technical Cooperation Network on Plant Biotechnology in Latin America and the Caribbean/Food and Agriculture Organization of the United Nations]. 1998. *REDBIO'98— Plant biotechnology on food security*. Conference proceedings of the third Latin American meeting on plant biotechnology. Havana, Cuba (June 2–5).

Rohter, L. 2001. Model for research rises in a third world city. *The New York Times*. April 24. <http://mindfully.org/GE/GE2/Brazil-Research-Rises.htm>. Accessed September 27, 2001.

SAGAR. (*Secretaría de Agricultura, Ganadería, Desarrollo Rural, Pesca y Alimentación*) [Secretariat for Agriculture, Livestock, Rural Development, Fish and Nutrition] Mexico. 2001. *Regulación de Organismos Genéticamente Modificados de Uso Agrícola* [Regulations for genetically modified organisims in agriculture]. <http://www.sagar.gob.mx/Conasag/svtransgen.htm>. Accessed September 2001.

Salazar, S., C. Falconi, J. Komen, and J. I. Cohen. 2000. *The use of proprietary biotechnology research inputs at selected Latin American NAROs*. Briefing Paper 44. The Hague, the Netherlands: International Service for National Agricultural Research.

Shoemaker, R., J. Harwood, K. Day-Rubenstein, T. Dunahay, P. Heisey, L. Hoffman, C. Klotz-Ingram, W. Lin, L. Mitchell, W. McBride, and J. Fernandez-Cornejo. 2001. *Economic issues in agricultural biotechnology*. Washington, D.C.: ERS (Economic Research Service of the U.S. Department of Agriculture).

Trigo, E. J. 1999. Strategic elements for the development of agricultural research in Latin America. San José, Costa Rica: Inter-American Institute for Cooperation on Agriculture.

———. 2000. The situation of agricultural biotechnology capacities and exploitation in Latin America and the Caribbean. In *Agricultural biotechnology in developing countries: Towards optimizing the benefits for the poor*, M. Qaim, A. F. Krattiger, and J. von Braun eds. Dordrecht, the Netherlands: Kluwer Academic Publishers.

Chapter 12

Biotechnology Policies for Asia: Current Activities and Future Options

John Skerritt

Introduction

The application of modern biotechnology to agriculture in developing countries could conceivably have as great an impact on farmers as the Green Revolution of the 1970s. However, if indeed it does, it will differ from the Green Revolution in several ways (Conway 1997). Modern biotechnology has the potential to affect many crops, and benefits could accrue in both irrigated and rainfed areas. The private sector will dominate technology development and dissemination, with the public sector playing the role of facilitator and regulator. Much of the intellectual property (IP) involved will be protected, and the capital costs of research and development (R&D) will be comparatively high. Finally, a broad spectrum of expertise will be required, spanning molecular and cell biology, conventional plant and livestock breeding, and other agricultural sciences.

It is perhaps unfortunate that the term "biotechnology" is often equated with plant and animal genetic manipulation, as a host of other technologies have been developed and have significantly affected on developing-country agriculture. These other biotechnologies, including disease diagnostics, vaccines, molecular markers, micropropagation techniques, and rumen manipulation, are not considered controversial. Table 12.1 provides information on a range of these techniques and their current applications.

To date, most of the practical impacts of genetically modified (GM) crops are in developed countries and with crops and traits that developed-country farmers are

Table 12.1   Non-GM biotechnologies and their current applications

Technique	Description	Application
Crop diagnostics	Use of antibodies or nucleic acid technologies combined with simple testing formats	Improving the specificity, sensitivity, and ease of diagnosis of plant pests and pathogens, contaminants, and quality traits. Particularly useful in the study of pests and diseases and in rapid identification in quarantine.
Crop micropropagation	Tissue culture and other in-vitro micropropagation technologies	A practical means of providing disease-free plantlets of current varieties with significant yield gains by the removal of pests and pathogens. Especially useful in vegetatively propagated species such as sweet potatoes and bananas.
Marker-assisted selection	Use of genetic markers, maps, and genomic information	Means of improving both the accuracy and time to commercial exploitation of single and polygenic traits in plant breeding. Starting to be used for selection of superior reproductive, growth, or meat-quality characteristics and disease resistance in livestock.
Livestock health	Diagnostics for the major diseases of livestock	Identifying the cause of poor performance of livestock in developing-country situations and understanding the spread of certain diseases.
Vaccine development		Enhancing the control of epidemic viral diseases of livestock, such as foot-and-mouth disease. Though vaccines have yet to be developed for many important diseases, notably parasitic diseases, modern biotechnology offers great promise.

Source: Compiled by author.

most interested in. The most recent figures, as discussed by Marra (this volume), show a leveling off in world area planted to GM crops, partly due to increasing scrutiny and debate over public acceptance. Asian developing countries nevertheless have pockets of good R&D capacity in agricultural biotechnology.

Biotechnology In Asian Developing Countries

Several governments in Asia—notably China, India, Indonesia, Malaysia, Pakistan, the Philippines, and Viet Nam—have committed significant public resources to modern biotechnology research of potential use in agriculture. Seldom, however, has this biotechnology R&D been matched by coherent biotechnology policy or close interactions with those able to put the results of the work to practical use. There is relatively little industry involvement in Asian biotechnology R&D, with the bulk of the research being done by government or international organizations (although the same can be said of Australia).

People's Republic of China

China accords high priority to the use of biotechnology to increase food production and product quality in an environmentally sustainable manner. It has moved quickly to adopt new biotechnologies and perceives a competitive edge in rapid uptake of technologies such as plant genetic engineering. Some of the technologies have been imported, but government has made a multihundred-million-dollar investment in biotechnology R&D. Institutes of the Chinese Academy of Agricultural Science (CAAS), leading agricultural universities, and three or four of the top provincial agricultural institutes in biotechnology all house world-class programs. A program of "key open centers," which includes biotechnology, also has been established targeting a variety of crops and traits for improvement. These include rice, wheat, corn, cotton, tomatoes, peppers, potatoes, cucumbers, papayas, tobacco-disease resistance, pest resistance, and herbicide resistance, as well as crop quality improvement. Some 50 GM varieties have been approved for large-scale release or small-scale field testing in China; the most widespread of these are insect-resistant varieties of cotton cultivated on some 500,000 hectares in 2000 (James 2000).

India

India has invested significant amounts of public funds in human resource development and infrastructure in the field of biotechnology, and the national government created a department of biotechnology in the early 1980s. Active R&D programs in agricultural biotechnology exist in institutes within the Council for Scientific and Industrial Research (CSIR), the Indian Council of Agricultural Research (ICAR), and some agricultural universities. Nongovernmental organizations (NGOs) such as the Swaminathan Foundation near Chennai and the TATA Energy Research Institute in Delhi play an important role in biotechnology education and policy debates. R&D in India is directed toward agricultural productivity; environmental bioremediation; vaccines, diagnostics, and drugs; crop genetic engineering; molecular marker technology; and bioinformatics (Sharma 2000). Tissue culture work has included new regeneration techniques for the rapid multiplication of citrus, coffee, mangrove, vanilla, and cardamom.

Indonesia

In Indonesia, applications of biotechnology in agriculture are primarily the responsibility of the Agency for Agricultural Research and Development (AARD), with World Bank loan support. In recent years an extensive training program has been undertaken nationally and abroad to upgrade the skills of the scientists involved. In the 1980s, a major World Bank loan financed the creation of three interuniversity centers, including one in agricultural biotechnology. The Bogor Agricultural University and Gajah Mada University have strong programs in plant and livestock biotechnology, respectively. The Indonesian Institute of Sciences (LIPI) also has a biotechnology R&D center with world-class facilities. Emphases include crop genetic engineering, application of molecular markers in selection in forestry and livestock breeding, livestock embryo transfer, biofertilizers, microbial engineering, and microalgal culture.

The Philippines

The Philippines created its National Institutes of Molecular Biology and Biotechnology in Los Baños in 1980 to focus on agricultural biotechnology. In 1997, the Agriculture Fisheries Modernization Act recognized biotechnology as a major strategy to increase agricultural productivity. In 1998, five major biotechnology research projects were funded by government: development of new varieties of banana resistant to banana bunchy top virus and papaya resistant to ringspot virus; delayed ripening of papaya and mango; insect-resistant corn; marker-assisted breeding in coconut; and coconut oil with high lauric acid content. However, public opposition to GM crops has constrained field trials and commercial use of modern biotechnology in agriculture.

Thailand

Thailand's National Center for Genetic Engineering and Biotechnology has adopted a holistic approach to biotechnology, not only conducting research (both in-house and involving universities, government departments, and other institutes), but also programs of technology transfer to the private sector, training, and public information. Crop transformation work involves tomato (yellow leaf-curl virus resistance), papaya (ringspot virus resistance), chili pepper (vein banding virus resistance), and cotton (transformation of local cultivars with *Bacillus thuringiensis* [*Bt*] genes). Biosafety guidelines and facilities are reasonably well developed, but they are not backed by legislation. Permits to import transgenic plants are still difficult to obtain, and only *Bt* cotton and corn are likely to be grown (in small amounts) over the next few years. Transgenic soybeans were imported with little attention to segregation, recently causing problems when canned fish exports containing soybean oil were rejected by Middle Eastern countries. Thailand is focusing on applications of biotechnology for traditional foods, fruits, and export commodities. Additional R&D priorities are to raise production and cut costs on crops such as rice, cassava, sugarcane, rubber, durian, and orchids. An early success has been using biotechnology to develop new molecular diagnostics for viral diseases in shrimp.

Regional and International Programs in Asia
In addition to national programs in the developing countries and bilateral cooperation activities (generally project-specific and forming part of official development assistance from Australia, Japan, and the United States), Asia's biotechnology programs are being strengthened through a number of multilateral programs as outlined in Table 12.2.

International Agricultural Research Centers
International R&D programs using modern biotechnology are being conducted by the international agricultural research centers, particularly the International Rice Research Institute (IRRI), the International Maize and Wheat Improvement Center (CIMMYT), the International Crops Research Institute for the Semi-Arid Tropics (ICRISAT), and the International Livestock Research Institute (ILRI). The Center for International Forestry Research (CIFOR) uses biotechnology in the characterization of forest diversity in its Asia program. ICLARM—The World Fish Center uses new technologies in research to improve fisheries and aquaculture systems. ILRI is initiating a program to improve Asian livestock. The biotechnology service of the International Service for National Agricultural Research (ISNAR) assists Asian countries in developing human resources for managing biotechnology research programs and institutions. This includes training in strategy building, priority setting, managing biosafety and regulatory aspects, resource generation and deployment, product delivery, and information sharing, as well as establishment and management of linkages. The International Food Policy Research Institute (IFPRI) conducts policy research in several related areas, including IP rights, genetic resources, and trade. In total, the Consultative Group on International Agricultural Research (CGIAR) centers invest some US$25 million per year in modern biotechnology.

Biotechnology and Australian Development Assistance
In 2000 and 2001 the Asian Development Bank (ADB) and the Australian Government, through the Australian Centre for International Agricultural Research (ACIAR) and with the support of the Australian Agency for International Development (AusAID), commissioned a study to assess the potential contribution of modern biotechnology to reducing poverty and achieving food security in Asia

Table 12.2   Regional and international programs in Asia

Donor(s) and contributing organization(s)	Activity
APEC (Asia-Pacific Economic Co-operation) through its Agricultural Technical Cooperation Experts Group (ACTEG)	High-level workshops were held to stimulate cooperation among countries on information, biosafety risk assessment and harmonization, public assessment, and risk communication. This includes training and development of guides on IP, risk management, plant variety protection and public communication on biotechnology. The work links with other APEC working groups on quarantine, plant and animal genetic resources, and IPR.
Asian Development Bank (ADB) *Budenministerium fur Technische Zussammenarbeit* (BMZ)	The Asian Rice Biotechnology Network (ARBN) was initiated by the International Rice Research Institute (IRRI) in 1993 to provide a vehicle for collaborative research in programs in tissue culture, wide hybridization, genetic engineering, DNA marker technology, and DNA fingerprinting of pests, diseases, and rice germplasm with universities and rice research institutes of national agricultural research systems (NARSs) in Asia.
Asian Development Bank (ADB) International Wheat Improvement Center (CIMMYT)	The Asian Maize Biotechnology Network (AMBIONET) emphasizes the development of molecular markers for specific traits and their use in plant selection. Member countries are China, India, Indonesia, the Philippines, and Thailand.
Asian Development Bank (ADB) International Crops Research Institute for the Semi-Arid Tropics (ICRISAT)	Support for capacity building in biotechnology as part of loan components for agriculture and education projects in countries including the Philippines, Sri Lanka, and Thailand, and support for improvement of sorghum, chickpeas, and groundnuts through ICRISAT.
International Service for the Acquisition of Agri-Biotech Applications (ISAAA) CAB International (CABI) SEAMEO Regional Center for Graduate Study and Research in Agriculture (SEARCA)	Facilitation of technology transfer, training in biosafety and public/private-sector partnerships through a brokering role. Current regional projects focus on improving the productivity of corn, papayas, and sweet potatoes. ISAAA is also establishing a new Asian knowledge center for crop biotechnology based in the Philippines, in partnership with CABI and SEARCA. Papaya networking has been used as a pilot project. ISAAA has played a role in negotiating with private companies that own proprietary technologies such as Zeneca's delayed ripening gene and Monsanto's papaya ringspot virus resistance gene. Member countries are Indonesia, Malaysia, the Philippines, Thailand, and Vietnam. The company gives member countries license-free use of technology and the technology can be used only for papaya transformation; products can be commercialized only within the country and among member countries.

(ADB 2001). The study, which also assessed the associated risks to human health and the environment, had three objectives:

- to examine the impact of agricultural biotechnology on human health, the environment, and agriculture, and to examine measures to minimize adverse impacts;

Table 12.2   (continued)

Donor(s) and contributing organization(s)	Activity
U.S. Agency for International Development (USAID)	USAID's Agricultural Biotechnology for Sustainable Productivity project at Michigan State University has played an important brokering role in crop biotechnology, especially in Indonesia (Maredia et al. 1999).
Asia-Pacific International Molecular Biology Network	Established in 1997 in the belief that molecular biology and biotechnology can benefit humanity, the network intends to facilitate developments in molecular biology and biotechnology through cooperation and collaboration with various organizations.
Rockefeller Foundation Rice Biotechnology Network	Operational since 1984, the network has two objectives: to create biotechnology applicable to rice, producing improved rice varieties suited to developing-country needs, and to ensure the scientists in developing countries know how to use the techniques and adopt them to their own objectives.
Food and Agriculture Organization of the United Nations (FAO) United Nations Development Programme (UNDP)	The FAO/UNDP project Biotechnology Development Network for Animal Production and Health operated from 1989 to 1993 involving China, India, Indonesia, Malaysia, Pakistan, the Philippines, Republic of Korea, and Thailand. It encompassed capacity building, use of the recombinant DNA techniques in animal improvement, embryo transfer technology, animal disease diagnosis, development of vaccines, modification of rumen microbial ecosystems, production-related hormones, and improvement of feeds.
International Center for Genetic Engineering and Biotechnology (ICGEB) United Nations International Development Organization (UNIDO)	ICGEB, New Delhi, India, is one of two centers sponsored by UNIDO and has an active agricultural biotechnology program, particularly in plant molecular biology. The focus is biotechnology applications to biotic and abiotic stresses on rice and other important crops in the region.
World Bank	The World Bank has supported infrastructure and human resource development for biotechnology in several Asian countries over the past 15 years through loans in the agricultural sector (India and Indonesia) and the science, technology, and education sectors (Indonesia and Korea). It is also a main supporter of the CGIAR.

Source: ADB (2001).

- to explore the use of biotechnology to reduce poverty and achieve food security in Asia; and

- to develop policies and strategies for funding agencies to support biotechnology in developing countries in Asia.

ACIAR's Interest in Biotechnology

ACIAR, a government statutory authority within the Foreign Affairs and Trade portfolio, forms, with AusAID, Australia's official overseas development assistance effort. ACIAR has initiated more than 100 biotechnology projects in R&D partnerships with more than 10 Asian countries over the past 15 years. The projects have emphasized development of diagnostics and vaccines for a large suite of diseases affecting tropical livestock, along with some recent work on fish and shrimp. Projects have also included work on molecular marker methods for disease resistance and prolificacy in livestock and biotechnology for rumen manipulation. Crops and forestry work has focused on diagnostics for diseases (viral, fungal, mycoplasma, and bacterial) and contaminants in tropical crops and application of biofertilizers, bioremediation technology, and biofumigants. Molecular markers have been developed for improvement of cereals and tree species, and attempts are being made to develop apomictic systems for rice in cooperation with IRRI. Other research involves tissue culture methods for micropropagation and conservation of several species, including sweet potatoes, taro, tropical fruits, coconuts, green tea, and tree species such as mangroves.

Seven of ACIAR's current or completed projects have included aspects of plant genetic engineering, with target crops being cereals and pulses, peanuts, and several tropical fruits. Among the target characteristics are virus resistance and quality defects related to ripening processes. ACIAR developed these collaborative projects at the request of its Asian partner countries, with their full approval of procedures. The projects also fall within the context of a much larger program of more than 600 active or completed projects (Table 12.3). ACIAR provides core funding to many CGIAR and other international agricultural research centers; a proportion of this support is applied to biotechnology R&D. Priorities for future collaboration in biotechnology between ACIAR and its Asian partners are determined through high-level consultations with scientists and policymakers held every 3–5 years in partner countries. Table 12.4 lists some biotechnology priorities.

Through AusAID, Australia supports an agricultural technical cooperation experts group for a regional biotechnology network under the Asia-Pacific Economic Co-operation (APEC) agreement. The Crawford Fund for International Agricultural Research has sponsored several master classes in biotechnology for senior technical individuals and policymakers over the past decade. Several other activities relate to capacity building in biosafety in countries such as China, and the Australian Quarantine and Inspection Service (AQIS) has provided risk analysis training to quarantine staff from a number of Asian countries. Finally, IP Australia has carried out training in Asian developing countries, not only to strengthen IP sys-

Table 12.3   Work under way or recently completed on GM crops, supported by ACIAR

ACIAR[a] project number	Project title and description	Partner countries or CGIAR[b] centers
CS1 94039	*Improved diagnosis and control of peanut stripe virus* Developed gene transfer system for peanuts and established virus-resistant commercial cultivars by inserting a virus coat protein gene	China and Indonesia
CS 1 92026	*Control of papaya ringspot virus in papaya and cucurbits through transgenic resistance* Incorporation of virus coat protein gene into papayas and cucurbits	Thailand
CS 1 97119	*Pulse transformation technology transfer*	International Center for Agricultural Research in the Dry Areas (ICARDA), Syria
CS 1 95125	*Molecular tools for achieving apomixis in rice*	International Rice Research Institute (IRRI), the Philippines
PHT 94045	*Control of ripening in papayas and mangos by genetic engineering* Modification of genes for ethylene production through antisense transformation	The Philippines and Malaysia
PHT 94097	*Pineapple quality improvement* Transformation of pineapples to reduce polyphenol oxidase	Malaysia
PHT 99040	*Genetic engineering of pineapples with blackheart resistance* Peroxidase expression to reduce blackheart	Malaysia

Source: Compiled by author.
a. Australian Centre for International Agricultural Research.
b. Consultative Group on International Agricultural Research.

tems but also to share expertise in protecting and commercializing biotechnology inventions.

A Synthesis of Ideas and Recommendations

This section presents a synthesis of recommendations from a range of discussions and studies along with several of the author's own ideas.[1]

Establishing Benchmarks to Facilitate Policy and Priority Setting

A sizeable amount of R&D in biotechnology is already being carried out in Asian developing countries. Yet few have studied the cost-effectiveness of these national

Table 12.4   Priorities of ACIAR's Asian partners for Australian collaboration in biotechnology

Partner country and date	Description
India, July 1997	Molecular genetics in livestock breeding and selection Livestock disease diagnostics and vaccine production Genetic transformation for insect and drought resistance in chickpeas and pigeon peas Genetic transformation and markers for salt and water-logging tolerance, high-temperature tolerance and bread-making properties in wheat Cotton integrated pest management, including use of *Bt* transgenics Molecular characterization of phytoplasmas affecting palm crops and forest plantation species Biotechnology in aquaculture including fish nutrition Biotechnology improvement of Acacia, Casuarina, and Eucalypts
The Philippines, February 1998	Biotechnology policies affecting agricultural production and marketing Biotechnology for crop breeding (bananas, mangos, papayas, coconuts, corn, citrus, and legumes) Disease diagnostics (potatoes, bananas, sweet potatoes, citrus, and coconuts)
Indonesia, September 1998	Vaccines and diagnostic procedures to control cattle diseases Applications of biotechnology to improve field crop yields Biotechnology for reduction of mycotoxin levels in food crops
China, October 1999	Microorganisms to improve the nutritional value of crop byproducts Animal health vaccines and disease diagnostics Potato, tomatoes, and brassicas with resistance to diseases and pests and improved quality through molecular techniques Pesticide residue and mycotoxin monitoring using biotechnology
Viet Nam, March 2000	Application of biotechnology in crop improvement Diagnostics in protection of fruit trees Pig disease management through diagnostics and vaccines Biotechnological techniques in tree selection
Thailand, November 2000	Molecular technologies in forest and food crop propagation and animal and fish breeding Diagnostic tests for plant pests and plant, animal, and fish diseases and vaccines for the treatment of livestock diseases Development of transgenic crop plants with virus and abiotic stress resistance, improved storage characteristics and quality Risk assessment and biosafety of transgenic crops Conservation of genetic resources using biotechnology tools, including molecular profiling and culture collections

Source: Compiled by author.
Note: ACIAR denotes Australian Centre for International Agricultural Research.

biotechnology programs or whether priorities may be research-driven rather than demand-driven at the expense of less glamorous but necessary research. At the same time, countries have a justifiable concern at being "left behind" if they do not get involved with biotechnologies early.

Biotechnology R&D needs to be strongly linked to extension programs to ensure that benefits reach poor farmers. A useful starting place here is the analogy of the Green Revolution for provision of improved seed. Another consideration is who the winners and losers from biotech crops will be. Economic concentration in industry means that companies in developed countries increasingly own biological processes and products. Will the income gap therefore widen between the rich and poor with insufficient attention to farmers who may lose their livelihoods because GM crops replace their own?

Detailed information still needs to be obtained and disseminated in several areas:

- the state of development of IP protection and plant variety rights (PVR) systems in target countries;

- current and planned biotechnology research in Asia via the development of an extensive database; and

- the policy environment for release of genetically modified organisms (GMOs) and biosafety assessment in individual countries given that private-sector investment and government decisions on biotechnology regulations are often clouded by lack of current and accurate information.

Information is also lacking on whether regional harmonization of IP law would actually enhance trade and investment in developing countries and lower the costs of creating and enforcing IP regulations.

The best scientific information available must support biotechnology policy choices. Situations where biotechnology has a comparative advantage need to be better defined (for instance, where it can deliver varieties with traits that conventional breeding cannot produce). Biotechnology work must also be integrated with breeding programs and good agronomy. Donors could support national governments' decisionmaking, focusing on the more advanced developing countries, which have greater capacity and therefore are more likely to adopt biotechnology.

Some Asian developing countries may want help in setting priorities for biotechnology R&D, in implementation, and in planning for investment based on demand. For example, is plant biotechnology emphasized at the expense of animal biotechnology, given that the livestock sector is growing faster? Comparative economic analyses of the use of biotechnology versus conventional approaches for target crops and traits could help programs allocate resources more rationally.

Regional and national coordination of policy on GMOs and consistent distribution of responsibilities among agencies in different countries needs to be encouraged. This may be difficult to achieve, but the European experience has highlighted problems of poor coordination (Levidow et al. 1999). How developing countries are likely to be affected by proprietary interests in biotechnology must be assessed, including the implications of ownership of IPR and issues of access to biotechnology, "licensing in" of technology owned by developed countries or multinational companies, and freedom to operate. Assessment should also be made of the legal, economic, and technological environment of developing countries in the region and how these environments affect the ownership of IP rights.

Training Needs in IP Management

Changes over recent decades in the IP environment related to agriculture include patenting of living organisms and the establishment of plant breeders' rights. The protection of target genes for particular traits and of enabling technologies requires that developing-country organizations be conversant with a variety of licensing arrangements (see Nottenburg, Pardey, and Wright this volume). Proprietary biotechnology inputs are vital to the use of modern biotechnology, and yet many developing-country (and for that matter, several developed-country) organizations use these inputs without formal permission. This becomes important at the time of commercialization or release of a variety, which is often too late to change direction or incorporate alternative technology in a research or breeding program.

The recent ISNAR survey of five Latin American countries (discussed by Trigo et al. this volume) shows that NARS laboratories utilize proprietary technologies widely, but in many cases without formal agreements (Salazar et al. 2000). Most of the proprietary technologies were related to plant genetic engineering, such as selectable markers, transformation systems, promoters, and specific genes, but marker techniques and diagnostics were also included. Both academic and administrative personnel knew little about IPR. Many institutes had focused training on the technical aspects of biotechnology R&D, with less training in areas such as biosafety, IP management, licensing skills, and biotechnology business management.

IP management of biotechnology inventions is complex. Kryder, Kowalski, and Krattiger (2000) recently reviewed the example of *Golden*Rice™—high in provitamin A, otherwise known as beta-carotene—the development of which involved a large number of proprietary technologies (Ye et al. 2000). *Golden*Rice™ is a multitransformant, because three genes were introduced into a biosynthetic pathway to produce the high beta-carotene levels. Other proprietary technologies included three transformation vectors, *agrobacterium* transformation, and plant regeneration, and DNA amplification technologies. About 40 patents are associated with these technologies across the United States and Europe. But the number differs significantly among Asian developing countries (11 in China, 5 in India, 6 in Indonesia, 1 in the Philippines, and none in Thailand or Malaysia), complicating the export process. Alternative strategies to gain freedom to operate may include "inventing around" current patents, redesigning constructs to synthesize genes to reduce reliance on external technical property, asking IP owners to relinquish claims or provide royalty-free licenses, ignoring all intellectual and technical property, and seeking licenses for all intellectual and technical property. That last strategy is certainly the safest route to build cooperation between the public and private sectors.

There is an obvious need for information to support decisions related to modern agricultural biotechnology and for development of the necessary regulatory arrangements. Training in IP regulations is also needed, to facilitate technology transfer in evolving IP rights systems, to provide clear understanding of the Trade-Related Aspects of Intellectual Property (TRIPs) agreement, and to develop knowledge of the steps required to secure consent for the use of a given technology in a partner country. Systems must be in place to enable countries to protect their own technology while at the same time minimizing barriers between countries that could hinder technology spillovers.

Better Public Awareness of Biotechnology

The news media in several countries (for example, India, Indonesia, the Philippines, and Thailand) regularly mention biotechnology and the controversy surrounding GMOs, while such publicity seems less common in China and Viet Nam. Some aspects of the debate are similar to those in Australia. For example, "technocrats" are often perceived as encouraging the use of biotechnology, opposing average people who are unsure of and uninformed of its benefits and risks. In developing countries, however, as illustrated by Pinstrup-Andersen and Cohen (this volume), additional imperatives such as hunger come into play. On the other hand, countries like Thailand are major exporters of processed foods and are also concerned about attitudes toward GM foods in their export markets. The resulting issue is whether the potential economic benefits of GMO adoption outweigh the advantages of targeting GM-free export markets.

The future of biotechnology lies in public awareness and acceptance; good technology alone is not enough. One need only look at the substantial disadoption of low-cost nuclear power in recent years to grasp this point. Strategies for informed public debate about the true benefits and costs of biotechnology—recognizing the validity of freedom of choice—are imperative. Major institutions undertaking biotechnology R&D should launch public awareness programs involving community groups and using simple messages in local languages (as in Thailand and the Philippines).

Facilitation of Public-Private Partnerships

Many of the technologies used in modern biotechnology are privately owned, so public agencies need to establish new modes of operation in an increasingly private-sector world. The private sector—especially seed companies—is gaining importance in countries such as India and China. As in Europe and North America, several seed companies have formed alliances with global life science companies, and developed-country companies have established joint ventures with Asian agrochemical and floriculture companies. The private sector needs mechanisms to assist in extending and distributing the products of biotechnology; this will likely require innovative arrangements, special funding, and other financial incentives. Segmentation of markets will be important to help developing-country farmers to take advantage of biotechnology products under realistic conditions. The public sector can encourage private-sector research for poor people by converting some of the private benefits of research into social gains. For example, government might buy exclusive rights to a newly developed technology and make it freely available (or available at a nominal charge) to small farmers. The private research agency would still bear the risks, as it does when developing technology for the market.

Economic examination of the balance between developing technologies in-country and "licensing them in" will be important. The increasing concentration of ownership of technology raises its own set of issues; it is often said that Thailand's main concern regarding GMOs is not biosafety, but the risk of Thai agriculture's dependence on U.S. technology. "Escape" or poor protection of IP limits private-sector investment in biotechnology in some Asian developing countries. Stimulating the development of small and medium-sized bioenterprises in rural areas is particularly important to create more jobs and deliver affordable and useful products such as seed, biofertilizers, and biopesticides to farmers.

There is a further need to establish whether major organizations should have a brokering role. The size and influence of an organization like the ADB could make it a positive force in brokering deals and philanthropy between large companies and developing-country organizations. An incentive for multinationals to pursue philanthropic developing-country partnerships is their need to counter negative public perceptions. A neutral broker can have significant advantages. The International Service for the Acquisition of Agri-biotech Applications (ISAAA), for example, claims its comparative advantages are cosponsorship by public- and private-sector institutions, independence, and neutrality (that is, financial disinterest in the technology). Centralizing technology transfer offices for agricultural biotechnology in individual countries would also facilitate the brokering of agreements.

Technical (R&D) Interventions

Obtaining a clear view of which crops and characteristics should be targeted for genetic manipulation in partner countries is a critical step, but it has rarely been addressed systematically. Research should focus on crops such as bananas, cassava, yams, sweet potatoes, rice, maize, wheat, and millet, along with livestock—all relevant to small farmers and poor consumers. The limitation is that relatively little biotechnology research is being undertaken on many of Asia's basic food crops or on the problems of small farmers in rainfed (that is, less productive, nonirrigated) and marginal lands. The private sector is unlikely to do much in these areas because it perceives limited potential for returns on investment.

If Asian countries are to participate more fully in biotechnology, they will need to expand their own national and regional capacity to undertake biotechnology research linked to the problems of small farmers and orphan crops. In certain situations, it may make sense to purchase, license, or import particular technologies rather than reinventing them.

A first option is to identify crops and animals with short- to medium-term potential for applying existing biotechnology in developing countries. Orphan crops would almost certainly be included. In some cases, the research might be done by developing more efficient methods of crop improvement through the use of marker-assisted selection for complex traits such as drought tolerance. In other cases, the best approach may be to develop transgenic varieties with specific characteristics, such as disease resistance or improved nutritional quality. Herbicide-resistant crops increasingly have a place in developing countries, as labor available for weeding dwindles. Other applications of crop engineering require close investigation. Apomixis (production of seeds without fertilization) in a wider range of crops has huge potential to simplify breeding of adapted genotypes, to preserve hybrid vigor, and to improve propagation of crops that currently rely on vegetative propagation (see Jefferson this volume).

Closer linkages between biotechnologists and plant breeders should be supported. One of the most profitable applications of crop biotechnology in the short to medium term is better implementation of molecular markers for selection in conventional breeding programs. It is important to ensure that the genomic knowledge of each of the major food crops in Asia is obtained and that this information is in the public domain, as it is the basis for the development of new crop varieties as public goods for the poor. The rice genomics program provides a good model for others (Sasaki 1999). Building capacity of Asian developing countries to undertake laboratory and on-site testing of GMOs is vital. An increasing number of published, collaboratively trialed protocols is available, as well as simple commercial test kits. Table 12.5 lists some potential applications for biotechnology in Asian developing countries.

Table 12.5   Potential biotechnology applications in Asian developing countries

Target	Application
Crop productivity	Reduce pressure to expand cultivated areas to forest and marginal areas
Tolerance of existing high-yielding varieties to drought, flooding, salinity, heavy metals, and other abiotic and biotic stresses	Stabilize and improve the yields of crops grown in rainfed areas, such as cereals with aluminum tolerance for production on acid soils
Crop quality and nutritional quality, including the enhancement of vitamin and micronutrient contents of food grains	Benefit consumers in the developing world who cannot afford to buy supplementary vitamins and micronutrients on a regular basis, for example, rice and Indian mustard with elevated beta-carotene, rice with elevated iron, tomatoes with elevated lycopene
Disease and pest resistance	Lessen pesticide use
Postharvest defects	Delay ripening in papayas and eliminate blackheart disorder
Vaccines and disease prognosis for livestock and aquaculture	Increase productivity and quality of farm animals
Nonedible substances of food crops	Produce medicinal products, fuel alcohol, and industrial oil
Virus resistance	Resistance to potato virus x, y, and leaf roll; sweet potato FMV (figwort mosaic caulimovirus) resistance; papaya ringspot virus; and cassava mosaic virus disease resistance
Insect resistance	Sweet potato insect resistance, *Bt* maize, and *Bt* cotton
Bacterial resistance	Rice with bacterial blight resistance
Oral vaccines for humans	Bananas containing vaccines against cholera and hepatitis B

Source: Compiled by author.

Biosafety

Biosafety has been reviewed extensively elsewhere (Mikkelsen et al. 1996; Altieri 1998; Skerritt 2000; Wolfenbarger and Phifer 2000), so it is only briefly summarized here. Biosafety concerns relate to both food safety and human health (potential for allergens or toxins in GM food) or to the environmental impact of GM crops (for example, the unintended spread of genes to nontarget species). The major food-safety issues relate to consumer perceptions that GM foods are unnatural and that new allergens (or other unhealthy substances, such as toxic lectins) can be introduced into foods. A key principle in biosafety guidelines is that of "substantial equivalence" to identify differences between biotechnology-derived and traditional foods (Miller 1999). The main ecological risks relate to potential loss of genetic diversity in cropping systems; potential transfer of genes from herbicide-resistant crops to wild relatives, creating "super-weeds"; ability of herbicide-resistant crops to act as weeds in rotation crops; escape of transgenes, especially antibiotic resistance markers, to soil bacteria; vector recombination to create new viruses; and with *Bt* toxins, insect resistance to the toxin and direct ecological effects of the toxin on nontarget organisms.

The need for developing countries to have functioning biosafety systems has strengthened since the adoption of the Cartagena Protocol on Biosafety in January 2000. The protocol established an international framework for regulating international trade in transgenic crops and has implications for individual countries as users, developers, and exporters of "living modified organisms." Its major components are described below:

- International shipments that "may contain" transgenic food products must be so labeled. This labeling provision applies only to large-scale shipments and does not affect labeling requirements on consumer products, which are determined by each country.

- Governments may use the so-called "precautionary principle" to bar import of a transgenic product even without conclusive evidence that the product is unsafe. The protocol does not, however, override other international agreements including the World Trade Organization (WTO) requirement that import decisions be science-based.

- To assist countries in making import decisions, a database will make available uniform information on transgenic crops.

The need to harmonize regulations is not just an issue for Asian developing economies, but for developed countries as well. For example, Levidow, Carr, and Wield (1999) report that Europe has had difficulty harmonizing regulatory criteria, despite an expressed position of using science-based criteria. Countries disagree about the amount of scientific evidence needed to resolve uncertainties and the evidence required in recent approval processes for *Bt* insect-resistant maize and herbicide-tolerant canola (oilseed rape). Countries have a range of options in designing and implementing a national biosafety system geared to their particular technical, legal, and institutional realities and in adapting the system to local needs, priorities, and capacities. Asia needs to assess the adequacy and effectiveness of biosafety procedures for testing, release, import, production, and utilization of GMOs. Regulatory systems must be flexible to allow for either increased scrutiny or relaxation of controls (for example, for containment of field trials) based on scientific evidence.

Harmonization of regulations between agencies is important, but it may be simpler and less expensive to embed biosafety regulations within existing institutions rather than building new institutions. Australia's official view has been to develop national policies and regulations for trade in GMOs within the country's existing regulatory framework, instead of setting up a whole new infrastructure. Aid could build the infrastructure to manage GMOs in the context of developing quarantine policy, managing sanitary and phytosanitary issues, and the capacity for assessing risk and environmental impact. This process should strengthen collaboration between quarantine/regulatory officials and environmental policymakers. Governments and international agencies should receive support for participatory field studies—involving local communities—that would evaluate the ecological impact of the first generation of genetically modified crops, such as insect-resistant cotton and rice.

Several countries have introduced labeling systems for foods containing GM products and others are considering such systems. In some cases, industry has expressed concern about the extra costs involved in testing, tracing ingredients, and labeling. Several options have been proposed: labeling based on presence of detectable transgenic DNA or protein only; introduction of special labeling for GMO-free foods; labeling of all foods derived from GMOs, irrespective of whether the final product contains traces of transgenic DNA or protein; and labeling of foods and any food ingredients produced with GMOs (for example, meat from animals fed with transgenic crop residues). The likelihood that certain countries (both Asian developing countries and their agricultural export customers) will adopt labeling of food containing GM products needs to be assessed. The impact of such labeling on the production, distribution, marketing, and exports of GM foodstuffs also must be considered.

Conclusion

Biotechnology is not a single solution to feeding the poor, but a suite of technologies to be embedded in established breeding and selection programs. Several biotechnology approaches could have major impact. A range of options are available to ensure that future biotechnology initiatives can reach their full potential for alleviating poverty and securing food security. It should be emphasized that many developed countries face the same challenges, including, but not limited to, the lack of harmonization of regulatory systems, poor linkages between biotechnology research and its use in practical plant breeding, and differences in national approaches to labeling and acceptance of GMOs. Assistance by international donors from developed countries and ongoing cooperation in biotechnology can have immediate, mutual benefits for both developed and developing countries. Some of the developed-country benefits may include greater confidence in the protection of IP internationally, facilitated two-way trade, better regional quarantine surveillance, and commercial opportunities through joint ventures in potentially huge markets such as China and India.

Notes

The author gratefully acknowledges ACIAR and the Asian Development Bank colleagues from the Australia study on biotechnology—Dimy Nangju, Carliene Brenner, and Gabrielle Persley—along with Ken Fischer and Philip Pardey for stimulating discussions and suggestions. Views expressed are the author's and should not be understood to represent ACIAR or the Australian Government.

1. Studies include the recent ADB—Australia study on biotechnology (ADB 2001); the National Academy of Sciences report *Transgenic plants and world agriculture* (2000); the Nuffield Council on Bioethics study (1999); the World Bank Agricultural Knowledge and Information Systems Thematic Team study (Byerlee and Fischer 2000); IFPRI's 2020 focus series on developing-country biotechnology (Persley 1999); and the proceedings of the October 1999 CGIAR conference *Agricultural Biotechnology and the Poor* (Persley and Lantin 2000).

References

ADB (Asian Development Bank). 2001. Agricultural biotechnology poverty reduction and food security. Working paper. Manila.

Altieri, M. A. 1998. The environmental risks of transgenic crops: An ecological assessment. *Agbiotech News and Information* 10(12): 405N–410N.

Byerlee, D., and K. Fischer. 2000. *Accessing modern science: Policy and institutional options for agricultural biotechnology in developing countries.* Washington, D.C.: World Bank.

Conway, G. 1997. *The doubly Green Revolution: Food for all in the 21st Century.* Ithaca, N.Y., U.S.A.: Cornell University Press.

De la Fuente, J. M., V. Ramirez-Rodriguez, J. L. Cabrera-Ponce, and L. Herrera-Estrella. 1997. Aluminum tolerance in transgenic plants by alteration of citrate synthesis. *Science* (276): 1566–68.

Department of Foreign Affairs and Trade, Australia. 2000. Capacity building activities in the field of biosafety: Australian submission. <http://www.dfat.gov.au/environment/bsp/bio_sub/capacity.html>.

FAO (Food and Agriculture Organization of the United Nations). 1995. Agricultural biotechnology in the developing world. FAO Research and Technology Paper No. 6. Rome.

Goto, F., T. Yoshihara, N. Shigemoto, S. Toki, and F. Takaiwa. 1999. Iron fortification of rice seed by the soybean ferritin gene. *Nature Biotechnology* (17): 282–86.

Gressel, J., J. K. Ransom, and E. A. Hassan. 1996. Biotech-derived herbicide-resistant crops for third world needs. *Annals of the New York Academy of Science* (792): 140.

James, C. 2000. *Preview—Global status of commercialized transgenic crops: 2000.* International Service for the Acquisition of Agri-Biotech Applications. Brief No. 21. Ithaca, N.Y., U.S.A.

Kryder, R. D., S. P. Kowalski, and A. F. Krattiger. 2000. The intellectual and technical property components of pro-vitamin A rice (*Golden*Rice): A preliminary freedom-to-operate review. International Service for the Acquisition of Agri-Biotech Applications Brief No. 20. Ithaca, N.Y., U.S.A.

Levidow, L., S. Carr, and D. Wield. 1999. Market-stage precautions: Managing regulatory disharmonies for transgenic crops in Europe. *AgBiotechNet* 1 (April) 414: 1–7.

Lipton, M. 1999. Reviving the stalled momentum of global poverty reduction: What role for genetically modified plants? Crawford Memorial Lecture, CGIAR International Centers Week. Washington, D.C.: Consultative Group on International Agricultural Research.

Maredia, K. M., F. H. Erbisch, C. L. Ives, and A. J. Fischer. 1999. Technology transfer and licensing of agricultural biotechnologies in the international arena. *AgBiotechNet* 1 (May) 017: 1–7.

Mascarenhas, D. 1998. Negotiating the maze of biotech "tool patents." *Nature Biotechnology* (16): 1371–72.

Mikkelsen, T. R., B. Andersen, R. B. Jorgenson. 1996. The risk of crop transgenic spread. *Nature* 380: 31–32.

Miller, H. I. 1999. Substantial equivalence: Its uses and abuses. *Nature Biotechnology* (17): 1042–43.

National Academy of Sciences (NAS). 2000. *Transgenic plants and world agriculture*. Washington, D.C.: National Academy Press. <http://www.nap.edu/html/transgenic/pdf/transgenic.pdf>.

Nuffield Council on Bioethics. 1999. *Genetically modified crops: The ethical and social issues*. London: Nuffield Council on Bioethics. <http://www.nuffield.org/bioethics/publication/pub0010805.html>.

Persley, G. J., ed. 1999. *Biotechnology for developing country agriculture: Problems and opportunities*. 2020 Vision Focus Series 2. Washington, D.C.: International Food Policy Research Institute.

Persley, G. J., and M. M. Lantin, eds. 2000. *Agricultural biotechnology and the poor*. Proceedings of an international conference, Washington, D.C., October 1999. Consultative Group on International Agricultural Research.

Pinstrup-Andersen, P., and M. J. Cohen. 2000. Agricultural biotechnology: Risks and opportunities for developing country food security. *International Journal of Biotechnology* (2): 145–63.

Qaim, M., A. Krattiger, and J. von Braun, eds. 2000. *Agricultural biotechnology in developing countries: Towards optimizing the benefits for the poor*. Dordrecht, the Netherlands: Kluwer.

Salazar, S., C. Falconi, J. Komen, and J. I. Cohen. 2000. *The use of proprietary biotechnology research inputs at selected Latin American NAROs*. ISNAR Briefing Paper 44. The Hague: International Service for National Agricultural Research.

Sasaki, T. 1999. Rice genomics for agro-innovation. *AgBiotechNet* 1 029: 1–4.

Sasson, A. 1998. Biotechnology in food production: Relevance to developing countries. In *Agricultural Biotechnology*, A. Altman ed. New York: Marcel Dekker.

Schauzu, M. 2000. The concept of substantial equivalence in safety assessment of foods derived from genetically modified organisms. *AgBiotechNet* 2 (April) 044: 1–4.

Sharma, M. 2000. India: Biotechnology research and development. In *Agricultural biotechnology and the poor*, G. J. Persley and M. M. Lantin eds. Proceedings of an international conference on biotechnology, Washington, D.C.: Consultative Group on International Agricultural Research.

Skerritt, J. H. 2000. Genetically modified plants: Developing countries and the public acceptance debate. *AgBiotechNet* 2 (February) 040: 1–8.

Spillane, C. 2000. Could agricultural biotechnology contribute to poverty alleviation? *AgBiotechNet* 2 (April) 042: 1–39.

Thro, A. M., N. Taylor, K. Raemakers, J. Puonti-Kaerlas, C. Schopke, R. Visser, C. Iglesias, M. J. Sampaio, C. Faquet, W. Roca, and I. Potrykus. 1998. Maintaining the cassava biotechnology network. *Nature Biotechnology* (16): 428–30.

Wambugu, F. M. 1999. Why Africa needs agricultural biotech. *Nature* (6739): 15–16.

Weil, A. 2000. GMOs in developing countries. *AgBiotechNet* 2 (July) ABN 052: 1–4.

Wolfenbarger, L. L., and P. R. Phifer. 2000. The ecological risks and benefits of genetically engineered plants. *Science* (290): 208–12.

Woodend, J. J. 1994. Biotechnology for cash crops of developing countries: Opportunities, prospects and threats. *Genetic Engineering and Biotechnology Monitor* (1): 75–81.

Ye, X., S. Al-Babili, A. Kloti, J. Zhang, P. Lucca, P. Beyer, and I. Potrykus. 2000. Engineering the provitamin A (beta-carotene) biosynthetic pathway into carotenoid-free rice endosperm. *Science* (287): 303–05.

Chapter 13

The U.S. Biotech Story:
As Told By Economists at USDA

Nicole Ballenger

he Washington Post featured more than 50 articles and op-ed pieces on agricultural biotechnology between January 1999 and November 2000 (Table 13.1). The titles alone reveal a lot about how the still unfolding biotech story is being told to the U.S. public, or at least to the readers of *The Washington Post*. (The coverage may surprise those who have thought that the perspective in the United States has been 100 percent positive.) The articles trace the evolution of the agricultural biotech story as it winds its way through several distinct points of tension, from scientific intrigue to concerns about butterflies, big business, European markets, and rights of U.S. consumers, and back to the promises for fighting human illness and disease. They portray the changing faces and viewpoints of the characters at each twist and turn in the storyline, and they map the shifting territory of public agency responsibility for guiding the story ultimately to a happy ending. The articles also record the public- and private-sector responses to new information and shifts in the balance of influence among the participants in the biotech debate.

The titles from *The Washington Post* archives provide a colorful backdrop for a subplot that is the subject of this chapter—how research economists at the U.S. Department of Agriculture (USDA) have been involved in the agricultural biotech issue. It will likely surprise no one that economists do not appear as prominent characters in the newspaper version. Indeed, only one op-ed piece in the *Post* was written by an economist (see "Biotech and the Poor," *The Washington Post*, October 27, 1999). Nonetheless, research economists at USDA and their research collaborators at universities have had something to say at each juncture in the story. The purpose of this chapter is to review the economic questions that have emerged, and

Table 13.1   *Washington Post* articles on agricultural biotechnology, 1999–2000

Date	Title
January 1, 1999	Biotech Stocks Made Healthy Gains in '98
January 9, 1999	Corn Seed Producers Move to Avert Pesticide Resistance
February 3, 1999	Seeds of Discord: Monsanto's Gene Police Raise Alarm on Farmers' Rights, Rural Tradition
February 8, 1999	Sowing Dependency or Uprooting Hunger
February 13, 1999	U.S. Observers Lobby Against Trade Curbs on Biotechnology: Accord Would Be First to Target Genetically Engineered Products
February 24, 1999	The Birth of Broccolini: Sometimes a Great Notion Becomes a New Vegetable
February 28, 1999	Cows and Clones on a VA. Pharm: Where Animals Make Drugs and Gene Research Goes to the Frontier
March 26, 1999	A Clone's Fleecing Fame: Dolly Finds Stardom as Her Scientific Value Wanes
April 11, 1999	Variety, the Vanishing Crop
April 24, 1999	In Europe, Cuisine du Gene Gets a Vehement Thumbs Down: Biotech Food Protests Reflect Cultural Contrasts, Health Fears
May 18, 1999	British Report: Label Gene Modified Food; Call by U.K. Doctors Group Adds to Trade Tension with U.S., Brings Strong Reaction on Hill
May 20, 1999	Biotech vs. "Bambi" of Insects? Gene-Altered Corn May Kill Monarchs
June 24, 1999	Europe's Food Fright (op-ed)
July 4, 1999	Starting Food Frights (op-ed reply)
July 7, 1999	The Right to Know What We Eat (op-ed)
July 17, 1999	Wars of the Plate (editorial)
August 15, 1999	Next Food Fight Brewing Is Over Listing Genes on Labels: Processors, Retailers Resisting Demand of Some Consumer Groups
August 15, 1999	Biotech Food Raises a Crop of Questions: Genetically Modified Foods Offer Benefits, But Is It Safe for Human Consumption?
August 31, 1999	Well-Tested Biotech Foods (op-ed)
September 10, 1999	Beware Engineered Foods (op-ed)
September 12, 1999	Food War Claims Its Casualties: High-Tech Crop Fight Victimizes Farmers
September 18, 1999	Caterpillars, Pollen, Science (op-ed)
October 6, 1999	Monsanto to Forego Work on Sterile Seeds
October15, 1999	Gene-Altered Food Study Fuels a Fire
October 26, 1999	Crop Busters Take on Monsanto: Backlash Against Biotech Foods Exacts a High Price
October 27, 1999	Biotech and the Poor (op-ed)
November 13, 1999	Gene-Altered Corn's Impact Reassessed: Studies Funded by Biotech Consortium Find Little Risk to Monarch Butterfly
November 19, 1999	A Biotech Food Fight: Two Sides Square Off at FDA Hearing
November 24, 1999	Biotech Crops Spur Warning: 30 Farm Groups Say Consumer Backlash Could Cost Markets
December 1, 1999	Consumer Groups Urge Labeling of Biotech Foods
December 15, 1999	6 Farmers in Class Action vs. Monsanto: Lawsuit Questions the Company's Testing of Genetically Modified Seeds
December 23, 1999	Southern Maryland Notebook: A Push to Put Tobacco to a Healthy Use
December 27, 1999	At USDA Unit, Seeds of Many Ideas
January 14, 2000	Gene-Altered Rice May Help Fight Vitamin A Deficiency Globally
January 16, 2000	EPA Restricts Gene-Altered Corn in Response to Concerns: Farmers Must Plant Conventional "Refuges" to Reduce Threat of Ecological Damage.
January 17, 2000	Down on the High-Tech PHARM: Researchers Tap Goat Milk for Genetically Enhanced Drugs
January 24, 2000	Talks to Open on Divisive Issue of Gene-Altered Foods
March 4, 2000	Tighter Rules for Organic Food Eyed: USDA Seeks Bans on Irradiation, Genetic Changes
April 6, 2000	Biotech Crops Appear Safe, Panel Says

Table 13.1	(continued)
Date	Title
April 28, 2000	Dolly's Premature Aging not Evident in Cloned Cows: Finding Hints at Curative Role for Cloned Human Embryos
April 30, 2000	Big Processors to Shun Biotech Potato
May 3, 2000	U.S. to Add Oversight on Biotech Foods: Proposals Cover Testing, Labels, and Public Notice
June 29, 2000	Cloning Sheep with Customized Genes: Advance in Scotland May Help Study of Human Diseases
July 11, 2000	Report Says Biotech Fails to Help Neediest Farmers: Panel Calls for Allowing Seed Saving, Other Steps to Eliminate Barriers
July 20, 2000	Groups Launch Campaign Against Biotech Foods
August 3, 2000	Biotech Research Branches Out: Gene-Altered Trees Raise Thickets of Promise, Concern
August 4, 2000	Monsanto Offers Patent Waiver on Rice Altered to Fight Illness
August 22, 2000	Second Study Links Gene-Altered Corn, Butterfly Deaths
September 18, 2000	Biotech Critics Cite Unapproved Corn in Taco Shells: Gene-Modified Variety Allowed Only for Animal Feed Because of Allergy Concerns
September 23, 2000	Biotech Corn Fuels a Recall: Unapproved Variety Used in Taco Shells
September 27, 2000	Biotech Firm Suspends Sale of Corn Seed After Recall
October 3, 2000	FDA Will Widen Probe of Biotech Corn Misuse
October 17, 2000	"Frankenfish" or Tomorrow's Dinner?: Biotech Salmon Face a Current of Environmental Worry

Source: Compiled by author.

some of the answers. It is also to elicit themes from the economic analyses that can potentially inform the public and influence the policy process in a way that could matter to the story when one looks back a year or so from now. At risk of giving away the punch line, economists can sometimes help diffuse tensions surrounding the biotech issue by asking the dispassionate question of whether or not markets are working and, where they are not, by helping design appropriate government response.

January 1, 1999—"Biotech Stocks Made Healthy Gains in 1998"

This optimistically titled article appeared in the *Post* on the first day of 1999. Although the content was not specific to agriculture, the title calls to mind the dramatic rise in private-sector agricultural research and development (R&D) that the U.S. was experiencing at the time. Total research expenditures by the private food and agricultural industry had nearly tripled in real terms between 1960 and 1996, from about US$1.3 billion to $4 billion (Figure 13.1). This rise meant that total agricultural and food R&D in the United States was larger than ever before. The fact, however, that it came at a time when public-sector R&D funds were more or less flat raised questions about why the public-private sector balance might be shifting

Figure 13.1 United States agricultural research and development

Billions of 1996 dollars

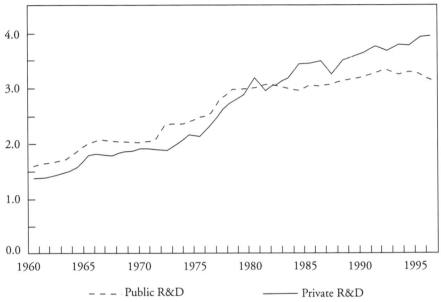

--- - Public R&D   —— Private R&D

Source: Klotz-Ingram (2001).

and what the implications might be for U.S. farmers and also for public R&D policy (Smith et al. 1999).

The rise in private-sector R&D was inextricably tied up with the rapid advances in agricultural biotechnology, but it is still difficult to unravel the various influences of advances in science, changes in intellectual property rights (IPR), structural change, new arrangements for public-private collaboration, and technology transfer and other factors. To single out the role of biotechnology, methods such as cell culture, genetic engineering, and molecular mapping have shortened the time needed to develop new plant varieties and increased the precision with which plant traits can be modified. Consequently, the development of new crop varieties with sought-after traits seems to be increasingly profitable for input firms such as seed and chemical companies. (Shoemaker et al. 2001.)

Along with the supposedly good news that biotech—coupled with enhanced IPR—was bringing more R&D to agriculture came the question of whether there should be a lesser or refocused role for public-sector agricultural R&D, and how the public and private research sectors ought to interact. Economists have long argued that the combination of a public-sector specializing in basic research and a private sector oriented toward applied research generates the highest return on society's R&D investment. Now, however, it was apparent that what was once considered basic science, such as genomic mapping, was being done by private "life science" firms such as Monsanto and Novartis (Smith et al. 1999).

A specific concern at USDA's Agricultural Research Service (ARS) was that some basic scientific knowledge, or enabling biotechnological tool, that could be critical to a public-sector research endeavor would be the property of private firms and therefore unavailable to public-sector researchers. Balancing this concern, economists pointed out, was the evidence to date of widespread licensing of many enabling technologies whose patents are owned by private firms (Shoemaker et al. 2001). Nonetheless, public-sector research (including that at universities) is increasingly complicated by the need sometimes to negotiate many such licensing agreements for every single project. This overlap of research endeavors makes it likely that separate domains of public and private agricultural research are going to be less and less the norm in the United States. If and how public-private interactions will be optimized for society's benefit through a variety of forms of collaboration is still an economics story in the making.

January 9, 1999—"Seeds of Discord: Monsanto's Gene Police Raise Alarm on Farmers' Rights, Rural Tradition"

The large private-sector investment in crop biotechnology moved into the commercial arena in 1996 when the United States saw the first wide-scale planting of newly approved biotech crops, including *Bt*-corn, *Bt*-cotton, and Roundup Ready® (RR) soybeans. Although industry estimates had been available for some time, it was not until farm-level survey data from the Agricultural Resource Management Study (ARMS), conducted by the Economic Research Service and the National Agricultural Statistical Service from 1996 to 1998, were analyzed that the U.S. government had official statistics on biotech crop acreage. ARMS data showed that U.S. acreage planted to biotech crops increased rapidly from 1996 to 1997, and even more sharply from 1997 to 1998. Area increased from about 8 million acres in 1996 to more than 50 million acres in 1998, accounting for about 16 percent of all U.S. crop acreage. By 1998, about 40 percent of U.S. cotton acres, one third of U.S. corn acres, and 44 percent of U.S. soybean acres were planted to biotech varieties (Fernandez-Cornejo and McBride 2000).

Early in 1999, *Washington Post* stories reflected concerns that private seed companies had garnered too much power vis-à-vis farmers through biotech crops. Adoption had clearly been rapid in the United States, suggesting to economists that farmers anticipated positive net benefits. However, there were concerns that through

Table 13.2   Econometric results on the impact of adopting herbicide-tolerant and
insect-resistant field crops

	Effect with respect to change in the adoption of		
	Herbicide tolerant soybean, 1997[a]	Herbicide tolerant cotton, 1997[a]	*Bt* cotton, 1997 (southeast) [a]
Change in yields	small increase[b]	increase[c]	increase[c]
Change in profits	0[d]	increase[c]	increase[c]
Change in pesticide use [d]			
Herbicides			
Acetamide herbicides	0[e]		
Triazine herbicides		0[e]	
Other synthetic herbicides	decrease[c]	0[e]	
Glyphosate	increase[c]	0[e]	
Insecticides			
Organophosphate insecticides			0[e]
Pyrethroid insecticides			0[e]
Other insecticides			decrease[c]

Source: Fernandez-Cornejo, Klotz-Ingram, and Jans (2000).
a. Based on Fernandez-Cornejo, Klotz-Ingram, and Jans (1999).
b. Small increases or decreases are less than 1 percent change for a 10 percent change in adoption.
c. Increases or decreases are less than 5 percent change for a 10 percent change in adoption.
d. In percent change in acre-treatments.
e. Underlying coefficients are not statistically different from zero.

technology fees, price premiums for the new seeds, and conditions specified in seed purchase contracts, the seed companies were reaping the primary rewards. The ARMS data allowed USDA economists to begin to rigorously sort out the impacts of adoption on farmer costs and returns on a much broader level than had previously been accomplished through various regional studies or field trials (see, for examples, Arnold, Shaw, and Medlin 1998; Stark 1997).

Based on econometric analysis of the 1997 ARMS data, Fernandez-Cornejo and McBride (2000) report a statistically significant relationship between increased yields and increased adoption of herbicide-tolerant and insecticide-resistant crops, although results are mixed across crops and regions due to the variety of growing conditions and pest-infestation levels. They find that the adoption of herbicide-tolerant cotton led to significant increases in yields, as did the adoption of *Bt* cotton and the adoption of herbicide-tolerant soybeans, although the latter increase was quite small. Turning to net returns, they find a similar pattern except for the adoption of herbicide-tolerant soybeans where they believe regional variations in the data mask detection of a statistically significant relationship (Table 13.2). The statistical results tend to back up farmers' own stated reasons for adopting biotech crops. In 1997, the majority of farmers surveyed (54–76 percent of adopters) said they adopted biotech crops with pest management traits in order to "increase yields through improved pest control." The second most important reason was "to decrease pesticide costs" (Fernandez-Cornejo and McBride 2000).

The economists' work at USDA lends support to research by other economists such as Falck-Zepeda and Traxler (1998) and Marra, Hubbell, and Carlson (2001), who find that farmers and companies have shared in the economic benefits of *Bt* cotton. It stops short, however, of dismissing concerns related to the structure of the seed industry. Between 1995 and 1996, six large multinational companies acquired or entered into joint ventures with about 68 seed companies, although three of them later announced plans to divest their seed operations (King 2001). U.S. seed sales have become generally more concentrated among fewer firms although there are significant differences across crops. (For an in-depth discussion of the different roles of private companies in plant breeding for different crops, see Heisey, Srinivason, and Thirtle 2000). For example, the leading private company accounted for about 70 percent of cottonseed sales in 1998 in contrast to less than 30 percent in the early 1970s (Shoemaker et al. 2001). In 1997, four leading companies accounted for 69 percent of corn seed sales and for between 37 and 49 percent of soybean acreage (Shoemaker et al. 2001 and Hayenga and Kalaitzandonakes 1999).[1] No evidence has yet determined whether U.S. farmers or consumers have been harmed by the increasing concentration in seed markets, and there have been no anti-trust investigations to date. The long-run commitment to agriculture by a few life science "giants" is still uncertain and the biotechnology industry is still experiencing rapid change including spin-offs of agricultural divisions (King 2001).[2] Nonetheless, considerable work still lies ahead for agricultural and industrial organization economists in assessing the balance of economic benefits and costs associated with structural change in the seed industry. Consolidation, along with enhanced IPR, appears to have motivated private crop research, but too much market power eventually may inhibit technological advancement by creating barriers to entry for new firms and may limit farmers' access to technological alternatives.

April 24, 1999—"In Europe, Cuisine du Gene Gets a Vehement Thumbs Down"

As the year progressed, it became more difficult to extrapolate future levels from observed levels of adoption of biotech crops in the United States. Regional differences in the likely occurrence of pest infestations were one reason that uniform adoption of the current varieties across the United States would be unlikely. Uncertainties were also emerging with respect to overseas markets.

The biotech issue began to be cited as a potential negative for U.S. agricultural and food exports when a number of biotech corn varieties that had been approved and planted in the United States were not approved in the European Union (E.U.). Although just a small portion of U.S. corn acreage was actually planted to these non-approved varieties, fears of having shipments delayed or halted if unapproved varieties were commingled with approved varieties prompted some U.S. exporters to forego the E.U. market. The value of U.S. corn exports to the E.U. (in particular to Spain and Portugal) dropped about US$200 million a year in FY1997–98 and FY1998–99 because of this so-called moratorium on E.U. approvals (Lin, Chambers, and Harwood 2000).

The bilateral tension over these "regulatory delays" seemed to grow over the months in the U.S. press, and maybe in the eyes of the world, into a U.S.–E.U. standoff over the future of biotech crops. The differences between the United States and the E.U. were clearly important because the world was watching and waiting for guidance on questions about the biotech approval process, risk-assessment methodologies and environmental monitoring, and consumer information. In contrast, however, the economic analyses tended to suggest minor impacts of the E.U.'s de facto moratorium on approvals on global and U.S. grain and oilseed markets. In particular, the loss of corn sales to the E.U. was unlikely to strongly impact the U.S. corn market because the U.S. domestic market (which is largely for corn to be used in animal feed) accounted for more than 80 percent of the total use of U.S. corn. Also, at their peak in the early 1990s, exports to the E.U. were only a small portion (less than 5 percent) of U.S. corn exports. Even prior to the advent of the biotech debate, the E.U. was almost self-sufficient in corn, making it unlikely that E.U. regulatory delays or more deliberate restrictions would seriously disrupt world markets (Ballenger and Bohman 2001).

The U.S.–E.U. trade issues served, however, to focus attention by USDA economists on how U.S. and global markets might respond and adapt should the demand begin to grow globally for nonbiotech commodities or should emerging foreign labeling proposals eventually restrict market access for biotech grains. Of particular interest in the USDA was how a marketing system that had become highly efficient over the years at handling huge volumes of grain (routinely commingled to achieve a particular export grading standard) would adapt to the potential demand for product segregation and even identity preservation (Shoemaker et al. 2001). Analysis by Lin, Chambers, and Harwood (2000) suggested that identity preservation could be quite costly and would require significant price premiums for nonbiotech grains to be cost effective. On the other hand, the U.S. marketing system had demonstrated its ability to respond and profit from foreign demand for products with specific quality attributes, such as organic and nonbiotech soybeans for the Japanese food-use market. An emerging perspective was that differentiation according to biotech status could become part of a general trend toward product differentiation and niche marketing in U.S. agriculture, already encompassing specialty crops, organic foods, specialized cuts of meat, and other value-enhanced grains and oilseeds (Ballenger, Bohman, and Gehlar 2000).

On close examination, the levels of foreign demand for nonbiotech commodities represented only a small share of the U.S. market. Nonetheless, it was apparent that should foreign regulatory restrictions come to include animal feedstuffs and strict labeling requirements for processed foods, the impact on the United States had the potential to be much more substantial.

May 20, 1999—"Biotech Versus 'Bambi' of Insects?"

Biotech crops began to be controversial in the United States, too, particularly after news articles reported results of laboratory tests showing that pollen of *Bt* corn killed monarch butterfly larvae (Losey, Rayor, and Carter 1999). Although several scientists pointed out how the popular press had overstated the risks and missed the nuances of the research, attention turned to potentially adverse environmental or ecological impacts and how those might compare to the potential environmental benefits from using crops with herbicide-tolerant or insect-resistant traits. The research economists at USDA were able to contribute to this issue by extending the econometric analysis of adoption to sort out the impacts of adoption on pesticide use in relation to the impacts of other factors. Statistically controlling for factors other than adoption of genetically modified (GM) seeds produced the following impacts on pesticide use between 1997 and 1998:

- Increases in adoption of herbicide-tolerant cotton were not found to be associated with significant changes in herbicide use.

- Increases in adoption of herbicide-tolerant soybeans were associated with significant decreases in herbicide use, and use of glyphosate herbicide increased while use of other more toxic and persistent synthetic herbicides decreased by a larger amount.

- In the case of *Bt* cotton (where the analysis was focused on the southern United States), an increase in *Bt* adoption was not associated with significant changes in the use of organophosphate insecticides and pyrethroid insecticides, but there was a significant decrease in the use of other insecticides such as aldicarb (Heimlich et al. 2000).

As is typical of economic studies (and presumably the reason they make poor press stories), the results were mixed but on balance they support the case for reduced pesticide use associated with biotech crops.

August 15, 1999—"Next Food Fight Brewing is Over Listing Genes on Labels"

No precise estimates are available, but extensive cultivation of biotech corn and soybeans in the United States has surely resulted in the introduction of biotech ingredients into a wide variety of processed food products consumed by Americans. The use of biotechnology in flavoring and enzyme production adds to the likelihood of consuming foods containing biotech ingredients. Additionally, many meats and meat products are derived from livestock fed biotech corn, soybeans, or cottonseed meal or oil.

Despite safety assurances and strong evidence that most U.S. consumers are not concerned about the safety of their food, some U.S. consumer groups have become strong advocates for labels that can distinguish between biotech-based and non-biotech foods. Industry groups were opposed to labeling requirements because they felt a label proclaiming the possibility of biotech content would have a negative safety connotation, and would stigmatize the product for consumers who would otherwise be accepting of biotech ingredients. The policies of the U.S. Food and Drug Administration (FDA), which has the responsibility for labeling requirements for all foods except meat and poultry, and the USDA, which handles labels for meat and poultry, tended to support the industry stance. Both agencies would require labeling of biotech food if the food's composition were found to differ significantly from that of its nonbiotech counterpart; however, since most biotech foods approved for the market have been found to be essentially the same, foods are not required to be labeled just because they have biotech-based ingredients (Golan, Kuchler, and Mitchell 2000). Additionally, U.S. food policy has been generally disinclined to use labels to protect consumers from potentially risky food additives (Hadden 1986). Consequently, if a biotech ingredient is suspected of posing safety risks—of having unknown or widespread allergenic properties, for example—there is no need for a label because the ingredient simply would not be approved for food use.

Economists at USDA sorted out the immensely complicated questions related to consumers' interest in biotech information—and how labeling might address those concerns. Economists explained that, should a market develop for nonbiotech foods, private firms would have an incentive to weigh the costs and benefits of eliminating biotech ingredients from some of their food products and of then labeling the products as nonbiotech. In fact, several food companies took such steps, for example Gerber and Heinz for baby foods, and Frito-Lay, Inc. for snack foods (ERS 2000). Economists demonstrated that a limited government role in this voluntary approach by firms could promote a more efficient matching of product attributes with consumer preferences. In contrast, using government policy to mandate that firms indicate their food products "may contain biotech ingredients" would work against firm incentives (given that current biotech products have no obvious consumer attributes), and send potentially confusing signals about the safety of the product.

Economic theory was also used to help decisionmakers work through the relationships between labeling options and various social objectives. Proponents of mandatory biotech labeling, for example, seemed to suggest that labeling could be used to help nonbiotech producers deal with the added costs of producing nonbiotech products, such as preventing commingling and ensuring against cross-pollination. Golan et al. (2000) show that even if biotech producers were to label their products, nonbiotech producers would still bear the costs of certifying that their products are nonbiotech, and that nonbiotech producers and consumers would still be the ones to bear the costs of market segregation, testing, certification, and so on.

September 12, 1999—"Food War Claims Its Casualties: High-Tech Crop Fight Victimizes Farmers"

By fall 1999, concern was growing that shifts in consumer preferences might hurt not only biotech crop producers but also nonbiotech crop producers who might not be able to guarantee delivery of a biotech-free product. USDA economists were asked to work together across agencies to consider the potential need for government involvement in the markets for biotech and nonbiotech corn and soybeans. That effort produced a report, "Biotech Corn and Soybeans: Changing Markets and the Government's Role," which is posted on the Economic Research Service website at <http://www.ers.usda.gov/whatsnew/issues/biotechmarkets/governmentrole.htm>. The report found that private markets for corn and soybeans were showing flexibility in reacting to differentiating consumer demands. A significant (though uncertain) percentage of grain handlers and elevators had begun to segregate biotech and nonbiotech varieties, and surveys of elevators indicated some were offering premiums for the nonbiotech commodities. There was also evidence that private firms had developed and begun to market biotech testing products to help elevators and processors provide assurances of nonbiotech status.

The report explored concerns, however, with how market mechanisms were allocating the benefits and costs of biotech and nonbiotech product differentiation. Those concerns were divided into three categories. The first was with the distribution of economic risks associated with nonbiotech production. Most important in this category was the concern that the responsibility and liability for assurances that a delivered product was biotech-free would fall mostly on nonbiotech farmers—for example, that these farmers were being pressured to sign contracts with elevators agreeing to accept liability. The second area of concern was the risks being borne by biotech producers. In particular, in this category was the worry that overseas markets for biotech crops were increasingly unreliable and that producers would again bear all of the costs of this economic uncertainty. Seed companies, for example, had developed "growers agreements" that assigned farmers the responsibility for finding domestic market outlets for their crops if export markets closed to some biotech varieties. Storage constraints associated with demands for segregation could also impose additional risks and costs on farmers.

The third area concerned the distribution of costs and benefits related to impacts on consumers. The report noted that the process of market differentiation created both winners (consumers supportive of or unconcerned about biotechnology who would gain through lower commodity and food prices) and losers (consumers who did not want to consume biotech products who must now pay premiums for biotech-free foods). The costs imposed on those consumers who prefer nonbiotech foods could be perceived as unfair, and there could be a potential role for government policy in redistributing these costs. A key distinction between the United States and Europe, the report pointed out, seemed to be that U.S. society was weighting these consumer benefits and costs differently than was European society. An important reason for this difference may have been national differences in peoples' trust of regulatory agencies (Gaskell et al. 1999). Sustaining and building public trust in the regulatory authorities at USDA, FDA, and the Environmental Protection Authority (EPA) was, then, clearly important to perceptions of costs and benefits of biotech foods. Government initiatives to ensure that regulatory capacity appeared warranted and, therefore, the regulatory authorities' credibility with the general public would continue to advance in step with new developments in biotechnology.

May 3, 2000—"U.S. to Add Oversight on Biotech Foods: Proposals Cover Testing, Labels, and Public Notice"

By the end of 1999, the U.S. administration had announced several initiatives to ensure that the U.S. regulatory programs would keep abreast of the science. A standing committee under the auspices of the U.S. National Academy of Sciences (NAS) was tasked with reviewing USDA's biotech approval process and evaluating ways in which it might be strengthened. The Secretary of Agriculture at the time, Dan

Glickman, asked the committee for recommendations on environmental risk-assessment processes, gaps in the science base for risk assessment, and a system for environmental monitoring. The Secretary also created USDA's Advisory Committee on Agricultural Biotechnology (ACAB) to advise him on a broad range of issues relating to agricultural biotechnology and to bring together the many diverse voices and opinions regarding this technology. The U.S. administration also called for significant funding increases for competitively awarded university research to examine safety issues surrounding biotechnology and to support U.S. regulatory decisions (Glickman 2000).

In May 2000 significant developments in U.S. policy reflected the willingness to address some consumers' questions about the biotech status of a food product. First, a presidential initiative announced that companies would now be required to notify the FDA in advance of their intention to market new biotech-based products, a step that had been voluntary. The intent of this advance notification is to give the FDA sufficient time and means to identify any safety issues, although the FDA still finds that substances introduced into food through bioengineering are generally "substantially the same" as other substances found in the diet. Second, the FDA announced it would develop guidance for voluntary labeling by food companies, with guidelines focusing on whether genetic engineering was or was not used to develop a food or whether biotech ingredients were or were not added to a food product. There would be no health or safety implications of such a voluntary label.

At the same time, the U.S. government announced steps to enhance the effectiveness with which the U.S. marketing system could deliver both biotech and non-biotech products in response to differentiating consumer demand. USDA's Grain Inspection, Packers, and Stockyards Administration (GIPSA) moved to establish a reference laboratory that would evaluate and verify analytical tests and procedures for detecting and quantifying bioengineered traits; evaluate the performance of detection methods; evaluate and accredit non-USDA testing labs; and establish sampling procedures for use in testing biotech grains and soybeans (GIPSA 2000). USDA also announced it would assess the need for a "quality assurance program" to provide an independent, third-party verification and certification system for the processes used by private firms to differentiate and segregate biotech and nonbiotech commodities. The purpose of the program would be to strengthen consumer confidence in industry claims.

The Economists' Version of the Biotech Story

Probably the most telling evidence of the importance of economics in the biotech story is the estimates collected in June 2000 of farmers' planting intentions.

Randomly selected farmers across the United States were asked by the USDA's National Agricultural Statistics Service (NASS) if they had planted seed that was bioengineered to resist herbicides, insects, or both. The acreage survey found that 54 percent of U.S. soybean acreage was planted to biotech varieties; 25 percent of corn acreage; and 61 percent of upland cotton acreage (NASS 2000). A formal analysis of factors accounting for the changes from previous years has not been done, but one might hypothesize that biotech varieties continue to be seen as good news by U.S. farmers although market uncertainties may have dampened corn farmers' enthusiasm.

Biotechnology has helped many U.S. farmers in the form of higher yields and lower input costs. Some farmers have undoubtedly felt that their decisions about what to plant are more complicated and they have discounted these benefits because of market uncertainties. At the same time, markets have responded to some (still relatively small) consumer demand for nonbiotech commodities and foods both abroad and at home by introducing new biotech diagnostics and marketing arrangements. Unlike other instances of technological change in agriculture, the nonadopters may be able to tap into a new niche market that stems from a preference for nonbiotech technology. Meanwhile, the life sciences industry is clearly engaged in an ongoing assessment of the profitability of continued expansion in agricultural biotechnology.

Although known as the dismal science, economics is actually often quite optimistic about the ability of markets to help sort things out. In the case of biotechnology, economists have tended to see the question not as one of whether biotechnology is good or bad, or has a future or not, but one of whether agricultural and food markets can efficiently match global consumers with the commodities and food products they want. While the magnitudes differ, in all countries consumers can be found that accept biotech crops and foods, along with those that prefer nonbiotech crops and foods. As farmers and food companies across countries respond to these differing demands with products differentiated by biotech status, the biotech story need no longer feature U.S. interests aligned with biotech crops and E.U. interests focused on preventing biotech crops. It may be a less interesting story, but it would reflect the realties of modern agricultural and food markets.

Economists have an ongoing role, however, in assessing options for public-sector intervention in differentiated agricultural product markets. Recent events surrounding the detection in a food product of a biotech corn variety that had been approved only for feed use heightened concerns that the U.S. marketing system cannot by itself effectively segregate crop varieties (*The Washington Post* articles dated September 18, 23, and 27, and October 3, 2000, Table 13.1). The economists have argued that it is not a matter of physical impediments, but one of incentives—if it pays to segregate, the marketing system will. In the Starlink® case, none of the parties involved—that is, the seed company Aventis, the farmers, and the grain handlers—seem to have anticipated that commingling would be detected; they therefore lacked incentive to ensure against it by assuming the added costs of preventing Starlink® corn from entering foodgrain channels. Segregation and identity preservation can be done but not without someone paying the extra costs. The private costs of segregation can be reduced, and they can also be redistributed from one actor in the marketing system to another, if government decides to intervene. To date, USDA has marked out a measured role for itself in evaluating, verifying, and certifying biotech testing services and the segregation and identity preservation services provided by private firms.

Economists have highlighted some important questions about how markets are working. One is whether new intellectual property rights are conferring too much market power on private firms, and whether there are constraints to the public sector's pursuit of public-goods research because of the complex web of licensing and ownership issues. A second and related dimension is not a U.S. issue per se, but certainly is one for the world—that is, the problem of insufficient incentives to private firms to deliver the benefits of biotechnology research to developing countries (see "Biotech and the Poor," *The Washington Post*, October 27, 1999, Table 13.1).

Finally, the agricultural biotech story in the United States is a story about the intersection of technological change in agriculture and an increasingly consumer-driven food system. Consumer preferences for biotech are shaped, among other things, by their confidence in the public agencies with responsibilities for regulating new biotechnology-based products. At the same time, regulatory agencies and their decisions may be increasingly affected by consumer preferences. Although the United States has taken important steps to upgrade and ensure continued confidence in its regulatory approval processes, it will be impossible for new science to bring certainty to every regulatory decision pertaining to biotechnology. How, then, will other factors that influence consumer preferences, which may be cultural, ethical, social, or economic, be taken into account? As some of the recent *Washington Post* articles suggest, biotech regulatory issues for trees and fish are likely to be as or more challenging and complex than those for crops (see *Post* articles dated August 3 and October 17, 2000, Table 13.1).

Notes

1. The range in soybean acreage estimates has to do with farmers' decisions to plant saved GMO seed.

2. Monsanto's decision to cancel a US$1.9 billion deal to buy Delta and Pine Land, which would have significantly increased their combined share of the cotton seed market, may have been motivated in part by the likelihood of an anti-trust investigation.

References

Arnold, J. C., D. R. Shaw, and C. R. Medlin. 1998. Roundup Ready programs versus conventional programs: Efficacy, varietal performance, and economics. *Proceedings of the Southern Weed Science Society, Southern Weed Science Society* 51: 272–73.

Ballenger, N., and M. Bohman. 2001. Toward common ground: Roles of markets and policy. In *Genetically modified organisms in agriculture: Economics and politics,* G. C. Nelson ed. London: Academic Press.

Ballenger, N., M. Bohman, and M. Gehlar. 2000. Biotechnology: Implications for U.S. corn and soybean trade. *Agricultural Outlook* AGO–270 (April): 24–28.

ERS (Economic Research Service of the U.S. Department of Agriculture). 2000. Biotech Corn and Soybeans: Changing Markets and the Government's Role. <http://www.ers.usda.gov/whatsnew/_issues/biotechmarkets/>. Accessed April 12, 2000.

Falck-Zepeda, J. B., and G. Traxler. 1998. Rent creation and distribution from transgenic cotton in the U.S. Paper prepared for the symposium Intellectual Property Rights and Agricultural Research Impacts, NC–208, International Maize and Wheat Improvement Center (CIMMYT), El Batan, Mexico, March 5–7.

Fernandez-Cornejo, J., and W. D. McBride. 2000. *Genetically engineered crops for pest management in U.S. agriculture: Farm level effects,* AER No. 786. Washington, D.C.: Economic Research Service of the U.S. Department of Agriculture.

Fernandez-Cornejo, J., C. Klotz-Ingram, and S. Jans. 2000. Farm-level effects of adopting genetically engineered crops in the U.S.A. Chapter 4 in *Transitions in agrobiotech: Economics of strategy and policy,* W. L. Lesser, ed. Proceedings of the 1999 NE–165 Conference, Storrs, Conn. and Amherst, Mass. U.S.A.: Food Marketing Research Center, University of Connecticut and Dept. of Resource Economics, University of Massachusetts.

Gaskell, G., M. W. Bauer, J. Durant, and N. C. Allum. 1999. Worlds apart? The reception of genetically modified foods in Europe and the U.S. *Science* 285: 5426 (July 16): 384–87.

GIPSA (Grain Inspection, Packers and Stockyards Administration). 2000. <http://www.usda.gov/gipsa/biotech/biotech.htm>. Accessed August 30, 2001.

Glickman, D. 2000. Remarks to National Academy of Sciences First Meeting of Standing Committee on Biotechnology Food and Fiber Production and the Environment, Washington, D.C., May 4, 2000. <http://www.usda.gov/news/releases/2000/05/0146>. Accessed August 30, 2001.

Golan, E., F. Kuchler, and L. Mitchell. 2000. *Economics of food labeling,* AER No. 793. Washington, D.C.: Economic Research Service of the U.S. Department of Agriculture.

Hadden, S. G. 1986. *Read the label: Reducing risk by providing information.* Boulder, Colo., U.S.A.: Westview Press.

Hayenga, M., and N. Kalaitzandonakes. 1999. Structure and coordination system changes in the U.S. biotech seed and value-added grain market. Proceedings of the International Food and Agribusiness Management Association 1999 World Food and Agribusiness Congress, Florence, Italy, May.

Heimlich, R., J. Fernandez-Cornejo, W. McBride, C. Klotz-Ingram, S. Jans, and N. Brooks. 2000. Genetically engineered crops: Has adoption reduced pesticide use? *Agricultural Outlook* AGO–270 (August): 13–17.

Heisey, P. W., C. S. Srinivasan, and C. Thirtle. 2000. Privatization of plant breeding in industrialized countries: Causes, consequences, and the public sector response. Paper prepared for the XXIV International Conference of Agricultural Economists, Berlin, Germany, August 13–18.

King, J. 2001. *Concentration and technology in agricultural input industries.* Agriculture Information Bulletin No. 763. Washington, D.C.: Economic Research Service of the U.S. Department of Agriculture.

Klotz-Ingram, C. 2001. Personnal communication, Economic Research Service of the U.S. Department of Agriculture (March 5).

Lin, W. W., W. Chambers, and J. Harwood. 2000. Biotechnology: U.S. grain handlers look ahead. *Agricultural Outlook* AGO-270 (April): 29–34.

Losey, J. W., L. S. Rayor, and M. E. Carter. 1999. Transgenic pollen harms Monarch larvae. *Nature* 399 (May 20): 214.

Marra, M., B. Hubbell, and G. Carlson. 2001. Information quality, technology depreciation, and the adoption of a new technology: The case of *Bt* cotton in the Southeast. *Journal of Agricultural and Resource Economics.* 26 (1): 158–75.

NASS. (National Agricultural Statistics Service of the United States Department of Agriculture). 2000. Acreage. Report released June 30, 2000. Available at http://jan.mannlib.cornell.edu/reports/nassr/field/pcp-bba/acrg0600.pdf. Accessed December 2000.

Shoemaker, R., J. Harwood, K. Day-Rubenstein, T. Dunaway, P. Heisey, L. Hoffman, C. Klotz-Ingram, W. Lin, L. Mitchell, W. McBride, and J. Fernandez-Cornejo. 2001. *Economic issues in agricultural biotechnology.* Agricultural Information Bulletin No. 762. Washington, D.C.: Economic Research Service of the U.S. Department of Agriculture.

Smith, K. R., N. Ballenger, K. Day-Rubenstein, P. Heisey, and C. Klotz-Ingram. 1999. Biotechnology research: Weighing the options for a new public-private balance. *Agricultural Outlook* AGO–265 (October): 22–25.

Stark, Jr., C. R. 1997. Economics of transgenic cotton: Some indications based on Georgia producers. In *Proceedings of the Beltwide Cotton Conference*, Vol. 1, 251–54. Memphis, Tenn., U.S.A.: National Cotton Council.

Part 6

Concluding Comments

Rural R&D Technology Policy

Jock R. Anderson

On previous occasions, I have had recourse to a Weinberg (1975, 12) aphorism to the effect that "The future will be like the past because, in the past, the future was like the past." But today I must depart from this view of the future because some of the challenges the world faces in the new century are different from those in the past in several significant ways, ranging from genetic engineering and related intellectual property protection to better custody of rural natural resources, including biodiversity.

One form of public investment that has an outstanding track record in assisting the poor, especially in Asia, is agricultural research. Precisely how the benefits of such productivity gains in agriculture play out in reducing poverty per se, however, depends on the relative magnitudes of several direct and indirect effects that, as set out by Byerlee (2000), are determined by a variety of factors such as the distribution of poverty between rural and urban areas, market structure, geographic concentration of the poor, economic policies, and the extent to which particular commodities are important in incomes of poor producers or expenditures of poor consumers.

Perhaps inspired by the successes of the Green Revolution beginning in the 1960s, the 1970s and 1980s saw a rapid growth in national and international investment in agricultural research. This strengthening tendency rather stagnated during the 1980s, as nations struggled to sustain their support to the large national agricultural research institutes (NARIs) that had been built. The World Bank, for one, actively supported this process of investment growth, especially in the bricks and mortar phase, but concern has grown about the effectiveness as well as the sustainability of many of the investments (for example, Purcell and Anderson 1997). And there are new challenges, some of which are broached below.

Engaging in Modern Biotechnology for Agricultural Advance

Some would convincingly argue that the future of crop-improvement, for example, will definitely not be like it has been in the recent past, because of several major changes in the scientific and legal environments. As the chapters in this volume and papers from other meetings vividly document, modern biotechnology is generating revolutionary advances in genetic knowledge and the capacity to change the genetic structure of organisms that can be used or farmed for humanity's use. The rapidly expanding field of genomics provides molecular tools to greatly accelerate and better target conventional breeding. This same knowledge is being applied to transfer genes across (and within) species to create transgenic varieties. These approaches, which are increasingly concentrated in a few global "life science" companies, require special skills, focused research laboratories, increasingly the capacity to manage intellectual property, and, most importantly in the case of transgenics, the ability to evaluate environmental, food-safety, and health risks. These topics link to other matters that are not trivial, such as marketing chain analysis, product registration, and trade policy issues (see Ballenger, this volume).

Modern biotechnology has an increasingly recognized potential in developing countries to significantly raise agricultural productivity in an environmentally acceptable manner, supply cheaper and more nutritious food, and help alleviate poverty (for example, Conway 2000 and Pinstrup-Andersen and Cohen 2000). This potential, along with the attendant possible environmental and health risks (for example, Wesseler 2000), should be the subject of careful policy analysis as part of the considerable challenge of increasing food security in the developing world, particularly as gains from conventional sources of technology are slowing. Fortunately, there is active dialogue on these topics, for example in Asia (Gupta 2000; Sharma and Ortiz 2000), but the public at large is not yet effectively involved and, perhaps influenced by the strong activist lobbies in the West, there is a risk that biotechnology may not get to play its needed role as early as it should.

Application of molecular biotechnology has thus far been limited to a few traits of interest mainly to commercial farmers, developed primarily but not exclusively by the larger-than-life science companies. Few applications that directly benefit poor consumers or resource-poor farmers in developing countries have been introduced, although there is much in the works. According to James (2000), less than 20 percent (that is, only some 8 million hectares) of the global area of transgenic crops is in developing countries.

Although much of the science and many tools and intermediate products are probably relevant to solving high-priority problems in developing areas, it is unlikely that the private sector itself will invest sufficiently to make the needed adaptations. Consequently, national and international public sectors in the developing world will have to play a key role, much of it inevitably by accessing proprietary tools and products from the private sector. Against this background, some observers have called for public-private partnerships to begin to harness for the poor the benefits of the new science. There has been, however, little detailed analysis of the incentives and mechanisms by which such partnerships can be realized, although Byerlee and Fischer (2000) have recently made a good start, and the wide-ranging discussion in this volume, especially that of Nottenburg, Pardey, and Wright, represents a significant advance.

The public sector, both national and international, will necessarily remain the principal source for investments in biotechnological R&D in developing countries in the years to come (Horstkotte-Wesseler and Byerlee 2001). Although biotechnology applications targeted at resource-poor, drought-prone farmers are being made in developing countries, deployment of these products has been slowed for a number of reasons, including:

- lack of an appropriate regulatory framework for the testing and release of transgenics, which constitutes a perverse type of social risk aversion, although perhaps an understandable one given the costs and information demands of setting one up;

- lack of capacity to carry out risk assessment, even where a regulatory framework is nominally in place, which is implicitly highly precautionary, but again is understandable given the many constraints on capacity in the developing world;

- constrained use of proprietary tools and technologies, and lack of capacity and resources to negotiate access to intellectual property; and

- lack of capacity to manage effective public dialogue with respect to release of transgenics.

These problems are not trivial to overcome, and represent major challenges for development agencies such as the World Bank in programs of assistance to client countries and for concerned research agencies such as the International Food Policy Research Institute (IFPRI). If they are not addressed effectively and soon, not only will opportunity to alleviate poverty be lost, but also agencies themselves increasingly risk their reputations from lost and botched opportunities.

Knowledge is key: research and policy ought to be, and indeed has been, increasingly shifting to a more holistic approach to the long-term management of the broad rural resource base. The situation relating to the adoption of integrated natural resource management techniques is analogous to this broader picture in its demands, both for cogent new knowledge (much of which will link directly to advances in biotechnology), and for reforms in and fine-tuning of the policy environment.

Summary

These abbreviated notes have touched on several issues that will affect the future of global agriculture, but they are not a complete catalogue of challenges and risks. Science offers many solutions to finding productivity-driven escape routes from poverty and to answering questions of better rural natural resource sustenance. The growth of agricultural productivity will continue to be a crucial driver of economic development, as is persuasively argued by Rosegrant and Hazell (2000). Policymakers therefore need to come to grips with these opportunities and those related to postharvest, processing, and other linked economic activities.

Biotechnology brings new risks, as yet poorly understood and not a priority to rural policy analysts. How these risks sit with the many others encountered in rural areas is beyond the present discussion, tackled elsewhere (Anderson 2001). The big risk is that, through various institutional failures, resource-poor farmers of the developing world may largely miss out on the benefits that could and should come from well-articulated investment in this domain, unless we somehow get cleverly proactive in facilitating novel arrangements between public and private players. Complicating the picture are other implicit risks, such as the "reputational risk," which seems to be growing more important to cautious, and apparently risk-averse agencies, such as the World Bank, which are guided by representatives with diverse national perspectives on such matters as transgenics. Clearly, there is great scope for better informing policy development and sensible risk management in this area.

References

Anderson, J. R. 2001. Risk in rural development: Challenges for managers and policy makers. *Agricultural Systems*, special issue, in press.

Byerlee, D. 2000. Targeting poverty alleviation in priority setting for agricultural research. *Food Policy* 25 (4): 429–45.

Byerlee, D., and K. Fischer. 2000. Institutional and policy options for accessing modern biotechnology for the poor. Paper presented at the fourth international conference of the International Consortium on Agricultural Biotechnology Research, Ravello, Italy, August 24–28.

Conway, G. 2000. Crop biotechnology: Benefits, risks, and ownership. <http://www.rockfound.org>. Accessed January 19, 2001.

Gupta, D. D. 2000. Is biotechnology needed for agricultural growth? *The Financial Express on Sunday*, September 24, Chennai, 7.

Horstkotte-Wesseler, G., and D. Byerlee. 2001. Agricultural biotechnology and the poor: The role of development assistance agencies. In *Agricultural biotechnology in developing countries: Towards optimizing the benefits for the poor*, M. Qaim, A. F. Krattiger and J. von Braun eds. Dordrecht, the Netherlands: Kluwer.

James, C. 2000. *Global status of commercialized transgenic crops: 1999.* International Service for the Acquisition of Agri-biotech Applications Brief No. 17. Ithaca, N.Y., U.S.A.

Pinstrup-Andersen, P., and J. I. Cohen. 2000. Modern biotechnology for food and agriculture: Risks and opportunities for the poor. In *Agricultural biotechnology and the poor*, G. J. Persley and M. M. Lantin eds. Proceedings of an international conference on Biotechnology. Washington, D.C.: Consultative Group on International Agricultural Research.

Purcell, D. L. and J. R. Anderson. 1997. *Agricultural extension and research: Achievements and problems in national systems.* A World Bank operations evaluation study. Washington, D.C.: World Bank.

Rosegrant, M. W., and P. B. Hazell. 2000. *Transforming the rural Asian economy: The unfinished revolution.* New York: Oxford University Press.

Sharma, H. C., and O. Ortiz. 2000. Transgenics, pest management, and the environment. *Current Science* 79 (4): 421–37.

Weinberg, G. M. 1975. *An introduction to applied general systems theory.* New York: Wiley.

Wesseler, J. 2000. Uncertainty, irreversibility, and the optimal timing of agricultural policy: The case of transgenic crops. Paper for the mini-symposium on New Investment Theory in Agricultural Economics, XXIV conference of the International Association of Agricultural Economists, Berlin, August 13–18.

Biotechnology Policy Issues

Walter J. Armbruster

A range of policy issues has arisen involving food production, consumer concerns, and environmental issues in the context of international markets and the rapid adoption of biotechnology. James Bonnen, in his International Association of Agricultural Economists Elmhirst Lecture, argued that the introduction of biotechnology has been badly managed and hence politicized because adequate distinction has not been made between biotechnology innovations, which are little more than extensions of traditional breeding technologies, and those biotechnology applications involving transgenic applications (Bonnen 2000). Many of the issues identified involve genetically modified organisms (GMOs). Though no evidence of consumer health problems has surfaced to date, scientists disagree over whether biotechnology products threaten consumers' health and endanger the environment. This uncertainty is exacerbated, according to Bonnen, when the public doesn't understand the difference between transgenic and nontransgenic biotechnology. He argues that risk analysis has focused on the level of risk that deals primarily with specific products and their potential harm, while little attention has been paid to risk analysis in the context of what is socially acceptable (Bonnen 2000, 14). This is a product of the system under which biotechnology has been introduced; the public sector's role in biotechnology research is being rapidly eclipsed by the private sector, which increasingly plays an important research, product development, and marketing role.

Policy Issues

Food safety issues center around the approval process for biotechnology products. Is mandatory or voluntary testing required to get products into the market? United States policy allows products to be introduced under the assumption that product characteristics do not change just because biotechnology techniques are used to produce the products. The U.S. Food and Drug Administration (FDA) allows firms to voluntarily test and submit data for obtaining approval unless there are changes in product characteristics that are known to be linked to potential problems such as allergenicity. In those cases, the FDA requires specific testing for approval. A major challenge is that biotechnology products introduced to date have no visible consumer benefits, but make profits for the input supplier, producer, and marketing firm. Hence, consumers have reason to be concerned about any possible food safety risks, however minor they may be.

Biotechnology opponents argue that the U.S. approval process leaves too much discretion in the hands of the firms standing to gain from introducing products without enough objective testing, and little is known about long-term potential consumer implications of gene-altered products. The scientific community and the biotechnology industry have strongly supported science-based evaluation of technologies and products as the driving force for adopting biotechnology products. Opponents argue that long-term tests have not been conducted and past technologies have been introduced and subsequently found to have adverse effects not suspected initially. While companies introducing the products have tested for risks focused on the particular characteristic that they are selling, concern is whether adequate testing has been done for possible effects of alterations in plant cells (Eichenwald, Kolatam, and Petersen 2001).

Environmental risks and benefits from biotechnology products are not widely understood and, some argue, not well established scientifically. Ervin et al. (2001, 6), argue that "The varieties and uses of genetically altered (transgenic) crops have grown much more rapidly than our ability to understand or appropriately regulate them." Further, they argue that the limited knowledge of environmental impacts of transgenic plants results in risks to the environment and to the agricultural industry.

Concerns center around the potential of biotechnology crops to cross-pollinate with other varieties of the crop and, in particular, to cross-pollinate with related wild species, thus creating super weeds for which there are no control mechanisms available. The Starlink® problem of recent months raises concerns about cross-pollination with other varieties of the crop planted in nearby fields. Refuges have been established to prevent cross-pollination and to maintain biotechnology-free insect populations, but the Starlink® product appears to have cross-pollinated beyond the established refuge limits. It may be that the refuge concept is impractical given the increased level of management required to assure system integrity. Alternatively, the problem may have developed in the harvesting and marketing processes through an inability to assure market channel integrity.

The environmental benefits of using less protective chemicals are not clearly evident to the public. While biotechnology products target a particular disease or insect, there are other diseases and insects for which producers use pesticides or herbicides that may require continued chemical applications. Biotechnology products may allow the application of lower-toxicity chemicals, but this is not well understood by the general public.

Developing and developed countries have different socioeconomic perspectives on biotechnology as discussed by Pinstrup-Andersen and Cohen (this volume). The question of whether the risks are socially acceptable is driving much of the controversy surrounding biotechnology, although most of the research emphasis has been on evaluating known risks in a biological or environmental context.

The shift from publicly funded research to the private sector may be at the root of much of the difficulty in obtaining acceptance of biotechnology products. The land grant system in the Untied States and various institutional structures in other countries have long used the public research, education, and extension approach to discover and adopt new technologies. Increasing private-sector funding and dissemination of research results through patented products has short-circuited the education and extension functions that created a better understanding of previous new technologies and allowed objective assessment of their impacts before widespread adoption. The private-sector model puts a premium on secrecy until the product is ready for marketing and then introduces it using a sales rather than an educational approach.

Policy Options

A variety of policy options are available to deal with these issues. One option is mandatory testing over a long time period for impacts of genetically altered products on food safety, as well as on the environment. Mandatory testing would slow the adoption of new products and shift more of the burden for research on safety and efficacy back to the public sector. This may be necessary, at least in some cases, to establish greater public trust in the products available, especially where problems have arisen or substantial doubts have been raised by those opposed to the technology. The Starlink® incident has raised concern about adequately controling the presence of products not approved for use in the food system and our ability to assure product integrity.

Another approach for dealing with the issues is mandatory or voluntary labeling. Current U.S. policy relies on voluntary labeling if companies see an advantage to promoting a certain characteristic in a biotechnology product. U.S. policy has opted for a product rather than a process-based labeling regime. There are increasing calls for mandatory labeling—even within the United States—and a number of countries have adopted mandatory labeling as an official policy. The level of tolerance established for a product to be declared free of genetically modified product varies by country and is a political decision.

An international committee established under the United States-European Union Biotechnology Consultative Forum recently recommended safety reviews and mandatory labeling for genetically engineered foods. Representatives of consumer groups, academia, and industry from the United States and the E.U. participated in this panel, formed during 2000. Although the recommendations are not binding, U.S. regulators will be under pressure to consider such recommendations as they struggle to manage biotechnology, according to Lueck and Kilman (2000).

With a few notable exceptions, the development of coherent national policies for regulating biotechnologies, managing intellectual property rights, establishing food safety standards, and mitigating environmental impacts has failed to keep pace with the availability of genetically modified product application (see Skerritt this volume). Further, regulations within countries and among countries must be harmonized. Whether biotechnology can be adequately dealt with through the existing regulatory frameworks or whether it requires setting up whole new infrastructures remains to be seen. Bonnen (2000, 15) argues that biotechnology will require international standards and regulation. Moschini (2001, 114) concludes that lack of harmonization in intellectual property rights and in government regulations can greatly affect the adoption of biotechnology products.

The lack of acceptance in some countries and disputes between countries around biotechnology products indicate that serious challenges must be addressed by policymakers, the industry, and the professionals involved, including agricultural economists. It may take the introduction of the second generation of biotechnology products offering clear-cut nutritional or health benefits to obtain market acceptance.

References

Bonnen, J. T. 2000. The transformation of agriculture and the world economy: Challenges for the governance of agriculture and for the profession. Elmhirst Memorial Lecture, XXIV conference of the International Association of Agricultural Economists, Berlin, August, 13–18.

Eichenwald, K., G. Kolatam, and M. Petersen. 2001. Biotechnology food: From the lab to a debacle. *The New York Times*, January 25: A1.

Ervin, D. E., S. S. Batie, R. Welsh, C. Carpentier, J. I. Fern, N. J. Richman, and M. A. Schulz. 2001. *Transgenic crops: An environmental assessment*. Policy Studies Report No. 15. Arlington, Va., U.S.A.: Henry A. Wallace Center for Agricultural and Environmental Policy, Winrock International.

Lueck, S., and S. Kilman. 2000. Gene-altered food needs labels, safety review committee says. *Wall Street Journal*, December 19: B6.

Moschini, G. 2001. Biotech—who wins? Economic benefits and costs of biotechnology innovations in agriculture. *The Estey Centre Journal of International Law and Trade Policy* 28: 93–117.

Public Policy Responses To Biotechnology

Bob Richardson

My few remarks will focus on public policy in relation to biotechnology against the background of recent legislative initiatives in Australia. It is not highly informed by involvement in technical or economic aspects of potential effects of biotechnology.

The recent legislative initiative in Australia seems to me to have been a strong response to the emotive position taken by some consumer and environmental lobby groups. Governments have looked to a coordinated federal/state regulatory response, which led to passage in Parliament of the Gene Technology Bill 2000. In time it may replace the role of the Genetic Manipulation Advisory Committee (GMAC) in nationally coordinating genetically modified (GM) crops and biotechnology.

The new bill establishes an Office of the Gene Technology Regulator (OGTR) "to protect the health and safety of people, and to protect the environment, by identifying risks posed by or as a result of gene technology, and by managing those risks through regulating certain dealings with GMO's" (Parliament of Australia 2000). The legislation has the usual limited scope of federal legislation in Australia, relying on complementary state legislation. The OGTR will have a degree of statutory independence, will establish three advisory committees (Technical, Community Consultative, and Ethics), and will issue licenses previously issued by GMAC.

While no doubt a need exists for coordinated regulatory controls in relation to biotechnology, my initial impression is of an excessively regulatory framework being established. It seems excessive in the sense of concentrating mainly on risk-averse and risk-minimization mechanisms that could hold back beneficial technology developments. Given the diversity of potential impacts of different types of biotechnology, it seems unlikely that a single regulatory system with extensive processes of review, community consultation, and licensing will be sufficiently flexible and responsive. The likelihood is that regulatory response will be too exposed to political pressures, through the advisory committee process.

The introduction of *Bacillus thuringiensis (Bt)* cotton and trials on genetically modified canola in Australia have produced differing responses by state, by industry groups, and nationally. In the rural media some people have argued for a complete ban on genetically modified organisms (GMOs), claiming there will be net gains in international marketing of Australian food and feed products from being GMO-free (Carson 1999, quoting Doug Shears). The State Government of Tasmania has announced a moratorium on GMO field trials on similar grounds. Given the diversity of potential impacts of GMOs, such blanket arguments would seem difficult to sustain. In Victoria the state government has partially funded a major investment in health-related biotechnology, Bio21, at the University of Melbourne. This presents a major opportunity for agriculture as a platform to undertake basic research on issues in biotechnology.

Government policy settings seem likely to respond to emotional public opinions. This public opinion is in turn driven by:

- perceptions of greed among agribusiness corporations (the "terminator gene" proposed by Monsanto has been a public relations disaster for biotechnology); and

- food safety and health issues (public trust of biotechnology has been caught up in this, perhaps by association with such problems as mad cow disease).

On both counts there is a lack of public trust of biotechnology as it affects food and feed. Restoration of trust could be a long, slow process unless strengthened by independent scrutiny of the impact of biotechnology. Food safety issues must be taken seriously and not dismissed as extremism and scaremongering.

This brings me to the issue of the need for better-informed markets, and whether publicly funded research (for example, at universities and government agencies) is equal to the task of generating information that can credibly remove uncertainties about biotechnology. In Australia at least, with declining public funding of university research (and thus "basic" research), academics are sourcing private-sector funding and building commercial relationships. This could compromise their creditability and independence in evaluating the food safety, environmental impacts, and other aspects of biotechnology-based products.

Some economists seem concerned that anticompetitive mergers will control intellectual property arising from biotechnology research. If the costs of R&D and its transformation to marketable products have risen radically, old competitive structures with larger numbers of competitive firms simply may no longer be appropriate. Increased concentration may be essential to generate investment capital and absorb the market risks associated with the adoption of new technology. Like Ron Duncan, I think the appropriate response to concerns about anticompetitive activity is to focus policies on making markets contestable, rather than on regulatory responses.

Better-informed public debate seems essential to introduce sound public policy on biotechnology. I have been struck by the complexity and diversity of the forms of the new biotechnology. These new technologies need to be clearly and simply presented so the wider community can understand the implications of real policy issues.

References

Carson, J., 1999. Little support for GMO ban. *Stock and Land.* September 9: 1–2.

Parliament of Australia. 2000. *Gene Technology Bill 2000.* Bills Digest No. 112000–01, Parliamentary Library, Canberra, ACT, March.

Acronyms and Glossary

AARES	Australian Agriculture and Resource Economics Society
AAFC	Agriculture and Agri-Food Canada
ACAB	Advisory Committee on Agricultural Biotechnology (USDA)
ACIAR	Australian Centre for International Agricultural Research
Bt	*Bacillus thuringiensis*
CAMBIA	Center for the Application of Molecular Biology to International Agriculture
CABBIO	*Centro Argentino Brasileño de Biotecnología* / Argentine-Brazilian Biotechnology Center
CATIE	*Centro Agronómico Tropical de Investigación y Enseñanza* / Tropical Agricultural Research and Higher Education Center
CBD	The United Nations Convention on Biological Diversity
CGE	Computable General Equilibrim (model)
CGIAR or CG	Consultative Group on International Agricultural Research
CIDA	Canadian International Development Agency
CIAT	*Centro Internacional de Agricultura Tropical* / International Center for Tropical Agriculture (Colombia)
CIMMYT	*Centro Internacional de Mejoramiento de Maíz y Trigo* / International Maize and Wheat Improvement Center (Mexico)
CIP	*Centro Internacional de la Papa* / International Potato Center (Peru)
CLIMA	Centre for Legumes in Mediterranean Agriculture (Australia)
CRC(s)	Cooperative Research Centre(s) (Australia)

CSIRO	Commonwealth Scientific and Industrial Research Organisation (Australia)
DNAP	DNA Plant Technology
EC	European Community
EPA	Environmental Protection Agency (United States)
FAO	Food and Agricuture Organization of the United Nations
FAPESP	*Fundação de Amparo à Pesquisa do Estado de São Paulo* / The State of São Paulo Research Foundation
FDA	Food and Drug Administration (United States)
FONCYT	*Fondo para la Investigación Científica y Tecnólogica* / National Fund for the Promotion of Science and Technology
Freedom to operate	The permissive use of other people's technology
GAMS	General Algebraic Modeling System
GIPSA	Grain Inspection, Packers, and Stockyards Administration (USDA)
GM	Genetically modified
GMAC	Genetic Manipulation Advisory Committee (Australia)
GMO(s)	Genetically modified organism(s)
GRDC	Grains Research Development Corporation (Australia)
GTAP	Global Trade Analysis Project (model)
GURTs	Genetic use restriction technologies (including variety-specific V-GURTs, and trait-specific T-GURTs)
HARTs	Homologous allelic recombination (or replacement) technologies
HT	Herbicide tolerance
IARC(s)	International Agricultural Research Center(s)
IDB	Inter-American Development Bank
IFPRI	International Food Policy Research Institute (United States)
INGER	International Network for Genetic Evaluation of Rice
In situ	In place of origin, as compared with ex situ—away from place of origin
IP/IPR	Intellectual property/Intellectual property rights
IRRI	International Rice Research Institute (the Philippines)

ISAAA	International Service for the Acquisition of Agri-Biotech Applications
LAC	Latin America and the Caribbean
Landraces	Plant varieties developed through farmer selection
LDCs	Less-developed countries
MAS	Marker-assisted selection
Mercosur	*Mercado Común del Sur* / Common Market of the South
MTA	Material transfer agreement
NARS(s)	National Agricultural Research System(s)
NIC	Newly Industrialized Countries
NIH	National Institutes of Health
OECD	Organisation for Economic Co-operation and Development
OGTR	Office of the Gene Technology Regulator (Australia)
PCR	Polymerace chain reaction
Procisur	*Programa Cooperativo para del Desarrollo Tecnológica Agropecuaria del Cono Sur* / Cooperative Program for Agricultural Technology Development in the Southern Cone
PVPC	Plant variety protection certification
PVRs	Plant variety rights
RAFI	Rural Advancement Foundation International
R&D	Research and development
REDBIO/FAO	Technical Cooperation Network on Plant Biotechnology in Latin America and the Caribbean/Food and Agriculture Organization of the United Nations
Sida	Swedish International Development Cooperation Agency
Southern Cone	Subregion generally including Argentina, Bolivia, Brazil, Chile, Paraguay, and Uruguay
SNP	Single nucleotide polymorphisms
Sui generis	Rights designed for a specific field of technology
TRIPs	Trade-Related aspects of Intellectual Property agreement (WTO)
UBMTA	Uniform Biological Materials Transfer Agreement (United States)

UNDP	United Nations Development Programme
UNESCO	United Nations Educational, Scientific and Cultural Organization
UNIDO	United Nations Industrial Development Organization
UNU/BIOLAC	United Nations University Programme for Biotechnology in Latin America and the Caribbean
UPOV	International Union for the Protection of New Varieties of Plants
USAID	United States Agency for International Development
USPTO	United States Patent and Trademark Office
USDA	United States Department of Agriculture
WARDA	West Africa Rice Development Association (Côte d'Ivoire)
WTO	World Trade Organization

Contributors

Jock Anderson is an emeritus professor of Agricultural Economics at the University of New England, Armidale, Australia, and adviser, Strategy and Policy, to the Rural Development Department of the World Bank. He is a fellow of the Australian Institute of Agricultural Science, the American Agricultural Economics Association, and the Academy of the Social Sciences in Australia.

Kym Anderson is professor of Economics and executive director of the Centre for International Economic Studies at Adelaide University, South Australia. He has authored or edited 20 books and published around 200 articles in the areas of international, agricultural, and development economics. Since working in Geneva during 1990–92 with the secretariat of the economic research division of GATT (now WTO), much of Kym's research has been directed toward strengthening the global trading system.

Walter Armbruster is president of the Farm Foundation, Oak Brook, Illinois. As chief executive officer of the nonprofit Farm Foundation, he works as a catalyst, facilitator, and stimulator of research, education, and dialogue on private-sector and public policy issues related to agriculture and rural communities. Walt is a past president and fellow of the American Agricultural Economics Association.

Nicole Ballenger is chief of the Diet, Safety, and Health Economics Branch of the U.S. Department of Agriculture's Economic Research Service. She directs a program of economic research on consumer issues such as factors affecting dietary choices, demand for food quality attributes, the role of information and consumer education in improving nutritional status, and the benefits and costs of food safety policy.

Marc Cohen is special assistant to IFPRI's director general. His current research focuses on the world food situation and outlook, biotechnology and food security, and conflict and food security. Before joining IFPRI in 1998, he edited the annual world hunger report at Bread for the World, a U.S. nongovernmental organization. Marc received his Ph.D. in political science from the University of Wisconsin-Madison.

Dan Dierker is a doctoral candidate in the Department of Agricultural Economics at the University of Saskatchewan in Saskatoon, Canada. He has worked on freedom-to-operate provisions under different intellectual property rights regimes and on endangered-species protection legislation.

Kate Dreher holds bachelor's degrees in biology and economics from Williams College in Williamstown, Massachusetts, and is pursuing a doctorate in Crop Science at the University of California at Davis. She was previously a Research Assistant in the Economics Program of the International Maize and Wheat Improvement Center (CIMMYT).

Ron Duncan is director of the Asia Pacific School of Economics and Management and executive director of the National Centre for Development Studies at the Australian National University. In these roles, Ron is primarily concerned with postgraduate education of students from developing countries in the Asia Pacific Region. His research interests are agricultural and trade policy and natural resource management in the Pacific Island countries. Ron is president-elect of the Australian Agricultural and Resource Economics Society.

Ruben Echeverría is the chief of the Rural Development Unit of the Inter-American Development Bank (IDB). His main activities include the preparation of agricultural and rural development strategies and policy documents, technical workshops, coordination of the Inter Agency Working Group for Rural Development of Latin America and the Caribbean, assistance to IDB investment project preparation and evaluation, and technical support to the Regional Fund for Agricultural Technology (FONTAGRO).

Brian Fisher is executive director of ABARE, the Australian Bureau of Agricultural and Resource Economics. He is an agricultural economist with interests in public policy and trade research. In the past decade he has dedicated much of his effort to disseminating information on the benefits of trade reform both in OECD and developing countries. Brian is currently one of Australia's leading climate change negotiators.

Richard Gray is a former director of the Centre for Studies in Agriculture, Law and the Environment (CSALE), at the University of Saskatchewan. In July 2001 Richard became head of the Department of Agricultural Economics at the same institution.

His research interests include international trade, the economics of research, and environmental issues.

Richard Jefferson is the founder, chairman, and CEO of CAMBIA. His work has been cited in the primary literature over 5,000 times. He is the inventor of a number of technologies, including the GUS system, the most widely used tool in plant biotechnology, and in 1987 conducted the first field release of a transgenic food crop. Prior to founding CAMBIA, he was the first Molecular Biologist for the FAO, and has been responsible for troubleshooting the Rockefeller Foundation's rice biotechnology activities in Asia, Latin America, and Africa. He has been plenary or keynote speaker at numerous international symposia and given more than 300 invited seminars in over 35 countries, and plays a pretty mean blues guitar and newgrass mandolin.

Mireille Khairallah, a molecular geneticist and plant breeder, is a private biotechnology consultant based in Texcoco, Mexico, previously a senior scientist in the Applied Biotechnology Center at the International Maize and Wheat Improvement Center (CIMMYT). Her fields of expertise include use of molecular marker techniques for improvement of maize and wheat germplasm.

Bob Lindner is executive dean of the Faculty of Agriculture and professor of Agricultural Economics at the University of Western Australia. Bob's research focuses on the economics of research management and research policy including measuring benefits of research, the adoption of innovations, and intellectual property rights in plant genetic resources.

Michele Marra is a professor in the Department of Agricultural and Resource Economics at North Carolina State University. Her research concentrates on issues surrounding the economics of new technology and farmer decisionmaking under uncertainty.

Michael Morris, an agricultural economist, is assistant director of the Economics Program at the International Maize and Wheat Improvement Center (CIMMYT). His research interests include projecting the likely impacts of crop biotechnology on research organizations, seed producers, farmers, and consumers. In addition to his other duties, he also dedicates time to communicating technical scientific issues to nonspecialists, especially the general public.

Carol Nottenburg is chief legal officer and director of Intellectual Property at the Center for the Application of Molecular Biology to International Agriculture (CAM-

BIA) in Canberra, Australia. Carol is responsible for the strategic development and licensing of CAMBIA's patent portfolio, and in addition, spearheads its Intellectual Property Resource, an Internet-based resource comprising a patent and patent application database, white papers, and tutorials in the area of agricultural biotechnology intellectual property.

Philip Pardey is a senior research fellow at the International Food Policy Research Institute, Washington, D.C., where he leads the institute's Science and Technology Policy Program. His current research interests include the investment and institutional dimensions of agricultural R&D, genetic resources and agricultural biotechnology policy, and evaluation of the consequences of R&D. As of 2002, Philip will be professor of Science and Technology Policy in the Department of Applied Economics at the University of Minnesota, at the same time maintaining his institutional ties with IFPRI.

Peter Phillips is a professor of agricultural economics with a five-year NSERC/SSHRC Chair in Managing Knowledge-based Agri-food Development at the University of Saskatchewan in Canada. His current research concentrates on issues related to intellectual property rights for agricultural biotechnology and trade, and marketing issues related to GM foods. Peter is a member of the Canadian Biotechnology Advisory Committee, Director of the Canadian Agri-food Trade Research Consortia and founding member of the International Consortia on Ag-biotechnology Research, based in Rome.

Per Pinstrup-Andersen, a native of Denmark, joined the International Food Policy Research Institute (IFPRI) as its director general in 1992. Prior to this, he was director of the Cornell Food and Nutrition Policy Program, professor of food economics at Cornell University, and a member of the Technical Advisory Committee to the CGIAR. Per is a member of several committees, including the Committee on Agricultural Biotechnology, Health, and the Environment under the National Research Council; the Working Committee on Biotechnology under the State Department's Advisory Council on International Economic Policy; and the World Health Policy Forum and its General Council. He is a Fellow of the American Agricultural Economics Association and the American Association for the Advancement of Science (AAAS). Per has received numerous honorary degrees and awards, including the *2001 World Food Prize*, and he is the author of more than 300 books, articles, and papers.

Chantal Pohl Nielsen is an economist with the Danish Institute of Agricultural and Fisheries Economics (SJFI) and a doctoral candidate at the University of Copenhagen in Denmark. Her research interests include analyzing the consequences of the use of biotechnology in agricultural production in various parts of the world, and the conflicting views as to its potential benefits and risks on developing countries' trade and production possibilities. Chantal is currently working on analyzing the trade barriers and domestic policies that affect international trade in rice, with a particular focus on Viet Nam.

Carl Pray is professor of Agricultural, Food, and Resource Economics. Carl has been at Rutgers University since 1986 and prior to that was at the University of Minnesota from 1980–85. He earned his Ph.D in Economic History from the University of Pennsylvania.

Jean-Marcel Ribaut, a plant physiologist and molecular geneticist, is assistant director of the Applied Biotechnology Center at the International Maize and Wheat Improvement Center (CIMMYT). His research interests include genetic dissection of maize and wheat and the use of molecular marker-based breeding techniques for development of improved maize and wheat germplasm with tolerance or resistance to abiotic stresses, with particular emphasis on drought.

Bob Richardson is an agricultural economist and dean of the Institute of Land and Food Resources at the University of Melbourne, Australia. The Institute is involved in research on plant and animal biotechnology and is a major provider of vocational and higher education and research training in agriculture and food, forestry, horticulture, and resource management.

Sherman Robinson is the director of the Trade and Macroeconomics Divison at the International Food Policy Research Institute (IFPRI). He was previously a professor at the University of California at Berkeley, a division director in the research department at the World Bank, an assistant professor at Princeton University, and a lecturer at the London School of Economics. Sherman's research interests include international trade, macroeconomic policy, income distribution, and methodological developments in policy-oriented general equilibrium modeling.

John Skerritt is deputy director of the Australian Centre for International Agricultural Research (ACIAR). He oversees a team of senior managers involved in designing and managing collaborative research projects in a range of agricultural disciplines, including crop sciences, animal sciences, fisheries, forestry, land and water resource management, postharvest technologies, and agricultural economics. John also directly manages a portfolio of short-course and postgraduate training.

Michael Taylor is secretary of the federal government department Agriculture, Fisheries and Forestry–Australia. Previously he was secretary of the department of Natural Resources and Environment and it predecessor agencies for the state government of Victoria. Michael has been extensively involved in preparing and negotiating commonwealth and state agreements and legislation on a wide range of agricultural and related environmental issues.

Karen Thierfelder is an associate professor of Economics at the U.S. Naval Academy, specializing in international trade, using empirical trade models to analyze the effects of changes in domestic and trade policies on global trade patterns. Karen's research interests include the effects of NAFTA on member countries, regional trade agreements in southern Africa, OECD agricultural policy reforms and WTO negotiations, and consumer attitudes towards genetically modified food.

Eduardo J. Trigo is an Argentine agricultural economist, currently the director of Grupo CEO, a consulting firm specializing in agricultural economics and policy. He also serves in the Board of Directors of the National Agency for the Promotion of Science and Technology of Argentina and is an adviser to the Secretary of Agriculture on biotechnology policy issues. Eduardo's primary research focus is science and technology policy and organization, emphasizing the agricultural sector.

Greg Traxler is a professor of agricultural economics at Auburn University, Alabama, and affiliate scientist in the Economics Program at the International Maize and Wheat Improvement Center (CIMMYT). Some of his recent studies have examined the distribution of benefits from biotechnology innovations, the impacts of the introduction of *Bt* cotton in Mexico, and the effect of technology spillovers and economies of size in agricultural research.

Brian Wright is professor of Agricultural and Resource Economics at the University of California, Berkeley. His interest in agricultural economics dates from his early experiences on his family's sheep station in the Riverina district of New South Wales, Australia. Brian's current research topics include dynamic analysis of patenting of research inputs, the theory of commodity price behavior and speculation, and the economics of conservation of genetic resources.